THE COMING WAR WITH JAPAN

THE COMING WAR WITH JAPAN

GEORGE FRIEDMAN

MEREDITH LEBARD

St. Martin's Press New York

Design by Karin Batten

Library of Congress Cataloging-in-Publication Data

Friedman, George.
    The coming war with Japan / George Friedman and Meredith LeBard.
        p.   cm.
    ISBN 0-312-07677-5
    1. United States—Foreign relations—Japan.   2. Japan—Foreign
relations—United States.   3. United States—Foreign
relations—1989–   4. Japan—Foreign relations—1945–   I. LeBard,
Meredith.   II. Title.
E183.8.J3F72   1991
327.73052—dc20   91-28088
                                                                   CIP

First Paperback Edition: April 1992

10 9 8 7 6 5 4 3 2 1

To Dorothy and Lee

During the twentieth century as a whole, no country has more consistently regarded itself as in essential conflict with the United States than has Japan, and no country has been more uniformly looked upon as a potential enemy by Americans. The burden of proof, perhaps, should rest on those who assume Japanese–American friendship, rather than those who expect the contrary.

> —Edwin O. Reischauer,
> Former Ambassador to Japan,
> writing in 1953

Contents

x • Contents

PART IV: JAPAN'S SECOND PACIFIC WAR

List of Maps

Preface

Imagine being alive in the summer of 1900. Europe was powerful, peaceful, and rich. Could you have imagined the devastation of 1920, the fall of the Kaiser, the Russian Revolution? Could anyone, then, have imagined the summer of 1940? Germany resurgent, France crushed, Britain fighting for its life. Or, in the summer of 1940, could anyone have imagined 1960? Europe divided and occupied by Americans and Soviets, the British and French empires gone, a nation called Israel arisen. In 1960, could anyone have imagined the summer of 1980? America in retreat, defeated by Vietnam, reeling before the Iranians, allied with Communist China. One would ask about the man in the summer of 1980 trying to imagine the summer of 2000, but by the summer of 1990 he would already be so flabbergasted that there would be no need to force him to strain his already stricken imagination.

The conventional wisdom holds that what happened yesterday will also happen tomorrow. Anyone who in 1980 dared predict the collapse of communism would have been ridiculed. Yet, if there is one thing that the twentieth century ought to have taught us, it is that the commonsense approach to history is almost invariably doomed to be wrong, and that the most preposterous expectations are usually closer to the mark.

Thus, a book that predicts war between the United States and Japan is bound to be ridiculed by the conventional among us. The United States and Japan are friends. If you were to speak with the decision makers in either country, they would, with genuine sincerity, insist that whatever the tensions between the U.S. and Japan, they are nothing compared to the ties that bind the two countries. That may well be right. But what statesman in 1900 would have predicted 1920?

There are in fact many things that bind the U.S. and Japan today. There are also many things that divide them. The task of a scholar is to weigh the relative importance of such things, and then, using a most imprecise methodology, his imagination, try to envision the weight of these things twenty years hence. The chances of being wrong are great. But those who predict that the world in twenty years will look pretty much as it does today almost certainly run a greater chance of error than we do.

Our arguments are, we hope, not as preposterous as our conclusion might appear to be. We have begun by considering the history of U.S.–Japanese relations, to try to uncover the deep patterns that gave rise to the first U.S.–Japanese war. Then we consider the last forty-five years of friendship, to try to uncover the depth and permanence of that friendship. Finally, we try to imagine, using the prisms provided by the past, the future of U.S.–Japanese relations.

Our conclusions are not ones we welcome. We are both parents of young sons, and we do not celebrate the thought of war. We both hope that we are wrong, but we do not think that we are. We have thought long and hard on this matter, and it seems to us difficult to imagine an outcome other than what we have projected.

We have not blamed anyone in this book. This is most emphatically not an attack on Japan or an exercise in "Japan bashing." As we will show, both the United States and Japan are victims of forces they can neither control nor resist. The tragedy of this war, as in many of history's great wars, is that it will be fought by two altogether decent nations, neither of which harbors real ill will toward the other. Yet the fear that seems to dominate the human condition quite as much as love is supposed to will overwhelm the decency of each.

Neither can we claim to be neutral on the subject. We are both Americans, and our affections are with our own people; our fates are bound up with that of our country. The Olympian pose of indifference to the outcome of this conflict that so many scholars might affect is beyond our capacity. We can see clearly that if fault is to be laid, it lies with our own country perhaps more than with Japan. But the margin is small, and there is precious little that America can do to rectify the situation. If war comes, we are not indifferent to its outcome. Nor do we expect our counterparts in Japan to be indifferent. That is the tragedy of political life.

Thus, we are driven by two motives to write this book. One is the pleasure of scholarship. There is a certain very real joy in thinking and reading about a subject such as this. To be able to produce a book that others will read—to participate, in some small measure, in the life of the mind and the spirit of our age—is a pleasure in itself.

But we are citizens as well as scholars, and as citizens we are engaged in a very old and respected tradition, that of pamphleteers. On what we hope is a more learned level than that of some other practitioners of the art, we wish to inform our compatriots of a coming danger, and to urge them to beware. We Americans have a tendency to be too ready for wars that never come and to be taken by surprise by the ones that do.

There is another reason for this book. The leaders of both countries are today willfully engaged in a well-intentioned deception, indeed, a self-deception. By pretending that there is nothing basically wrong in the relationship between our two countries, by pretending that we can go on this way indefinitely, they are permitting the tensions that are driving our two countries apart to develop beneath the surface, out of sight and utterly out of control.

If there is any hope in avoiding a second U.S.–Japanese war, it rests in our leaders becoming frightened. These are the two wealthiest nations in the world, with the finest minds, laboratories, and, one might add, publics. They both have notable records of waging ruthless wars. The prospect of a war between the minds, spirits, and bodies of these two relentless nations ought to frighten anyone.

It is easier to predict a war than to know how to fight one, and both are easier still than knowing how to prevent one. Aside from the usual bromides of the would-be peacemakers, we have little to offer on that score. But it is possible that finer minds than ours might be moved by what we say to discover what we have been unable to discover: the key to peace.

It is customary to thank certain people for the help they have given us in this project, but we are embarrassed by the vast number to whom we are indebted. We will limit our thanks to J. Mark Ruhl and Douglas Stuart of Dickinson College for the many wise comments and hours of thoughtful conversation they have provided us; Lee LeBard for his help with the maps and graphs; Bob Oskam, whose advice and encouragement were of enormous value; and Keith Kahla for his care and energy in moving the manuscript along. Also, we must thank Leonard Hochberg of Stanford University for his careful and illuminating comments; we were enriched by his learning and scholarship. We must also express our deepest gratitude to our editor, Michael Denneny, who encouraged and guided us with meticulous care and patience on all aspects of this book. Finally, we must thank our families, who endured the ordeal of this book with patience, kindness, and occasional good humor.

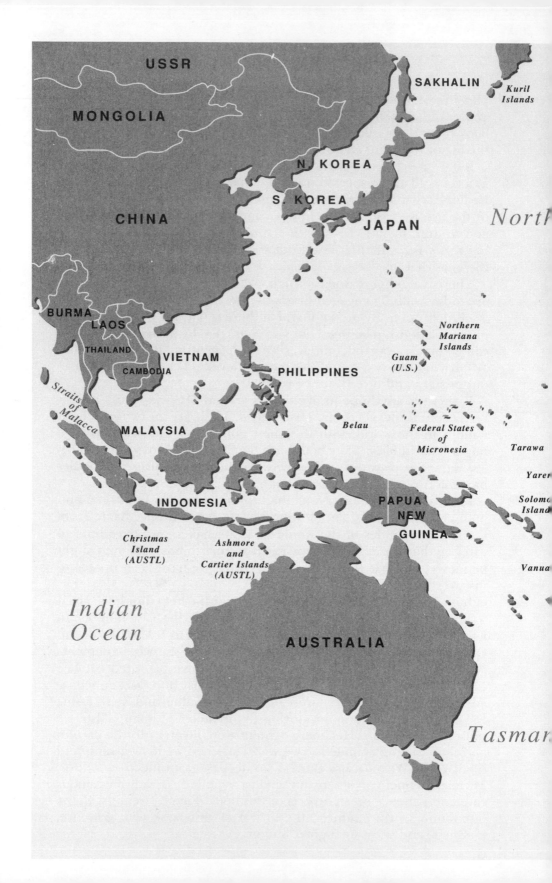

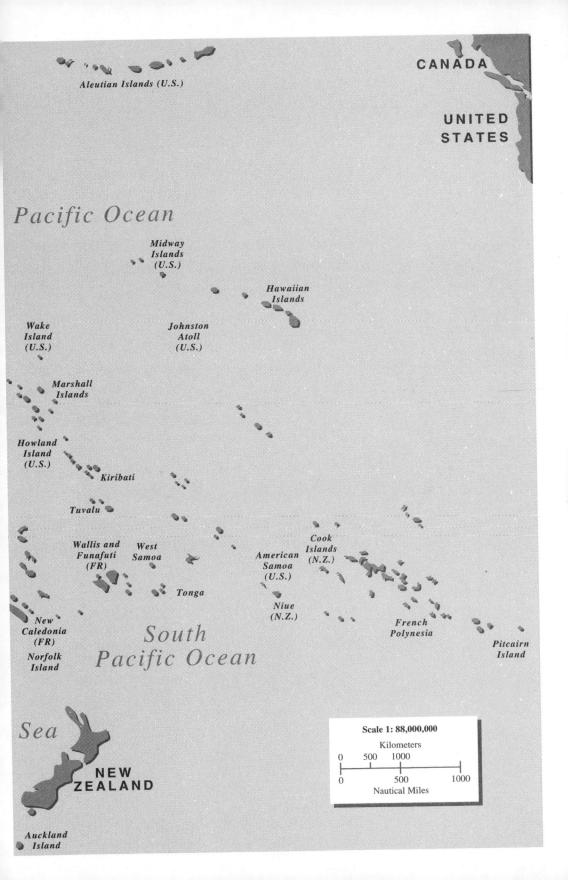

CANADA

UNITED
STATES

Pacific Ocean

Aleutian Islands (U.S.)

Midway
Islands
(U.S.)

Hawaiian
Islands

Wake
Island
(U.S.)

Johnston
Atoll
(U.S.)

Marshall
Islands

Howland
Island
(U.S.)

Kiribati

Tuvalu

Wallis and
Funafuti
(FR)

West
Samoa

American
Samoa
(U.S.)

Cook
Islands
(N.Z.)

Tonga

Niue
(N.Z.)

French
Polynesia

New
Caledonia
(FR)

*South
Pacific Ocean*

Pitcairn
Island

Norfolk
Island

Sea

NEW
ZEALAND

Auckland
Island

Scale 1: 88,000,000

Kilometers

| 0 | 500 | 1000 | |

0   500   1000
Nautical Miles

Introduction

Enemies to Friends;
Friends to Enemies

Philosophers have said that history repeats itself, that everything happens twice. This is an understatement. History, particularly the history of nations, repeats itself many times. It is difficult to name a war of any consequence in antiquity or modern times that did not repeat itself on innumerable occasions. How many times did Sparta and Athens come to blows? Or Rome and Carthage? England and France? France and Germany? Poland and Russia? Conflicts that are of profound importance continually resurface, finally to end only in the triumph of one nation over the other, or in their mutual annihilation. Observers expect each war to settle the matter once and for all. Yet, phoenixlike, the vanquished seem repeatedly to arise anew, to try their hand at making history again.

To date, the United States and Japan have fought but a single war. But it was a war of fundamental and enduring importance, since the fight was for control of the Pacific Ocean, the world's largest body of water. As with the conflict between Carthage and Rome for control of the Mediterranean, control of the Pacific meant not merely control of trade, but also control of economic life on the lands surrounding the ocean.

At first glance, the Japanese surrender in 1945 appeared to settle

1

permanently the question of Japan's claim to domination of the western Pacific. With the Japanese Imperial Fleet annihilated, the United States emerged from the war as the major naval power in the Pacific. Japan was both militarily destroyed and economically shattered. Under the terms of unconditional surrender, the United States appeared to be in a position to remove permanently any possibility of a future challenge from Japan. Indeed, this was the intent of General Douglas MacArthur's clause in the Japanese constitution that had the Japanese forswear war as a matter of fundamental political principle. In fact, should the United States have chosen to destroy Japan as a civilized culture, there would have been little to prevent it.

That this did not happen resulted not so much from the nobility of the American spirit as from the need of the United States to preserve its hard-won hegemony over the Pacific from the new challenger, the Soviet Union. Where the Americans had become the world's preeminent naval power, the Soviets had become Eurasia's preeminent land power. As powerful as it was on land, that is how weak the Soviet Union was at sea. Still, the potential for a Soviet challenge in the Pacific was real: the Soviets had political cards to play, and they could always build a navy. Therefore, after Mao's triumph in China and the outbreak of the Korean War, a sense of concern, indeed panic, gripped American policy in the Pacific. As America panicked, Japan changed from a defeated enemy into a potential bulwark against the Soviet Union.

Thus, the question of Japan, apparently settled for good in 1945, was reopened only a few years later. Ironically, the Japanese came to honor as sacrosanct the antiwar clause of their constitution more than its American authors did. The Japanese saw little profit in joining in America's crusades when America was quite capable of taking care of itself and its allies without help against a threat the Japanese could not take altogether seriously. Thus, while the Japanese were quite content to peacefully rebuild their economy, the United States sought to coax them into a more active military role.

As long as the Soviet–American competition remained the central fact of the international system, the United States was dependent on Japan. Geographically, Japan was indispensable; not only did its position effectively block the Soviet Far Eastern fleet from access to the Pacific, but Japan also provided the United States with unsinkable bases for air attacks on the Soviet mainland. Additionally, Japan was both a major U.S. supply depot for Korea and a reserve industrial plant for the production of war materials. As a vital link in America's strategic and industrial planning, the United States had an overriding interest in maintaining cordial relations with Japan. It needed an active ally rather than a compliant prisoner.

The United States clearly had mixed feelings about the treatment of Japan following the war, as it had mixed feelings about the handling of Germany. There were those who felt it vital to crush Japan, to deny it any possibility of revenge. While this thinking was logical in the context of the old political order, it made little sense in the new one. The new order pitted America against the Soviet Union, and America needed every ally it could get in its struggle—Japan more than most, for its location, manpower, and industrial potential.

The American decision to reindustrialize Japan obviously met with approval from Japanese interests, because it repudiated the position of those who sought to brutalize Japan. In order to secure its own interests, Japan was pleased to become a cog in the American Far Eastern war machine. This role was particularly satisfactory in that it guaranteed Japan's access to much needed raw materials through American-controlled waters while not requiring any major military exertion on the part of Japan.

Thus, there was a perfect synergy between Japan's economic interests and America's political interests. Japan was so important to America's strategic interests that the United States was willing to endure substantial discomfort from Japanese economic competition. Indeed, as Japan became an increasingly formidable economic power, the United States became increasingly dependent on it politically. Its importance as a consumer of raw materials throughout the Pacific Basin, but particularly in Southeast Asia, made it a subtle but powerful political force, drawing mineral suppliers into the Western camp. Japan proved useful in helping the United States achieve its political, anti-Soviet aims in the region. Its political importance to the United States forced America to cede to Japan substantial economic autonomy, far beyond what normally would be enjoyed by a nation that had surrendered unconditionally.

Without the Soviet–American rivalry, Japan's economic development could have been aborted at any point by the United States. What made this impossible was the prospect of Japan, in the face of such pressures, deciding to throw itself at the mercy of the Soviet Union, or, through internal instability, making the American military presence difficult or impossible to maintain.

If Soviet–American rivalry is the foundation of Japanese prosperity, then what would Japan's condition be without this rivalry? In the past, this question has been academic, since that conflict was understood to be the permanent foundation of the international system, certainly for the past forty years. But with the arrival of glasnost, entirely new relationships are inevitable.

In an extraordinarily short period of time, the Soviet Union has gone from being the apparently ascendant power on the world scene to being the sick man of world politics. American foreign policy must be prepared to follow either of two courses. In one, the Soviets recover as quickly as they collapsed and the prior status quo is restored; frankly, a dubious proposition. In the other, the Soviet Union becomes an increasingly marginal actor on the world scene, either collapsing entirely or returning to a more passive and inward role in foreign affairs, as it did during the interwar period.

One of the reasons for glasnost was the inability of the Soviet Union to compete with the United States militarily. In spite of tremendous expenditures on defense since 1962, the year of Soviet humiliation during the Cuban missile crisis, the Soviets failed to break free from their containment, or pose a direct challenge to America's control of the oceans.

The only sphere in which the Soviet Union competed effectively was in strategic nuclear weapons. It is particularly ironic that the Soviet Union's success in the most dreaded sphere of modern warfare should have meant so little in its struggle for world power. On one hand, the Soviets had succeeded in matching, or exceeding, American nuclear capability. On the other hand, they failed to overawe China or NATO on the ground, or the U.S. Navy at sea. Their success in nuclear weapons meant little compared to their failure in conventional weapons. Even as the Soviet Union writhes with internal instability and is increasingly disregarded in international affairs, the Soviets still retain their massive nuclear arsenal. This should be a cautionary thought for all who believe that the rules of international relations have been abolished or rewritten by the advent of nuclear weapons.

The United States defeated Soviet strategy through a combination of statecraft and naval power. Its statecraft was quite simple, the fruit of a hard-learned lesson from the years between World Wars I and II. American isolationism was understood to have had catastrophic results for the U.S. After World War II, the United States set about establishing a system of alliances, binding together a vast coalition on three principles: hostility to the Soviet Union, collective security, and free trade. Behind this strategy was a deeper one: using American economic strength to entice nations close to the Soviet Union to risk war with the Soviets in return for the substantial economic benefits of membership in the American bloc. This system of relationships was pursued vigorously by the United States, and with particular energy in East Asia, where China's threat supplemented that of the Soviets.

America's Asian strategy had two parts. First, the United States wished to remain in mainland Asia, to create a counterweight to China. South Korea, South Vietnam, Thailand, and Malaysia were all key positions in this perimeter strategy. The second part was to control both the waters surrounding Asia and Asia's offshore islands. This ring of islands, including Indonesia, the Philippines, Taiwan, Okinawa, and finally Japan, constituted a cordon around Asia. It was the final line beyond which communism was not to pass, as well as the forward base for adventures on the Asian continent.

The purpose of this archipelago strategy was twofold. First, to prevent communist navies from breaking into the Pacific with a fleet strong enough to challenge America's navy. Second, to have a platform from which to interdict the flow of materiel along the Asian coast, as well as to project U.S. air and ground forces onto the mainland. Thus, Clark Airbase in the Philippines served a critical function during the Vietnam War, as did Japan during the Korean War. During both wars, Japan served as a forward logistical base, an air platform, and a defense plant.

In addition to serving as another island platform in the archipelagoes surrounding the mainland, Japan was uniquely situated for another purpose. Its position effectively blocked the Soviet Far Eastern fleet's access to the Pacific. Japan is a crescent offering Vladivostok four main lines of access to the sea. Two are internal waterways, each passing through channels less than ten miles wide. The other two are larger passages but still closable. From Japan, the United States could close the door on Soviet operations in the Pacific.

In order to operate in the Pacific, the Soviets would first have to conduct a war against Japan. Indeed, this would be a war in which the United States could content itself with inflicting heavy losses on the Soviets, sapping their strength, while allowing Japan to be overrun, since it could then fight the Soviets on more favorable terms in the vastness of the Pacific.

The greatest threat to United States interests in the Pacific, therefore, would have been some internal development in Japan that would have made it pro-Soviet. There were two possible sources for such an evolution. The first was the very real presence of a radical political movement in Japan. The second threat came from the right. On the far right were figures such as Yukio Mishima, who wanted to resurrect the Japanese Bushido tradition and wreak vengeance on the United States. This faction could in the long run prove a threat, but was only of "aesthetic" interest in the short run.

The main faction in Japanese politics center-right ruling Liberal Democratic Party, dominated postwar Japan and was normally pro-American in its outlook. In fact, the center-right is simply pro-business. And therein lies a threat, for there has always been a basis for Japan and the Soviet Union to do business. Japan needs raw materials, and the Soviet Union needs technology and capital. Each has what the other needs. There has always been a real possibility that the Japanese Liberal Democratic elite would make a deal with the Soviets, one element of which would be a guarantee of Japanese neutrality and the expulsion of U.S. forces from Japan.

This deal has never been made for a number of reasons. First, so far the Japanese elite has properly calculated that neutralization might bring short-term benefits but long-term disaster. Any alliance with the Soviet Union might turn into domination. Second, the terms of a business relationship between the two nations might not necessarily be favorable to Japan. In previous cases, 1905 and 1939, the Japanese thought about securing Soviet resources by invasion. Even if successful, such a course would not have proved profitable, since Soviet resources are inconveniently located and difficult to extract. Finally, the Japanese were given access to cheaper materials by the United States, which guaranteed low prices by securing Japan's sea-lanes while absorbing the cost of that security. Since most of the resources came from American-controlled or -allied areas, the United States managed to make Japan dependent on it for the supply and transport of materials.

Obviously, this relationship was mutually satisfactory. The United States absorbed the largest expense of any mercantile economy, sea control. This gave Japan a real economic advantage, producing spectacular economic growth and undermining the appeal of radicals in the universities and labor unions. Additionally, the United States created a web of alliances in which Japan was included. Paralleling this alliance system was a free-trade regime that was created by the United States for several purposes, not the least of which was political. The postwar free-trade regime, which continues to reign today, had the effect of opening markets to the exports of recovering economies. The Japanese, in particular, traditionally oriented toward an export-driven economy, took full advantage of the opportunities available both in the U.S. and in allied countries and grew prosperous.

Thus, the United States provided Japan with access to raw materials as well as a system of trade relations that gave substantial advantage to the Japanese. In this way, the U.S. kept the Japanese within its system of alliances. Japan, in turn, provided the United States with substantial strategic and political advantages that were infinitely precious in the context of the Cold War.

It was a fair bargain by any measure.

With glasnost, however, the equation shifts, for if the Soviet Union accepts its encirclement, then the foundation of the United States–Japanese alliance dissolves. It is not Japan that will seek to free itself from the relationship. Quite the contrary, the Japanese will fight long and hard to maintain it, since they clearly have benefited handsomely.

Rather, the relationship will dissolve because the United States will no longer need to endure Japanese economic encroachments, since the strategic payoff that Japan provides will cease to have meaning after the Cold War.

The United States has paid an extremely high price for its relationship with Japan. The U.S. has permitted Japan to close its consumer and capital markets to American companies, while allowing Japanese companies access to American markets. In 1989 America's trade deficit with Japan was about 52 billion dollars. This means that the U.S. sent about 1 percent of its Gross National Product to Japan, an astronomical figure for a country as large and developed as the U.S. The costs of sea control have been borne by our own producers in the form of deficits, inflation, and high interest rates, while the Japanese have operated with much lower interest rates and inflation. The U.S. has periodically disrupted its society with wars against Soviet surrogates, while Japan has avoided conflict, although fully benefiting from U.S. hegemony. This has meant that the Japanese have been able to undercut the U.S. throughout the former colonies of Europe, and even in the United States itself.

To a great extent, this was the theme of the 1988 Presidential primaries, in which one candidate, Richard Gephardt, ran an explicitly anti-Japanese campaign, indeed one that was called racist by some. For the first time since World War II, the Soviet Union was hardly an issue in an election. Instead, Japan took its place as the bogeyman of American politics. Since 1988, poll after poll has found that Americans have come to regard Japan as a greater enemy than the Soviet Union. For example, a McGraw-Hill poll found that while 22 percent of all Americans regarded the threat of the Soviet Union to be serious, 68 percent thought that Japan was the greater threat faced by the United States.[1] While not fully rational, these increasingly hostile sentiments toward Japan provide psychic fervor to fuel the more rational aspects of United States–Japanese rivalry.

In attempting to envision the shape of this coming rivalry, it is necessary to recall the fundamental grievance of the United States against Japan. It boils down to the claim that Japan is able to sell more of its products through unfair practices. On one hand, there is the suspicion that Japan's government subsidizes its exports, and on the other, the belief that deliberate impediments are placed in the way of American exports to Japan. There is little truth to the former claim. A government that subsidizes exports is a government on its way to bankruptcy, and that certainly is not the case with Japan. As to impediments in the way of exports to Japan, while more nearly true, that charge misses much of the point, which is that at this moment in history Japan is simply more efficient than America in producing some key products. The reasons for this have more to do with the age of Japan's capital stock and the current low price of imported minerals than with unfair practices. Which also means it is not a permanent condition.

Nevertheless, states, like people, are never as reasonable or as patient as they might be. Thus, the pressure grows on the American government to take action. So far, the United States has concentrated on the export question, seeking to control Japanese exports to the United States while opening up Japan to American exports. But this is not an area in which the U.S. is likely to outmaneuver Japan. Nor does it matter, because Japan is far more vulnerable in other areas, areas to which American attention will inevitably be drawn in the coming years.

Japan must export in order to grow, and it must grow in order to maintain its peculiar financial system. While the prosperity of Japan may depend on exports, Japan's very life depends on imports. Japan's dependency on the United States for its imports is far, far greater than its dependency on the U.S. for its exports. Indeed, while the debate in the United States has focused on Japanese exports, Japan has been concerned with the availability of the minerals it must import to survive. Fear of being cut off from vital imports is becoming a critical dimension of the Japanese political culture. And it is becoming increasingly noted that those imports are guaranteed by the United States, a power potentially hostile to Japan's economic interests.

Consider the following data:

TABLE I-1. Percent Japanese Imports of Mineral Commodities, 1987—by Weight.

COMMODITY	% IMPORTED
Coal	87.66
Oil & Petrol	99.72
Natural Gas	99.94
Iron Ore	99.76
Copper	99.20
Nickel	100.00
Bauxite	100.00
Lead	91.36
Zinc	85.46
Manganese	100.00
Molybdenum	100.00
Chromium	79.39

TABLE I-1. Percent Japanese Imports of Minerals (continued)

COMMODITY	% IMPORTED
Tungsten	82.18
Titanium	100.00

(Sources: *Japan Statistical Yearbook*, 1949–, Statistics Bureau, Management and Coordination Agency, Government of Japan [prior to 1963, issued by the Bureau of Statistics, Office of the Prime Minister]. Additional data from *Minerals Yearbook* [1947–], Bureau of Mines, U.S. Department of the Interior.)

More than any other great nation in the world, Japan is dependent on its imports of minerals—the lifeblood of the Japanese economy and Japanese prosperity. It does not require great insight to understand that should these imports be cut off, within a matter of months Japanese exports would cease to exist. Indeed, the Japanese have an acute awareness of this, and have been stockpiling key commodities —in the case of oil, a 142-day supply. But this is only a temporary solution. Were there a cutoff in supplies, in due course there would be a reckoning. And in that reckoning, Japan would cease to be an industrial power and its threat to the United States would disappear. This is a fact fully familiar to the Japanese. Nobutoshi Akao, chief economic officer at the Japanese Embassy in Washington during the late 1970s and 1980s, and currently director of the Japanese Foreign Ministry's United Nation's Bureau, wrote in 1983:

> This high dependence on overseas sources of raw materials makes the Japanese economy extremely vulnerable to any interruption in their supply, and also to any sharp rise in prices—as the oil shocks of 1973 and 1979 demonstrated. As a result, the Japanese have become preoccupied with ensuring access to overseas raw materials, especially to oil and food. A recent best-selling novel, *Yuddan*, vividly, though somewhat exaggeratedly, depicts what the consequences would be for Japan if oil imports were reduced as a result of an outbreak of a major war in the Gulf region: if oil imports were cut by 70% for 200 days, three million Japanese people would die and 70% of all property would be severely damaged or completely lost, with results more tragic and devastating than the losses in World War II.[2]

As Akao points out, these figures are an exaggeration. They are not, however, a gross exaggeration. The effect of a cutoff of oil and other minerals on Japan would be absolutely devastating.

Thus, it should be the starting point of all thinking in Japan on this matter that should the United States cease to view Japan as an important strategic asset, it would be free to base its relationship with Japan on economic considerations, all of which militate against friendly relations. Barring the animosity of the Soviet Union—and that is precisely what glasnost is intended to do—there is much to divide the United States and Japan and precious little to hold them together. Should the United States wish to put an end to Japanese competition, it could do so by blockading Japan either through direct military means or through political intervention with its suppliers.

It can also threaten Japan indirectly. During the 1990 Kuwait crisis, the United States intervened in the region to protect the long-term stability of the international oil markets. In doing this, the U.S. ignored the fact that Japan, importing over 60 percent of its oil from inside the Straits of Hormuz, cannot have a long-term perspective on oil. Japan cannot withstand even a short-term disruption of oil exports from that region. Thus, American and Japanese interests during the crisis were quite different. Japan needed a rapid settlement of the crisis, even on less than satisfactory political terms, while the U.S. had far more room for maneuver on the matter. Where the U.S. was extremely solicitous of Japan during the oil crisis of 1973, in 1990 it treated Japan rather cavalierly. Japan responded to U.S. demands for support coolly, and the beginnings of a U.S.–Japanese divergence became more visible.

From the Japanese point of view, the situation became dangerous once the United States stopped worrying about the Soviets. The Japanese find themselves in a position where their most important and resourceful economic adversary is the guarantor of their supply of raw materials. For the Japanese to accept this situation, they must accept the premise that the United States is not only infinitely generous but also infinitely fair. Nothing in the Japanese experience teaches them this. Recalling the Nixon Shock of 1973, when President Nixon unilaterally cut off supplies of soybeans to Japan in order to reduce the price of meat in the U.S., it can be seen that there is precedent for American interference in the vital interests of Japan.

On a much more important level, there are strong parallels between the current situation and the relationship of the United States to Japan prior to World War II. At that time, Japan's key imports were petroleum products, rubber, food, and iron ore. Japan's primary sources of supply were in Malaya, the Dutch-controlled East Indies, and the United States. All their goods passed through U.S.-controlled waters and up to 80 percent of their oil came directly from the United States. The United States was in a position to disrupt these supplies at will, and following Japan's invasion of Indochina that is precisely what it did.

It was partly to solve this problem that the Japanese invaded China, seeking a source of supply under their direct control. The United States responded to the invasion of China by engaging in boycotts and waging escalating economic warfare against Japan. From the Japanese point of view, it was this hostile behavior by the United States that forced them to seek to secure the raw materials necessary to their survival. The result was their move into Indochina, which resulted in a general cutoff of trade with the U.S. The Japanese responded with an attack on Pearl Harbor, the seizure of the Philippines, and the great offensive of 1942 that made Japan the master of Southeast Asia, in control of its own economic fate for the first time. It is important to note that the aggravating matter of Japanese exports to the United States and their effect on the American economy was not then a factor.

Without the binding element of the Soviet Union, the economic dispute between the United States and Japan will inevitably become political. As the title of the now-infamous book co-written by the chairman of the Sony Corporation and a leading Japanese politician, *The Japan That Can Say "No,"* implies, growing Japanese economic self-confidence will inevitably lead to growing political self-confidence. On the other side, growing irritation with Japan will inevitably lead to an unwillingness on the part of the United States to continue to underwrite Japanese security. Paradoxically, it will be the demand on the part of the United States that Japan share more of the burden for its own defense and rearm more vigorously that will make Japan a more and more formidable military force in the region and a potential threat to the United States. As Japan is forced to assert itself politically, it follows that it will also assert itself militarily.

No great power can tolerate a situation in which the very lifeblood of its society and economy are in the hands of another nation, let alone a nation that has interests fundamentally opposed to its own. Japan can never be secure, nor in control of its own destiny, until it controls the sources of its mineral supplies and the transportation routes that carry those supplies to Japan. Nor can it guarantee its prosperity until it can guarantee access to markets for its exports and security for its investments. While the United States had strategic reasons for supporting Japan, and while Japan was a relatively weak player on the international scene, this situation was tolerable. With today's dramatically changed strategic situation and the emergence of Japan as an economic superpower, Japan will inevitably need to control the elements of its own survival.

No nation can control its destiny without a military force equal to its needs. During the Cold War, the U.S. provided Japan with sufficient benign force so that Japan had no need to develop its own military power. Indeed, Article 9 of the Japanese constitution bans warfare and the maintenance of an army. It therefore comes as a surprise to many to learn that Japan today spends more money on defense than any country except the United States and the Soviet Union. It spends more on defense than China, Germany, Britain, or France. Thus, the question is no longer whether Japan will rearm, but to what extent and to what end. This will be determined by Japan's strategic needs.

In considering Japan's future strategy, attention is drawn to the first U.S.–Japanese war. As in World War II, if for different reasons, Singapore must be the focus of Japanese strategy. If an enemy were to seize Singapore and its Malaccan Straits, Japan would be strangled. The bulk of Japan's oil, as well as other mineral supplies, passes through these straits. Japan cannot help but be aware of this fact, nor can it avoid the conclusion that the one power that could close Malacca is the one power with a motive to do so. The Japanese must plan for the worst case, as must all great powers, and that means they must take steps to ensure that the United States does not close the Straits of Malacca.

One does not have to argue that Japan is preparing for war. It is sufficient to note that Japan would be insane not to prepare for war. And, in turn, the United States must prepare its defense by carefully considering what it is forcing Japan to do. With the end of the Cold War, conflict is no longer global. Events in Cuba are no longer connected to events in Vietnam or Germany. In one sense, the world is free from the threat of global conflagrations. In another sense, nations freed from the responsibility of globally consequential actions are free to engage in vicious local conflicts without fear of escalation. This regionalization of conflict frees the last superpower, the United States, to impose its will ruthlessly, without fear of global consequence. The U.S. now lives in a more unruly world, but the world clearly faces an unleashed giant.

The essential political and military fact in the world today is the domination of the seas by the U.S. Navy. All of the world's oceans belong to one country: America. This is a novel fact in recorded history, a goal Britain strived to attain for a century without success. This means that, should it choose to do so, the United States can determine the pattern of world trade, dictating what goes where and how. If this is intolerable for Japan, then Japan must try to challenge that power, at least in the Pacific.

The desire for Japan to control its own economic destiny cannot be achieved without displacing the United States Navy from its preeminent role in the Pacific. This cannot be done without generally undermining American power throughout the world's oceans. The Japanese political and military challenge cannot be achieved unless the United States contents itself with becoming a hemispheric rather than a global power. After nearly a half-century of refusing to take this role vis-à-vis the Soviets, it is unlikely that the United States will accept the role vis-à-vis the Japanese. Thus, the seeds of conflict are planted.

Japan lost its last war with the United States for several reasons. First, it was vastly inferior to the United States industrially. Second, its adventure in China proved a quagmire, diverting men and materiel from the later war with the United States. Finally, Japan was not prepared to cope with the unrestricted submarine warfare of the United States Navy. Things have changed.

Japan is still inferior to the United States industrially, but not nearly to the extent that it was in 1941. It is not bogged down in China. And it is developing one of the most advanced antisubmarine warfare systems in the world. Today, Japan would be an easy target for the United States. It is Japan's task to make certain that this is not the case a generation from now.

There are serious barriers to the development of a militaristic Japan. For nearly half a century the Japanese have lived under a constitution banning war as a matter of principle. Even more important, Japan has been psychologically defeated. The generation that fought World War II was discredited, and the following generation confined itself to private, economic pursuits. But today's new generation feels less of the burden of what went before and feels less responsible for the failures of Japan in war. Quite the contrary, its members feel pride in the enormous achievements of Japan and are ready for Japan to take its place among the leading powers of the world. As has happened in Germany, World War II is ending, psychologically speaking, forty-five years after it ended militarily. And with that ending, the constitution, a product of the war as much as of Japanese shame and modesty, loses its significance.

The defeat of Japan by the United States was traumatic. The first response was guilt and shame. But in the face of Japanese success, and in the face of growing differences with America over economic and political matters, the shame of World War II will inevitably give way to a more natural, and more fierce, national sensibility. This will particularly be the case should Japan experience a decline in its economic miracle and blame the United States for that decline. Pacifism is not native to Japan, nor is national modesty. Resentment will corrode both very efficiently.

We can therefore see quite clearly that there are underlying reasons—economic, political, and military—that must put the United States and Japan on a collision course. Essentially, the issues are the same as they were in 1941. Japan needs to control access to its mineral supplies in Southeast Asia and the Indian Ocean Basin and have an export market it can dominate politically. In order to do this, it must force the United States out of the western Pacific. The United States will see this attempt to force it out of the western Pacific as Japanese aggression and imperialism, as well as the desire to reduce the United States to the status of a second-class power. As in the 1930s, both will engage in a cold war against each other which will, in extremis, spill over into a hot war.

One obvious argument against a U.S.–Japanese war is the existence of nuclear weapons. There are those who contend that nuclear weapons make war impossible. Vietnam and Afghanistan, along with the willingness of the Arabs to attack a nuclear-armed Israel in 1973, all argue against this easy and comforting assumption. True, the U.S. and the Soviets never fought a war, but it is unclear that there was any issue dividing them that would have justified a general war even had nuclear weapons never been invented. The existence of nuclear weapons has permitted analysts the easy solution of arguing that nuclear weapons have made war impossible, even as the bloody reality of the nuclear age has belied this claim. Thus, while nuclear weapons might in some way change the shape of a U.S.–Japanese conflict, limiting it in some areas, intensifying it in others, the facile assumptions that conflict between these two powers is impossible because of the existence of nuclear weapons does not withstand the scrutiny of either theory or history.

At the same time one must not simply assume that war is inevitable. If the past forty-five years have shown anything, it is that nothing is inevitable in history, not even war. But while it might not be inevitable, it is a real and troubling possibility, one that can more easily be prevented now than later. However, in order to prevent such a war it is important not to dismiss it as mere paranoia or neurotic need for conflict. Wars have reasons, and denying the reality of those reasons can be as dangerous as making too much of them.

Thus, the proper beginning is to consider the underlying reasons for wars and not the passing events that appear so gripping. In looking beneath the surface, we ought to start by considering the grand strategies of America and Japan.

1. Business Week/Harris Poll, in *Business Week*, August 7, 1989, p. 51.
2. Nobutoshi Akao, *Japan's Economic Security* (New York, 1983), p. 17.

PART I

THE FIRST U.S.- JAPANESE WAR

1

The Grand Strategies of the United States and Japan

In studying international affairs, it is necessary to focus on permanent things. Personalities and ideologies change, yet the same constellation of nations engages in the same sorts of conflict. It is necessary to understand the reasons for the extended animosities that have marked history. In order to do this, one must examine the underlying forces that have conditioned the choices nations have made. This will illuminate whether the U.S. and Japan are permanent enemies who have merely put aside their animosity for a time or whether their first war was a passing event, now permanently behind them.

Nothing is less permanent in the history of nations than ideology. Germany went from monarchy to social democracy to fascism and then to communism and liberal democracy in less than thirty years. Yet, in international affairs, Germany behaved in rather consistent ways. The paradox of modern politics has been the instability of personalities and political values, as opposed to the consistency of political behavior in the international arena.

The search for permanent things is the goal of any scholar. It should also be the goal of any statesman. The task of statesmanship is to look beyond the background noise of daily events and the cultural eccentricities that distinguish nations and to focus on the substructure of events, the layer that gives rise both to culture and to the ordinary events of public life that shape the history of nations. Grand strategy resides in this layer.[1]

Grand strategy is the intersection of choice and necessity in the life of a nation. Strategy is concerned with choosing among actions. Grand strategy is concerned with a level at which choices cease to exist except in the broadest sense. Statesmen choose among strategies, but they obey grand strategy. The unavoidable realities of geography are of particular importance. Factors like a nation's location, its neighbors, its terrain and climate, shape a nation indelibly and are permanent features.[2] These constraints permanently shape the needs and fears of nations, and all too often these needs and fears collide with those of other nations. Where neither nation is able to obliterate the other, these permanent necessities lock nations into apparently endless cycles of war. Mere goodwill is impotent against this brute necessity. In examining the relationship between the United States and Japan, we must begin by considering these permanent forces and calculating how they are likely to intersect in the future.

The United States has a grand strategy, one that it has pursued with ruthless consistency and great success over two centuries. Japan also has such a strategy, although one that it has not been nearly so successful in following. So fundamental were these grand strategies that many times citizens and politicians were unaware of them. All of us know that the reasons we have for doing things do not exhaust the actual causes of our actions. Both in success and failure, our conscious reasoning frequently fails to explain our motives. We are constrained to act in certain ways by forces outside ourselves. This is even more true in the case of nations.

In looking back over history, it is striking how often the men who shaped events had intended to create quite different outcomes. Indeed, frequently they were unaware of what they had created. One might define a statesman, as opposed to a politician, quite simply: a politician is so concerned with his tiny role in events that he neither understands the forces that shape his actions nor the ends to which he is working. By contrast, a statesman has at least some awareness of the hidden structure, the underlying forces, that shape his actions.

The tragedy of international relations is that wars occur not when men are driven by uncontrollable greed but when they act out of fear. The Israelis genuinely believe that they are defending themselves when they attack the Arabs, and in a sense they are correct. The Arabs genuinely believe that they are defending themselves when they attack the Israelis, and in a sense they are correct. Both have every reason to fear the other and, given that, they are behaving in utterly rational ways.

Ideology, the method by which nations justify what they do, lacks this tragic dimension. It reduces politics to moralizing. Ideology acts as if men were infinitely free to choose among different courses. Grand strategy gives us a standpoint from which to see the necessity, and therefore the tragedy, of international politics.

Japan and the United States are equally driven by fear. Indeed, each nation has a series of fears, born of this underlying necessity, which can be soothed only by national self-assertion. This self-assertion must, in due course, conflict with the self-assertion of other nations. Each new border, no matter how distant or how secure, must be defended lest the entire defensive web unravel. The collision of Japan and the United States will not occur because either is a monster. It will occur because both powers will be afraid of losing what they already have. Each will see the other as the aggressor, as both know that they themselves mean the other no harm. This was the tragedy of the first U.S.–Japanese war and it will also be the tragedy of the next.

THE GRAND STRATEGY OF THE UNITED STATES

Let us begin by considering the grand strategy of the United States and consider first the obvious: America's geographical position in the world.

The world is round, and contains two large land masses, the eastern and western hemispheres. The eastern hemisphere is larger, more populous, and richer (although not on a per capita basis). When the eastern hemisphere encountered the western during the period 1500–1900, that is, when Europe encountered the Americas, the result was the overwhelming victory by one over the other. This was in spite of the fact that the eastern hemisphere was involved in continual internal conflicts during this period.

There were many reasons for Europe's victory, not the least of which was that, like the native peoples of South America, the North American Indians were badly outnumbered. But the most important strategic explanation was military: the Europeans controlled the sea. Control of the sea is the key to both prosperity and safety.[3] Since the Europeans controlled the sea, they could come ashore where and when they chose, with as much force as they wished. The American Indians could not cut the supply line to Europe, nor could they attack Europe. Their only strategic option was the systematic annihilation of all settlements, and this was impossible because of their lack of coordination and the ability of Europeans to land unlimited numbers and superior firepower. Lacking sea power, it was inevitable that the American Indians would be overwhelmed. The permanent strategic imperative of the United States is to prevent a repetition of the invasion of the western hemisphere by the eastern.

The layers of American strategic interests might be stated as follows:

1. That the U.S. Army should completely dominate North America.
2. That no power or group of powers should exist in the western hemisphere capable of challenging U.S. hegemony.
3. That the U.S. Navy should be able to keep eastern hemispheric powers out of the western hemisphere by controlling the North Atlantic and eastern Pacific oceans.
4. That no eastern hemispheric power should be able to challenge U.S. domination of the oceans, having their energies diverted by land threats.

The United States is extraordinarily rare among nations in that it has achieved all of its strategic goals. The peaceful and prosperous continental nation we take for granted is the result of this success. Other nations, Japan included, have not been so successful. It is therefore useful to sketch briefly how the United States achieved its goals.

At its founding, the U.S. occupied a narrow strip of land between the Appalachian mountains and the Atlantic. West of these mountains was the Ohio Territory, recently wrested from the French by the British; the vast French Louisiana Territory; and to the south and west, Spanish holdings that stretched from Florida to Texas and California. Indian nations were scattered throughout these territories. The initial position of the U.S. was precarious, as it was vulnerable to attack from two directions on an extended front and also lacked strategic depth. Thus, the U.S. needed to defend its coast while expanding beyond the Appalachians. In a broader sense, the U.S. had to conquer North America and destroy any military force capable of challenging its dominion.

In order to accomplish this, the U.S. had to achieve three goals on land, while keeping the British from seizing or blockading the East Coast of the United States:

1. Gain control of French possessions on the continent.
2. Expel Spain from North America, incorporating strategically significant territories into the U.S., while emasculating any successor state.
3. Destroy the Indian nations that still dominated North America west of the slowly advancing line of settlements.

MAP 1-1. Conquest of North America.

First, and perhaps most important, the U.S. executed the Louisiana Purchase in 1803, resulting in the acquisition of the entire Mississippi–Missouri River complex and, from this, access to the interior of the continent. Jackson's victory at New Orleans in 1815 gave the U.S. control of the mouth of the Mississippi and unfettered access to the continent, as well as the ability to ship goods and materials from the middle of the country to Europe and the East Coast.

Using the lure of free land, the U.S. induced masses of European immigrants to move westward. The settlers served both a military and economic function. Militarily, each family was well armed and able to match, at least defensively, the poorly armed Indian forces. Further, each settlement was able to mobilize an armed militia in emergencies. The U.S. Army, garrisoned at strategic points, served as reinforcement for settlers in hard-pressed areas and as shock troops against enemy concentrations. Using the mobility of light cavalry, the army was able to cover substantial amounts of territory while concentrating overwhelming force at given points. Army forts were virtually impregnable and were able to shelter settlers who lived in the surrounding countryside. With this force, the U.S. set out to conquer the continent and succeeded.

During this settlement period, the U.S. encountered its second enemy on the continent, the Mexicans. With the expulsion of the Spanish from Florida, the state succeeding Spain, Mexico, was a substantial power in the early nineteenth century. Its army numbered about 40,000 at the start of the Mexican War, while the United States Army was only about 8,000. It was by no means certain that the U.S. would emerge as the dominant North American power. Nevertheless, the same settlement process that was underway in the Louisiana Territory brought settlers into Mexican territory north of the Rio Grande. This had already undermined Mexican control of the region, so that the smaller U.S. force was able to break Santa Anna's army and both seize Texas and California and permanently destroy Mexico's military might.

From this point until near the end of the century, the only task the U.S. Army had left was to liquidate the remnants of North American Indian life. Making their final stands in the southwestern deserts and the foothills of the Rockies, the last autonomous Indian nations were nearly annihilated. With this, the U.S. gained absolute control of the continental United States and domination over North America.

Following the defeat of Mexico, there was no force in North America that could not be defeated by the U.S. Army. Canada lacked the population and the will to challenge the U.S., while Mexico survived its humiliation in a state of perpetual chaos. The only land threat that could be posed to the U.S., therefore, came from the rest of the western hemisphere, from Latin America.

Such an attack was never very likely. The only land route from the south was via a narrow peninsula that was seized by the U.S. at the turn of this century. Still, a strong power in Latin America could threaten the United States by sea as well as by land. Thus, the U.S. sought to achieve three goals in Latin America:

1. That no foreign power use Latin America as a base from which to launch attacks on the north.
2. That no alliance of Latin powers emerge that could challenge U.S. domination of the hemisphere.
3. That no single Latin power become strong enough to achieve this end.

The Monroe Doctrine was the expression of the U.S. desire to achieve the first goal. At the time it was promulgated the doctrine was an empty bluff. It announced that the entire western hemisphere was under the protection of the United States and that the United States was the guarantor of the independence of Latin America. Coming a mere decade after the ignominious burning of Washington during the War of 1812, the assertion that Britain would not be permitted into the western hemisphere was utterly unenforceable. Fortunately, however, this was of little importance, as the Monroe Doctrine was a strategic principle to be pursued rather than a reality.

At various points since 1823, the United States has been concerned with the presence of Spanish, French, British, German, and Soviet forces in its hemisphere. For example, in the case of Cuba, the U.S. has opposed the presence of Spanish, Germans, and Soviets with equal vigor. Some have claimed that the U.S. has an inordinate fear of communism, and point to its treatment of Cuba as an example. But the opposition to Castro is no more obsessive than was fear of the Spanish or paranoia about the Germans. The underlying motive in each case was not ideology, but strategic principle expressed as ideology. The United States has been ruthlessly consistent in pursuing one end: absolute safety for North America. Strategy, not ideology, will determine American thinking about Japan as well.

In terms of the other two goals underlying this principle, over the past century the U.S. has pursued a consistent policy of dividing and disrupting Latin American governments in order to keep them preoccupied and unable to threaten the U.S. At various times the U.S. has subverted them, invaded them, and brought them to the brink of war with each other. As a result, Latin America has never been able to challenge American hemispheric power; neither has any European power found a firm foothold in the hemisphere.

Having gained domination of North America and hegemony over the hemisphere, the U.S. faces only one remaining threat: attack from the sea. Invasion by sea is the most costly and difficult of all military operations. Ships are more expensive than any other item in a nation's arsenal. From ancient times, the acquisition of ships was sometimes beyond the means of even great powers. But invasions do occur. In World War II the U.S. simultaneously invaded Europe and the Japanese empire. There is no reason that the U.S. could not be invaded in turn. It only appears preposterous because of the success of the United States in preventing it from happening.

In a way, the doctrine of naval defense is the one that has been most consciously held by Americans.[4] As heir to the British tradition, American political culture was aware of the benefits of naval power even while conquering North America, a task requiring little naval support. The U.S. was aware of the vulnerability of its coastline and its trade routes to Europe. In addition, toward the close of the nineteenth century, the strategic and economic possibilities resulting from the domination of the Pacific also became quite attractive to the U.S.

The domination of the Atlantic was a long process, requiring patience in constructing a navy and prudence in challenging the British, the dominant Atlantic power. First, the U.S. needed to construct a fleet that would deter a repetition of 1812. This was achieved during the Civil War. Then it had to drive all other navies, except the British, from the western Atlantic. This it achieved in the Spanish-American

War and World War I. Finally, it had to supplant the British fleet as the paramount power in the Atlantic (which it did in size after World War I) as well as finally expel Britain from the Atlantic.

In 1940–1941, when the British had their backs against the wall, the U.S. agreed to transfer to them large amounts of equipment, particularly destroyers. This is well known. Less well known is that the British reciprocated by transferring to the U.S. control of all of its key naval facilities in the western hemisphere. In effect, what the U.S. did was to take advantage of British desperation to throw the Royal Navy out of the western Atlantic. The U.S. thereby gained control of all oceans abutting the U.S. It was a coup of epic proportions, as it made U.S. domination of the Atlantic a reality and forced Britain to express gratitude for American willingness to take advantage of its plight. With the end of the war, the U.S. pressed its advantage further, establishing naval facilities in Britain itself. It also created NATO, which effectively placed the Royal Navy in the Atlantic under joint command, or in practical terms, American command. By the end of World War II, the U.S. was in total control of the Atlantic.

The U.S. did not want to be excluded from the imperial game in the western Pacific for fear of being forced out of the Pacific altogether. At the same time, while there was no immediate threat to the West Coast, there was a real possibility of a threat somewhere down the line. With British, French, German, Russian, and Japanese fleets all present in the Pacific, the possibility of such a threat could not be discounted. The key to preventing such a threat was Pearl Harbor.

Hawaii occupies an important position in the Pacific. It is the only land for 2,100 miles west of San Francisco. It is also the only substantial land mass on a direct line between Japan and the United States. Pearl Harbor is the Pacific's finest anchorage. Held by America, Pearl Harbor provides America access to Asia, and denies Asia access to North America. Other powers, including England, France, Germany, and Japan,[5] coveted Hawaii in the nineteenth century. By annexing it, the U.S. blocked their ambitions. It opened the door for other, greater ambitions.

The U.S. had decided, not without controversy, that it needed to become the predominant naval power in the Pacific. The seizure of Manila Harbor from the Spanish gave America that prize as well. Manila, along with Guam, also ceded by the Spanish, gave the U.S. excellent harbors in the Pacific. The victory over Spain made the U.S. a player in the European sacking of Asia, the profitability of which would prove more than a little problematic. Most important for our purposes, with the Philippines the U.S. occupied a position from which it could choke off Japanese trade with Southeast Asia.[6] While not of great significance in 1898, this would emerge as the critical reason for the first U.S.–Japanese war.

The growing American naval power posed a new problem for the United States. It was increasingly possible for the U.S. Navy to fight and win battles against European navies. The key to maritime success, however, is in having the strongest navy not because of a nation's own efforts, but because of the inability of competitors to find resources to build a navy of their own. One way to ensure this is to manipulate the political environment in such a way as to cause competitors to be preoccupied with land enemies.

Great Britain in the eighteenth and nineteenth centuries faced a problem similar to that of the U.S. A strong maritime power, its land forces were inadequate in the face of the French, Austro-Hungarian, or Russian armies. A united Europe would be able to sail a fleet strong enough to sweep the Royal Navy from the oceans. Therefore, it became British policy to prevent this by making certain that Europe was never united. So long as France, Prussia, Russia, and Austria-Hungary, in whatever combination, were locked in land wars or preparations for land wars, none could possibly afford to construct a decisive navy. Thus, the Royal Navy won its sea battles before the ships sailed by manipulating the balance of power in such a way as to make European instability permanent. Great Britain did not care who won, so long as nobody won.

On a far larger, global scale, this has been United States policy ever since the U.S. emerged as a world power. From World War I onward, the U.S. has manipulated the European balance of power in order that no nation might impose a peace. The U.S. did not intervene in World War I until it appeared that Germany might win and until Germany began to threaten U.S. interests in the Atlantic.

After the war, the U.S. acted to ensure that peace in Europe was temporary. There are those who view Woodrow Wilson's behavior at Versailles as idealistic.[7] Yet his actions could be seen as utterly cynical. The basic interest of the U.S. after World War I was that no power become strong enough to impose a Pax Europa and then use its vast resources to create a global navy. With the simultaneous collapse of Germany, Austria-Hungary, and Russia, it appeared possible that the Anglo-French alliance, or even France alone, might be able to achieve this. Because of Wilson's machinations at Versailles, French attempts to impose hegemony on the continent were thwarted and Germany was saved to fight another day. The U.S. went home, luxuriating in its isolation and leaving Europe in chaos.

The result of this chaos was World War II. Here again, the U.S. was quite content to let Europe make war on itself until it began to appear as if one power, again Germany, might win. Then America intervened with just enough wealth and just enough force to prevent a German victory. Having intervened, the U.S. refrained from active combat beyond the bare minimum required to keep the alliance intact until just before the German collapse. Then it introduced massive force and, suffering minimal casualties, reaped enormous rewards from victory.

The U.S. was a bit more active toward Japan, which was reasonable given that Japan was a naval power, directly challenging an American strategic interest. Japan, an island like the U.S., was a maritime power. Even if the Asian balance of power were maintained, a powerful Japan always posed a threat to U.S. control of the Pacific. Thus, the U.S. needed to take action against Japan.

The U.S. emerged as the war's greatest victor. It controlled all the oceans of the world, the western and more prosperous half of Europe, as well as the entire Japanese empire. Moreover, it had created a situation where the British and French empires had to collapse and, in effect, fall into the hands of the Americans. For this, the U.S. paid with about 300,000 dead. The Soviet Union, on the other hand, managed to move its empire a few hundred miles to the west and, in the east, seize a few minor Japanese islands, while remaining surrounded by enemies. The Soviets paid with about 20 million dead.

The victory of the United States in World War II was total. It consummated all four strategic principles. The Soviet Union, although able to expand somewhat, remained trapped, surrounded on all sides by enemies (a situation temporarily relieved by the Chinese revolution, but quickly lost again in the Sino-Soviet split). Containment, the postwar doctrine of the U.S., had a simple purpose: to surround the Soviets with hostile American clients and thereby force the Soviets to spend their resources on ground forces rather than naval forces. The wars in Korea and Vietnam, as well as other lesser interventions, were examples of this policy. In all cases the U.S. used minimal force (compared to what was available) and absorbed negligible casualties. Winning and losing was irrelevant as long as Soviet resources were diverted from naval construction.

Navies are expensive to build. A single aircraft carrier battle group costs about $18.2 billion. Considering that fielding a mechanized division costs about $6.4 billion, creating a navy requires either enormous resources or the freedom not to have to field a very extensive land army.[8] This is not a new problem, but rather one of the most ancient. If nations were preoccupied with land problems they would not have the wherewithal to construct navies. Thus, if the U.S. could ensure crises in the eastern hemisphere, it could avoid challenge on the oceans.

Chaos suits U.S. interests perfectly. The U.S. does not actually care what happens in the eastern hemisphere, as long as it does not spill into the oceans. The collapse of the Soviet Union promises instability in Europe and Asia. In the end, land warfare, or at least great tension, will absorb the resources and energies of the eastern hemisphere once again. Minor ancient squabbles, between Hungary and Romania, Albania and Serbia, Armenia and Azerbaijan, are but the beginnings of a chaos that will last for generations, and which are the norm in Eurasia. While this goes on, the U.S. will exist serenely behind its wall of ships.

There is only one fly in this ointment, one major power that must inevitably become a maritime power, and therefore one threat to the United States: Japan. The Japanese alone have the ability and the need to have a navy. Japan's emergence as an economic superpower makes the development of a navy a necessary complement to its wealth, status, and vulnerability. In order to understand this, it is necessary to turn to the Japanese grand strategy.

THE GRAND STRATEGY OF JAPAN

Japan is an archipelago, a group of four large islands and numerous smaller ones, running about 1,200 miles from the southern tip of Kyushu to the northern tip of Hokkaido. The largest island, Honshu, is about 800 miles long, and about 200 miles at its widest and 70 miles at its narrowest. The four islands are divided by straits less than 30 miles wide. The terrain of all the islands consists of coastal plains, with interior mountains usually less than 5,000 feet but rising to over 10,000 feet at certain points. Thus, Japan has a vast coastline and little physical depth. An invader, if he made it ashore, would have an easy time splitting any of the islands in two, or at least capturing the populous coastal plain.

It is therefore odd that Japan has never been successfully invaded. Not even the U.S. actually invaded the islands. Rather, it laid siege to them and then bombarded Japan into submission. Given the fact that Japan is close to some of the hungriest and most populous nations in the world, this record of security needs to be explained. How was it that masses of Chinese, at the height of Chinese power, did not regularly sail to Japan to loot and occupy it?

Japan is shaped like a crescent, with the two points of the crescent closest to the mainland of Asia. The distance from Fukuoka, the port on southernmost Kyushu, to Pusan, Korea's southernmost port, is about 140 miles. On the Asian coast facing Japan, there are relatively few usable ports. In the north, facing Hokkaido, there are none. In the center, there is Vladivostok, but there the distance to Japan balloons to around 500 miles. In the south, on the Korean Peninsula, there are several harbors, at Pusan, Wonsan, and Chongjin. However,

MAP 1-2. Japan and the Northwest Pacific.

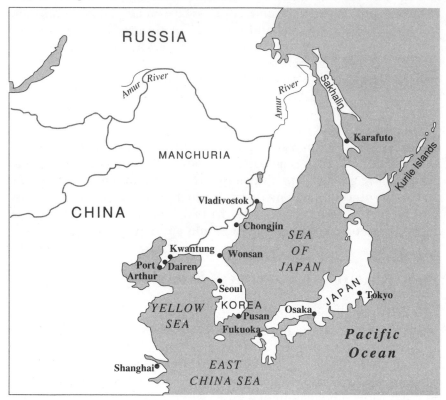

the waters of the straits between Korea and Japan are extremely treacherous, more so even than the English Channel.[9] Historically, invasions of Japan from Asia have failed. Kublai Khan tried twice and failed. Japan has never once undergone direct assault from the sea.

Thus, in its grand strategy Japan, unlike the U.S., did not have to struggle to achieve its first goal, the security of the homeland. But unlike the U.S., everything further up the scale proved painful, difficult, and thus far even impossible. The goals of Japan's grand strategy might be organized as follows:

1. To keep the home islands under the control of a central government and a unified army.
2. To maintain control of the seas around Japan's islands.
3. To dominate land masses abutting this area of sea control.
4. To be the dominant naval power in the northwest Pacific as far

south as Formosa, as far southeast as Iwo Jima.

5. To secure and maintain control of access to Japan's mineral sources in either mainland China or Southeast Asia by dominating the entire western Pacific and excluding all foreign navies.

Japan is ethnically homogeneous and geographically protected from foreign incursion. Therefore, it is not accurate to say that Japan's first goal must be to secure the home islands from foreign enemies. This was already achieved. The Japanese dominated their islands and were secure from foreign aggression. Japan was not united internally, but was divided instead among various warlords. It was not until the Emperor Meiji restored the emperor's throne to its archaic glory, in 1868, that centralized government returned to Japan.

Thus, Japan secured its first goal virtually without effort, at least until the advent of the steamship, which was not only impervious to the treacheries of straits, but which also came from an unprecedented direction, from the Pacific. The European intrusion brought about

MAP 1-3. Japan's Geopolitical Spheres.

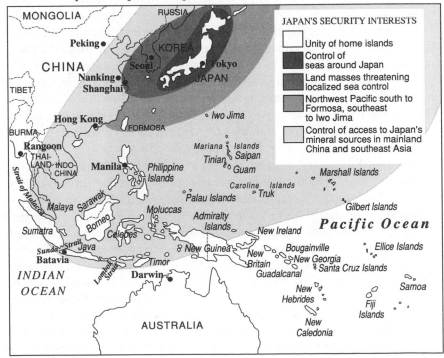

the first real threat of foreign domination since the failed Mongol invasions. Japan quickly realized that the best way to combat this threat was to expand its power militarily and keep the foreigner at arm's length.

The growth of Japanese power brought Japan into competition with the Chinese Ching dynasty during the 1880s and 1890s. It was the intention of the Chings, and not an improbable one, to invade Japan, using the new naval technology, in order to assert Chinese authority and impress Westerners.[10] In this whirlwind of strategic intrigue, Japan began to construct the sinews of modern power. As early as 1865, the Yokohama Iron Works began constructing warships for the Japanese fleet.[11] In its shipbuilding program, Japan would confront, for the first time, the nature of industrial war. It would come face to face with a stark reality, which was that by most measures of national economy Japan was a very poor country and a financially disorganized one.

In order to achieve their second goal, control of the waters around Japan, the Japanese had to invest enormous economic resources relative to the size of their economy. In fact, the Chinese threat was insignificant except for Japan's lack of natural resources. This points to an important feature of Japanese strategic history. Frequently, it was the scarcity of internal industrial resources, more than any external opposition, that endangered Japanese strategy and Japan itself.

For the U.S., industrialization and its military benefits came easily. In the event of war, the first recourse of American military planners has been to turn to its industrial base: the U.S. has produced its way to victory. Japan's industry had little surplus capacity and there was great scarcity of raw materials. In order to produce the weapons it needed, Japan first had to engage in political and military actions to secure the natural resources that industrial production required. In other words, for Japan, war was the foundation of industry, while for the U.S., industry was the foundation of war.

Aritomo Yamagata, a prime minister during the 1890s and leading figure in Japan's political renaissance, represented the Japanese view on this in 1890. He argued that Japan had secured its "line of sovereignty," but that it had also to secure a "line of interest." This line of interest was an outer line from which foreigners could encroach on Japan, and included both ocean and land areas.[12] In 1893 he went on to call for a vast expansion of the navy, saying that "within ten years, we shall be at war. At that time, our enemy will be neither China nor Korea, but Britain, France, and Russia."[13] However farseeing Yamagata might have been, Japan had to settle more immediate problems first. The most immediate problem was that of Korea. Jacob Meckel, a German adviser to the Japanese Army, put it most succinctly when he said that "Korea was a dagger pointed at the heart of Japan."[14]

With the waters around Japan secured, Japan pursued Yamagata's line of interest. It stretched from Russia's Kamchatka Peninsula to Sakhalin Island to Vladivostok. It then went south to include the Korean Peninsula, the Chinese coast from the Shantung Peninsula south to Fuzhou, then east to Formosa, the Ryukyus, and out into the Pacific to the Bonins and the rest of Micronesia.

The first problem was the islands directly north and south of Japan, the Kurils and the Ryukyus. The Kurils were secured from Russia by treaty in 1875, and the Ryukyus from China in 1879, in a complex deal that included recognition of Chinese ownership of Formosa.

The second problem was the threat posed by the Korean Peninsula. This threat was not primarily Korean. The fear was that some other power, particularly a European power like Russia, would seize the peninsula. Rough water would be no safeguard against their navy. Thus, pursuit of the third goal (domination of immediate land masses) and the fourth (becoming the dominant naval power in the northwestern Pacific) were intimately linked. In 1894, at a time advantageous to Japan, war broke out with China, ending in a complete Japanese victory. The Treaty of Shimonoseki, which ended the war, gave Japan control of Korea, Formosa, and the Liaotung Peninsula in China.

By 1895, the Japanese had gained the essentials of the line of interest that was the foundation of their third strategic principle. They had not, however, managed to become the dominant naval force in the northwest Pacific. As a result, the fruits of victory were taken away by a combination of European powers, who together could field an overwhelming navy, one that Japan could not yet match.

The rise in Japanese power disturbed the Russians more than any other nation. Russia did not have sufficient forces in the Pacific to resist, by itself, an aggressive Japanese policy. Russia persuaded France and Germany, both weak but aspiring naval powers in the Pacific, to intervene against Japan's claim to the Liaotung Peninsula. They did so for reasons having more to do with the European balance of power than with Asian considerations. This Triple Intervention had two results. First, it temporarily forced Japan out of China. Second, it fixed Japan with a resolve to achieve the fourth principle and become the dominant naval power in the region.

Germany had no significant anchorages in the region and therefore could not be a long-term threat. France had interests in Indochina and the South Pacific, far from Japan. England had refused to be a party to the intervention, fearing France and Germany more than Japan. Thus, the only guarantor of the treaty, really the only interested party, was Russia.

With cold calculation, Japan understood that war with Russia was inevitable if it was to achieve control of its line of interest. Only if its navy was unchallenged in the northwest Pacific could Japan be secure. This meant that Russian naval power in the Pacific had to be smashed. Russia foolishly allowed Japan to choose the time and place for the attack. The Japanese scored a decisive victory by launching a surprise attack on the Russian fleet at Port Arthur. This victory was later confirmed at the Battle of the Tsushima Straits, the first time in the modern age that a European country had been defeated by a non-white power.

Japan was on the verge of becoming the only great naval power in the northwest Pacific when Theodore Roosevelt intervened. The United States did not want to see Russia annihilated, inasmuch as it would have left Japan with too free a hand in the region. The U.S. intervention resulted in the Treaty of Portsmouth, which brought peace to the area, saved Vladivostok for the Russians, and won Roosevelt the Nobel Peace Prize. Korea, the Liaotung Peninsula, and southern Sakhalin all passed into Japanese hands, and the results of the Triple Intervention were nullified by the two new great northern Pacific powers, the U.S. and Japan. Saved from Japan, however, was the Pacific coast of Russia, which meant that Japan would have Russia at its back indefinitely. This, of course, was exactly what the U.S. wanted.

The Japanese victory meant that Japan had fulfilled its fourth goal. It was the fifth goal (securing access to the natural resources of the mainland of Asia and the southern archipelagoes) that would be Japan's undoing. Pursuing this goal would turn Japan from a powerful regional power into a challenger of broad imperial significance. Japan's shortage of minerals had not been unbearable to this point. The level of industrialization achieved by Japan was not enough to require much in the way of outside resources.

The need for more raw materials coincided with Japan's emergence as a major power after World War I. Japan played a minor role but was a major beneficiary in that war. An ally of Britain ever since the Triple Intervention, Japan chose to enter the war on the allied side. There was little it could do for the war effort, but Japan did seize, with British agreement, Germany's Pacific empire north of the equator. The conquest of Micronesia gave Japan an empire of sorts. More important, it caused Japan to be viewed, for the first time, with alarm by the Americans.[15]

As the interwar period developed, Japan's industrialization continued, and Japan began to experience a shortage of raw materials. Nowhere was this shortage greater than in oil, of which Japan needed to import 65 percent in 1930, and 80 percent in 1935. It was also short of a wide range of other materials. Given that Japan was importing the bulk of its oil from the U.S., a potential enemy, it was clear that Japan had to search for a source of minerals that it could control.

There were three possible controllable sources. One was China, another was Siberia, and the third the imperial holdings of England, France, and the Netherlands in Southeast Asia. By 1930 there was no longer any question but that Japan had to act. The problem was which way to turn? China was the obvious solution, but the least satisfactory, since it had its own need for these minerals and its deposits were limited and undeveloped.

The Japanese invasion of China had two separate strategic purposes. One, of course, was to secure minerals as well as a cheap labor supply. The other was strategic. A subdued China was a point from which Japan could strike in one of two directions: north into Siberia or south into Indochina and the Netherlands East Indies.

Had all gone as planned and wished, the Japanese would have quickly conquered China and could have dealt with the longer-term question at their leisure. Unfortunately for Japan, China did not prove to be a pushover. No matter how many Chinese the Japanese were willing to kill, the Chinese had more. In short order Japan found itself bogged down, and even farther away from solving its resource problem.

The question was whether to go north or south: into Siberia or into the Netherlands East Indies? Theodore Roosevelt bequeathed this problem to Japan. Had Roosevelt left matters alone, Japan would have absorbed Siberia, and its hunger for oil and minerals might have been satisfied. By keeping the Siberia question open, Japan was forced into the decision to head south.

Japan decided to go south because the Siberian deposits were difficult to get to and needed much development. In addition, with the fall of France in 1940, Indochina fell into Japanese hands with ease, and the need to hold Indochina gave logic to much that came after.

Japan, in order to have secure control of Southeast Asia, had to have a secure line of supply. The U.S.-held Philippines lay astride that line. For the U.S. to give the Japanese free access to its Southeast Asian resources would have meant abandoning the western Pacific and trusting Japan not to threaten Pearl Harbor and the rest of the Pacific. For Japan to accept U.S. domination of the western Pacific would have meant trusting the U.S. not to interfere with Japan's access to Southeast Asia. There was no basis for trust in either direction, nor could there be. World War II was fought over whether the ultimate principles of the U.S. or the Japanese grand strategies would take precedence; would the U.S. dominate the Pacific or would Japan have free access to its supplies of raw materials? It was impossible to satisfy both imperatives. The result was war.

The outcome of World War II was that Japan was first stripped of all of its strategic goals. It lost control of everything, including, for the first time in its history, its national sovereignty. In effect, Japan ceased to exist as a state, and its fate as a nation was in the hands of its enemy. Not a single strategic principle was still held by the Japanese, while every one of America's principles was attained. The U.S., for reasons of its own convenience, returned the first principle, control over the home islands, and even the Kurils and Ryukyus, to Japan.

Since then, Japan has been permitted, indeed urged, by the U.S. to pursue the second goal, domination of the waters around Japan, and, lately, even its fourth goal, domination of the northwest Pacific. The United States, in pursuing its own fourth goal, the maintenance of the balance of power in Eurasia, needs allies. Japan's usefulness in limiting Soviet power made attractive an increase in Japanese naval forces. Thus, as frequently happens in history, the pursuit of higher strategic goals sometimes causes nations to be casual with lesser concerns. In this case, the Eurasian balance of power has caused America to permit the growth of the Japanese Navy, a natural threat to American domination of the Pacific. Yet, if the balance of power is to be pursued, there is little choice but to permit this and hope for the best.

If Japan is to move up the scale of its strategic goals, it must clash with the United States. Only if Japan accepts the idea that its economic and political well-being will be guaranteed by a foreign power, one increasingly hostile in tone to Japan, and with fundamentally different interests, can a clash be averted. This is extremely problematic.

Neither the U.S. nor Japan is a wicked country. Each is a frightened one, and their fears are well founded in history. Each nation tries to protect itself as best it can. For the U.S. this has been extremely easy, once its first goal was achieved. For Japan, everything has come hard, as it has for most countries. But the fatal necessity of moving up the scale of strategic principles is still there. As will be seen, Japan is already beginning the journey, one that must culminate in a clash with the United States' desire for a stable, peaceful, and unchallenged hegemony over the world's oceans.

Principles remain constant. Japan's basic interests are unchanged from the nineteenth century. Only its ability to pursue these goals, and its tactics, have shifted. So, too, with the U.S. This is the stuff of which great and lasting animosities are made. Nothing was settled by World War II. It is not clear that, short of the annihilation of one of the parties, anything can be settled. This is the tragedy of U.S.–Japanese relations, a tragedy that we must understand by studying the origins and nature of World War II with some care.

---

1. Grand strategy has been defined in two ways. One has been sociologically, as the social process behind politico-military action. See, for example, Philip Egner, *Grand Strategy* (New York, 1915), or J.R.M. Butler, *Grand Strategy*

(London, 1956). Another definition posits grand strategy in terms of geopolitics. See Halford J. Mackinder, *Democratic Ideals and Reality* (New York, 1919), for the foremost theorist of geopolitics. Geopolitics fell into disfavor when the Nazis embraced it wholeheartedly. While something of an oversimplification, geopolitics is more successful in predicting the long-term behavior of nations than are allegedly more sophisticated methodologies.

2. As Hans Morgenthau, the greatest contemporary theorist of realpolitik, put it, "The most stable factor upon which the power of a nation depends is obviously geography. For instance, the fact that the continental territory of the United States is separated from other continents by bodies of water three thousand miles wide to the east and more than six thousand miles wide to the west is a permanent factor that determines the position of the United States in the world." Hans Morgenthau, *Politics Among Nations* (New York, 1967), p. 106.

3. Alfred Thayer Mahan, the greatest American strategist, wrote that "the history of the seaboard nations has been less determined by the shrewdness and foresight of governments than by conditions of position, extent, configuration, number and character of their people—by what are called, in a word, natural conditions." See Mahan, *Mahan on Naval Warfare*, ed. Allan Wescott (Boston, 1948), p. 21.

4. The foremost American strategist, indeed, we might say the only American who contributed to the intellectual tradition of grand strategy, was Alfred Thayer Mahan. Mahan's work is important because his treatment of sea power in American foreign policy was midwife to the emergence of the U.S. as a global military power. See his *The Influence of Sea Power upon History, 1660–1783* (Boston: Little, Brown, 1940), and *The Influence of Sea Power on the French Revolution and Empire, 1793–1812* (1892; repr. Westport, Conn., Greenwood, 1968).

5. For a study of Japanese views of Hawaii, see Hilary Conroy, *The Japanese Frontier in Hawaii: 1868–1898* (Berkeley, 1953).

6. For a discussion of Japan's view of the U.S. seizure of the Philippines, see James K. Eyre, *Japan and the American Annexation of the Philippines* (New York, 1942). Initial approval gave way to concern and later fear as the occupation began to interfere with what were seen as vital Japanese interests.

7. Hans Morgenthau, *Politics Among Nations*, p. 256, is one example of this.

8. This would include an aircraft carrier, a wing of aircraft, six escort vessels, two attack submarines, four supply vessels, and four escorts for the supply vessels. See William W. Kauffman, *A Thoroughly Efficient Navy* (Washington, D.C., 1987). Note that a lone carrier costs about $2.8 billion without support or aircraft.

9. Hisahiko Okazaki, *A Grand Strategy for Japanese Defense* (Washington, D.C., 1986), p. 4.

10. Ibid., p. 19.

11. Michael A. Barnhart, *Japan Prepares for Total War* (Ithaca, 1987), p. 22.

12. On Yamagata's views, see Marius Jansen, in *Political Development in Modern Japan*, ed. Robert Ward (Princeton, 1968).

13. James W. Morley, *Japan's Foreign Policy: 1868–1941* (New York, 1974), p. 14.

14. Peter Duus, *The Rise of Modern Japan* (Boston, 1976), p. 125.

15. Mark R. Peattie, *Nanyo: The Rise and Fall of the Japanese in Micronesia* (Honolulu, 1988), pp. 47–49.

2

The Emergence of the U.S. and Japanese Empires

If great conflicts repeat themselves, it is because the causes of these conflicts are permanent and intractable. If we are to understand the coming U.S.–Japanese war, we must begin by understanding the causes and course of the first clash of the two Pacific giants, beginning with the basic elements of that conflict. As America moved west across the Pacific and Japan moved south, geography dictated that the two powers would come into contact. That alone did not guarantee conflict. In due course, however, the geopolitical merged with the economic, as the United States and Japan searched for markets and Japan for resources. This quest intensified the fear each had of the other, until the geography of trade turned into the geography of war.

The United States and Japan became major actors in the Pacific at about the same time, the turn of the century. For the U.S. the rite of passage was the Spanish–American War of 1898, which gave America the Philippines. For Japan, the event was the Russo–Japanese War of 1904–1905, which made Japan the preeminent naval power in the northwestern Pacific. The first Japanese–American war, therefore, was a conflict between the first two native Pacific maritime powers over which would determine the political and economic order in the Pacific.

Both the U.S. and Japan had expansionist ideologies. For the U.S. this was summed up in the doctrine of Manifest Destiny, now extended to include the Pacific.[1] Japan, too, had a doctrine of expansion, based on theories of population growth.[2] America and Japan shared a common arrogance and insecurity, which gave rise to similar ethnocentric ideologies hiding intractable fears. For America, the fear that the eastern hemisphere would return and overwhelm the western was a primordial concern. For the Japanese, the fear that Asia's weight would descend on them and that Europe would turn their islands into prisons were enduring concerns. Celebratory ideologies compensated for these deep insecurities.

Along with ideology, there were some practical arguments for imperialism as well. Both the U.S. and Japan sought to expand in order to secure markets for their goods:

> The appearance of the United States in the circle of world powers having possessions in the Orient, although seemingly sudden and unexpected, has been a natural evolution of recent political and economic tendencies. The time has come when the intensity of the struggle for new markets and for opportunities for investment has forced the great commercial nations, by the instinct of self-preservation, to demand that the field of competition be kept open, even by the exercise, if necessary, of paramount military force.[3]

On the Japanese side:

> We have closer diplomatic and geographical ties with China than do the other powers; accordingly, our rights and interests must be expanded in China more extensively than those of other countries. This is our heaven-given right, and we must also make it so.[4]

The ideology of expansion overlaid an economic interest in expansion. Both the U.S. and Japan were commercial regimes; their futures were tied to trade. In many ways, Japan's interest in this was more desperate than America's. It needed to export goods more than America did, and it needed to import raw materials far more than did the U.S. Thus, the conflict over markets and resources was something of an uneven battle. Whether the victory would go to the more or less intense player is, of course, the continuing question.

THE PACIFIC AFTER 1905

When the United States and Japan emerged as great Pacific powers, they were not immediately enemies. Quite the contrary, they viewed each other as friendly, if distant, powers engaged in roughly the same pursuit: expelling the European imperialists from the Pacific Ocean. This was particularly true with Germany, which both nations feared and whose Pacific domain lay between the two empires. But on the whole, the sphere of Japanese influence and the sphere of American influence were clearly demarcated and not in conflict.

Japan emerged from the Russo-Japanese War in an excellent strategic position. It had secured complete control of the Sea of Japan, and was effectively in control of the Yellow Sea and the Pacific as far south as Formosa. Formosa, the Korean Peninsula, and portions of China fronting on the Yellow Sea were in Japanese hands. Yet Japan's position was not as strong as it might have been.

The Russo-Japanese War had been settled through American mediation. The Treaty of Portsmouth, which ended the war, won the Nobel Peace Prize for President Theodore Roosevelt, but American motives were not fully altruistic. Had the war concluded with total Japanese victory, had Japan been able to seize Vladivostok and the rest of Siberia, Japan's position would have been even more powerful. Japan would have been in a position to expand much more freely in both the Pacific and Asia. The American diplomatic intervention was motivated by fear of what total Japanese victory would have meant to the American position in the Philippines and the western Pacific in general. Portsmouth resuscitated the Russians. If they were no longer a threat at sea, they remained a permanent threat to the rear of any Japanese adventure in China. Thus, Japan was prevented in part by diplomacy—as well as by certain very real military weaknesses—from achieving total victory over the Russians. Through Portsmouth America strengthened its own hand.

In Tokyo, this American triumph was not missed. The response in Tokyo to what was to earn Theodore Roosevelt a Nobel Peace Prize was "a scene of bloodshed, fire and fighting. Never in the history of the Meiji era has the popular indignation been given vent to in such a terrible manner as in the last twenty-four hours."[5] Although the crowd was angry at its government, it was more angry at the Americans. The American legation was singled out for attack. The Americans could not grasp the basis for Japanese unhappiness, that they had been robbed of the fruits of their victory: complete domination of northeastern Asia. The Japanese could not believe that the American glee came from genuine concern for peace and the end of bloodshed rather than from a sinister anti-Japanese plot. The first scene of the U.S.–Japanese struggle had been acted out. The arena for this struggle would be the Pacific, still very much under the sway of European imperialists.

There were no navies capable of attacking Japan from Asia and therefore the western and southern approaches were secure. To the east, the vast Pacific shielded Japan from attack. So, in a way, the Japanese had managed to restore the isolation of the pre-Meiji period.

There were three other great powers in the Pacific. The British had the largest navy but were no threat to Japan, as they rarely operated north of Hong Kong. Between 1895 and 1903, the Royal Navy kept more ships on Asiatic station than the U.S. had in its entire navy.[6] In addition, Britain had entered an alliance with Japan, seeking a northern Pacific force to counter the German and Russian presence. The Germans were in the Pacific by default; latecomers to the imperial game, they were scavenging for unclaimed territories, picking up what was still available and trying to bluff their way into the rest.

The United States Navy was the third presence in the Pacific. Geographically, it was the best placed to cause trouble in the new Japanese area of operations, but it lacked the inclination and the ability to do so. The closest point to Japan was the Philippines, whose northernmost point in Luzon was only 200 miles from Formosa. This was not particularly troubling to the Japanese. Indeed, the Japanese were quite favorably disposed to U.S. seizure of the islands, fearing a German Philippines more than they feared an American one.[7]

Japan was much more powerful than the U.S. in the Pacific. By the end of the 1905 war, the Japanese Navy displaced 451,000 tons.[8] Although in number of capital ships the U.S. outclassed the Japanese, the U.S. had a severe strategic problem: it had two oceans and a gulf to patrol. In 1906, the Atlantic was the dangerous ocean. Thus, while the entire Japanese fleet was in the western Pacific, the U.S. had only one battleship there and only one small dry dock on the entire Pacific Coast of the U.S.[9]

While Japan was quite secure in the aftermath of the Russo-Japanese War, the seeds of conflict between the U.S. and Japan were already present. The U.S. Navy in Manila could potentially block Japanese trade routes to the south. This mattered little at the time. Japan was still concerned with consolidating its control over the northwest Pacific and had not yet developed a hunger for raw materials. The American presence, therefore, seemed innocuous.

Yet, beneath the surface, Japan's mineral hunger was beginning to show itself. From 1907 until the beginning of World War I, Japan's total imports, measured in yen, rose by 47.3 percent. The quantity of raw material (defined as cotton, oil cake, wool, ammonia sulfate, coal, flax and hemp)[10] rose by 75.7 percent. These figures would translate into an insatiable appetite over the coming years.

It is useful to consider the structure of this growing dependency

MAP 2-1. Imperial Division of the Pacific Basin, 1913.

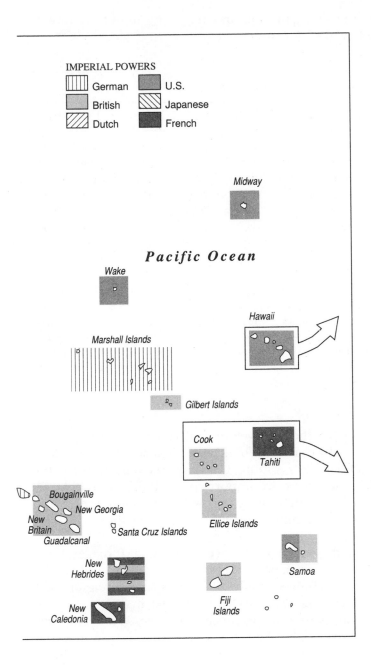

IMPERIAL POWERS

German   U.S.

British   Japanese

Dutch   French

Midway

Pacific Ocean

Wake

Hawaii

Marshall Islands

Gilbert Islands

Cook

Tahiti

Bougainville

New Georgia

New Britain

Guadalcanal

Santa Cruz Islands

Ellice Islands

New Hebrides

Samoa

New Caledonia

Fiji Islands

in greater detail. In viewing this import surge in terms of tons, rather than yen, the following pattern emerges:

TABLE 2-1. Imports of Raw Material by Ton.

	1907	1908	1909	1910	1911	1912	1913	1914
Wheat	54,243	35,627	21,020	49,092	54,517	61,457	168,884	117,726
Rice	406,216	291,213	198,786	137,794	257,935	335,166	545,590	303,397
Sugar	197,783	199,412	134,490	120,207	78,872	136,270	326,196	198,573
Soybean	159,385	199,229	217,403	158,199	176,043	129,725	106,831	150,965
Wool	10,223	4,149	5,980	7,899	6,775	10,063	9,477	9,374
Cotton	254,180	200,640	239,125	297,192	247,977	364,604	402,131	372,047
Skin	4,750	3,225	4,254	3,581	2,237	3,752	4,243	—
Rubber	312	468	599	716	925	902	1,207	1,038
Iron Ore	123,000	190,000	188,000	188,000	125,000	198,000	280,000	299,000
Phosph.	128,000	120,000	71,000	168,000	230,000	285,000	331,000	285,000
Coal	19,000	31,000	117,000	176,000	184,000	311,000	581,000	965,000
Salt	10,000	33,000	26,000	19,000	38,000	21,000	40,000	49,000
Total	1,367,092	1,307,963	1,223,657	1,325,680	1,402,281	1,856,939	2,796,559	2,751,120

(Source: The Bank of Japan)

Between 1907 and 1914, the total weight of all commodities imported more than doubled. But, as a harbinger of what was to come, key industrial commodities rose far more. Coal imports went from 19,000 to 965,000 metric tons; iron ore imports from 123,000 to 299,000 metric tons. Of the 1,384,028 tons of growth in imports, therefore, over 80 percent of the tonnage growth came from these two key industrial commodities.

Japan's emerging dependency on places like China, India, and the Netherlands East Indies was a pattern that would endure until World War II, and even later. Indeed, much of Japan's later foreign policy can be foretold by looking at a map of its imports in 1913.

The reason for an American presence in the western Pacific was somewhat more murky. The Americans had come to the imperial game late and, like Germany, searched for targets of opportunity. Such a target was the Spanish empire; the result was the American Philippines. Those searching for an economic motive in the American presence were frequently disappointed. Economic gain was something hoped for, but in its absence there were other benefits from being in the Philippines.

MAP 2-2. Japan's Imports by Country, 1913.

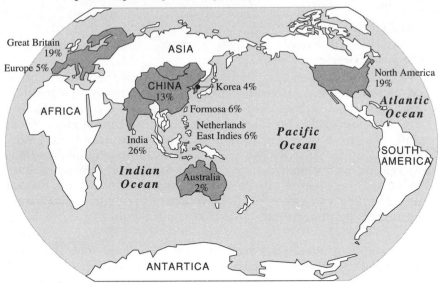

American interests were essentially defensive. The Philippines might not have been very lucrative, but they were strategically positioned to be a bone in the throat of any power that would seek to control the Pacific. It was not clear who would pose this challenge. At first, it seemed that Germany or Britain would be the threat, rather than Japan,[11] but both could survive without dominating the Pacific.

Japan could not. Its security would always be threatened by other Pacific competitors. But the fate of any blocking power is, inevitably, to come into conflict with some other power. The position of the Philippines both blocked secure Japanese access to the south and provided a base for any U.S. move north. That the U.S. intended neither was not important. By being aggressively defensive, the U.S. put itself in a position where war with someone, sometime, was inevitable.

Nevertheless, the first encounters between the emerging Pacific indigenous empires were cordial. Each had favorable views of the other. For example, Alfred M. Low, speaking before the University Club in Providence, in February 1905, said of Japan during its war with Russia:

Japan fights for us the battle of freedom, of liberty, of progress, of advanced civilization. If Japan is defeated the whole of Northern China falls under the grim shadow of Russia, and what that shadow means all the world knows. . . .

For the Japanese although yellow in face are not yellow in mind.[12]

On the Japanese side there seemed an awareness that this could not last. In 1910, Kiyoshi Kawakami wrote:

> We realize that when once we begin to take away the Chinese trade of Western nations, the latter will cease to be effusive, sympathetic and cordial towards us. But that is one thing we cannot help. We are poor; our natural resources are limited; we cannot grow wheat and corn, raise hogs and cattle and "live on the fat of the land," as you of great America can. . . . And like all poor families ours is increasing with embarrassing rapidity—such is the irony of fate. What will become of our ever-increasing children if we do not manufacture and export as best we can? If we entice away your customers by underselling, that is no fault of ours.[13]

Kawakami's predictions were not long in coming true. By 1917 warm American sentiments had changed to the following:

> Japan is jesuitical, leveling everything to attain progress toward her far-flung ultimate end. The world is pretty well assured now that the moral sense of Japan is totally different from that of the Anglo-Saxon countries, or that it is still a fluid and indefinite body. That accounts for Japan out-distancing us in the political game in the Pacific, to be sparing of our vanity. It took arms to do it, and arms is what it takes to oppose it. Japan's policies are such, both political—in her foreign relations and domestic—in her ethical teachings and education of her people to their peculiar, blind patriotic duties to the sovereign, that we could not but be obliged to inculcate among coming and present Americans the principle of war with Japan.[14]

The question is: What happened between Low's speech of 1905 and Frederick McCormick's broadside of 1917 to make Kawakami's prophecy come true?

One significant cause was American racism. Immediately after the end of the Russo-Japanese War, Japanese immigrants on the West Coast became a major issue. Nearly 40,000 Japanese had settled on the West Coast by 1904.[15] American views of the growing Japanese presence were less than enthusiastic. In 1906 a surge of anti-Japanese agitation arose, beginning in San Francisco and spreading up and down the West Coast. The Japanese, claiming that these incidents violated their treaty with the U.S., demanded action by the federal government.[16] The matter grew into an international crisis of the first order, in which, for the first time, each side was forced to think of the other as a potential enemy.[17] Inevitably, such thinking led to an assessment of their relative military strengths.

The United States had to face the inferiority of its Pacific forces and of its strategic position in general. The essential problem was not the size of the fleet, but the need to defend both the Atlantic *and* the Pacific. Even after the opening of the Panama Canal, the principle of never dividing the fleet still required stripping the Atlantic in order to wage war in the Pacific. With growing concern about German intentions in the Atlantic, this was an impossibility.

Thus, for the first time, triggered by a trivial racial incident, the U.S. turned its energies to considering the problem of defending its interests in the Pacific. This led the U.S. to its first rough plan for creating an independent Pacific fleet. It was a momentous decision for the U.S., because orthodox naval doctrine taught that a nation ought never to divide its fleet. On paper at least, the U.S. plan called for constructing a vast new fleet, indeed, two full fleets rather than one divided one.

For the first time the world was to confront the awesome potential industrial power of the U.S. The U.S. found that it could construct, simultaneously and in two years, twelve large warships, and could also commandeer vessels under construction in the U.S. for third parties. Of course, very little was done. As would become a mark of American warmaking, grand plans and execution were very different things. Nevertheless, the basic American strategy against Japan was set. In the event of war, the U.S. would try to hold on while rapidly constructing a fleet. The Japanese strategy would be to defeat the United States before the new fleets could be launched by concentrating its unified fleet for a single, fatal blow.

Between the mutual admiration of pre-World War I relations and the hostility after the war, an important event took place: the emergence of Japan as an imperial power outside the confines of the northwest Pacific. This breakthrough had a profound impact on the United States. What had once been a distant, friendly relationship became much more intimate and much less pleasant. The distant European war changed the Pacific balance permanently.

THE PACIFIC IN WORLD WAR I

World War I was primarily a European conflict. It affected the Pacific only insofar as the empires of the European combatants were affected. In German thinking, their Pacific empire was not useful in itself, but was a means for acquiring more desirable territories. In a war in which Germany was fighting for its life, these colonies were of no value. Thus, the German fleet that was present in the Pacific at the outbreak of the war ran for home. Conveniently, this left Germany's Pacific empire free for the taking.

From the British viewpoint, their alliance with Japan was based on Japan's usefulness in limiting German expansion in the northwest Pacific. From the Japanese side, the alliance had provided access to material and technology with which to build the Japanese Navy. It had also provided support against France and Germany in China.[18]

Britain was ambivalent about Japan's entry into the war. It was both fearful of long-term Japanese intentions and, with Germany gone and France bound to Britain, no longer in need of its services. The Japanese were more eager to become involved than the British were in having them. Much to Britain's chagrin, the Japanese insisted on honoring the terms of the Anglo-Japanese Alliance.[19]

Early in the war, the Japanese and British governments came to a hasty agreement that would shape the Pacific for a generation. Germany's holdings would be divided between Japan and the British Empire. Japan could take the German colonies north of the equator while those holdings south of the equator were to be held by Australia and New Zealand, as British proxies.

In this way the Japanese gained control of a vast array of economically worthless but strategically critical islands: the Marianas, the Marshalls, and the Carolines. With control of these islands, Japan for the first time came into a hard, strategic collision with the United States.

In order to hold and defend the Philippines, the U.S. needed a string of coaling stations across the Pacific. The U.S. had to hold the Hawaii–Midway–Guam–Philippines line.[20] Previously, only Germany was in a position to break that line. What U.S. naval planners realized immediately after the Japanese seizure of Germany's Pacific colonies was that Japan was now in a position to block U.S. access to the Philippines.

This reveals the strategic weakness of the U.S. position in the western Pacific. The Philippines were over 4,000 miles from the main U.S. base at Pearl Harbor, which, in turn, was 2,000 miles from the west coast of the U.S. With the Pacific fleet based at Pearl Harbor, the U.S. Navy had a narrow corridor to traverse to reach Manila fully coaled. U.S. bases in the Pacific were so meager and distant that an enemy holding the surrounding islands would be in a position to block any naval movement. Even more ominously, Japanese forces were suddenly discovered in the eastern Pacific. One ship, the *Asama*, actually ran aground in Baja California in December 1914. This incident set off feverish speculation in the U.S. about a possible alliance between Japan and Mexico.[21] The response to these and other crises was another program to expand the U.S. Navy.[22]

The end of the war brought the question of the naval balance in the Pacific to a head. Japan seemed, suddenly, to be in a position to seize the western Pacific. In both the U.S. and Britain there was growing uneasiness about Japanese intentions. Ironically, Britain had been instrumental in creating the Japanese Navy and in allowing it to seize Micronesia. But by 1918 Britain, as a result of Japanese pressure in China as well as its growing naval power, felt that the alliance could not be maintained.[23]

The Americans, while not indifferent to growing Japanese influence in China, were far more concerned with the Pacific.[24] The challenge led the U.S. to develop its first full-scale war plan against Japan, which bore the code name Orange. Plan Orange was one of a series of plans developed by the Joint Army-Navy Board. JANB developed its first, rudimentary plan against Japan in 1904, along with a set of other contingency plans.[25]

In 1913, Plan Orange contained the following principles:

1. The Philippines would be the primary target of Japan.
2. Defending the Philippines depended on the concentrated battle fleet being in the western Pacific.
3. A line of communications via Hawaii and Guam was necessary.

Since the Panama Canal was not yet complete and the fleet was still concentrated in the Atlantic, and since neither Pearl Harbor nor Guam had yet been developed sufficiently to serve an entire battle fleet, it followed that Plan Orange had merely demonstrated the inability of the Navy to defend the Philippines.[26]

Plan Orange focused on two problems. The first was that if the doctrine of the concentrated fleet was adhered to, then a war in the Pacific meant the Atlantic would have to be stripped of its fleet. Second, it demonstrated that, given the distances in the Pacific, U.S. planning had to concentrate on developing fortified, defensible bases at reasonable intervals.

Assume a fleet consisting of thirty battleships, twenty large cruisers, forty destroyers, twenty colliers, three supply ships, and a fleet repair ship, all cruising at ten knots in good weather. The fleet is ordered to reinforce Manila, and travels from Panama via Magdalena Bay–Honolulu–Guam–Manila with layovers, and begins the trip with full bunkers. The fleet would be able to carry with it 249,000 tons of coal and 45,000 tons of oil. This would leave only 6,800 tons of coal and 3,400 tons of oil on arrival in Manila. Since the ships would then be expected to fight as well as return, and since this assumes flawless operations throughout the journey, not to mention a speed of only ten knots in submarine-infested waters, it is obvious that the U.S.

MAP 2-3. Imperial Division of the Pacific Basin, Post 1914.

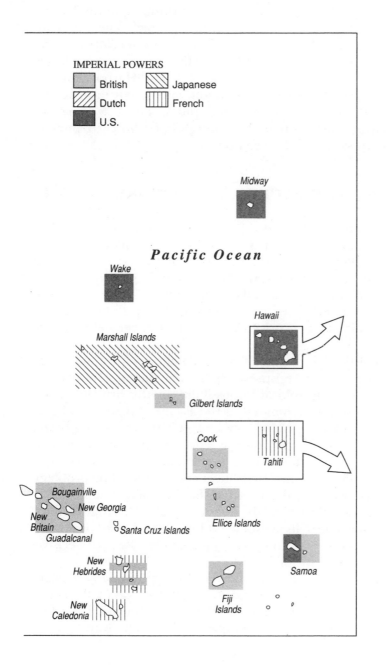

could not defend the Philippines without a string of intermediate bases for supply.[27]

This equation, analyzed more fully following the Japanese move into Micronesia, was the basis for all strategic thinking in the Pacific until the advent of the nuclear-powered naval vessel. The U.S. had essentially three choices. First, it could fortify and develop Hawaii, Midway, and Guam. Second, it could divide the fleet and base a large portion of the Navy in the Pacific, preferably at Pearl Harbor. Finally, it could try to reach some accommodation with Japan in order to guarantee peace and access to the Philippines. The U.S., torn by internal dissension and bureaucratic infighting, chose to pursue watered-down versions of all three options.

THE U.S. AND THE PACIFIC AFTER WORLD WAR I

In 1919 the U.S. finally created a Pacific fleet consisting of sixteen battleships, equaling the Atlantic fleet's total, but smaller and more heavily armed.[28] With this move, Secretary of the Navy Josephus Daniels said that "by this means, the Navy not only protects each of our long coastlines, but places a wall of steel round our ocean boundaries, and gives us a sense of security such as we have never before enjoyed."[29] If so, it was at a price the Navy had never before been willing to pay.

The division of the fleet violated fundamental principles laid down by America's foremost strategist, Alfred Thayer Mahan. However, it faced squarely the geographical impossibility of the principle now that the U.S. was firmly committed to the Pacific. An Atlantic fleet, even utilizing the Panama Canal (opened in 1914), was simply incapable of reaching the Pacific quickly enough and with sufficient remaining fuel to launch the decisive attack that U.S. naval doctrine called for. Only an indigenous Pacific fleet could do so. The problem with this measure was that the Japanese fleet remained superior to the American Pacific fleet.[30] In the event of war, the Atlantic fleet would still have to come to its assistance. Thus, the U.S. had not really solved the problem of how to defeat the Japanese fleet in decisive combat with concentrated force.

Fortifying Guam and Midway, and developing Manila and Pearl Harbor, also met with half-measures. In 1919, the Navy's Plans Division, analyzing the Pacific battle problem, recommended the following shore-facilities projects to complement the fleet transfer:

1. A new base at San Francisco.
2. Expanded facilities at Puget Sound.

3. An air station and submarine base at San Diego.
4. Fuel-storage facilities and air defenses at Panama.
5. Expanded air defenses in Hawaii.
6. A fortified base in Guam.
7. Increased antisubmarine defenses in Manila.
8. An expanded merchant marine to ship 3.225 million tons of cargo to the Pacific in war.

The price of Pacific domination was high. The cost of the Plans Division's proposal would have been $157,738,350 over five years just for the Pacific Coast and Hawaiian plans.[31] The Senate Naval Affairs Committee approved only $2.4 million for naval facilities in the Pacific.

There was a sharp split among American strategists at this point. The General Board of the Navy (a group of senior, retired officers) said that they:

> . . . could not subscribe to the opinion that without Guam a successful campaign in the Pacific cannot be conducted by us. As long as the present comparative strengths of navies of the United States and Japan are maintained and Manila Bay remains in our possession, the General Board believes that the United States could and would conduct successful operations in the Western Pacific or against Japan. . . . It disagrees with the proposal to abandon our Far Eastern possessions at the outbreak of war with Japan unless Guam has meanwhile been so heavily fortified as to repel any force that can be brought against it until the United States can come to its rescue.[32]

This posed the strategic question for the next generation: could the U.S. hold the Philippines and the western Pacific without fortifying Guam? The younger officers in War Plans, freer of Mahan's influence, were looking at the logistical dimension of the problem, and said it couldn't be done. They argued for a strategy of withdrawal, regrouping, and counterattack. In short, in 1917, the Navy had already devised the general strategy of the first U.S.–Japanese war.

The older officers on the General Board were more concerned with concentrated fleet action and less concerned with intermediate logistical support. They wanted to spend money on ships rather than on bases. The planners felt that the U.S. fleet was adequate, and that in 1924 the U.S. would have 300,000 more tons of capital ships than Japan. They preferred to build aircraft carriers, cruisers, submarines, and bases, rather than more battleships.[33] The argument, at least over Guam, was settled practically in favor of the General Board: on December 7, 1941, Guam had still not been fortified and, therefore, the Philippines could not be held. The War Plans officers were proven right.

The twin issues of a stable and favorable ratio of naval forces and the fortification of Pacific islands could have been handled in another way: diplomatically. Ideally, these questions could have been by-passed in a general political settlement with Japan. Such a settlement never occurred because there was little room for compromise. Geo-politically, both needed to dominate the western Pacific. Japan could not tolerate a large American naval presence threatening its supply lines. The U.S. could not permit the Japanese to control East Asia and the western Pacific, since it would have threatened its domination of the Pacific. Similarly, both desired access to China's markets, and Japan in particular, with its need for export-driven growth, could not afford to share. Thus, where diplomacy is meant to bridge the gap between nations of goodwill, in this case goodwill was not enough. The dispute between the two Pacific powers was ultimately not ne-gotiable. Thus, diplomats tried to solve fundamental issues with stop-gap arrangements. Paradoxically, the U.S. was neither prepared to negotiate away its interests nor prepared to spend the money nec-essary to defend them.

Given that the U.S. and Japan were not in a position to negotiate their differences and that the U.S. was not prepared for an all-out commitment to the domination of the Pacific, the U.S. followed the diplomatic course in a half-hearted way: collective security and dis-armament. The U.S. attempted to secure its position in the Philip-pines by negotiating an agreement on naval forces with the other two major Pacific players, Japan and Great Britain.

The Royal Navy, although exhausted by the war, was still the largest in the world. But Britain could not hope to match the ambitious ship-building programs of Japan and the U.S., both of which had come through the war unscathed. Since Britain had no desire to expand its Pacific empire and was content to hold on to what it had while it recovered from the war, it shared the American interest in limiting the naval power of Japan. It also hoped to use the agreements to hamstring American power in the region.

The Washington Conference of 1922 was called to refound the Pacific military and political order. Its essential goal was to limit the Japanese ability to threaten British and American interests. Essen-tially, it sought to confine Japan to the box it had seized during the Russo-Japanese War. The means toward this end was imposing a force ratio of 5:5:3, in which the Japanese Navy would be held to 60 percent of the British and American force levels. The rationale for this was simple. The sole purpose of a navy was self-defense. The Japanese could defend themselves quite well with 60 percent of the U.S. Navy inasmuch as the Japanese occupied a more compact area.

Similarly, since its possessions were easily within range of land-based aircraft, it had little need of aircraft carriers. The U.S. and Britain, however, had far more extensive interests in the Pacific, interests that were far away from home.

The American reasoning was accepted by the Japanese. Their quid pro quo involved the fortification of the Pacific islands. The U.S. was to agree to freeze the fortification of its Pacific holdings at current levels. This meant that the central Pacific avenue of approach to the Philippines could be closed at will by the Japanese. The superior size of the U.S. Navy was irrelevant if there were no intermediate bases for refueling. Moreover, Japanese naval air power in Micronesia could close off key channels of approach, something the U.S. could not do with its sparse air fields.

Thus, the outcome of the Washington Conference was an agreement not to wage war in the Pacific. In fact, none of the three powers had any intention or interest in waging war, at least at that moment. The vehicle for achieving this end, the 5:5:3 ratio, was of little significance. The Japanese might have had an inferior force, but they were clearly able to maneuver it far more freely than the Americans. Ironically, the U.S. force could protect the eastern Pacific, where there was no threat. But in the western Pacific the problem was the islands, not the Navy. However, with the signing of the Five-Power Treaty at the Washington Conference, the U.S. had given away the right to fortify its islands. So had the Japanese, but they had already begun the process of fortification and had less need of fortification than did the Americans, being much less vulnerable to U.S. attack.

Thus, the playing field was set. Japan had the strategic upper hand although numerically inferior forces. But the real issue for Japan was economic: industrializing and taking its place among the world's great economic, as well as military, powers. Although the value of Japan's empire was minimal, it did secure Japan physically.

The Naval Limitation Treaty of 1922, which grew out of the Washington Conference, set the tone for the interwar period. Deepening mistrust between the two great Pacific powers led them to engage in complex political maneuvers designed to attain political ends without recourse to war. The fact that the growing industrialization of Japan would create a hunger for raw materials that could not be satisfied by its already enlarged empire was unanticipated in any of these maneuverings. These raw materials were obtainable only from other, more distant countries like the Netherlands East Indies, Indochina, and the United States itself. Japanese hunger for oil, steel, and aluminum, the blood and sinews of a modern industrial society, would set in motion events and passions that could not be contained by diplomacy and goodwill. The will to compromise in 1922 would be washed away by reality, and would culminate at Pearl Harbor and Hiroshima.

1. See Dan E. Clark, "Manifest Destiny and the Pacific," *Pacific Historical Review*, 1 (1932).
2. For an American attack on this notion, see Thomas Millard, *Japan and the "Irrepressible Expansion Doctrine"* (Shanghai, 1921). See Robert T. Pollard, "Dynamics of Japanese Imperialism," *Pacific Historical Review*, 8 (March 1939), for an analysis of the Japanese notion of population expansion as a justification of imperialism.
3. Charles A. Conant, *The United States in the Orient* (New York, 1900), p. 156.
4. See Akira Iriye, "The Ideology of Japanese Imperialism: Imperial Japan and China," in Grant K. Goodman, *Imperial Japan and Asia: A Reassessment* (New York, 1967), p. 36.
5. John Albert White, *The Diplomacy of the Russo-Japanese War* (Princeton, 1964), pp. 318–324.
6. Seward W. Livermore, "American Naval-Base Policy in the Far East, 1850–1914," *Pacific Historical Review*, 13 (June 1944), p. 116.
7. James K. Eyre, Jr., "Japan and the American Annexation of the Philippines," *Pacific Historical Review*, 11 (1942), p. 59.
8. Gichi Ono, *War and Armament Expenditures of Japan* (New York, 1922), p. 93.
9. Ibid., pp. 193–194.
10. United States Tariff Commission, *The Foreign Trade of Japan* (Washington, D.C., 1922), pp. 45–46.
11. The U.S. always suspected that it was the real target of Germany both in the Pacific and the Atlantic. See William Reynolds Braisted, *The United States Navy in the Pacific, 1909–1922* (Austin, 1971), pp. 18–19.
12. Alfred Maurice Low, *Japan and the World's Future* (Providence, 1905), p. 18.
13. Kiyoshi K. Kawakami, *American–Japanese Relations* (New York, 1910), p. 139.
14. Frederick McCormick, *The Menace of Japan* (Boston, 1917), p. 346.
15. Akira Iriye, *Pacific Estrangement: Japanese and American Expansion, 1897–1911* (Cambridge, 1972), p. 85.
16. For a Japanese view of the 1924 Immigration Act and its discrimination against Japanese, see Motosada Zumoto, *Japan and the World* (Tokyo, 1928), pp. 109–111.
17. "How long will Japan be patient under the pin-pricking attitude of those States? Will she sit eternally unruffled under the rebuffs accorded to her in the shape of discriminatory laws restricting the rights of her nationals residing in the West? I have not sufficient confidence in Japan's equanimity to hazard the prediction that, whatever the Western States may do against her nationals, Japan will never go to the length of appealing to the tribunal of arms." K. Kawakami, *Japan in World Politics* (New York, 1917), p. 23.
18. See Ian Nish, *Alliance in Decline: A Study in Anglo-Japanese Relations, 1908–1923* (London, 1972).
19. Mark R. Peattie, *Nanyo: The Rise and Fall of the Japanese in Micronesia: 1885–1945* (Honolulu, 1988), pp. 38–40.
20. See Seward W. Livermore, "American Naval-Base Policy in the Far East, 1850–1914," *Pacific Historical Review*, 13 (June 1944), for a discussion of this in the American context.
21. Braisted, *The United States Navy in the Pacific*, p. 164. In 1912, Henry Cabot Lodge had accused the Japanese of trying to establish a naval base at Magdalena Bay in Mexico. See K. Kawakami, *Japan and World Peace* (New York, 1919), p. 95.

22. Outten Jones Clinard, *Japan's Influence on American Naval Power, 1897–1917* (Berkeley, 1947), pp. 161–165.
23. Peter Lowe, *Great Britain and the Origins of the Pacific War* (Oxford, 1977), p. 4.
24. It is true, however, that the General Board of the Navy, in its first sketch of an anti-Japanese war plan in 1919, held that the flash point between the two powers would be China. See Roger Dingman, *Power in the Pacific: The Origins of Naval Arms Limitation, 1914–1922* (Chicago, 1976), p. 98. The U.S. obsession with a naval-limitation agreement indicates that concern with the Japanese Navy was a prior concern.
25. Red was Britain; Crimson was Canada; Scarlet was ANZAC; Orange was Japan. The plans were not ranked in order of probability. See Thaddeus Holt, "Joint Plan Red," *Military History Quarterly*, 1:1 (Autumn 1988), p. 49.
26. Louis Morton, "War Plan ORANGE: Evolution of a Strategy," *World Politics*, 11:2 (January 1959), p. 224.
27. Hector C. Bywater, *Sea Power in the Pacific* (Boston, 1921), p. 273.
28. Braisted, *The United States Navy in the Pacific*, p. 459.
29. Bywater, *Sea Power*, p. 243.
30. Ibid, p. 245.
31. Braisted, *The United States Navy in the Pacific*, p. 473.
32. Letter to Secretary of the Navy, August 10, 1920, ibid., p. 483.
33. Ibid., p. 485.

3
Struggle for Supremacy

The first U.S.–Japanese war evolved naturally out of the geopolitical and economic conflicts that began to emerge early in the twentieth century. Concerns for national security and for access to markets shaped U.S.–Japanese relations much as they shaped those of other nations. In the Pacific, however, there was an additional factor that added an element of desperation to the conflict. Japan was as impoverished in natural resources as America was blessed with them. All of the moves and countermoves of the 1920s and 1930s took place against the backdrop of industrializing Japan's search for raw materials. Every action of the United States that unwittingly threatened Japan's access to these supplies brought the U.S. and Japan closer to war.

In order to understand the process that led to Pearl Harbor, it is necessary to consider the political consequences of Japanese industrialization carefully. The manner in which Japan's growing hunger for resources translated into foreign policy and the reaction of the United States to that policy is critical not only from a historical point of view, but also because it may provide hints as to the future course of U.S.–Japanese relations.

JAPAN'S ECONOMY IN THE TWENTIES AND THIRTIES

Japan emerged as an industrial power following World War I, a remarkable fact, since as late as 1868 Japan had been an agrarian, feudal society. Japan had been thoroughly preindustrial at a time when American, Western European, and even Russian industrialization was well under way. When Perry arrived, he found that Japanese warriors employed swords, shields, and bows and arrows,[1] while Europeans were using massed artillery, armored trains, and breech-loading rifles.

Japan's annual growth rate from 1880 to 1940 ranged from 3.2 to 5.5 percent; during the 1890s and 1930s the decade-long growth rate was about 65 percent.[2] It is noteworthy that the 1920s, normally regarded as a calamitous time for the Japanese economy, still showed substantial growth compared to other industrial economies. In 1937, less than seventy years after the Meiji restoration, Japan ranked fifth in the world in production and consumption of electricity, sixth in steel production, second in cotton yarn production, and first in rayon manufacture.[3]

Japan's industrialization carried an enormous financial and political price tag. Alone among the industrial nations, Japan had to import most of the raw material that fueled its factories. The more dependent Japan became on imports, the greater was the risk of mortgaging itself politically, for the suppliers of its raw materials obviously were in a strong position to make demands.

In 1920 Japan for the first time ceased to be self-sufficient in food and deepened its dependence on other imported materials as well.[4] This was just the beginning. Between 1920 and 1931, the quantity of raw material required to run the Japanese economy nearly tripled; oil imports soared to twenty times the 1920 level, coal quadrupled, iron ore more than doubled.[5] The very success of the Japanese economy was its undoing. It could not continue to grow without becoming more dependent on other countries and this inevitably would undermine Japanese autonomy. If Japan was not to give up its independence, the only solution was that it gain control of its sources of supply or be strong enough so that others would fear to tamper with those supplies.

Unlike Britain or France, Japan did not have wealthy colonies to draw on. The empire Japan had won during World War I had its strategic uses, but it did not come close to satisfying Japan's need for raw materials. Economically, Micronesia was more of a burden than a benefit to Japan. In 1922, Japan lost over 4 million yen in Micronesia, and did not make money off Micronesia until 1932, when it was able to report a profit of 122,000 yen. In no year did Japan show a profit greater than about 700,000 yen.[6]

During the interwar period, Japan generally had a negative balance of trade. With exceptions only in 1935 and 1938, Japan imported more than it exported. In fact, losses were covered by income from invisible exports, including shipping service, profits from Japanese overseas enterprises, remittances of Japanese emigrants in foreign countries, and tourism.[7] From 1935 through 1939, Japan actually enjoyed an average positive balance of payment of about 6.5 million yen. In the worst year, 1937, the net loss of trade unadjusted for invisible exports equalled about 3.2 percent of the gross domestic product—bad but bearable.

But money is only one measure of a commodity's worth. There is a difference between the use value of an object and its exchange value. Air, for example, has an infinitesimal price, but its use value is infinite: it is life itself. There are other commodities, such as iron ore and tin, with trivial monetary value but with a use value vital to any economy. Money does not measure the full worth of these minerals, nor the consequences of not being able to obtain them at any price. When such goods become scarce for political or military reasons, then the real barrier to obtaining them is not their price but their physical characteristics: weight, bulk, and the difficulty of transporting them.

Japan's standing as an industrial producer was surpassed only by its standing as a consumer of tonnage. Measured in terms of loadings and unloadings of freight, Japan unloaded 37 million tons, while shipping out only 13 million tons of goods in 1937. With the exception of Britain and the U.S., both of which imported for reexport purposes as much as for internal consumption, Japan topped every country in the world in the weight of goods imported. In terms of net loadings (goods shipped in minus goods shipped out), Japan had the worst record of all.[8]

The potential problem was not financial but political. Japan was fully able to pay world market prices for all its commodities, but the United States chose to use Japan's dependence on purchases from the U.S. for political advantage. In a strategy that was to become common in the postwar period, the U.S. tried to restrain Japanese political influence and military power by threatening to stop sales of raw materials. This threat heightened Japan's sense of vulnerability, causing it to become even more aggressive. In turn, American apprehension at the rise of Japanese militarism increased and caused the U.S. to seek more effective sanctions against Japan, in a cycle that culminated on December 7, 1941.

The search for raw materials has been a driving force in Japan's foreign policy since it industrialized. Japan could not survive as a modern nation without steady imports of minerals. This is a permanent feature of Japanese life. Indeed, the more successful Japan is industrially, the more dependent it is on these imports.

The accident of geography that impoverished Japan's soil carried a cruel twist. The most readily accessible supply of many minerals was in the hands of its geopolitical rival, the United States. Thus, over and over again Japan found itself in a position in which it depended on cordial trade relations with its geopolitical enemy. Throughout the twentieth century, this paradox forced Japan to look elsewhere for alternative supplies to buy or seize. Japan's search for autarky, for complete economic self-sufficiency, was understood by America to be a geopolitical challenge. This collision course, first undertaken in the 1920s, is one of the permanent and unavoidable forces driving U.S.–Japanese relations.

THE PACIFIC BALANCE

On the surface, the 1920s were a relatively stable period in the Pacific. Boundaries remained fixed and the military balance, reinforced by the Naval Limitation Treaty of 1922, remained constant. Japan's willingness to accept an inferior naval position was balanced by the Anglo-American agreement not to challenge Japan's World War I territorial gains. While the Pacific basin was stable, the Asian mainland was in chaos as the Chinese revolution raged on. The unrest in China both threatened imperialist interests there and opened up the possibility of new types of exploits. The newer imperialist powers—Japan and America foremost among them—were given opportunities to increase their power at the expense of the older European imperialists as well as the Chinese.

While China held center stage in the region, there were other, growing tensions beneath the surface in the Pacific. Most of these arose from Japan's growing need for raw materials and its concern that it could not adequately support its population. Many in Japan saw the need for a more aggressive foreign policy to secure these supplies. One should not think, however, that the Japanese were eager for war. In 1922, Prime Minister Korekiyo Takahashi said, "The war taught us that it is impossible to undertake national expansion through the use of force." He went on to say, "While armed conflict has cooled off, economic competition is becoming more and more intense."[9] As is the case today, there were those who believed that competition could be confined to economic life and not spill over into military confrontation.

There were others, of course, who argued that Japan's problem was not economic but political and military. They felt that Japan could not guarantee its economic growth unless it had more direct and secure control of its resources and markets. The key to this was military power, and particularly naval power. But Japan's military and naval power was strictly limited by the arms-limitation agreements of the early 1920s. By 1930, Japan had decided that it could no longer tolerate limitations on its naval force, since this also limited Japan's ability to achieve economic autonomy. Japan demanded parity with Britain and America, and that required a renegotiation of the Washington Naval Limitation Treaty of 1922.

Throughout the 1920s, the three Pacific powers had pressured each other for treaty revisions based on different strategic needs. This divided America and Britain from each other more than from Japan. Britain wanted treaty revisions permitting large numbers of light cruisers, important for protecting its long and complex lines of supply. Britain had numerous bases and therefore would exchange range for more and cheaper ships. The U.S., lacking refueling stations, preferred revisions allowing larger and more powerful cruisers with longer ranges.[10] As with nuclear weapons today, matters of strategy turned on obscure technical details.

The Japanese also had a problem with force projection, one that was much more threatening to its national interest. Force projection, the ability of a nation to send military forces to distant battlefields, is essential for any major power, particularly island powers. By 1931, Japan was importing vast amounts of raw materials for its factories: 90 percent of its iron ore, 66 percent of its oil, 100 percent of its rubber, 94 percent of its lead, and 85 percent of its phosphates were coming from overseas. The most important suppliers were the United States, Canada, China, the Netherlands East Indies, and Malaya.[11] Given the potential for rising tension with the United States, Japan simply had to have alternative suppliers that it could control. If Japan was not willing to accept the limits placed on it by the United States, then it had no choice but to seek more direct control over its raw materials. And for that, any island needs a powerful navy.

Japan had two basic interests it needed to protect. These were, according to the cabinet led by Prime Minister Hamaguchi:

1. To preserve the safety of our national territory by resisting in the western Pacific the naval forces employed by a certain country.
2. To protect the sea communication our special national circumstances have made vital to our national existence.

Thus, Hamaguchi wanted three treaty revisions:

1. The standard for our auxiliary vessel strength should be the actual amount we will possess at the end of fiscal 1931, and the ratio of our forces to those of the United States should be overall at least 70%.
2. We should have a 70% ratio vis-à-vis the United States, particularly in the category of 20-cm gun heavy cruisers.
3. Submarine tonnage should be the actual amount we will possess at the end of fiscal 1931.[12]

Hamaguchi had clearly stated the dual structure of Japanese foreign policy. On one hand, Japan had to protect the physical, territorial integrity of the northwest Pacific against American encroachment. At the same time, Japan's "special national circumstances"—resource scarcity—made it essential that Japan control extended sea-lanes. The key to this latter goal was a limitation on the U.S. Navy and expanded rights for Japan's.

The outcome of the London Conference, forced by Japan, was not what Japan had hoped for. The fundamental issue was the number and type of cruisers that would be permitted, inasmuch as cruisers had become the primary means of force projection. By forcing Britain to cut almost 20,000 tons more than it did, America substantially weakened Britain's power in the Pacific.[13] Although still a great power in the region, Britain's ability to protect its holdings east of Singapore was significantly damaged at the London Conference, a fact that would have great significance ten years later. Japan remained in third place, managing to increase its overall tonnage to about 67 percent of each of the U.S. and British fleets. Moreover, with limitations placed on its heavy cruisers, Japan was still confined to its corner of the Pacific. Thus, the real winner of the London Conference was the U.S. Navy, a fact that concerned the Japanese greatly.

The decisive diplomatic breakout had eluded the Japanese. The Supreme War Council met, following the conclusion of the negotiations, and argued that accepting the treaty would require the following secret reservations on the part of the Japanese government:

1. Complete utilization of the strength allotted under the agreement; the maintenance and improvement of the capabilities of existing vessels; full development of the categories of vessels upon which no limitations are placed by the treaty.
2. Full provision of the air strength necessary to support and implement operational plans.
3. Improvement of defense facilities; full development of experimental research agencies; improvement of educational facilities; rigorous implementation of every kind of training exercise; im-

provement and full development of personnel, materiel, amphibious equipment, arrangements for dispatching expeditionary forces, etc.[14]

The London Treaty stifled Japanese naval expansion. Its limitations prevented the navy from reaching the strength required to engage in the amphibious operations necessary to seize Asia's periphery. Thus, by default, Japan was given only one direction in which to expand: toward China, where a continental, army-oriented operation was practicable. Since 1895, Japan had entertained the belief that it had the right to expand into China. An informal domination of China by Japan had long existed, and many Japanese statesmen had argued for its formalization.[15] However, the choice of China as a target for expansion had less to do with ideology than with lack of better options.

The result of the London Treaty was a phenomenon we are familiar with from contemporary nuclear arms control agreements. Those areas and weapons not specifically controlled become objects of intensified competition. The London Treaty was an invitation to an arms race. The Supreme War Council's response to the treaty concluded by saying that "as soon as this treaty expires, it is necessary immediately to perfect our national defense in accordance with the policies regarded as the best for our empire."[16]

JAPAN'S CHINA CARD

Prior to the Sino-Japanese War, Japan's involvement on the Chinese mainland, except for specific treaty rights, had been economic and informal. The informal dimension is important. Japan's influence in large parts of China had resembled the European, or British, presence more than anything else, with one exception: Britain's fundamental strategic interests were not involved in China, whereas Japan's were. The informal economic arrangements that sufficed for Britain were not enough for Japan.[17] Parts of China were within that area defined by Japan as its natural security zone, other areas could fulfill Japan's need for raw materials, and yet other areas had to be secured in order to defend the parts that were useful, and so on, in an ever-expanding pattern.

Japan had developed important financial interests in China. In fact, Japan had even greater economic interests in China than did Britain. For example, in 1931 Japan's trade with China was three times as great as Britain's; four times as many Japanese firms did business in China as did British, while total investments were almost identical, Japan at $1.13 billion and Britain at $1.19 billion.[18] Moreover, Japan's investment in China was a far higher proportion of its total foreign investments than Britain's. This presence in China was important enough to defend, but it was not enough to solve Japan's fundamental problems—a dangerous combination.

Manchuria was of particular interest to the Japanese, geopolitically and economically. It was part of Japan's geographic security zone and held, in the minds of some, the key to solving Japan's economic problems. Domination of Manchuria by a hostile power might have led to the collapse of the Japanese position in Korea and could then have threatened Japan's control of the Sea of Japan. An added factor was the fear that the Soviet Union, just twenty-five years after its war with Japan, would come to dominate Manchuria through the growing Chinese Communist Party, which was particularly strong in Manchuria.

Whatever the geopolitical significance, Manchuria's economic worth was badly overestimated. Japan ran a deficit in its Manchurian trade in 1927. Japanese investments in Manchuria tended to have modest rates of return.[19] One Japanese observer tried to explain the Japanese interest in Manchuria in the face of the relatively poor economic performance there:

> The question then arises as to why Japan and the Japanese continue to invest such large sums of capital in Manchuria in the effort to promote industrial activities there? The answer is that investments in Manchuria are not viewed exclusively from the standpoint of immediate profit. The wider significance of the relationship lies in the expectation that Manchuria offers to Japan a solution of serious national problems that seem to threaten her future development. . . . It is in this view of an organic economic relationship between Japan and Manchuria, that a solution of Japan's problems of food and raw materials seems to emerge.[20]

It is not clear what the author of this statement, Masamichi Royama, a professor of Public Administration at Tokyo Imperial University, had in mind here. Manchuria was quite limited in the types of commodities it could potentially provide.

Japan imported only five major commodities from Manchuria—coal, iron ore, salt, wheat, and soybeans. Of these, Japan was heavily dependent on Manchuria for only two. It imported almost all of its soybeans from Manchuria and about three-quarters of its coal.[21] Some of the most important commodities—rice, petroleum, and cotton—were unobtainable there. Japan had hoped that Manchuria would solve Japan's coal problem, and that it would help alleviate Japan's iron ore shortage.[22] But not even the strongest booster claimed that Manchuria could help much with the deeper petroleum problem.

Japan's original ambitious plans for Manchuria, developed after Japan's invasion in 1931, were never realized. By 1936, the end of the first five-year plan, Manchuria had met expectations only in coal and salt. It fell short in all iron and steel categories (only 29 percent of planned steel ingot production was achieved) and shale oil. The next five-year plan, ending in 1941, was no less a disappointment.[23]

Japan's seizure of Manchuria cost Japan internationally. It was a violation of both the Nine Power Treaty, which created the postwar relationship in China, and the Covenant of the League of Nations. Japan's fig-leaf solution, nominal Manchurian independence under a puppet emperor, did not assuage international opinion. The end result was that Japan was forced out of the League of Nations and became an official pariah state. But the point was that Japan had begun the process that would lead to breaking out of its 1905 box, and had become a major factor on the mainland of Asia. Formal sanctions aside, however, no other power, not even China, was inclined to challenge its seizure of Manchuria. It was simply not important enough to anyone.

In retrospect, Japan may have been the biggest loser in Manchuria. Manchuria was a salient, bracketed by the Chinese to the south and, more ominously, Soviet forces to the north. Japan could not passively hold Manchuria. It had to be defended actively. Since the best defense is the preemptive offense, Japan had to spoil the plans of China and the Soviets.[24] This meant that Japan was drawn further and further into Asia in an attempt to protect an entity whose real value to Japanese economic and political security was dubious.

The Japanese Navy was appalled by the China adventure. Where the Japanese Army leadership pressed for operations deeper into China, to Mongolia, the navy demanded a move down the coast instead. It was the south, beyond China, that was the natural goal of the navy. It was there, in the Netherlands East Indies, Indochina, and Malaya, that the resources necessary to construct and maintain a navy were found. Southern operations were naval operations, which played to Japan's technological strength, while China played to Japan's weakness, its manpower shortage.

It should be understood that from the American standpoint, Japan's China quagmire was not all bad. While a Japanese victory would have been a threat, a long, drawn-out conflict that bled the Japanese Army would be an excellent outcome for the United States. U.S. policy was to make certain that Japan did not win outright. On the other hand, it was not U.S. policy to use direct force to stop Japan. In other words, the U.S. intended to use just enough pressure to prevent a Japanese victory, but not enough to cause a defeat that would free the Japanese Army for adventures elsewhere.

There were three tracks. The first was to develop international diplomatic support for China. Franklin D. Roosevelt's famed "quarantine speech" was a late example of this policy: it sought to harass the Japanese without risking any real American interests in the process. As one critic has charged, the decision to ask for a collective quarantine against Japan "was and remained a confused and unsuccessful attempt to solve the dilemma of how to restrict aggression without resorting to threatening measures such as sanction."[25] This misses the point that a Japanese defeat in China would have been more harmful to the U.S. than an ongoing war. When war finally came between the U.S. and Japan, Japan lacked sufficient land forces to exploit its early victories. Because of China, Japan could not invade Australia, lacked sufficient forces for a move on India, and did not even have enough strength to occupy Hawaii. By doing nothing to defeat Japan in China, yet preventing a Chinese collapse, Roosevelt, far from being confused, managed to tie up the bulk of the Japanese Army without firing a shot.

The second U.S. policy track was to supply the Chinese nationalists with sufficient materiel to avoid defeat. Early in the conflict, the U.S. provided financial aid to the Chinese government and encouraged other nations to do so as well. Additionally, while the U.S. government officially refused to provide military assistance, unofficial and covert help was given. For example, as early as 1933, the U.S. Commerce Department arranged for a group of Army Air Force Reserve officers to go to China under contract in order to train China's air force.[26]

Finally, the U.S. tried to use Japan's need for imports as a leash with which to control Japan. Informal embargoes led to more formal ones, until, just prior to Pearl Harbor, the U.S. cut off all trade with Japan and intervened with other countries to halt their trade. If the U.S. had succeeded in this policy, it would not itself ever have had to fight Japan. Instead, Japan would have bled itself to death in China, diverted resources from naval development, and finally collapsed from war and resource exhaustion, leaving the U.S. free to pick up the pieces. The virtue of this strategy was that, should the Japanese follow it faithfully, the U.S. would fall heir to Japan's empire without exertion or danger. The danger was that if the Japanese recognized the likely catastrophic outcome of their policy in time, they might act to avert their fate. Japan did act, at Pearl Harbor.

JAPAN AND THE EMERGING GLOBAL CRISIS

By the late 1930s, the world situation had become less stable. Germany had once again emerged as the major economic and political power in Central Europe. Hitler's desire to abolish the Treaty of

Versailles meant that the Franco-British *pax* which had established the postwar political order would come to an end or would have to reassert itself. The Anglo-French alliance found it more attractive to use an indirect approach to contain Germany. Britain sought to surround Germany with a shifting coalition of powers whose combined strength was consistently greater than Germany's. Britain used the threat of a renewal of the 1914–1918 war to intimidate the Germans, but tried to do this without putting itself at direct risk, and therefore the strategy became increasingly less credible.

More than Europe's internal balance was at stake in these maneuvers. The fate of empires and of the entire international order was at stake. Whatever Hitler's intentions—and there is a good deal to indicate that he did not wish to break Europe's or Britain's hold on their empires[27]—the logic of his position could not help but undermine the European imperial system. Germany could not break the power of France or the sovereignty of Belgium and expect them to retain their empires. Britain, without the concert of European imperialists alongside her, could not survive as the sole European empire.

If Germany were to break the power of the European imperialists in Europe, then control of their Pacific empires would suddenly be up in the air and Germany would not be able to fill the vacuum. In such disorder, it was inevitable that Japan would benefit greatly. On the other hand, should Japan be able to gain control of the Pacific empires prior to a German strike, it would inevitably weaken the imperialists' power in Europe. This was what made Germany and Japan natural allies. The two countries actually needed no formal agreement to cooperate; the natural inclinations of each could not help but benefit the other. Germany's demand for a New Order in Europe would inevitably lead to a new world order in general. Japan's demand for a new order in Asia would help undermine the existing European order.

In such a reshuffling of empires, Japan was the likely heir to the European imperium in Asia, at least as far west as Singapore and as far south as New Guinea. Indeed, it was possible that Japan's naval power might be capable of penetrating beyond Singapore, into the Indian Ocean and toward India itself.

Only one power could stop Japan in this: the United States. The United States was deeply divided on the question of European imperialism. Ideologically, the idea of empire offended the American sensibility. After all, the U.S. fought the world's first modern war of national liberation. On the other hand, the internal ideologies of the European imperialists were much more congenial to Americans than the ideology of those nations seeking to undermine those empires.

Germany and Japan might, in some sense, have been enemies of the old imperial system, but the nature of their regimes was infinitely distasteful to Americans, particularly when compared to Europe's imperial democracies.

The U.S. had no strategic interest in preserving the European imperial system. On the other hand, these empires had decayed to the point where they posed no threat to the U.S. In the Pacific, the United States wanted the Japanese Navy to be confined in the northwest. The British, French, and Dutch served a useful purpose in containing the Japanese. Thus, without being ideologically attracted to the concept of imperialism, the U.S. wound up in a position of supporting European imperial interests as long as they served American purposes. Of course, once the Europeans proved incapable of serving these purposes and the U.S. was forced to take a more direct hand against Japan, the U.S. showed its indifference and even hostility to the European empires.

The formal instrument of German–Japanese alignment was the Anti-Comintern Pact of 1936.[28] Its official target was the Soviet Union, and both Japan and Germany were certainly interested in bracketing the Soviets on the east and the west. But the alignment had a deeper meaning. Germany and Japan were both revolutionary powers; their survival required an upheaval in the international system. From both their points of view, whatever destabilized the great powers could only benefit them.

After 1917, Britain had become a genuinely conservative force. The great adventures of the nineteenth century were over and Britain was no longer changing the face of the earth; it was more than content to try to preserve what it had. As a conservative power, Britain adopted a policy that was both defensive and manipulative. In the Pacific this meant that its primary interest was defending Singapore, its "hinge of empire."[29] With Singapore, it could defend New Zealand and Australia, and possibly even Hong Kong. In defending what it already had, Britain needed to manipulate the Pacific balance of power to its own advantage.

Britain's concern with Singapore was not matched by an equal financial commitment. Like its European equivalent, the Maginot Line, the fortress of Singapore was never quite completed, nor was its function ever clearly thought out.[30] The Singapore strategy depended on the main body of the fleet being based there in a crisis, but this was never to be. It was assumed that a Pacific crisis would not be accompanied by a simultaneous European crisis. When the crisis with Japan came, Britain was fighting for its life in the Atlantic and Mediterranean, and had few resources to spare for the Pacific. Or, to be more precise, Japan did not precipitate the crisis until

Britain was desperately preoccupied. British strategy ought to have been to deal with Japan at a time and place of its own choosing; this would have been Britain's approach in the nineteenth century. But in the twentieth century Britain hung back, hoping the worst would not happen. It did.

Britain's strategy in the Pacific, therefore, was to support China and make sure that it did not capitulate to the Japanese. At the same time, Britain was determined not to go to war with Japan. Sir John Simon and Neville Chamberlain summed up the British position in October 1934, writing to the Cabinet:

> Whatever may be the outcome of the present regime in Germany, we need not anticipate that we should have to fight her single-handed, and although the results of any war between civilized peoples must necessarily result in appalling loss and suffering, we might reasonably hope to escape ultimate disaster if the hostilities were confined to European nations.
>
> But if we had to enter upon such a struggle with a hostile instead of a friendly Japan in the east; if we had to contemplate the division of our forces so as to protect our Far Eastern interests while prosecuting a war in Europe, then not only would India, Hong Kong and Australasia be in dire peril, but we ourselves would stand in far greater danger of destruction by a fully armed and organized Germany.[31]

Thus, Britain found itself in a position of having more extensive interests than it had the power to protect. It could neither deal with Japan nor give in to her. In such a case, Britain had no choice but to come to terms with the other Pacific power, the United States. Such accommodation would not come easily. As Chamberlain put it in 1937, "It is always best and safest to count on nothing from the Americans but words."[32]

Ever since Versailles in 1919, Britain had harbored the suspicion that the U.S. strategy was to maneuver Britain into ever weaker positions. Britain had felt great pressure from the American naval buildup and the U.S. had not been at all sympathetic in international forums about Britain's imperial needs. Britain was convinced that the U.S. meant to strip her of empire. But then, it felt the same about Japan. World War I had ended with Britain and Japan allied in the Pacific and the United States the odd man out. Twenty years later, Britain's inability to protect its interests in the Pacific caused it to throw its lot in with the U.S. Ultimately, Britain would be forced to place the British empire east of Singapore under American protection. This would cost Britain its role in the Pacific.

By the time war formally broke out between China and Japan in 1937, the British were in full consultation with the Americans, both at first taking rather mild positions on the war. The mildness of the British was the result of their weakness, but they did expect the Americans to do something. Alexander Cadogan, British Undersecretary of State, exclaimed, "The time has come to tell the Americans we must do *something* and ask whether they will take parallel action."[33]

Japan was acutely aware of the danger of a U.S.–British alliance against them. As early as January 1936, an editorial in the *Oriental Economist* noted with alarm Senator Key Pittman's call for a combined effort with the British to stop the "international bandits" of Japan, pointing out (not unfairly) that "if Japanese acquisition of more land will restrict American markets just that much, by the same token, America's (and a few other Powers') present control of vast territory is actually restricting Japanese markets."[34]

Whatever bluster came from the direction of Washington, the danger from the north was both more real and more immediate. The Soviet Union had long had interests in China, particularly in Manchuria and Inner Mongolia (it had effectively seized Outer Mongolia in 1922). Japan's growing presence along its Siberian border necessarily concerned the Soviets, who feared a land–sea attack on Siberia in concert with a German attack. With only the single track of the trans-Siberia railway, and a navy far weaker than the one defeated by Japan in 1905, the Soviet Union could not defend Siberia adequately.

Ideally, from the Soviet point of view, the Japanese would be so deeply engaged with the Chinese that they could not afford to divert forces northward. However, given the desultory nature of the war, Japan did have surplus forces available. And given the growing tension in Europe during late 1937 and early 1938, the Soviets had to take very seriously the possibility of a war with Germany. Since diplomacy seemed of no avail, as the British and French were not prepared to join the Soviet Union in an anti-German alliance, the two-front war dreaded by the Soviets seemed altogether possible.

The Soviets tried to turn the tables on the Japanese by an alliance with Germany securing their western flank. The Hitler–Stalin Pact of August 1939 had a strong Asian component to it, from the Soviet point of view. Whatever the diplomatic fictions, the agreement was a deadly threat to Japan. The first response of Hiroshi Oshima, Japan's ambassador to Germany, was to tell Foreign Minister Ribbentrop that:

This action of the German government violates the protocol attached to the Anti-Comintern Pact of 1936. The Japanese government and people will never accept it. The German Government must bear the responsibility for any unfortunate results.[35]

With this treaty, Stalin seemed to have solved his problem of the two-front war. The Japanese fear was that the Soviets would now be free to strike at them in the east without Japan's German ally being in a position to open a two-front war against the Soviets. The pact effectively paralyzed Japan.

To make matters worse, the United States began to tighten the screws on Japan by notifying it in July 1939 that by January 1940, the American–Japanese Treaty on Commerce and Navigation would be terminated. The 1911 treaty regulated U.S.–Japanese trade relations and guaranteed Japan's access to U.S. raw materials at market prices. By abrogating this treaty, the U.S. raised the possibility of an embargo on shipments of oil and other commodities to Japan. The U.S. wanted to clear the decks legally if it became necessary at a later date to actually cut supplies to Japan. Abrogation would give Roosevelt much more leeway in determining the level of deliveries to Japan.

The U.S. had no real desire to fight the Japanese. Embargo, as a strategy, had the advantage of attacking Japan's war-making ability without requiring direct military risk. By resorting to embargo, the U.S. could try to curb Japanese aggression in China without directly exposing the United States to military attack. If Japan accepted the embargo, it would, in effect, be capitulating to American wishes without a shot being fired. The key was whether Japan would capitulate.

The Japanese were deeply disturbed by the treaty abrogation. From their point of view they had acted with utmost correctness toward the United States. Japanese actions in China were no more America's concern than U.S. behavior in Latin America was Japan's. Moreover, Japan had always been a good customer, running a consistent deficit in trade with America. The Japanese tried to put the best face on the threat:

> The abrogation of the commercial treaty is to be regretted as showing an unfriendly attitude on the part of the United States toward Japan. Unless a new treaty is concluded to replace the old within a period of six months, and if the Washington Government resorts to the wholesale prohibition of exports from Japan, it will not only subject Japan to some inconvenience, but will also cause American traders and industrialists to suffer. If events actually reach such a pass, Japan will surely be placed at a disadvantage, but at the same time she will be able to take measures to cope with the situation and these measures will demonstrate that a fatal blow cannot be dealt to her by that method.[36]

The critical issue for Japan was the extent of any American embargo and the extent to which the U.S. intended to interfere with other sources of raw materials.

The year 1940 found Japan in a precarious position. It still did not control its natural resources; they remained in American, British, and Dutch hands. It was bogged down in an unwinnable war in China which, even if it were won, would not solve Japan's basic economic problems. The British and the Americans were moralizing and talking about cutting supplies to Japan, while the Americans prepared the administrative ground for such an action. To make matters worse, the Soviet Union was in a position to attack without worrying about its rear.

Hitler's sudden and brilliant success against France made the situation much worse for Japan. The fall of France, along with that of Belgium and the Netherlands, threw open the question of who controlled their colonies. Of particular interest to Japan was the status of French Indochina and, even more so, the Netherlands East Indies. Were the British and Americans to seize them, particularly the East Indies, their chokehold on Japan would be complete.

As dangers opened up, so did opportunities. Japan could now proceed on two fronts. It could try to seize the orphaned colonies of France and the Netherlands, or it could move north against the Soviet Union. Fundamental strategic decisions on the part of Japan could no longer be postponed.

NORTH OR SOUTH

Since 1932 the Japanese Army and Navy had been at odds. The army had favored a continental policy against northern China, yet lacked the strength to force a conclusive decision. The navy had argued that Japanese power was being squandered on the continent and, from the navy's point of view, the continent did not even offer a solution to the fundamental Japanese problem: lack of oil.

The navy, more than the army, was acutely aware of the limits imposed by Japan's lack of oil, since it required large amounts of oil in order to operate and it was continually aware that Japan did not have enough for sustained fleet action. That oil came from the United States. The only alternative source was in the south, in the Netherlands East Indies. Thus, the navy was pressing a move to the south and had been for quite a while.[37]

The alternative strategy was an expansion of the army's continental approach. According to this reasoning, the basic enemy facing Japan was the same one that had faced it since the turn of the century:

MAP 3-1. Japan's Strategic Position Prior to Pearl Harbor, December 1941.

Russia. Japan could never be secure while the Soviet Union menaced the Japanese position in China and in Japan proper. Additionally, Siberia had the potential to supply all of Japan's economic needs. Thus, this line of reasoning held that the solution to Japan's China problem, as well as the solution to Japan's import problems, lay in dealing the Soviets a fatal blow in Siberia.

Decisions on this question could not wait. The fall of France had opened an historical moment that, if not seized rapidly, would quickly disappear. Two great European empires, the French and Dutch, were suddenly cast adrift. In short order someone would anchor them again.

In the wake of these events, Ichizo Kobayashi, Japan's Commerce and Industry Minister, announced:

> With Japan, Manchoukuo and China as the nucleus and embracing Great Eastern Asia, a common economic sphere should be created. The sphere ought to be able to adopt and carry out an economic policy of self-sufficiency without the assistance of Britain or America forthwith and in the future that of any other country. The proposed common economic sphere could be made independent and to rest on a secure basis so that it might push with vigor the policy of self-sufficiency in the truest sense of the word.[38]

From Kobayashi's point of view, the return to autarky, away from free trade, had been forced on Japan by the United States and Britain, which were engaged in economic warfare against Japan at a time of great uncertainty for it as a nation. The Japanese saw this as a case of the Americans taking advantage of their weakness.

With this in mind, the question was, In which direction should Japan move? A move against the Soviet Union had two disqualifying aspects. First, although Siberia was potentially capable of supplying Japan's needs, in practice developing Siberia's resources required time and money. Infrastructure development alone—roads, port facilities, railroads, which were essential for the transport of materials—would take years and cost billions of dollars. Japan had neither. Second, at the moment of decision the Soviets were allied with Germany. By extension, Japan was in the same bloc as the Soviet Union. This diplomatic nicety was of little consequence. What was critical, however, was the fact that for the moment, the Soviets faced no threat from the west and therefore could concentrate their forces against Japan. Japan chose to decline one-on-one combat with the Soviet Union.

Instead, Japan turned her attention southward, the direction in which it had been drawn since the attack on Nanking in 1938—the first occasion on which the U.S. had placed an embargo on the shipment of material to Japan (in that case, on the export of aircraft).[39] The decision to abrogate the 1911 treaty forced Japan to urgently consider alternatives to supplies from the U.S. Inevitably, Japan's attentions focused on the Netherlands East Indies.

Japan already imported substantial quantities of raw materials from the East Indies. Over half of Japan's bauxite and about 6 percent of its oil came from there. More important still, the Indies were potentially able to supply a great deal more of Japan's needs. One problem, of course, was that it was unclear precisely how much the Indies could supply. Nevertheless, Japan's hopes ran high.

On May 10, 1940, the German Army invaded Holland. On May 20, as soon as the outcome was certain, Japan's ambassador to the Netherlands asked the Dutch government to guarantee the annual sale of key commodities to Japan from the Indies. The demands were for 1 million tons of petroleum, 20,000 tons of rubber, 200,000 tons of bauxite, 150,000 tons of nickel, 100,000 tons of scrap iron, and assorted amounts of tin, manganese, tungsten, chrome, and molybdenum.[40] Japan also demanded that it be permitted to supervise the transfer of these materials and send prospecting teams to the Indies.[41]

These were substantial demands; the demand for oil exceeded the total annual exports of the Netherlands East Indies. Japan, aware that Germany could not control the East Indies if the Netherlands capitulated, wanted to enter into a binding legal relationship with the Dutch before it fell in order to stake a legal claim to Indies resources. Using the veiled threat of a move against the Indies, the Japanese hoped to lay claim to the bulk of the territory's mineral exports. It was also hoped that such an agreement would prevent Japan's greatest fear, which was that the U.S. and Britain would seize the East Indies, using as a pretext the fall of the Netherlands.

The Dutch government, before moving into exile, accepted most of the Japanese demands except for the placement of Japanese personnel in controlling positions in the East Indies. This last appeared trivial compared to the Dutch acceptance of import levels. However, it represented the real weakness in the Japanese position: Japan had no direct control of its resources. They were dependent on the willingness of the Dutch colonial authorities to stand by their treaties.

Americans were divided on their course of action. One group demanded the immediate embargo of oil and steel. Another group feared that this would trigger a Japanese attack on the Netherlands East Indies and on Britain's Asian assets. Roosevelt vacillated and then sided with the latter group. The U.S. still wanted to limit Japanese access to East Indies oil, and therefore pressured the Standard Vacuum company (a subsidiary of what is today Exxon and Mobil Oil and, along with Royal Dutch Shell, the key producer of Indies oil) to limit shipments to Japan. The strategy was to agree to fulfill Japanese purchase orders while consistently holding back on deliveries.[42]

The U.S. bypassed the Dutch authorities and dealt directly with Standard Vacuum because they felt that the Dutch in the East Indies were not in a position to resist Japanese demands. The Dutch were also initially pleased to have private corporations deal with the Japanese, since this gave Dutch colonial authorities plausible deniability in their failure to execute contracts. But as time wore on, a sense developed in Batavia, the colonial capital, that the Americans were trying to have their cake and eat it too. They wanted to resist Japan but would not commit themselves to the defense of the East Indies. The Japanese, observing the machinations of American diplomats in the Indies, astutely came to the conclusion that the Americans intended to prevent Japan from having access to Indies oil, but that they intended to do so covertly, using their commercial assets.[43]

French Indochina, which was left adrift after the fall of France, was another concern. Indochina was interesting to Japan strategically. It flanked China, allowing an entire new front to be opened. In addition, Haiphong Harbor was the main port through which China received foreign supplies.[44] Seizing Indochina would close that supply line. Furthermore, in the event of war with Britain, Indochina was an excellent base from which to launch attacks against Malaya and Burma. Although Indochina could supply the Japanese with some rice and corn, as well as tin, rubber, and zinc,[45] it lacked oil and bauxite. This meant that Indochina could not be the end of the line for Japan.

But Indochina was a case about which both the Japanese Army and Navy agreed. From the army's point of view, Indochina was helpful in its continental strategy. From the navy's point of view, it was a step forward in its southern strategy. Thus, on September 5, 1940, Japan formally occupied northern Indochina; it was the beginning of the end of Pacific peace.[46]

The American response was to gradually tighten the embargo on Japan. Throughout the summer of 1940, Japan was permitted to purchase oil and gasoline in the U.S., while the United States tried to define its embargo policy.[47] A shortage of tankers in the Pacific squeezed Japanese imports badly, and was ultimately more important than anything Washington could do.[48] By the beginning of 1941, the Japanese were feeling the full effect of Washington's intrigues and the effect of the European war on merchant shipping. The Japanese condition grew increasingly desperate throughout 1941. In 1940, Japan had imported over 5 million metric tons of petroleum; in 1941, it was able to secure only 1.1 million tons.

An editorial in the *Oriental Economist*, an authoritative Japanese periodical, said:

As petroleum is an indispensable product in the existence of a modern state and Japan's oil supply is at the mercy of America's whim and pleasure, Japan's only method of survival would be to curry obsequiously to the favor of the United States. But no self-respecting race or nation can tolerate an existence of this kind.[49]

The choice was to become a vassal or go to war.

If a full embargo were to go into effect, Japan would have to dig deep into its oil reserves, fully utilize its small domestic production, and resort to inefficient methods of synthetic oil production. In mid-1941, Japan had about 58 million barrels of oil in reserve. During the blockade (which began in earnest that summer), the Japanese used 7 million barrels from this reserve.[50] Without any major exertion, Japan would run out of oil in about four years. All the U.S. had to do was wait.

But this figure did not take the high consumption rates of war into account. Japan could not go to war on its own resources, as it was estimated that a single major fleet action by the Japanese Navy would, by itself, require over 3 million barrels of oil.[51] When requirements for aviation fuel, war production, and other uses were added in, it became clear that Japan could not afford to go to war either, unless the war was short or Japan quickly captured oil resources that could rapidly be brought on line.

Oil defined Japan's strategic problem. If the U.S. persisted with its blockade, Japan could not remain passive. Japan had only two choices. First, it could negotiate its differences with the U.S. This was the desired course for Japan, except that the U.S. price was too high. The U.S. expected, as the price for lifting the embargo, that Japan would end its imperial ambitions. If Japan did this, of course, it would mean that it would never achieve economic independence and would be permanently at the mercy of the U.S. Japan's second choice was to forcibly seize what it needed.

Japan's position in minerals was even grimmer. In August 1941, Japan had the reserves indicated in Table 3-1.

Japan could follow two war strategies. It could avoid war until after its stockpile had grown large enough to endure an extended embargo, or go to war quickly, seizing areas that could rapidly produce the needed minerals. Put plainly: it could wait, using diplomacy to buy time and material, or attack the Netherlands East Indies and Malaya immediately. U.S. intransigence made the former course impossible.

There was another reason for going to war sooner rather than later. The United States had launched a major fleet-construction program, the Two Ocean Naval Expansion Act of 1940. The first major units under this program would come on line in 1943, while the entire program was to be completed in 1946–1948. The U.S. would probably be unbeatable by 1943.[52]

TABLE 3-1. Japan's Mineral Stockpiles in Months, 1941.

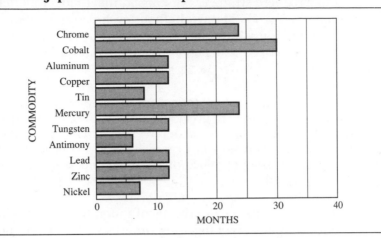

(Source: British Ministry of Defense, Enemy Resources Department)

Japan could not launch its attack immediately after the American embargo; it was still in the process of accumulating necessary material. More important, Japan was afraid that if it struck southward, the Soviets would use this as an opportunity to attack Japanese forces in China and Manchuria. This fear paralyzed the Japanese from the fall of 1940 until June 22, 1941. On that date, Germany attacked the Soviet Union and the fear of a two-front war disappeared. While there was a passing temptation to take advantage of the Soviet's plight and attack northward, and while Stalin was himself terrified of this, Japan's interests clearly lay in the south.

THE FIRST U.S.–JAPANESE WAR: THE STRUGGLE FOR RESOURCES

Japan's purpose in World War II was to attain self-sufficiency in industrial minerals. Its strategic goals, therefore, were:

1. To occupy those areas that could rapidly be utilized for the production of these materials.
2. To secure the sea-lanes necessary for seizing these areas and transporting the raw materials to Japan.

The first problem was the definition of the area necessary for Japan's mineral needs.

In theoretical discussion and planning, the Japanese had identified this area as the Greater East Asia Co-Prosperity Sphere. This concept originated in Japanese strategic thinking in the 1930s. Colonel Ishiwara Kanji and Miyazaki Masayoshi first developed the notion of an East Asian Federation whose purpose it would be to expel Western imperialism from East Asia and create a series of autonomous nations in its wake. Miyazaki wrote:

> Japan, chief advocate of Federation, must perceive the psychology of the suppressed people in every stage of the Federation program and should refrain from replacing Western style exploitation by Japanese style suppression in organizing the Federation . . . the right of political independence of the liberated peoples must be completely assured.[53]

The chief defect in the benign theory of federation was that Japan and its mineral suppliers had divergent interests. The economic motive behind confederation was for Japan to secure a noncompetitive position for scarce resources. Since this, by definition, would suppress prices below world levels, as well as infringe on the sovereignty of the supplier, Japan could not secure its national interest and guarantee independence at the same time.

The other defect of Miyazaki's theory, as well as of others that came in its wake, was that it concentrated on Sino-Japanese relations, ignoring the fact that China was incapable of supplying Japan's needs. This point was realized by Yabe Teiji, who wrote a position paper for the Navy Ministry in 1940:

> If America dares to carry out a total blockade against Japan, the Empire will face a very difficult situation regarding scrap iron, oil, especially fuel for airplanes, machinery, copper, molybdenum, vanadium, cotton, etc. And if Canada, Australia, New Zealand, India, British Malay, the Philippine Islands, etc., do not cooperate, Japan will have additional problems as to wool, cotton, rubber, pulp, nickel, lead, copper, bauxite, steel, etc.[54]

The goal of the Japanese Navy was, therefore, to seize those of Japan's suppliers that were both important and accessible: British Malaya and, above all, the Netherlands East Indies. Australia and India were distant dreams, beyond the Japanese imagination for the moment.

By seizing just the East Indies and Malaya, Japan would solve a wide range of its mineral problems, especially its lack of oil. Together, they could supply 151 percent of Japan's oil needs (as of 1940), 202 percent of its tin needs, and 98 percent of its bauxite requirements. In addition, 37 percent of its nickel and 22 percent of its iron ore requirements could be satisfied.[55] Taking into account that these figures represent only immediately available supplies, it is obvious that, given time and capital, Japan would have been able both to expand production and develop production of other resources. The East Indies already had proven reserves of phosphates, chromite, tungsten, and copper (developed by a Japanese firm).[56]

Seizing the Netherlands East Indies might appear to solve Japan's oil problems, but, in fact, it would produce a new set of problems: transporting the oil safely back to Japan. The rapid seizure of the Indies would have to be followed by the establishment and maintenance of secure sea-lanes. These lanes were located in an arc ranging from the Malay peninsula to the eastern end of the Indonesian archipelago, and would need to be defended from counterattack by the combined power of the United States and the British Empire. No small problem.

The obvious Japanese strategy would have been to launch a strike against the East Indies and then wait for the American fleet to counterattack, using America's extended supply lines to advantage.[57] The weakness in this strategy was that the U.S. did not necessarily have to counterattack. It could use a forward defensive strategy by reinforcing the Philippines and sitting astride the line of supply to Japan.

Clark Airfield in the Philippines was about 850 miles from Quang Ngai, the nearest point on the Indochinese coast. Mindanao was about 300 miles from Halmahera, the easternmost island of the Netherlands East Indies. The range of the Grumman F4F Wildcat was 900 miles, and that of the F4U Corsair 1,000 miles, without either requiring auxiliary external fuel tanks.[58] The long-range B-17 bomber and the Douglas Dauntless precision dive-bomber gave the U.S. the capability, from bases in the Philippines, of closing off the South China Sea without even needing to involve aircraft carriers. The only passage through the islands would have been the straits between Halmahera and New Guinea. Since that was a Commonwealth possession, British participation in the war, which was certain given the necessary seizure of Malaya and Singapore, would have closed off that exit.

Thus, Japan could not content itself with the seizure of Malaya and the East Indies. The Philippines, along with New Guinea, would have to be seized as well. However, in order to seize the Philippines it was necessary that they be isolated from reinforcements. Since only Guam and Wake Island, both relatively undefended, barred the way to complete control of the central Pacific, this seemed as if it would be an easy task.

However, taking Guam and Wake was simpler than holding the central Pacific against the U.S. Navy. Japan might well have defeated the U.S. fleet in a surface battle, or at least fought them to a standstill,

MAP 3-2. Japanese Transport Routes and Allied Airpower Prior to
Pearl Harbor, 1941.

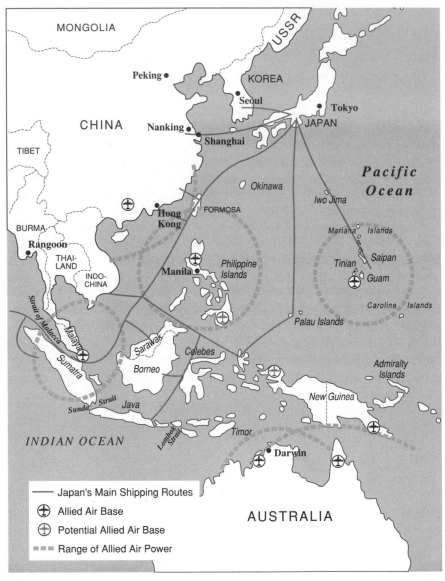

since the battle would have been fought within range of Japanese
land-based aircraft in the Marshalls and Gilberts. But this would
have meant tying down substantial elements of the Imperial fleet
to static, defensive duty, when the urgent task was seizing the East
Indies, landing amphibious troops in Malaya and New Guinea, and

standing by to block any British effort to move east of Singapore with its fleet.

Japan could not afford to wait for a U.S. countermove, even though that would have allowed it to fight a battle on more favorable terms. Time was of the essence. And this meant that the decisive naval battle of the Pacific would have to be fought at the beginning of the war. The decision to attack Pearl Harbor increased the risks of failure, but it would free the Imperial fleet for urgently required action elsewhere.

From the beginnings of strategic planning in the 1920s, U.S. naval planners realized that they could not hold the Philippines owing to the weakness of the U.S. position in the central Pacific. The decision not to fortify Guam troubled many, but it was a case of, Why bother? No amount of fortification would have allowed it to function as a corridor for U.S. forces coming to the aid of the Philippines. The only U.S. option was prepositioning troops and supplies in the Philippines, but this would have meant a static defense. Or the U.S. could have taken the offensive and seized the Carolines and Marshalls themselves, widening the corridor and setting up a blockade south of Japan. Such a move was politically impossible for Roosevelt, as he could not afford to initiate hostilities. More important, it might have forced Japan to move against Siberia, perhaps forcing a Soviet surrender and creating grave problems for the U.S. in Europe.

Instead, the U.S. chose a dynamic defense. Recognizing that the Japanese would take the Philippines, as well as the Netherlands East Indies and Malaya, the U.S. plan was to accept this loss, marshal the fleet, attack through Micronesia, engaging and defeating the Japanese fleet decisively, and conclude with a blockade of the Japanese home islands. The Japanese recognized this to be the American plan, and all their thinking went into the problem of coping with the U.S. fleet when it sailed west. This was the conceptual origin of the Pearl Harbor operation.

Allowing Japan to seize its defensive perimeter had been built into the U.S. Pacific strategy. The U.S. never intended to break the first Japanese assault. The U.S. had all the time in the world. The reason for Japan's early success had, therefore, less to do with the success of Japan's Pearl Harbor strategy than it did with American planning. The Japanese understood the element of time fully. There were limits to their stockpiled food and minerals; their factories could not match American production; and their isolation increased whether there was war or peace. Japan went into the war fully aware of the dangers. It was a desperate strategic gamble. But from the Japanese point of view, U.S. demands were impossible. Yoshimichi Hara, President of the Privy Council, said at a meeting on December 1, 1941, while negotiations were progressing in Washington:

> The United States is being utterly conceited, obstinate and disrespectful. It is regrettable indeed. We simply cannot tolerate such an attitude. If we were to give in, we would give up in one stroke not only our gains in the Sino-Japanese War and Russo-Japanese wars, but also the benefits of the Manchurian incident. This we cannot do.[59]

The Japanese hope was that, following the first phase, the U.S. would accept a peace treaty ceding the western Pacific to Japan. Japan failed to understand three things about American thinking. First, that Pearl Harbor would be psychologically traumatic. Second, that senior planners would not be at all fazed by Japan's initial successes, but had planned for them and expected them. Finally, and most important, the Japanese did not understand that the Americans did not believe that they could hold the eastern Pacific if they lost the western Pacific to Japan. The Japanese, having modest goals, did not understand the level of insecurity the Americans felt in the Pacific. In the long run, the U.S. could not believe that Japan would stop at controlling the Asiatic Pacific. Thus, the Americans would spare no expense in driving out Japan; negotiations would not take place before the surrender.

The unwillingness of the Americans to make peace meant that Japan had to make plans for an extended war. Japan had three options. The first was to go west of Singapore into the Indian Ocean. The second was to move south against Australia. The third was to go east, against Hawaii. The virtue of the first move was that it would have knocked Britain out of the war and secured Indian raw materials for Japan. The weakness of the plan was that it would have required army troops far beyond what was available. The second strategy enjoyed the same benefit as the first, plus it would have knocked out the United States' forward operating base. But here, too, the Japanese lacked troops. The move against Hawaii would have gained Japan several years, but again, they lacked troops for an assault. Further, it would have risked the entire Imperial fleet. Thus, indecisively, the Japanese tried probes in all three directions: toward Columbo in Ceylon; toward Port Morseby and Darwin; and finally, the Midway Island operation.

It took three years for the Americans to fight their way back. But the war was won for the U.S. when in 1942 the Japanese failed to win it. The U.S. could now attack the Japanese at the time and place of its choosing. Japan was no longer capable of launching spoiling attacks on the order of Pearl Harbor. Every time a plane or ship was destroyed, or a man killed for Japan, at an equivalent cost for the U.S., the result was a net victory for the U.S.

It must be recalled that Japanese strategy had two goals. The first was seizing the south, but the second was the key: rapidly securing and transporting raw materials to Japan. Toward foiling the Japanese on this score, the U.S. had created the most ruthless and effective fighting force of the war: the U.S. Navy's submarine force.

Unrestricted submarine warfare had been tried by the Germans in both wars with substantial, but not decisive, effect. The U.S. campaign against Japan was the only strategic success of submarine warfare thus far in history. Among the reasons for this was the utter ruthlessness of the American campaign. Within hours of Pearl Harbor, and using it as justification, the U.S. Navy Commander, Submarines Pacific, ordered his boats to commence unlimited submarine warfare against all Japanese vessels, naval, merchant, and otherwise. Conventional rules of warfare, which had placed restrictions on the manner in which merchant vessels could be attacked, were immediately abandoned. Since these merchant vessels, particularly tankers, were the key to victory or defeat, the U.S. went for Japan's jugular immediately.

The effect of the submarine war against Japan's mineral imports was devastating:

TABLE 3-2. Decline of Japanese Merchant Fleet, December 1941– August 1945.

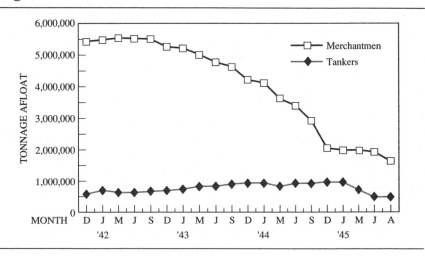

(Source: Roscoe, *U.S. Submarine Operations in World War II*)

Japan began the war with over 5 million tons of freighter capacity and a half-million tons of tanker capacity. This figure was barely sufficient for Japan's needs. By the end of the war, freighter capacity was down to 1.5 million tons and tanker capacity to 266,000 tons, woefully insufficient for their needs. This situation had a devastating effect on Japanese imports. Between 1940 and 1944, imports of coal were slashed by 62 percent, iron ore by 65 percent, and total bulk commodity tonnage by 54 percent. By 1945, Japan's imports of bulk commodities had plunged almost 90 percent from prewar levels.[60]

U.S. submarines, ranging themselves on the north–south routes from the Indies and along the Japanese coast, systematically interdicted the flow of raw materials, making it impossible for Japan to expand its industrial production to match its growing strategic needs. Many commentators have noted that Japan was able to maintain production levels. However, given the vast expansion of American production, merely maintaining production was woefully insufficient.

The United States won the war for the same reason that Japan started it: resources. The distance that Japan had to go for its resources made it too vulnerable to U.S. countermeasures, particularly submarine warfare, to cope with the problem. This was compounded by Japan's inability to formulate a satisfactory antisubmarine warfare campaign. It is one of the ironies of the war that Japan, which started the war because of its economic insecurity, never configured its forces to protect against this threat.[61]

The decision to submit to the American demand for unconditional surrender was made necessary by a number of events outside the control of the Japanese. First, the Soviet declaration of war on Japan in July 1945 meant that all room for diplomatic and political maneuver had disappeared. The Japanese undoubtedly hoped that their unwillingness to strike at the Soviets during the latter's darkest hour might be reciprocated in Japan's hour of need. This hope was misplaced.[62] With the Soviet intervention, Japan was now surrounded by a solid phalanx of enemies.

Second, Japan was no longer able to get the supplies it needed in order to maintain its armed forces. Between air attacks and naval blockades, Japanese raw material imports had collapsed. In the first quarter of 1945, Japan had available about one-half the iron ore it had had in 1943. By the second quarter, the rail ferry connecting Hokkaido and Honshu had been destroyed by U.S. planes, so that domestic production on Hokkaido could not reach the factories on Honshu.[63] By 1945, the Japanese had available only 5 percent of their cobalt needs, 10 percent of nickel, and similarly insufficient amounts of other essential raw materials.[64] The worst situation, of course, was in oil, the most essential commodity. By the second quarter of 1945,

Japan had no imports and produced only 492,000 barrels of refined petroleum products, compared with over 3½ million barrels in the same period of 1944.[65] Thus, Japan was simply no longer capable of producing the material necessary for a war of attrition.

Third, the air assault on Japan had made civilian life untenable. Well before the Hiroshima bombing, conventional massed bombing attacks by U.S. planes based in Micronesia had made life in Japan's major cities a living hell. With the massed B-29 bombings from Tinian, Japanese cities became unlivable. On May 14, 1945, Nagoya had three square miles of its city center burned to the ground. On May 23 and 25, sixteen square miles of Tokyo were reduced to a cinder. Over two-thirds as many people died in the Tokyo raid as at Hiroshima and, overall, more Japanese civilians died than did Japanese servicemen.

But most of all, Japan lost World War II because the U.S. was able to impose on it an effective blockade of mineral imports both before and during the war. At the end of the war, because of this power, the Japanese were in the condition they had feared most: they had lost their national autonomy.

The ability of the United States to control Japan's imports of raw materials was what the war had been about in the first place. Japan realized that it could not survive as a sovereign nation unless it could directly control the raw materials it needed for its economy. The United States, fearing for its domination of the Pacific, could not tolerate the power that Japan would have to exhibit in order to secure its raw materials. Thus, the U.S., out of geopolitical necessity, had to destroy Japan's empire, created out of economic necessity. America's fear that Japan meant to force it out of the Pacific, and Japan's fear that America intended to limit Japan's growth by cutting it off from its suppliers, combined. The result was the first U.S.–Japanese war. This war was not an accident. It was the inevitable result of two very real, quite intractable fears. It is these geopolitical and economic realities that continue to haunt the Pacific.

1. Michael A. Barnhart, *Japan Prepares for Total War: The Search for Economic Security, 1919–1941* (Ithaca, 1987), p. 22.
2. See Hugh T. Patrick, "The Economic Muddle of the 1920's," in *Dilemmas of Growth in Prewar Japan*, ed. James W. Morley (Princeton, 1971), pp. 214–215.
3. *Japan Statistical Yearbook, 1955/56*, "Production of Important Commodities Manufactures," pp. 532–533.

4. For a Japanese view on the pressure placed on Japan by population growth and lack of raw materials, see Seizaburo Takahashi, *Japan and World Resources* (Tokyo, 1938). He traces the growth of the problem as well as the perception of the problem.

5. Bank of Japan, *One Hundred Year Statistics of the Japanese Economy* (Tokyo, July 1966).

6. David C. Purcell, "The Economics of Exploitation: The Japanese in the Mariana, Caroline and Marshall Islands, 1915–1940," *Pacific Studies*, 6:1 (Fall 1982), p. 191.

7. Mitsubishi Economic Research Bureau, *Japanese Trade and Industry* (London, 1936), p. 486.

8. See *Japan Statistical Yearbook, 1955/56*, p. 535. The discrepancy between the two figures is due to the fact that the latter figure includes all cargo shipments and does not refine the data in terms of reexports.

9. Akira Iriye, *The Cold War in Asia* (Englewood Cliffs, 1974), p. 18.

10. Kobayashi Tatsuo, "The London Naval Treaty, 1930," in *Japan Erupts: The London Naval Conference and the Manchurian Incident: 1928–1932*, ed. James W. Morley (New York, 1984), pp. 12–16.

11. Bank of Japan, *One Hundred Years of Statistics on Japanese Trade* (Tokyo, 1968). Also, SCAP (Supreme Commander, Allied Powers), Natural Resources Section, *Mineral Resources of Japan Proper, 1925–1945* (1944).

12. Tatsuo, "The London Naval Treaty, 1930," *Japan Erupts*, p. 23.

13. Ibid., p. 347.

14. Ibid., pp. 104–105.

15. On the ideology of Japanese imperialism in China, see Akira Iriye, "The Ideology of Japanese Imperialism: Imperial Japan and China," in *Imperial Japan and Asia*, ed. Grant K. Goodman (New York, 1967), pp. 32–45.

16. Ibid., p. 105.

17. Peter Duus, "Japan's Informal Empire in China, 1895–1937," in Duus, Myers, and Peattie, eds., *The Japanese Informal Empire in China* (Princeton, 1989), pp. xi–xiv.

18. Ibid., p. 3.

19. Frank Dorn, *The Sino-Japanese War, 1937–41* (New York, 1974), p. 33.

20. Masamichi Royama, "Japan's Position in Manchuria," paper presented at the Third Biennial Conference of the Institute of Pacific Relations, Kyoto, 1929, p. 79

21. Bank of Japan, *One Hundred Years of Statistics of the Japanese Economy*.

22. Ibid., pp. 85–86.

23. Nakagane Katsuii, "Manchukuo and Economic Development," Duus, Myers, and Peattie, *The Japanese Informal Empire*, p. 145.

24. On this expansionist dynamic, see Masamichi Royama, *Foreign Policy of Japan: 1914–1939* (Tokyo, 1941), pp. 87–91.

25. Dorothy Borg, *The United States and the Far Eastern Crisis, 1933–38* (Cambridge, 1964), pp. 382, 383.

26. Ibid., p. 73–74

27. In *Mein Kampf*, for example, Hitler rejects competition with Britain for control of the sea, accepting that Germany will be a land power and Britain the great colonial sea power. See Adolf Hitler, *Mein Kampf*, trans. J. Murphy (London, 1939), p. 344.

28. On the Japanese view of this, see Ohata Tokushiro, "The Anti-Comintern Pact, 1935–1939," in *Deterrent Diplomacy*, ed. James W. Morley (New York, 1976).
29. On the strategic concept behind Singapore, and the strategic error, see Ian Hamill, *The Strategic Illusion* (Singapore, 1981), pp. 21–25.
30. Ibid., pp. 166–169.
31. William Roger Louis, *British Strategy in the Far East* (Oxford, 1971), p. 213.
32. Iriye, *The Cold War in Asia*, p. 43.
33. Ibid., p. 44.
34. "Anglo-American Combine to Check Japan Urged," *Oriental Economist*, 3:1 (January 1936), p. 19.
35. Chihiro Hosoya, "Japan's Search for an Independent Foreign Policy," in Morley, ed., *Deterrent Diplomacy*, p. 191.
36. *Oriental Economist*, 6 (September 1939), p. 600.
37. H.P. Wilmott, *Empires in the Balance* (Annapolis, 1982), p. 58.
38. *Oriental Economist*, 8 (August 1940), p. 473.
39. Nagaoka Shinjiro, "Economic Demands on the Dutch East Indies," in *The Fateful Choice*, ed. James W. Morley (New York, 1980), p. 138.
40. Ibid., p. 138.
41. Barnhart, *Japan Prepares for Total War*, p. 207.
42. W.N. Medlicott, *The Economic Blockade*, II (London, 1959), p. 84.
43. Irvine H. Anderson, Jr., *The Standard Vacuum Oil Company and United States East Asian Policy, 1933–1945* (Princeton, 1975), pp. 179–182.
44. Hata Ikuhiko, "The Army's Move into Northern Indochina," in *The Fateful Choice*, ed. James W. Morley, p. 157.
45. W.N. Medlicott, *The Economic Blockade*, p. 96.
46. Ikuhiko, "The Army's Move," *Fateful Choice*, p. 164.
47. Irvine H. Anderson, Jr., "The 1941 Defacto Embargo on Oil to Japan: A Bureaucratic Reflex," *Pacific Historical Review*, 44:2 (May 1975), p. 210.
48. Daniel Marx, "Shipping Crisis in the Pacific," *Far Eastern Survey*, 10 (May 5, 1941).
49. *Oriental Economist*, 6 (September 1941), p. 450.
50. H.P. Wilmott, *Empires in Balance*, p. 68.
51. Ibid., p. 69.
52. Ibid.
53. Masayoshi Miyazaki, "Theory of East Asian Federation (1936)," in Joyce C. Lebra, *Japan's Greater East Asia Co-Prosperity Sphere in World War II: Selected Readings and Documents* (Kuala Lumpur, 1975).
54. Teiji Yabe, in Lebra, *Japan's Co-Prosperity Sphere*, p. 32.
55. Sources: *Japan Statistical Yearbook*, and SCAP, Natural Resources Section, Report No. 44.
56. Alex L. Braake, *Mining in the Netherlands East Indies* (New York, 1944), pp. 99–100.
57. Shigeru Fukodome, "The Hawaii Operation," in David C. Evans, *The Japanese Navy in World War II* (Annapolis, 1986), p. 2.
58. Bill Gunston, *Allied Fighters of World War II* (New York, 1981).
59. Nobutake Ike, *Japan's Decision for War: Records of the 1941 Policy Conferences* (Stanford, 1967), p. 282.

60. Theodore Roscoe, *U.S. Submarine Operations in World War II* (Annapolis, 1949), p. 523.
61. On the failure of Japanese antisubmarine warfare methods, see Atsushi Oi, "Why Japan's Antisubmarine Warfare Failed," in Evans, *The Japanese Navy in World War II*.
62. Robert Butow, *Japan's Decision to Surrender* (Stanford, 1954), pp. 112–141.
63. Jerome B. Cohen, *Japan in War and Reconstruction* (Minneapolis, 1949), pp. 116–117.
64. Ibid., p. 125.
65. Ibid., p. 134.

PART II

THE ARMISTICE

4

U.S. Plans for Japan in the Postwar World

The surrender of Japan in 1945 left it utterly at the mercy of the United States. For the first time since the Indians, the U.S. had to deal with a victory so total that a mortal enemy was left completely within its control. This was, in a way, an unexpected consequence. Publicly, America talked about the war in only the broadest terms: of democracy, equality, justice. Underneath, a few Americans thought in strategic terms of trade patterns, sea-lane control, air superiority. War had broad strategic ends and broad moral ends. But in spite of a few bureaucrats and soldiers who had been quietly planning for the occupation of Japan, America, on the whole, was caught by surprise when the responsibility of ruling Japan fell to it. America was far more comfortable pursuing victory than administering it.

The war had been a moral project, and dealing with Japan was understood to be a moral problem. America was set the task of turning Japan into a humane, liberal, democratic society, founded on the rule of law, the equality of man, and the rights of the individual. It was understood that much of this went against the grain of Japanese culture, but there was a vast sense of American power after the war and this was a place where America was obligated to apply that power.

Thus, a mixture of mild vengeance and moral regeneration motivated American policy toward Japan at the beginning of the Occupation. In determining the mixture, the American attitude was that it was free to choose its course as it pleased, limited only by its duties and responsibilities toward humane values. Totally absent in this relationship was any sense that the Japanese might have something of use to Americans or that they might become useful in the future. There were no bonds of that sort.

Shortly after the peace began, a new threat of war emerged. The postwar break between the U.S. and the Soviet Union shattered the American daydream and turned America's sense of omnipotence into a sudden and terrible dread of the future. The gradual realization that the Red Army would not withdraw from Eastern Europe, coupled with growing communist activity in American- and British-dominated Europe, drove home to Americans that they now faced a new conflict. The U.S. sought allies, and as historical irony would have it, the two nations most strategically located were Germany and Japan, the U.S.'s erstwhile enemies and now its wards. Suddenly, the U.S. looked on both as if they were indispensable partners rather than despised enemies. Instead of seeking to reform Japan, the United States was content with resurrecting it, turning it into an anti-Soviet bulwark.

The Japanese naturally made the most of the situation, as any reasonable nation would. They crafted a relationship with the U.S. that allowed them, over time, to become the industrial giant they are today, while avoiding the dangers of conflict in the Cold War. Much of the history of U.S.–Japanese relations during the Cold War was put in place during the American occupation of Japan. No one can understand contemporary U.S.–Japanese relations unless they understand the beginnings of those relations in the occupation and the Cold War.

THE SURRENDER

When the United States occupied Japan, in September 1945, its intentions were simple: the U.S. wanted to make certain that Japan could never again wage war. In order to do this, the U.S. intended to impose an annihilating peace on Japan, one that would prevent Japan from rising again for at least a century. "Unconditional surrender" meant that Japan, on losing the war, would also lose its sovereignty, its very independence.

Just before the end, cut off from its army in China, isolated from suppliers in the south, no longer able to defend its skies, with a navy incapable of guarding its shores, Japan had a single military option left. It could allow the Americans to invade Japan and then engage them in a war of attrition. Japan could try to make the price of invasion so high that the U.S. would have to agree to an armistice rather than unconditional surrender.

Japan still hoped that a political settlement might be possible. It continued to hold this hope until the very last. After all, Japan had never intended to occupy and rule the United States. All that Japan hoped for was a political settlement with the U.S. which recognized Japanese rights in the western Pacific. Having no wish to annihilate America, it failed to penetrate the Japanese mind that the U.S. was intending to do just that to Japan; if not to the point of genocide, then certainly to the annihilation of the Japanese state. Thus, when Japan put out feelers concerning an end to the war, they had in mind the armistice between Germany and the allies in 1918. They expected a settlement to be harsh, but also to leave the basic sovereignty of Japan unchallenged.

The United States had something more drastic and permanent in mind. The doctrine of unconditional surrender was devised against Germany. The Western allies wished to preserve the anti-German alliance with the Soviets. At various points during the war, the Soviets and the Western allies each feared that the other would make a separate peace with Hitler. Churchill and Roosevelt were particularly worried about this following their failure to open a second front in France in 1943. At the Casablanca Conference, Churchill and Roosevelt (at Roosevelt's insistence) announced that the unconditional surrender of the Axis was the non-negotiable goal of the war. By simplifying the terms of the war, reducing them to the total destruction of the Axis, the allies sought to avoid misunderstandings. Obviously, by making total surrender the only goal, the Axis had less reason to end the war than if a more moderate end had been possible. But Roosevelt, having to choose between stiffened enemy resistance and intrigue in the alliance, clearly felt the latter to be a greater threat.

Since the Soviet Union was not at war with Japan, the matter of a separate peace never arose. Thus, the decision to demand unconditional surrender from Japan was not as compelling as with Germany. Roosevelt, however, had always framed the war as being of one fabric, a struggle of good against the unified evil of the Axis. Roosevelt actually made more of the Axis than it made of itself, but it was necessary for the American spirit to make the war a moral crusade in which all the enemies were equally wicked. This, coupled with the deep hatred Americans felt toward Japan after Pearl Harbor, meant that only absolute victory would satisfy the American spirit.

It is, of course, possible that, had Japan not capitulated prior to invasion, scheduled for October 1, 1945, the American view on unconditional surrender might have shifted. The invasion's toll was expected to be astronomical. Okinawa had deeply shaken U.S. military planners. Since Japan, stripped of its colonies, disarmed, and surrounded by the U.S. Navy, would not likely be a great threat to U.S. interests, it is conceivable that the decision would have been made to negotiate a harsh armistice in order to avoid invasion. This is pure speculation. There is nothing on the record to indicate that senior planners were thinking this way. Of course, these senior leaders were aware of the atom bomb.

This leaves the question of what unconditional surrender meant. Its official definition is in the Cairo Declaration of December 1, 1943, issued by Roosevelt, Churchill, and Chiang Kai-shek:

> The Three Great Allies are fighting this war to restrain and punish the aggression of Japan. They covet no gain for themselves and have no thought of territorial expansion. It is their purpose that Japan shall be stripped of all the islands in the Pacific which she had seized or occupied since the beginning of the first World War in 1914, and that all territories Japan has stolen from the Chinese, such as Manchuria, Formosa and the Pescadores shall be restored to the Republic of China. Japan will also be expelled from all other territories which she has taken by violence and greed. The aforesaid three great powers, mindful of the enslavement of the people of Korea, are determined that in due course Korea shall become free and independent.

The Cairo Declaration meant that Japan would return to its pre-1894 status. The Yalta accords were clear on this historical retrogression when they declared:

> The former rights of Russia, violated by the treacherous attack of Japan in 1904, shall be restored.

As draconian as this was, there was no mention of the fate of Japan internally. What did unconditional surrender mean to the life and sovereignty of the Japanese people?

PLANNING FOR THE OCCUPATION

While the public documents give no hint, there was a great deal of planning going on within the U.S. government concerning postwar Japan. The planning began as early as 1942, at a time when U.S. forces were struggling on Guadalcanal. The diversion of resources to planning the occupation of Japan indicated the superb self-confidence of the U.S. As early as 1942, the U.S. was certain that there would not only be victory, but absolute victory. Such confidence, in retrospect, was well placed.

The planning went on in the context of deep bitterness among the American people. In a Gallup poll taken in November 1944, fully 13 percent of the public was in favor of annihilating the entire Japanese population.[1] This attitude was not confined to the public alone. When the question of what to do with the Japanese was put to a group of officers training to be members of the military government, a few shouted, "Let the yellow bastards starve."[2]

The treatment of Germany was a more pressing issue for several reasons. First, the future of Germany was a bone of contention between the Western allies and the Soviet Union, while Japan's was not. Second, Germany and Europe in general were more important globally than Japan was. Finally, after June 6, 1944, the fall of Germany was a more immediate possibility than the fall of Japan. Planning for Germany sometimes spilled over into Japanese planning.

The first plan for the treatment of Germany was the so-called Morgenthau Plan. Henry Morgenthau, Secretary of the Treasury, posed a postwar vision of a Germany divided among its conquerors, left in the rubble of the war, and denied aid. Germany was to become a preindustrial society. Given the size of its population, this could only be accompanied by starvation, disease, and chaos. Morgenthau faced this prospect with equanimity.

The Morgenthau Plan surfaced in planning for Japan in a document called JCS 1380/15. Prepared for the Joint Chiefs of Staff by the Army's Civilian Affairs Division, the document transferred Morgenthau's draconian vision of an occupied and crushed Germany to Japan.[3] The Morgenthau view had influential supporters. Although Morgenthau was not himself particularly interested in Japan, his plan was adopted by what was known as the China lobby in the State Department as well as by liberals associated with the Institute of Pacific Affairs.[4] This faction saw America's future in the Pacific tied to China. A permanently decimated Japan increased the importance of China.

There was also a Japan lobby in the State Department, centered around the former American Ambassador to Japan, Joseph Grew. This faction, developing the State Department's plans as early as 1942, had much more influence on U.S. postwar policy than did Morgenthau and his allies. The Morgenthau plans were in the end applied to neither Germany nor Japan; instead, a much more modest and restrained set of plans emerged from the State Department Planning Group. While there was postwar controversy over whether MacArthur followed this group's suggestions or pursued an independently developed policy, there are clear precedents in the Planning Group's proposals for what happened later. Most of their planning centered on the political rather than on the social or economic future of Japan. They saw Japan's imperialism as a political problem, and intended to redeem Japan through political reform, rather than to write Japan off and destroy it.

The Emperor was at the center of the problem. His role in any future government was the key political question, as it symbolized whether the purge of the Japanese government would be limited or total, and whether the entire polity would be judged guilty or just certain officials. The Atlantic Charter, the basic document of the war, called for national self-determination for all nations, including the Axis. This was given to the postwar planners as their basic guideline. As inadequate as this may have been, one of the causes for American political unity during the war was the possession of a clear moral principle in fighting it. The State Department planners, as an exercise in applied political theory, sought to shape a new regime for Japan based on these moral principles. Naturally, when the planners hit the ground in Tokyo and theory had to be turned into practice, the purity of purpose was lost amid the jostle of political and economic interests.

However, even at this early stage, the moral project posed insoluble problems for the planners. In distinguishing between citizens and states, it was very hard to ignore the massive enthusiasm in Germany and Japan for those regimes. An excellent case could be made that both regimes rested on popular support, and that both were democratic regimes. Liberal theory also teaches that the masses, left to their own devices, will necessarily create liberal democratic regimes. If this were the case, then the obvious solution for Japan would be to treat the Emperor as a war criminal, try him, remove him as head of state, and dismantle the government apparatus of Japan. The result would be, if liberal theory were correct, the creation of democratic institutions by the Japanese people. The alternative, imposing a liberal democracy, was a theoretical impossibility. Liberal democracy must rest on the will of the governed and by definition cannot be imposed. Yet without intervention, the old regime would remain intact.

Since the war was officially a moral enterprise, occupation planners had to sort through these theoretical conundrums. In spite of all the planning by the State Department, the planning of the Army's Civil Affairs Division (CAD), and consultations of the State Department–War Department–Navy Department–Coordinating Committee (SWNCC), as the war came to an end, no one had made a clear determination as to the fate of the Emperor, nor had they really come to terms with the moral issues of the war. General Hildring, head of CAD, searching for guidance, complained that the State Department planners:

> . . . do not touch upon such issues of central importance as whether the emperor is to be treated as a war criminal or whether the property holdings of the Imperial Family are to be confiscated. Until these questions have been settled, it is impossible to say that the basic policy of the United States has been established.[5]

This statement was made on June 30, 1945!

The State Department group had not made recommendations on this because their views were running against the public mood. The key player in this was Joseph Grew, who had been named head of the Office of Far Eastern Affairs at the State Department in May 1944. By November, he was Undersecretary of State, and the Japan lobby had displaced the China lobby in the Far Eastern division of the department.

Grew did not feel that there could be any stability in Japan without the Emperor. It was his view that the U.S. ought not to carry out any large-scale reconstruction of the Japanese economy or society, and that the essential state structure should be left intact.[6]

The lines had been drawn between Grew's conservativism and Morgenthau's radicalism, or between pro- and anti-Japanese factions. U.S. postwar policy in Japan had to find a middle course between these poles. Douglas MacArthur, Supreme Commander, Allied Powers—known, along with the general headquarters that would govern Japan in the coming years, as SCAP—had almost no guidance as to his direction until well after his arrival in Tokyo. Final Presidential policy compromised: it left the Japanese state intact, but set loose a radical social and economic reform program. In his first directive to Supreme Commander, Allied Powers, President Truman included the following:

> You will require the Emperor and the Japanese Government to take all necessary steps to assure that all orders issued to effectuate the objectives of your mission are promptly and fully complied with by all persons in Japan.[7]

It is instructive to consider the difference with Germany. When Germany was defeated, all government, on every level, ceased to function. The Nazi regime had so completely penetrated German society that the defeat of the Nazis dissolved the state. Additionally, there was no legitimate head of state that could even theoretically be distinguished from the government's crimes. The Japanese case was different in that there was a genuine head of state, Emperor Hirohito, distinct from the head of government. The U.S. seized on this distinction to ease the burden of governing Japan. By retaining Hirohito, the legitimacy of the state bureaucracy remained intact, and therefore the U.S. did not need either to govern directly or to create a new bureaucracy. This also meant that the Japanese state, at least formally, remained in place, and the postwar regime was clearly a successor to the prewar regime. In addition, the radical reforms imposed by the Americans would be imposed in the name of the Emperor, in stark contrast to Weimar Germany, after World War I, where the Kaiser was deposed and lasting reform proved impossible.

There was another crucial difference between post-World War II Germany and Japan. Germany was occupied and divided by all the combatants against her. The U.S. in Japan ran the occupation alone. It both maintained the territorial integrity of Japan (save for minor territories lost to the Soviet Union) and never actually shared power in Japan with any of its allies, not even with Britain. There were 40,000 Commonwealth troops in Japan,[8] but the British experience became a painful lesson for Britain about its decline as a great power. Britain was shocked to discover that the ANZAC (Australia and New Zealand Army Corps) powers were no longer prepared to have it represent them in international councils, demanding their own representatives at the surrender ceremonies rather than a British general.[9] The Australians only agreed to cooperate in the occupation if units were composite Commonwealth forces, rather than British-led troops. These forces were made part of the U.S. Eighth Army, a further slight to Britain.[10]

Officially, the Soviets refused to participate in the occupation because they were unwilling to place their troops under American command. They proposed to occupy Hokkaido and govern it directly, as they did with their zones in Germany and Austria.[11] The Soviets did not press their objections. There were several reasons for this. First, the real Soviet interest was in Manchuria. The Soviets declared war on Japan in order to invade Manchuria and the Korean Peninsula. These two goals, pursued since the late nineteenth century, were far more important to Stalin than nominal participation in the occupation.

Most important was the fact that the Soviets would be in Japan at the sufferance of the Americans, in much the same fashion as the Commonwealth forces. In Europe the Soviet presence was a matter of conquest. The U.S. could not have pushed the Soviets out even had it wished to do so. This was not the case in Japan. Therefore, the Soviets could be in Japan only as a weak, indeed, hostage force. Stalin, understanding the disadvantages of mere symbolic representation, did not spend precious political capital trying to get it. The Soviets remained part of the occupation in two capacities. They were part of the Allied Council for Japan (ACJ), which consisted of the U.S., Soviet Union, China, and a British Commonwealth representative, and were also part of the Far Eastern Advisory Council (FEAC). However, since they were both primarily advisory to the Supreme Commander, Allied Powers, and since MacArthur paid singularly little attention to them, the Soviets had no influence and only used these forums for their propaganda effect.[12]

The Soviets were a more formidable presence via the Japanese Communist Party. The party had been founded in 1922, but its role in Japan had been marginal. Because it was weak, it had been under Moscow control far more than the Chinese Communist Party had ever been. During the war, however, many of the party's cadre had been trained by the Chinese Communists. The U.S. had actually attempted to use the Japanese Communist Party during the war to create some sort of underground in Japan and disrupt the Japanese rear during an American invasion. John K. Emmerson, part of the Dixie Mission to China, conducted these early contacts. While little came of them during the war, Emmerson became one of MacArthur's first advisors following his appointment as Supreme Commander, Allied Powers, and was placed in charge of creating political parties. Since the first project of SCAP was democratization, it followed that the Japanese Communist Party should be included in that process. It was therefore legalized and became a permanent part of the Japanese political landscape.[13] Thus, the Soviets, while losing out in the administration of the occupation, retained what was to be an important tool in Japanese political life through the legalization of the Japanese Communist Party.

THE OCCUPATION: THE FIRST PHASE

Having achieved almost total control over Japan, the Supreme Commander, Allied Powers, had to decide what he wished Japan to become. Everyone was haunted by the specter of Germany rising out of the rubble of the Versailles Treaty. A permanent solution to the Japanese problem was needed. It was understood that democratization was the key.[14] Behind this decision was a basic American assumption about the nature of conflict. The war did not originate in the interests or fears of the Axis powers, but from their ideology. Authoritarianism spawned aggressiveness, while the particular forms of authoritarianism, German National Socialism or Japanese Bushido, merely produced particularly virulent strains of aggression. In section 3A of the first Presidential directive to SCAP, this view is clearly enunciated:

> The ultimate objective of the United Nations with respect to Japan is to foster conditions which will give the greatest possible assurance that Japan will not again become a menace to the peace and security of the world and will permit her eventual admission as a responsible and peaceful member of the family of nations. Certain measures considered to be essential for the achievement of this objective have been set forth in the Potsdam Declaration. These measures include among others, the carrying out of the Cairo Declaration and the limiting of Japanese sovereignty to the four main islands and such minor islands as the Allied Powers determine; the abolition of militarism and ultranationalism in all their forms; the disarmament and demilitarization of Japan with continuing control over Japan's capacity to make war; the strengthening of democratic tendencies and process in governmental, economic and social institutions and the encouragement and support of liberal political tendencies in Japan. The United States desires that the Japanese Government conform as closely as may be to principles of democratic self-government, but it is not the responsibility of the occupational forces to impose on Japan any form of Government not supported by the freely expressed will of the people.[15]

To summarize American policy:

1. The primary interest of the Allies is to make certain that Japan can no longer make war.
2. Toward this end, the U.S. requires that Japan disarm and demilitarize, and that those supporting militarism, broadly defined, be suppressed.
3. That the U.S., in order to supplant militarism and nationalism, wishes to see the emergence of a liberal democracy in Japan as a safeguard.
4. The U.S. also supports the right of the Japanese people to choose their own form of government and cannot impose a liberal democracy.

The assumption was that liberal democracies are by nature opposed to nationalism and militarism. Nowhere was there any appreciation of the Japanese view of the origin of the war: that they had been forced into it against their will by American actions. By assuming that the key to the war was to be found in Japanese culture, the Americans were less ruthless than they might have been. Had the conflict been viewed as a struggle between competing *interests*, then the solution would have been to leave Japan prostrate, too weak to pursue its interests. Since the problem was seen as essentially *cultural*, there was no need to impose a Carthaginian solution. Cultural change would suffice. The American dilemma was this: how to impose cultural change and create a liberal democracy without imposing it against the will of the Japanese people?

The first stage of this process involved the demilitarization of Japan. This included several steps. First, the rather tricky task of apprehending, disarming, transporting, and demobilizing millions of Japanese soldiers. Next, the elimination of the leaders of the militarists and the military had to be achieved. The occupiers began with the assumption that "all Japanese in high positions had been selfish, brutal and malignant, but subordinates were usually good men and true."[16] This naiveté was compounded by a practical problem. In Germany, the enemy was clearly defined and placed: the Nazi Party. Membership in the Nazi Party, at least in the early stages of the occupation, was understood to be a debilitating point. No equivalent stigma could be found in Japan.

SCAPIN (SCAP Instruction) 550 lists five categories of Japanese for "Removal and Exclusion":

1. War criminals
2. Career military and special police
3. Important members of ultranationalist groups
4. Officers of financial organizations involved in Japanese expansion
5. Governors of occupied territories[17]

This was a rather narrow cross section of Japanese society. As of September 15, 1946, only 7,769 suspects had been screened, and only 894 purged.[18]

Still unanswered was the question of a new constitution. Indeed, no one seemed to know who had the responsibility for drafting one. MacArthur felt that the responsibility rested with FEAC. In the meantime, the Japanese government under Prime Minister Shidehara governed under the old Imperial constitution. When it became apparent that FEAC was impotent and that Shidehara had no intention of revising the constitution himself, MacArthur reversed himself. With elections scheduled for April 1946 and no constitution in sight, the Supreme Commander, Allied Powers, took it upon himself to produce one.[19]

The constitution retained the Emperor as symbolic head of state, and substituted popular sovereignty as the true legitimizer of the regime. For Japanese conservatives, who dominated the occupation cabinet, popular sovereignty was the antithesis of everything Japanese.[20] The cabinet split on the matter, but ultimately this was irrelevant. The occupiers had the power to force any constitution they wanted on Japan, and their need to pretend that the constitution met with the consent of the governed could not conceal this fact. The Diet had no choice but to ratify the new constitution. By forcing the drafting of the constitution and compelling the Diet to ratify it, MacArthur revealed two things. First, that whatever the theoretical problems involved, the American will to constitutional democracy could not be resisted by the Japanese. Second, that his power among Americans was so enormous that no real opposition to his action ever surfaced.

From the occupiers' perspective, the heart of the constitution was Article 9,[21] which stated:

> Aspiring sincerely to an international peace based on justice and order, the Japanese people forever renounce war as a sovereign right of the nation and the threat or use of force as means of settling international disputes.
>
> In order to accomplish the aim of the preceding paragraph, land, sea, and air forces as well as other war potential will never be maintained. The right of belligerency of the state will not be recognized.

With the ratification of this clause, the U.S. had achieved its strategic goal: Japan institutionally ceased to be even a potential threat to American interests.

The Americans came to have doubts about Article 9 before the Japanese. Article 9 makes the assumption that Japanese military strength was a permanent threat to the U.S., but the U.S. failed to note that nothing is ever permanent between nations. In the context of the postwar world, with its overwhelming preponderance of American naval power, it was difficult to imagine what sort of threat Japan could pose to the U.S. What was not difficult to imagine was the sort of help Japan could offer in America's new conflict with the Soviet Union. This conflict conditioned the remainder of the American occupation.

THE OCCUPATION: THE SECOND PHASE

The year 1947 was the turning point in the occupation. The Greek crisis and the proclamation of the Truman Doctrine drove home to Americans that war with the Soviets was a possibility. The U.S. began to reevaluate all of its postwar relationships in terms of the Communist threat, and emerged from World War II with two operational principles. They were the opposite of everything believed before the war, as is often the case. Prior to the war, U.S. policy had been to treat conflicts as localized and unconnected. After December 7, 1941, this view was held to be in error; everything was connected, and events in Greece would have consequences everywhere else.

Second, the U.S. had rejected collective security prior to the war, neither joining the League of Nations nor entering into any system of alliances. Conventional wisdom ascribed America's entry and initial disasters in World War II to its failure to engage in collective action early enough to stop the rise of the Axis. Thus, after the war, the U.S. decided never to be outside the international web of alliances again.

The crisis in Greece caused the U.S. to reevaluate the intentions of the Soviets, and therefore to reevaluate relations with all other nations. To stop the Soviets, the U.S. needed allies. Given the chaos in China, Japan was our natural ally in Asia. However, as the U.S. had not only defeated the Japanese but had just forced Article 9 on them, it was unclear how Japan, a vassal state, could function as an ally. From 1947 onward, the U.S. found itself with the task of creating an ally out of a nation whose sovereignty was still fully in American hands. Article 9 went from being the solution to Japanese aggression to being, in Richard Nixon's words in 1953, "an honest mistake."[22]

Prior to 1947, the main concerns of SCAP had been political and institutional: demilitarization and democratization. After 1947, a new imperative emerged: economic recovery, which had not been of primary concern in the first phase. In keeping with the remnants of the Morgenthau Plan, economic recovery was to be the task of the Japanese, not the occupiers; in other words, no investment in the Japanese economy would come from the United States. This is not to say that humanitarian aid was not sent to Japan, only that attempts to revive the Japanese economy through infusions of foreign capital did not occur.

Japan had been reduced to poverty. In 1945, production stood at 10 percent of prewar (not inflated wartime) production. Stocks of raw materials were practically gone, as was fuel. Rations were reduced to only 1,050 calories a day in the months after surrender, 20 percent of American levels and one-third of the minimum required by an active adult. While the Americans did begin bringing in food in 1946, they brought only about 800,000 tons, enough to avert starvation, but not malnutrition.[23]

With the sudden awareness of the Communist threat in Europe, American planners considered other matters as well. The Japanese Communist Party, legalized during the great democratization surge of 1945 and 1946, was not yet a serious problem. But given the level of misery in Japan, no one believed that this would remain the case. Furthermore, given the growing fear of the Soviets, it began to dawn on the U.S. that the physical well-being of Japan was a matter of strategic importance.

In 1947, the Supreme Commander, Allied Powers, began to take the first steps toward revitalizing the economy. The turning point came on October 9, 1948, with Truman's authorization of NSC 13/2. This document closed the first phase of the occupation and focused attention on the new goal: "To ready democratic Japan for entry into the free world's community of nations as a self-supporting trading partner."[24]

Two things came from this. The first was the decision to suspend reparations. Claims had become greater than the net worth of Japan,[25] and continued reparations would make economic recovery impossible. The other, and more controversial measure, involved the *zaibatsu*-busting laws. *Zaibatsu* were linked firms, operating in both vertical and horizontal monopoly. Their origins were rooted in the rise of Japanese capitalism, and in Japanese social forms. Some, like Mitsui, Sumitomo, and Yasuda, had been active in Japan's economic life for centuries, while others, like Mitsubishi, traced themselves back only to the Meiji restoration.[26]

The *zaibatsu* were few but powerful. Prior to World War II, four had risen to great prominence: Mitsui, Mitsubishi, Sumitomo, and Yasuda towered over Asano, Furukawa, Aikawa (Nissan), Okura, and Nomura.[27] Their interests were vast, including mining, manufacturing, banking, insurance, real estate, and shipping. Each *zaibatsu* was an economic universe unto itself. They were also closely linked to the state and, via the state, to each other. Japan, Inc., of which much is made today, has existed for decades and even centuries.

The *zaibatsu* were extremely successful as business ventures both within Japan and overseas. They were also natural to Japanese culture. First, they frequently descended from samurai, and integrated samurai principles of obedience, discipline, and courage with modern corporate values. They also invoked fundamental Japanese values such as the integrity of the family structure, hierarchy, and corporate and national pride. The *zaibatsu* were family affairs, governed by family councils, in which respect for age combined with respect for expertise.

The *zaibatsu* had been vital in creating both the modern Japanese economy and the modern Japanese war machine. One need only think of the role of Mitsubishi in creating the excellent Zero fighter airplane to see the importance of the *zaibatsu* to the military power of Japan. And the *zaibatsu* benefited from the war. In 1937, the Big Four owned 15 percent of heavy industry, the Big Ten 25 percent. By 1946, as a result of the war, these figures were 32 and 49 percent.[28]

The Americans saw the *zaibatsu* as the key problem in democratizing Japan. Not only were they anticompetitive in the American sense, but they also represented a locus of power that was antidemocratic. The *zaibatsu* was an elite of businessmen, linked by common interests and backgrounds, that could come to constitute an elite that could usurp Japanese democracy.[29] Thus, as the democratization process deepened, it was inevitable that the occupiers acted against them.

Almost as soon as the occupation began, SCAP acted to freeze the assets of the Big Ten and transfer them to the Holding Company Liquidation Commission. *Zaibatsu* family members were required to cease business activities for ten years. Finally, key subsidiaries such as Mitsubishi Soji were broken up. Other large companies, particularly public corporations run for government benefit, were included in the breakup.[30]

The assault on the *zaibatsu* continued and deepened, reaching its apex when the Deconcentration Law was passed in 1947 at the insistence of SCAP and with great reluctance by the Japanese Diet. The law gave the Supreme Commander, Allied Powers, great control over the *zaibatsu*, both in purging personnel and reorganizing the *zaibatsu*.

There was bitter opposition in Japan. The elite of Japan's society had not been liquidated by the Americans; they continued to govern in the Diet and elsewhere. Japan's elite was intimately bound together—more so, perhaps, than even the British—and it proved difficult to get the Diet to pass laws against their brethren. Where laws were passed, it was difficult to get the bureaucracy to administer those laws.

More important, the economic cost of breaking up the *zaibatsu* was enormous. One can imagine the chaos if the largest American corporations were suddenly purged and disorganized, without anything being ready to take their place. In already depressed Japan, economic disaster loomed. It quickly became apparent that if the 1,200 firms targeted for dissolution were actually dissolved, chaos would reign and the already dismal economic situation would become catastrophic.[31]

Growing fear of communism and the Soviet Union forced the Americans to shift their attention from democratization of Japan to promoting its economic recovery. The United States simply could not afford to conduct social experiments at a time of international crisis. It should be added that there were those among the Americans who felt that the reforms in Japan were getting too radical, and some feared that the antimonopolistic principles advanced in Japan might spill over into U.S. domestic policy.[32] Additionally, the Japan lobby, which had first suggested a conservative course in Japan, was quick to point out the failures of more radical approaches. But fear of the strategic implications of chaos in Japan were clearly more important in U.S. thinking than ideological concerns. The administration of Japan was running into the growing backlash in the U.S. against some of the more radical elements of the New Deal. Business interests wishing to do business in Japan as well as ideological enemies of social engineering combined to clamor for change, using the Soviet threat to drive their point home.

On January 6, 1948, Secretary of the Army Kenneth C. Royall gave a speech that marked the beginning of the new phase of U.S. policy. He said:

> It is clear that Japan cannot support itself as a nation of shop-keepers and craftsmen and small artisans any more than it can exist as a purely agricultural nation. We can expect continuing economic deficits in Japan unless there is some degree of mass industrial production.
>
> We are building in Japan a self-sufficient democracy, strong enough and stable enough to support itself and at the same time to serve as a deterrent against any other totalitarian war threats which might hereafter arise in the Far East.[33]

Royall's position was affirmed on October 9, 1948, in NSC 13/2:

> Second only to U.S. security interests, economic recovery should be made the primary objective of United States policy in Japan in the coming period. It should be sought through a combination of United States aid programs envisaging shipments and/or credits on a declining scale over a number of years, and by a vigorous and concerted effort by all interested agencies and departments of the U.S. government to cut away existing obstacles to the revival of Japanese foreign trade, with provision for Japanese merchant ship-ping and to facilitate restoration and development of Japan's ex-ports. In developing Japan's internal and external trade and industry, private enterprise should be encouraged.[34]

A sense of urgency, born of perceived danger from the Soviets, gripped U.S.–Japanese relations. The U.S. no longer wanted to pun-ish or educate the Japanese. It wanted a strong Japan to help defend the Pacific against the Soviets. Thus, the anti-*zaibatsu* program went by the boards, at least in practice, as private enterprise became U.S. policy. In order to revivify Japan, the Americans chose to revive the Japanese trading state.

There was a grim statistical background to this:

TABLE 4-1. Index of Industrial Activity.

YEAR	INDEX	CHANGE
1934	89.9	
1944	176.2	96.00%
1945	63.2	−64.13
1946	39.2	−37.97
1947	45.2	15.31
1948	61.8	36.73
1949	76.7	24.11
1950	88.0	14.73
1951	119.4	35.68
1952	131.8	10.39
1953	161.2	22.31

(Source: *Japan Statistical Yearbook*)

In 1944, the Japanese index of industrial production stood at almost twice the 1934 level. In 1946 the index had fallen to less than half the 1934 level. Industrial production in Japan had collapsed.

U.S. direct aid to Japan had been quite small during the first stage of the occupation. In 1945–1946, the U.S. had sent $108 million in aid, which rose to $294 million in 1946–1947.[35] Moreover, it was the policy of the Supreme Commander, Allied Powers (a policy not rescinded until January 13, 1949), not to permit foreign investment in Japan.[36] Under existing policy, Japan could not possibly recover and would remain an ongoing political liability to the U.S.

The strategic significance of Japan was clear to the Supreme Commander, Allied Powers, by September 1946, when, on the first anniversary of the surrender ceremony, MacArthur said:

> The goal is great—for the strategic position of these Japanese Islands renders them either a powerful bulwark for peace or a dangerous springboard for war.[37]

MacArthur also claimed that the economic warfare going on against Japan was more deadly than the atom bomb had been, and that the ongoing economic strangulation of Japan must stop.[38]

In the great "reverse course" of 1947, the decision was made that a vital Japanese economy was more desirable than an inert but egalitarian one. Obviously, many were morally offended by the reversal, and remain so today. They regard the decision as a repudiation of the principles for which the U.S. fought the war.[39] Perhaps so. More important from the U.S. point of view is the fact that this decision left intact the institutions that have come to constitute the contemporary Japanese corporation. Japan survived to flourish because of U.S. fear of the Soviet Union and the implications of Japanese instability in the face of that threat.

Throughout 1947, the U.S. studied the problem of what to do with Japan. In May 1948 the U.S. Army published the Johnston Report, prepared by a blue-ribbon panel of U.S. industrialists. They found:

> Defeat left Japan a ruined nation. The conquered empire was lost; with it the great investments which Japan had made. Within Japan proper, there was great destruction of houses, cities and factories. The merchant fleet, the means by which Japan carried on its trade, was also lost. Remaining inventories of raw materials, especially imported raw materials, such as oil, cotton, wool, coking coal, rubber and salts were small. Farm lands were neglected and supplies . . . insufficient. Food production within Japan was insufficient to supply even a minimum subsistence for the increased population for . . . some five or six million Japanese were returned from lost territories.[40]

The Johnston Report asked that Congress undertake a program to supply Japan with the means whereby its economy could recover—first and foremost, supplying the raw materials necessary for Japan. In order to finance these imports, Japan was to be permitted to resume its export trade. Additionally, the report warned that the uncertainties of the reparations program, which threatened to uproot entire factories for transfer to other nations, made production difficult. Finally, the uncertainties of the war on *zaibatsu*, as well as fears of government monopolies replacing them, made business difficult.

Thus, in allowing Japan to import raw materials once again, beginning the process that led to the termination of the reparations programs and reinforcing opposition to the anti-*zaibatsu* campaign, the Johnston Report laid the foundations of a renewed economy. Even so, it was not until 1951, the second year of the Korean War, that Japan started to experience a real surge in its production.

The United States had had no real, workable plans for Japan prior to its surrender. Victory seemed to give the U.S. infinite freedom in deciding what to do: in 1945 there appeared to be few constraints on American power and few threats to American interests. Japan was a blank canvas on which any picture could be drawn.

By 1947, reality had once more intruded and the U.S. found itself living in a dangerous world. Japan could not help but be important in that world, either as another threat or a crucial ally. The decision to help Japan recover economically was a decision to abandon turning Japan into a work of art and turn her instead into a powerful ally.

In order to make Japan an ally, the U.S. had to turn it into an economically viable nation. With its large, disciplined workforce, experienced managers, and memories of greatness, Japan would not be able to remain merely "viable." In order to create an ally, the U.S. set Japan upon a course that would end in its emerging as one of the great economic powers in the world, and the chief competitor of the United States. In so doing, the U.S. made Japan into a bulwark against Soviet expansion.

1. John Curtis Perry, *Beneath Eagle's Wings: Americans in Occupied Japan* (New York, 1980), p. 28.
2. Justin Williams, "From Charlottesville to Tokyo: Military Government Training and the Democratic Reforms in Occupied Japan," *Pacific Historical Review*, Vol. 51, (November 1982), p. 417.
3. Theodore Cohen, *Remaking Japan* (New York, 1987), p. 15.
4. Hata Ikuhiko, "Japan Under the Occupation," *Japan Interpreter*, 10:3 (Winter 1976), p. 362.
5. Robert E. Ward, "Presurrender Planning," in *Democratizing Japan*, ed. Robert E. Ward and Sakamoto Yoshikazu (Honolulu, 1987).
6. Cohen, *Remaking Japan*, p. 17.
7. Post-Surrender Directive to SCAP, forwarded November 8, 1945, in Edwin Martin, *The Allied Occupation of Japan* (Westport, 1972), p. 124.
8. Perry, *Beneath Eagle's Wings*, p. 12. The British troops arrived in February 1946, a year into the occupation. Chinese troops were also expected but they never arrived because of the civil war.
9. On the growing conflict within the Commonwealth, see Roger Buckley, *Occupation Diplomacy* (Cambridge, 1982), pp. 20–23.
10. E.J. Lewe Van Aduard, *Japan, From Surrender to Peace* (The Hague, 1953), p. 9.
11. Ibid., p. 9–10.
12. Rodger Swearingen, *The Soviet Union and Postwar Japan* (Stanford, 1978), p. 29. Also, George H. Blakeslee, "The Establishment of the Far Eastern Commission," *International Organization*, 5 (August 1951). There was a formal veto over U.S. policy given to the Soviet member of the FEAC, but this never had any practical effect in limiting SCAP's policies.
13. Takemai Eiji, "Early Postwar Reformist Parties," in Ward and Yoshikazu, *Democratizing Japan*, pp. 343–344.
14. Robert E. Ward, "The Legacy of the Occupation," in *The United States and Japan*, ed. Herbert Passin (Washington, D.C., 1975), p. 30.

15. "Basic Initial Post-Surrender Directive to Supreme Commander for the Allied Powers for the Occupation and Control of Japan," in Martin, *Allied Occupation*.
16. Harry Wildes, *Typhoon in Tokyo* (New York, 1978), p. 51.
17. Harold S. Quigley, "The Great Purge in Japan," *Pacific Affairs*, 20:3 (September 1947), pp. 299–300.
18. Ibid., p. 301.
19. Justin Williams, *Japan's Political Revolution Under MacArthur* (Athens, 1979), pp. 101–102.
20. Ibid., pp. 113–115.
21. On this clause, see Theodore McNelly, "The Renunciation of War in the Japanese Constitution," *Armed Forces and Society*, 13:1 (Fall 1986), pp. 81–106.
22. Meiron and Susie Harries, *Sheathing the Sword: The Demilitarization of Japan* (London, 1987), p. 213.
23. Kazuo Kawai, *Japan's American Interlude* (Chicago, 1960) p. 135.
24. Williams, *Japan's Political Revolution*, pp. 208–209.
25. Kwai, *Japan's American Interlude*, p. 141.
26. George C. Allen, *Japan's Economic Recovery* (London, 1958), p. 127.
27. Ibid., p. 128, and 128n.
28. Ibid., p. 131.
29. T.A. Bisson, *Zaibatsu Dissolution in Japan* (Berkeley, 1954), pp. 17–28.
30. Allen, *Japan's Economic Recovery*, p. 133.
31. Kwai, *Japan's American Interlude*, pp. 145–147.
32. E.M. Hadley, "Trust Busting in Japan," *Harvard Business Review*, July 1948.
33. Yakata Kosai, *The Era of High Speed Growth*, trans. J. Kaminski (Tokyo, 1986), p. 53.
34. Ibid., p. 54.
35. Robert A. Fearey, *The Occupation of Japan, Second Phase: 1948–50* (New York, 1950), p. 218.
36. United Nations, *Economic Survey of Asia and the Far East, 1949* (Lake Success, 1950), p. 429.
37. W. MacMahon Ball, *Japan, Enemy or Ally?* (New York, 1949), p. 12.
38. Ibid., pp. 12–13.
39. An example of this literature can be found in John W. Dower, "Occupied Japan and the American Lake, 1945–1950," in *America's Asia: Dissenting Essays on Asian-American Relations*, ed. Edward Friedman and Mark Selden (New York, 1971).
40. Ball, *Japan, Enemy or Ally?*, p. 211.

5

The Cold War and the Resurrection of Japan

On June 24, 1950, Shotaro Kamiya landed at Los Angeles International Airport to discover that war had broken out in Korea. The news added to his already grave concerns. Shotaro Kamiya was the president of Toyota, a small Japanese truck manufacturer in big trouble. Toyota had a large unsold inventory and was selling barely 300 trucks a month; Kamiya had come to America in a last-ditch effort to save his company. He hoped to persuade the Ford Motor Company to buy and market some of his trucks in the United States. Ford was not enthusiastic. It did not think that Japanese vehicles could ever have much success in the American market.

Kamiya stayed in the U.S. for two months and left dejected and defeated. But when he returned to Tokyo he discovered that he did not need Ford's help at all. To his shock, he was swamped with orders and could barely keep up with the demand. The American Defense Department had ordered Toyota trucks by the thousands. The Korean War had made the Far Eastern Command desperate for vehicles and equipment of all sorts. He was selling over 1,500 trucks a month, and his only limit was capacity. Using the profits from the truck orders, Toyota began producing passenger cars.[1]

More than anything else, it was the Korean War that began the process that turned Japan from a desperately poor, defeated, demoralized nation into the modern industrial giant that now challenges the world. American fear of communism and Soviet expansion caused the U.S. to stop viewing Japan as an enemy and view it instead as an ally in defense of the free world.

The Korean War was part of a greater conflict that gripped the world. The U.S. and the Soviet Union engaged in a vast, sometimes brutal conflict for domination of Eurasia, the eastern hemisphere, and indeed the world. It was an unprecedented event, in the sense that, for the first time, virtually the entire world chose sides and few could avoid the pressure of both superpowers.

The U.S. was fighting to achieve a fundamental strategic goal. At the end of World War II, the Soviets were Eurasia's supreme military power. The prospect of a Soviet-dominated Eurasia reasonably frightened the United States, as had the prospect of a German-dominated Eurasia a few years before. In order to avoid this threat and its consequences, and lacking sufficient forces to contain the Soviet Union on its own, the U.S. sought to create a system of alliances to encircle and contain the Soviet Union. In turn, the Soviets fought fiercely to break out of this encirclement and avoid the implosive force of the American strategy.

Japan played a part in this strategy, as did almost all other nations. Japan's geographical position was crucial. It effectively blocked the Soviet fleet at Vladivostok from the Pacific. It was also the most populous nation in northeast Asia, after China. With the triumph of the Communists in China, therefore, Japan became a crucial element in the American–Asian alliance system. Geography and history conspired to turn Japan from a despised enemy to a valued, indeed indispensable, ally. And nowhere was this relationship made more important than at the outbreak of the Korean War.

THE KOREAN WAR AND THE RESURRECTION OF JAPAN

It is not altogether clear why North Korea invaded South Korea when it did. It is clear that the North would not have done so without close consultation and approval from the Soviet Union. The most common explanation was that Stalin wanted to test the limits of U.S. commitment in Asia. In January 1950, Secretary of State Dean Acheson had described the boundaries of this commitment. Whether by oversight or intent, Korea had been excluded from America's security zone.[2]

Another, more cynical explanation might have had to do with Stalin's fear of Mao. Mao had made it clear to the Soviets that he intended to unite China and that a Soviet presence, particularly in Manchuria, was not necessary. Stalin understood, perhaps before anyone else, that a united China, whatever its ideology, was a threat to the Soviets in Asia. By fomenting conflict in Korea, Stalin diverted Chinese attention from Siberia. If the Republic of Korea fell, that was fine with the Soviets. If a protracted war brought the U.S. and the Chinese to blows, that was even better. The long, debilitating war and the mutual loathing of China and America that resulted were optimal outcomes for Stalin.

Whatever the reason, the U.S. interpreted the war as being part of the same probing that the Soviets had been doing in Germany, Greece, Turkey, and Iran. It was part of the search for weaknesses in the U.S. defense system, and therefore the U.S. felt obliged to respond. In addition, the fall of South Korea would place the Sea of Japan in jeopardy and threaten to undermine the U.S. defense system in the northwestern Pacific.

However good the reasons for defending Korea, the U.S. had not been prepared for war there. Its forces in Korea were insufficient, and reinforcements had to be scraped together from throughout MacArthur's Far Eastern Command to stabilize the situation. Along with troops, materiel had to be found to support the United Nations forces fighting in Korea.

Before North Korea crossed the 38th parallel on June 25, 1950, the Japanese economy was still very much in the doldrums. This greatly concerned American observers. *New York Times* correspondent Lindsey Parrott wrote:

What might result, if Japan's economy got into trouble, would be violent revolution to overthrow a profitless democratic connection and a turn for salvation to a new totalitarianism of the Left and a reliance on the resources of the Communist countries of Asia which could use Japanese industrial power.[3]

Revolution was a threat. Of equal concern was the possibility of Japan reaching some sort of political accommodation with the Communists. The People's Republic of China particularly worried U.S. analysts. Japan could not develop without both an export market and a source of raw materials. Prior to World War II, China served both functions to some extent. U.S. planners feared that, barring other solutions, Japan might drift back into prewar trade patterns with China and ultimately into some sort of political accommodation with the Soviets. This was certainly an increased danger if U.S. resolve in Japan was doubted.

Thus, in spite of Acheson's notion of a defensive perimeter, the U.S. intervened in Korea. There were good reasons for this. The failure of the U.S. to defend South Korea, however rational, would inevitably raise fears throughout the American alliance system that the U.S. did not intend to live up to its commitments. There was a suspicion that the U.S. would fight to the last drop of their allies' blood. Nowhere was this truer than in Japan, and the U.S. had to dispel it.

When the Korean War broke out, Japan was an occupied country without real sovereignty; it was not actually a nation-state in the conventional meaning of the term. Japan's internal and external security was in the hands of a foreign power, and its decision-making apparatus was subject to a foreign general. In addition, its economy was in shambles.

It had been recognized even before the outbreak of war that this situation could not continue. MacArthur said in March 1947:

> The Japanese nation and people are now ready for the initiation of negotiations leading to a Treaty of Peace—ready in the sense that Japan's war-making power and potential is destroyed, the framework of democratic government has been erected, reforms essential to the reshaping of Japanese lives and institutions to conform to democratic ideals accomplished . . .[4]

MacArthur was motivated by national interest as much as by altruism. A sovereign Japan was more likely to be of use to the U.S. than an occupied one. The problem for the United States was to make certain that in returning Japan to sovereignty, the United States would not give up the fruits of victory. Japan was to remain in the American camp, neither neutral nor pro-Communist. In addition, Japanese soil was to be available for use by American military forces without control or veto by the Japanese government. The question of a Japanese role in its own defense and the collective defense of the West was not yet at issue.

Just as the Americans were beginning to look forward to a peace treaty, so too, with even greater fervor, were the Japanese. Japan obviously wanted its sovereignty returned, but of course the terms of settlement were critical. Optimally, Japan wanted to be free of obligations for collective security. On the other hand, it wanted clear guarantees that the U.S. would come to Japan's defense in the event Japan was attacked. It did not want these guarantees to involve a large American military presence in Japan but, at the most, emergency facilities.[5]

The U.S. and Japan were agreed in principle on the return of sovereignty, but were deeply divided on what that sovereignty would entail. Negotiations on a peace treaty were hampered by factors outside of U.S.–Japanese relations. The other parties to World War II, particularly the Soviets but also the Commonwealth countries, were uneasy about a peace settlement with Japan. The Soviets were aware that any such threat would turn Japan from an occupied country into an active ally of the U.S. The Soviets had no wish to facilitate this process, assuming that the U.S. would do whatever it wanted in Japan anyway.

For Britain and the Commonwealth countries, the occupation of Japan represented the changing of the guard in the Pacific. During the late 1930s all serious matters had been coordinated by the British and Americans. This was no longer the case. Now, the U.S. was in a position to dictate terms.[6] The other Pacific Commonwealth nations, Australia in particular, were deeply suspicious of any return of sovereignty to Japan. William MacMahon Ball, Commonwealth Representative to the Far Eastern Advisory Council, said of American policy:

> The United States Government, with less experience than Britain in the conduct of foreign relations, with a shortage of experienced officers, and with a public opinion still capricious on world questions, is resolved to add to her foreign burdens those that Britain has laid down.[7]

Because of this, Ball went on, the U.S. had completely miscalculated in Japan:

> It is my thesis that since the surrender the Japanese Government, in response to the pressure groups that control it, has sabotaged economic recovery in the effort to frustrate the Allied aims of 1945, and that it has done this with frivolous indifference to the sufferings it has brought to the mass of the Japanese people.[8]

This sort of criticism held up a comprehensive peace settlement for several years. On June 14, 1950, John Foster Dulles arrived in Tokyo. He had been appointed Special Counselor to the Secretary of State, with special responsibility for the Japanese peace treaty. His appointment was one of a long trail of events that had led nowhere. His first trip was designed to sound out the Japanese and it was scheduled to end on June 29. On June 25, North Korea attacked South Korea, the U.S. found itself at war, and the tempo of urgency rose dramatically.

Immediately following the outbreak of war, the U.S. realized that it was in no position to maintain the internal security of Japan. U.S. ground troops were desperately needed in Korea. Even prior to the outbreak, the National Security Council had asked Japan to create a 150,000-man national police force.[9] This proposal fitted in with the thinking of figures like George Kennan, who felt that Japanese rearmament was going to contribute to stability in the region.[10]

U.S. pressure on Japan began to build in 1949. The U.S. had adopted the twin policies of containment and collective security. In order to make these policies work, U.S. allies had to be willing to play a role in the collective defense effort. U.S. troops were to be the mobile reserve of this crust defense. Native troops had to hold the line against the first assault. Thus, the Germans were slowly being reformed into the Bundeswehr; it was expected that Japan would be equally cooperative. It is ironic that this drive to rearm Japan occurred a scant two years after the Supreme Commander, Allied Powers had written Article 9 of the Japanese constitution. The United States had quickly lost interest in that clause. The Japanese had not.

Prime Minister Yoshida had vigorously resisted calls for rearmament. He saw Japan surviving in the world primarily as an economic entity.[11] Japan's Chief Justice Kotaro Tanaka said:

> The ideal setup for Japan, of course, would be to remain forever unarmed, and seek a security guarantee from the United Nations against both external and domestic dangers.[12]

The invasion of South Korea triggered some primordial Japanese fears. Korea has historically been crucial to Japan's security interests, and Japan had always been afraid that Korea might fall into hostile hands, since it is the closest point on mainland Asia to Japan.[13] In spite of these fears, Japan was reluctant to enter into a full alliance with the U.S. Rearmament would not have meant independence. It would have merely made Japan a cog in the U.S. military system. Whatever fears Japan might have over Korea, the only sphere in which it could triumph was an economic one.

The Korean War could not have been more helpful in economic matters. Along with its tradition of aggressive military expansionism, Japan also had a tradition of peaceful expansionism built on trade and emigration. Yoshida wanted to build on this tradition. Japan's basic prewar economic problem remained intact: it did not have sufficient resources internally to be a great industrial power. During World War II, Japan had attempted to gain direct military and political control over these resources. That had ended in catastrophe. Now, Yoshida was determined to try a new tack: attaining those supplies through purely economic means while leaving the security of those supplies in American hands. The problem, of course, was to persuade the U.S. that it was in its interest to undertake the role of guarantor of Japan's resource security. The Korean War was most persuasive. If the U.S. wanted to use Japan's factories for military purposes, it would have to make sure that Japan got the raw materials it needed.

The United States quickly turned to Japan for a wide range of products, ranging from trucks to gunnysacks. The result was a massive infusion of capital into the Japanese economy. The inflow of cash was so substantial that it made up for Japan's negative trade balance. In other words, Japan was able to finance its imports with U.S. orders, called Special Procurements. In 1950, these orders totaled $149 million. By 1951 they had soared to $592 million; in 1953 they were $809 million; they ended in 1955 at $557 million. In the five years of special procurements, the total income to Japan was over $3.5 billion.[14]

By March 1951, Japanese mining and manufacturing output had increased by 46 percent over March 1950.[15] Unlike previous booms in Japan, this one had a substantial effect on the standard of living of ordinary Japanese, as well as on economic activity and profits. So substantial was the war boom that by 1952 it was estimated that the Japanese standard of living had returned to prewar levels, something that had not been achieved during the previous six years of peace.[16] More important for Japan's long-term health, by 1953 there was a substantial investment boom underway.[17]

The effect of the war was felt throughout Japanese industry. It particularly affected shipbuilding, a key industry in an island economy. The initial intention of the Supreme Commander, Allied Powers, had been to severely limit Japan's shipbuilding. The industry had been earmarked for reparations. The Korean War changed this thinking. There was a sharp rise in demand by all Western powers for merchant ships, due to the war. Moreover, the U.S. was in no position to ship raw materials to Japan. Thus, SCAP agreed to relinquish control over Japan's shipyards and permitted the Japanese to begin constructing an ocean-going fleet again. Indeed, the U.S. government financed the startup of those yards, through the United States Aid Counterpart Fund, which allocated monies for strategically useful industries. Because of large orders, the shipyards reinvested over 22 billion yen in themselves, so that by the mid-1950s Japanese shipyards equaled or bettered the quality of those of other nations. Japan became the largest shipbuilder in the world by 1956, launching 26 percent of all ships in that year.[18] One might say that the U.S. paid to build the shipyards that ruined America's merchant shipbuilding industry.

The winners in the shipbuilding boom were corporations that had descended from the prewar *zaibatsu*: Mitsubishi, Hitachi, Kawasaki.

Profits from shipbuilding allowed these companies to resume activities in other industries, recreating the conglomerate nature of prewar industry in Japan. Mitsubishi, for example, used this money to finance the Fuji Precision Machinery Company (successor to the Nakajima Aircraft Co. of Zero fame) in its entry into the auto market, where it competed with Toyota and Nissan.[19]

An entire range of modern Japanese corporations, including Mitsubishi, Nippon Matai, and the rest of the modern giants, were saved from extinction by the Korean War. Even more important, the type of supplies needed by American troops allowed the Japanese to develop basic industries, useful in later development of broad-based consumer industries. They were also given the opportunity to use advanced American production techniques, which the Americans gladly transferred to the Japanese in the course of the war effort.[20] Finally, the war forced the U.S. to allow Japan to import as much raw materials as it required. By 1953, industrial output had grown to over twice the 1949 level.

The Korean War started Japan's postwar boom. So important was it and the Cold War to Japan that the Tokyo Stock Exchange plummeted on the news of Stalin's death in 1953. Stalin's bellicosity had been the salvation of Japan; the threat of peace terrified the Japanese investor. Indeed, the end of the war caused a recession in 1954. However, by the end of 1955, in spite of improving relations between the U.S. and the Communist bloc, the Japanese economy resumed its upward surge.[21] After the Korean War's kick, Japan was able to sustain rapid growth on its own, as long as its security was guaranteed by the United States.

FROM OCCUPATION TO ALLIANCE

The Korean War returned sovereignty to Japan very much along the lines envisioned by Prime Minister Yoshida. The desire to punish Japan was gone, and instead America wanted a healthy ally. The Japanese took full advantage of this. Writing in the January 1951 *Foreign Affairs*, Yoshida said:

> Then there is Korea. The United Nations relief and rehabilitation program will eventually call for quantities of building materials, rolling stock and machinery, besides clothing and all manner of miscellaneous articles. And we are right on the spot to supply them.
> But in order that Japan may become a real workshop of East Asia and contribute abundantly to its progress and prosperity, she must have a peace treaty. It is essential that we be guaranteed an

equitable and equal treatment in international commerce, the rights of travel and residence, and full freedom of trade and shipping in this and other quarters of the globe. Such conditions of commerce and navigation can be realized only after the conclusion of peace and Japan's restoration as a free and independent member of the society of nations.[22]

Yoshida was setting Japan's price for being a subordinate member of America's alliance system. Japan was to be permitted to become an economic power, and the United States was to guarantee the security of Japan's international trade. In return, the U.S. could have bases in Japan, but could not call on Japanese soldiers to fight.

The outbreak of the Korean War forced the U.S. to abandon the rather leisurely pace it had pursued in peace-treaty discussions with the Japanese. By August 7, 1950, seven weeks after the invasion, Dulles' staff had prepared a draft treaty.[23] The key issue in the American mind was the stationing of U.S. troops in Japan after the peace treaty had been signed. This was a tricky matter. The essence of the treaty would be the return of sovereignty to Japan, but the presence of troops would appear to compromise that sovereignty, particularly if the Japanese were not given the right to control the movement and function of those troops.

The Japanese position was mixed. Yoshida's government operated against a background of rather tepid public opinion. In a poll taken by the newspaper *Asahi Shimbun* in September 1950, after the San Francisco Conference had convened, 41 percent of the public felt good about a new treaty, 23 percent were "relieved but with mixed feelings," 9 percent were uneasy, and 21 percent had no opinion at all. As an indication of the importance of the matter, fully one-fourth of the population did not bother following events in San Francisco.[24] This actually played into Yoshida's hands. His political opponents could not mobilize public opinion against him, since the apathy cut both ways. The Americans, wanting Yoshida to be strong, would not push him against public opinion either.

Still, Yoshida's search for a comprehensive settlement met with opposition from both Left and Right. The two left-wing parties were united in wanting a return of sovereignty, but generally favored an unarmed neutrality.[25] Neutrality was, of course, anathema to the United States. In addition to opposition from the Left, Yoshida had to contend with pressure from his right wing. The Right was concerned that the peace treaty, when coupled with the Mutual Security Agreement desired by the U.S., would leave the Japanese with only the outer shell of sovereignty, exposed but not free. The United States, for example, wanted to retain base rights in Japan and have the right to call on Japanese participation. The U.S. did not want to reciprocate with a guarantee of U.S. intervention against an invasion of Japan. Japan would not be an equal partner in the alliance, nor (with bases) truly free of foreign domination.

U.S. thinking evolved over time. However, in his first memorandum on taking office as Special Counselor, Dulles sketched a set of U.S. interests that would be a permanent feature in the negotiations:

1. Japan should be a liberal democracy and part of the free world.
2. The West must make it impossible for Japan to fall to the Communists whether through invasion or subversion
3. A police force under SCAP supervision should be established.
4. Reparations should be abandoned.
5. A companion security treaty ought to be signed.[26]

Of concern in all of this was the matter of bases. As early as 1944, the U.S. had been studying the question of siting bases in Japan as a counter to Soviet power in the Pacific. Okinawa, in particular, was seen as a useful base from which to operate against the Soviets. A *U.S. News and World Report* article stated:

> Air dominance over Asia is the U.S. goal on Okinawa. . . . [The] U.S. aim now is to convert the former Japanese island into a stationary aircraft carrier from which U.S. bombers can dominate every Asiatic port from Vladivostok and Port Arthur to Singapore.[27]

The U.S. had other ambitions as well. Hokkaido was of great significance. The Soviets had requested that Hokkaido be turned over to them as part of their occupation zone, dividing Japan as Germany and Austria had been divided. When the U.S. rejected this request, the Soviets slowly built up military harassment in the region, culminating in a series of air intrusions in the early 1950s.[28] Hokkaido was a central concern of both sides because of its strategic placement. The Soviets had occupied all of Sakhalin Island. If Hokkaido fell into their hands, or was poorly defended, then the Perouse (or Soya) Strait between Hokkaido and Sakhalin would be open for Soviet naval use. This, of course, meant that the Soviet Far Eastern Fleet would have access to the Pacific. Thus, the U.S. wanted a continuing air presence on Hokkaido, defended by Japanese ground troops, as well as naval facilities throughout Japan.

Japan was prepared to accept the linkage of a peace treaty to a mutual defense agreement. However, Foreign Minister Hitoshi Ashida, who had been prime minister for a short time in 1948, did not want that agreement to include U.S. bases in Japan. Rather, he wanted the U.S. to defend Japan from "adjacent" territories, in order to minimize U.S.–Japanese friction and obviously to increase Japanese sovereignty.[29]

The truth was that the Japanese did not take the Communist threat particularly seriously. They did not believe that Japan would be invaded by the Soviet Union, in part because they thought the Soviets to be weaker than the Americans did and in part because they felt that the Soviets were too tied down in Europe to worry about Japan. The conservative Democratic Party, under Ashida's leadership, wanted Article 9 revised, Japan rearmed, and the Americans sent on their way.[30] Ashida knew that Japan could not be defended against the Soviets without American help, but he did not feel that Japan needed to be defended against them at all.

Yoshida did not disagree with Ashida's strategic analysis. On January 27, 1951, he said, "We do not have the slightest expectation that the Communist countries will invade Japan."[31] This was fundamentally at odds with the American understanding of the world. To be more precise, the Americans might not have expected the Soviets to invade Japan either, but they did expect a wider conflict than the Korean War. The Americans wanted the Japanese to commit themselves to active participation in the defense of the Pacific. The Japanese wanted no part of this. They were quite confident that, whatever the agreement, the U.S. would come to Japan's defense. Japan wanted to avoid making any military commitments to the Americans while extracting maximum commitments from them.

For Yoshida, the key to Japan's future was peaceful economic development. The United States, as the dominant military power in the Pacific, was important to this plan. First, the U.S. had to defend Japan against the unlikely threat of the Soviets. Second, the United States had to be a major trading partner with Japan. Finally, the U.S. Navy had to guarantee the flow of raw materials to Japan. The United States would have to guarantee Japan's economic success.[32] Thus, Yoshida was not willing to go as far as Ashida was in breaking with the U.S. altogether.

Yoshida did not want to alienate Japan completely from the Communists, and did so only at American insistence.[33] Yoshida himself, in a speech to the Diet in October 1951, said:

Japan will have to decide from a position of realistic diplomacy, whether or not to recognize the People's Republic of China. At the moment, the government is thinking of opening trade relations with that country and of establishing a commercial office in Shanghai.[34]

The U.S. responded with agitation. Dulles rushed to Tokyo and made it clear that a peace treaty was impossible if Japan did not remain faithful to the American line. Yoshida, who wanted ties with China in order to reestablish prewar trading patterns, bowed to American pressure. Sovereignty and security would require subordination to American strategic interests.

Thus, although Yoshida abandoned his opposition to American bases in Japan and refrained from opening Japan to China, these were the only major concessions that Japan made to the United States during the negotiations leading up to the signing of the Peace Treaty and Mutual Security Pact on September 8, 1951 (to take effect April 28, 1952).[35] On the other key point, that Japanese troops would be confined to an internal security role and would not participate in foreign expeditions, Yoshida remained firm and won.

AMERICA AND JAPAN AS ALLIES

From the beginning, the U.S. was dissatisfied with the Japanese role in the alliance. The U.S. wanted to see Japan do more and devote more resources. As the San Francisco Peace Conference was concluding, Dulles tried to persuade Yoshida to raise a force of 300,000 men. This desire for increased Japanese participation found its way into a National Security Council position paper, which wanted:

1. Japan to rapidly increase its defense capability.
2. That Japan should be prepared to contribute to the defense of other Asian neighbors.
3. That the U.S. take steps to prevent Japan from becoming too dependent on China or other Communist nations for the imports of its raw materials.[36]

The U.S. fear was that Japan's hunger for raw materials, bound to grow dramatically as the U.S. encouraged Japanese industry to grow and participate in collective defense production, would make it more and more dependent on China for its imports. The U.S. tried, therefore, to redirect Japan's trading activity to Southeast Asia—ironically, the same direction that Japan's import hunger had carried it in World War II. Perhaps even more ironically, the U.S. was now prepared to guarantee and protect the flow of those resources to Japan.

The divisive issue remained Japan's rearmament. The U.S. wanted Japan to do more, although there was never any great urgency in these demands. Dulles and the Americans had allies inside Japan. In

March 1951, a former admiral, Sokichi Takagi, called for the creation of an air force of 350 to 370 fighters, 180 medium bombers, a navy of three cruisers and ninety-six destroyers, and a mechanized army of up to 200,000 men. Takushiro Hattori, a member of former Prime Minister Tojo's staff (and among those purged and reinstated by Yoshida after the re-creation of Japan's military force), wanted a twenty-division army, which would have been one of the largest in the world.[37]

Yoshida resisted both the Americans and the Japanese Right. He was convinced that military growth would inevitably lead Japan to foreign involvements not in its interest, as well as to spending resources that could better be spent on economic activities. While the size of Japan's army crept upward (to 110,000 in 1952 and 130,000 in 1954), a navy was created in 1952, and an air force in 1954,[38] this did not represent a qualitative improvement. At no time under Yoshida's government, or after, did Japan possess sufficient armed force to defend herself in the unlikely event of a Soviet invasion, nor sufficient forces to fight elsewhere. Thus, for example, although Korean, Taiwanese, Australian, and Thai forces all fought in Vietnam, Japan, as it had done in Korea, committed no troops.

By 1954 the United States had soured on Article 9. Yoshida embraced it, not because he was a pacifist, nor because he did not foresee the possible uses of military force. Rather, Article 9 was a cloak behind which Japan could hide, avoiding making military commitments to the United States. Yoshida was well aware of the fate of West Germany in NATO. West Germany had become a potential battleground, and had to pay for that privilege by arming itself beyond what its economy could endure. Yoshida had no intention of allowing this to happen to Japan, and Article 9 was the perfect pretext, particularly since it had been written by MacArthur himself.

Yoshida wanted to implant his strategy permanently into Japan's political culture. His vehicle was a renegotiation of the Mutual Security Agreement with the U.S., as well as passage of two defense laws. None of these changed the strategic arrangements significantly, but Yoshida managed to codify his ideas:

1. It was agreed that defense required economic stability.
2. Military expansion must be in accord with the constitution.
3. Trade with China, while prohibited, was not part of the main body of the treaty.
4. Japan was permitted to accept aid from countries other than the U.S.
5. The cost of supporting Military Assistance Groups was reduced.[39]

Other things desired by the Japanese were not won. The U.S. did not agree to withdraw from Japan, and pressure would continue for rearmament. Partly as a response to these pressures, the Japanese created the Defense Agency (an alternative to a ministry, and part of the Office of the Prime Minister) and a Self-Defense Forces Law. This last dropped the fiction that Japan had no army, created an air force responsible for Japan's airspace, and further defined the role of the military. What Yoshida achieved in 1954 was the modest rearming of Japan, without actually accepting any part of collective responsibility.[40] Japan would be free to concentrate on economic matters, and would turn to military matters only as it suited.

Even though Yoshida fell shortly after this treaty, to be replaced by the more conservative Ichiro Hatoyama, the change meant little. Hatoyama was unable to change Article 9, as he might have wished, because it had ceased to be a limit on Japanese sovereignty. Quite the contrary, it made Japan freer than most other American allies. Japan could act militarily but only if it chose, and then it would be with the gratitude of the Americans, who had despaired of getting Japan to rearm. In short, Japan could simultaneously have an army, an alliance, and freedom from obligation.

The end of the Korean War in 1953 was the start of a period of apparent stability in the northwest Pacific. The ostensibly unshakable alliance between the People's Republic of China and the Soviet Union had nearly driven the U.S. off the Asian mainland. The Korean War was a strategic victory for the U.S. in the sense that it retained its perch on the Korean Peninsula. However, the Chinese intervention and the stalemate that followed made it clear that the U.S. would not be able to exploit that perch militarily.

Thus, the end of the war shifted attention to the only other region where U.S. forces or surrogates continued to operate on the continent: southern Asia. From Iran, through the Indian subcontinent, to Indochina, U.S. and Communist forces waged overt and covert wars for control and influence. This was particularly the case in Indochina, where 1954 brought the defeat of France and the advent of the United States as the guarantor of anti-communism.

U.S. policy remained centered on containment, but Indian independence and neutrality made a coherent South Asia policy impossible, as the region was now segmented. U.S. policy was therefore different west and east of India. West of India, southwest Asia was treated as an extension of the Middle East. East of India, however, stretching from East Pakistan through Burma, Thailand, and Indochina, Asia was seen as a distinct region. It became U.S. policy to resist the spread of communism in this tier of Asia.

The obvious problem in the region was economic. Communism was understood to thrive where there was poverty. The United States did not merely want to aid the region. It wanted to construct internal economies, linked to ongoing external relations, that would sustain strong social and political institutions. The phrase of the time was "nation building." The United States had plans for Japan in this regard.

World War II was fought precisely over the question of Japan's relationship to Southeast Asia. Now the United States wanted Japan to do what it had stopped them from doing in 1941. The U.S. wanted the Japanese need for raw materials to spur Southeast Asia's growth, and the availability of cheap raw materials from this region to drive Japan's growth.

The U.S. summed up this view in a report produced by Joseph Dodge entitled "United States–Japan Economic Cooperation in the Post-Treaty Period":

> There will be substantial reliance on Japan in the post-treaty period for:
>
> a. Production of goods and services important to the United States and the economic stability of non-Communist Asia.
> b. Cooperation with the United States in the development of raw material resources of Asia.
> c. Production of low-cost military material in volume for use in Japan and non-Communist Asia.
> d. Development of Japan's appropriate military forces as a defensive shield and to permit the redeployment of United States forces.[41]

The United States saw a trilateral relationship developing. Japan would import raw materials from Southeast Asia and manufacture products for the American market. The irony seemed to escape the Americans—the U.S. was offering Japan economic hegemony over Southeast Asia and full access to the U.S. market in return for not trading with China and the Soviet Union. If the Japanese were aware of the irony, they did not show it publicly.

The Dodge memorandum set the stage for Japan's growth over the next decades. The United States would provide political and military protection to Japan. Japan, in turn, would be an economic adjunct in this relationship, strengthening the economies of non-Communist Asia while supplying the U.S. with low-cost goods. Ultimately, the United States would be happy if Japan prospered, and would be doubly pleased if Japan's prosperity set off a boom in the rest of Asia.

THE CRISIS OF 1960

The sovereignty question still rankled Japan. Economic benefits would not be fully clear for years, but the limitations on Japan imposed by its relationship with the U.S. were quite clear. From the Japanese point of view, the treaty of 1952 had a series of inherent drawbacks. There was a provision in the treaty that permitted the Japanese government to request that American troops be used against internal unrest. The implication was that the United States was the guarantor of the Japanese state, and that the U.S. would not allow the state it had created to disappear under any circumstances, regardless of the popular will.[42] Implicit in this was the idea that the U.S. had an ongoing program of covert intervention already underway.

U.S. bases were another problem. The United States could use the bases in any way they chose, without consulting the Japanese government. Since operations from Japanese bases would surely invite Soviet retaliation, Japan could be plunged into war without even being consulted. The rumored presence of nuclear weapons did nothing to quiet fears, and grated on Japanese nerves in the wake of Hiroshima and Nagasaki. No matter how benign, how carefully controlled, the presence of foreign troops on a country's soil is a trying matter. In 1952 there had been about 210,000 U.S. troops in Japan. While this number had drifted downward, there were still some 65,000 troops in 1957.[43]

There were also inevitable problems with U.S. troops. One of these became a cause célèbre. In 1957, Specialist 3/c William S. Girard accidentally killed an old woman by firing an empty shell from a grenade launcher. The woman had been collecting brass on a U.S. firing range. Girard's commanding officer refused to place him under the jurisdiction of Japanese authorities, claiming that actions by servicemen while on duty were solely under the jurisdiction of the U.S. military. The case drove home the fact that the Japanese government was not fully sovereign in Japan. Eventually Girard was tried in a Japanese court, received a three-year suspended sentence, and was rushed out of Japan immediately after the trial.[44] The case set off a firestorm of protest in Japan. The Socialist Party in particular politicized the case, generalizing it into an attack on the U.S. presence in Japan.

It was against this backdrop that both sides agreed to revise the treaties of 1952 and 1954. The American interest in this revision was an old one: an attempt to get the Japanese to take a more active role in Asia militarily. The Japanese interest was to increase their sovereignty. In particular, the Japanese wanted a clear and direct American commitment to defend Japan in case of attack, to replace the implicit commitment that existed. It was necessary to show that the bases were somehow linked to Japanese as well as American interests. The clause allowing the use of troops for internal control was to be dropped, as was the purely symbolic clause barring Japan from granting basing privileges to any third party.

On the whole, the Japanese won the negotiations. They won on all the above points. The Japan Defense Forces were to be increased, but not dramatically or decisively. U.S. facilities in Japan could be used to support other U.S. operations in Asia, but there would be prior consultation before deploying troops based in Japan, and on major changes in weapons deployment in Japan, including nuclear weapons.[45]

The Americans felt that the concessions they had made were sizable. President Eisenhower planned to come to Japan to sign the new treaty and expected to receive a warm greeting. It was therefore a stunning surprise when the country exploded in bitter anger at the treaty revisions. The Americans ought not to have been surprised; the bases had never been popular in Japan with any segment of the public. The Left wanted to be neutral, the Right wanted to be sovereign, and the masses thought the bases spelled trouble. The anger over the Girard case ought to have warned the Americans to leave well enough alone.

The new treaty was a reminder to Japan of the dangers of involvement with the Americans. Japan had been extremely successful economically. Its annual growth rate of 13 percent between 1959 and 1961 was the highest in the world. Japanese exports had put many Western economies on the defensive, and several industries had become world leaders.[46] Business was good and the tensions between the Americans and the Communists promised nothing but trouble.

But one must speculate that there was a deeper cause behind the anger expressed during the riots that followed. Japanese pride and self-confidence had been shattered in World War II. The presence of the Americans was an ongoing reminder of the inadequacy of Japan, of its failure. Friction with the GIs was only the tip of the problem. Japan had lost a war and the Americans were there every day to remind them of the fact.

Anger confronted reality, however. The Japanese needed the Americans. An American withdrawal would not have meant neutrality. Given the importance of Japan to Soviet strategy in the Pacific and given the history of conflict between the two countries, the Soviets would inevitably have pressured the Japanese, forcing them to emulate Finland or even capitulate to more intrusive Soviet demands.

Japan swallowed its national pride and opted for the protection of the American nuclear umbrella and that of the Seventh Fleet. Eisenhower canceled his visit, signaling his fear that the Japanese government would not survive. This perhaps sobered the Japanese into considering the meaning of an American abandonment. Japan calmed down and went about its business, but not without implanting in the American mind a sense of Japan's political fragility.

VIETNAM AND CHINA

This sense of political fragility conditioned American thinking about Japan throughout the 1960s. The United States badly needed Japan for its strategic position and its ability to spur the economies of non-Communist Asia. The specter of 1960 haunted the Americans permanently, as it forced them to consider the defense of the Pacific without having Japan to anchor the northern end of its Pacific island line. This was in spite of the fact that, starting in 1965, economic relations between Japan and the U.S. were reversed. For the first time, Japan exported more to the United States than it imported. Except for 1975, at the height of the oil shortage, Japan ran a surplus with the United States in every year.[47]

In spite of the reversal in economic relations, the U.S. needed to maintain good relations with Japan, as the U.S. had its hands full in Indochina. First in Laos and then in South Vietnam, insurgencies supplied and directed by North Vietnam, which in turn were supplied by the People's Republic of China and the Soviet Union, began to flourish. The decision of the U.S., made after 1948, to maintain a presence on the periphery of Asia was being challenged.

The United States, like all young imperialist powers, did not take challenge lightly. The self-confidence of victory in World War II was only barely tarnished by the burdens and ambiguities of its new empire. The U.S. had policed its empire vigorously in the 1950s, and Indochina was only the latest in a series of probes by the Communists, still considered a monolithic bloc by most American analysts.

The decision to resist in Vietnam was made in the context of an expanding monolithic communism. There were only two alternatives: the U.S. could withdraw from the Asian mainland and try to hold a purely island line, or it could stand and fight, back against the sea. The third alternative, to manipulate the Sino-Soviet split so that the balance of power in Asia would not support the North Vietnamese adventure, was not considered. In part, the Sino-Soviet split is visible only in retrospect rather than at the point when the key decisions were being made. But more important, the American system of alliances required absolutes if it was to work.

Japan, for example, badly wanted relations with the People's Republic of China for its own economic advantage. Indonesia wanted to straddle the line as well. By operating subtly, the U.S. might have grasped a deeper truth about the world, but it would also have given license to U.S. allies to act with subtlety as well. The alliance could not be held together without imposing an artificial moral clarity on the world. It was, therefore, useful to act as if there was a monolithic and malignant communism. The U.S. was too young to have mastered the British art of public moralizing and private perfidy.

The war in Vietnam placed the U.S.–Japanese relationship in its clearest perspective. Under the treaty, U.S. bases in Japan could be used to assist the war effort in Vietnam; the issue was the extent to which those bases would be used, after consultation with the Japanese. Japan understood that it had to be pro-American in the war. Foreign Minister Shiina agreed, in 1965, that "Japan is not neutral in the Vietnam War."[48]

On the other hand, memories of 1960 were fresh in everyone's mind, and a deep discontent over the war was obvious. Neither the Americans nor the Japanese wanted to test that discontent, and both searched for a formula that would keep Japan in the American camp. For the U.S., being able to utilize its Japanese bases was more important than direct Japanese involvement.

The compromise reached left Japan free from contribution to the Vietnam effort. This distinguished Japan from virtually all other Asian allies of America. No Japanese troops fought in Vietnam. While U.S. bases in Japan were used for shipment of materiel, no aircraft took off from Japanese soil to carry out air strikes. Naval facilities were used by the Seventh Fleet, but ground forces were not based there.

For the U.S., the level of Japanese participation pointed out the problem in its relationship. By the late 1960s, the Japanese were becoming obviously and aggressively successful in their economic life. Frequently, they seemed to be doing that at the expense of American manufacturers. They carried no defense burden, but were simply defended by the U.S. For the first time some Americans began to voice the charge that the Japanese were taking advantage of them. At a time of deep American anguish, in spite of America's return of Okinawan sovereignty to Japan, the Japanese appeared to be more concerned about getting fat than about coming to America's aid. As the *Asahi Shimbun* put it:

> The American economy, being what it is at the moment, can hardly afford to allow Japan "special considerations" much longer. Japan, now a sharp competitor economically, is no longer the nation that she used to be either.[49]

The emerging tension between the U.S. and Japan was the beginning of a long process of competition within the confines set by the Cold War.

Japan's general opposition to the Vietnam War was not reflected in government policy. Aside from not wishing to alienate the U.S., there were strategic reasons for this. The war in Vietnam absorbed U.S. attention and, over time, decreased U.S. bellicosity in northeast Asia. The U.S. was much less interested in Korea and completely without stomach for conflict with China. Thus, the Japanese found themselves in an international backwater for the first time in nearly a century. If they simply avoided exciting American interest, they could go about their business in peace.

Japanese indifference turned to concern as it became apparent that the United States was being beaten in Vietnam. The change in the American mood was striking. Instead of the self-confident, arrogant adventurers of 1950, the Americans were becoming bitter and increasingly despairing of their ability to control events. As sentiment for withdrawal from Vietnam rose, a general isolationist disposition arose along with it. For the Japanese, a complete withdrawal from Asia by the U.S. would have been disastrous. While the Japanese did not want to be drawn into the war, neither did they wish to make their way outside the American security umbrella. The Japanese wanted American protection without overt presence and without paying too high a price.

After 1960, that is pretty much what they got. By 1970 the Japanese had to begin considering their fate outside the American protective barrier. The Japanese tried to keep a brave face, pretending that nothing would change were the U.S. to withdraw, but the sharp reaction at the news that the U.S. would withdraw some fighter squadrons from Japan betrayed that fear.[50]

The Japanese were prepared for the collapse of American power or its resurgence, but they were not prepared for America's next move. By 1968, after battles on the Ussuri River between Chinese and Soviet troops, it became apparent to the new American administration that the Sino-Soviet split was no chimerical event. Nixon and Kissinger therefore embarked on a twofold Asian policy. First, and less important, they decided to withdraw from Vietnam and hoped the Saigon government would survive. If it did not, the effect of this could be mitigated through their second move, which was to manipulate the Sino-Soviet split and become a de facto ally of China.

The Nixon Doctrine appeared to be a preface to withdrawal from the containment of the Soviet Union. In shifting the burden of defense on the periphery of the Soviet Union to the local power, and relying on guarantees to stabilize these countries, the U.S. seemed about to abandon its imperial role. The Nixon Doctrine, however, turned out to have another dimension: a return to manipulating the balance of power in Eurasia, of operating a fluid rather than fixed alliance system.

The Soviet Union had long sought an alliance with the U.S. against China. On occasion, it had even hinted that it might be interested in a joint operation with the U.S. against the People's Republic of China. Given the venomous feelings of Americans toward China after the Korean War, the Soviets certainly expected American neutrality in any Sino-Soviet split. Given the impending defeat in Vietnam and growing American weariness, they did not expect any further adventures in Asia. Nixon confounded them and the world.

Instead of aligning with the Soviets, Nixon used Soviet pressure on China to entice them into aligning with the United States. Kissinger's secret visit to Peking—and Nixon's later formal visit—were merely dance steps in a vast global realignment. On the surface it appeared that it was the two weaker powers uniting against the rising strength of the Soviet Union. In fact, it was the distant and secure power, the U.S., egging a weaker power into conflict with a stronger one, diverting the attention of both from possibilities less agreeable to the U.S. The U.S. was merely continuing the containment policy, but changing the definition of what had to be contained. Under Acheson and Dulles, communism had to be contained. Under Kissinger, it was only the Soviet Union, and the division in international communism could be used to achieve this end.

Nixon's opening to China stunned the Japanese. In part, this was because of the secrecy in which the preliminary negotiations had taken place. The U.S. had presented Japan with a completely new Asia without warning.[51] The Japanese were unused to such subtlety on the part of the vulgar Americans. Nor were they used to such amorality. The Americans had been great moralists. Both Douglas MacArthur and John Foster Dulles, key men in shaping Japan's image of America, were moralists. China's wickedness, not the balance of power, appeared to concern them. But America, in being defeated in Vietnam, had had its moral certitudes shaken, and the moral quality of China became less important than its uses for the Americans.

Nixon's move encircled the Soviet Union far more effectively than it had been before. The Soviets now faced the threat of conflict from the North Cape of Norway to Vladivostok, in a virtually unbroken line. Nixon's move reversed the outcome of the Vietnam War. America's defeat in that war seemed to lead to a weaker, more defensive America. Nixon understood that, for the present, the time for military adventures was at an end. But in substituting diplomatic adventure for military, Nixon managed to turn defeat into victory. The

Soviet Union's strategic position after the Vietnam War was qualitatively worse than before the war. Moreover, Nixon reinstituted a fundamental principle of alliance conflict: the stronger power forces the weaker to bear the burdens of conflict. In allying with the Chinese, Nixon used China's location to protect America's basic interest: that no single power should dominate Eurasia.

The effect on Japan of this Nixon Shock was mixed. As always, the Japanese wished to appear unperturbed. In fact, Japan was suddenly in uncharted waters. Japan was more than a little bitter at having been barred from access to the People's Republic of China for twenty years because of American moralism, only to see the Americans plunge into forbidden territory without blushing. They also felt themselves suddenly vulnerable. Sino-American friendship meant that the level of tension in northeast Asia had suddenly soared. Were there to be a Sino-Soviet war in which the United States supported the People's Republic of China, Japan would become an inevitable participant, as U.S. bases would certainly be used in any such conflict. When the Vietnam War was at its height, Japan felt the temporary pleasure of being in an uninteresting corner of the world. Suddenly, Japan felt that it had a front-row seat to Armageddon. Japan responded by doing nothing and hoped for the best.

The alliance between the U.S. and Japan had one advantage. Japan's own room for maneuver, particularly economic maneuver, opened dramatically. The U.S. could no longer frown on Japanese trade with the People's Republic of China, nor at Japan's flirtation with the Soviet Union over Siberian resource development. Since the U.S. had adopted the pivotal role in a three-player game, Japan, America's junior partner, was free to pivot as well. Thus, in the end, Japan found it useful to stay under the American umbrella and hoped to profit from it handsomely. And, as always, the Americans effectively exempted the Japanese from the Nixon Doctrine, carrying the burden of defense in return for stability and prosperity in Japan.

The U.S. resurrected Japan out of fear of the Soviet Union. One of the results of that resurrection was a Japan that was economically healthy and, indeed, aggressive. By the time of Nixon's visit to China, the U.S. was experiencing the pain of Japan's export boom, just as Japan had realized the pain of America's overwhelming political and military power. The Nixon Shock focused Japan's attention on the limits of America's attachment to Japan. The U.S.–Japanese alliance depended on America's ongoing interest in a strong Japan. With the creation of a triangular game in Asia, Japan's sense of vulnerability soared. Rising anger in the U.S. concerning Japan's exports of autos, steel, and textiles caused Japan to realize that one of the fundamental bases of the U.S.–Japanese relationship, the right of Japan to have unlimited access to the American export market, was not necessarily eternal. Thus, for the first time, Japan's certainty about its indispensability to the United States was opened to question. And, with the final shock of the early 1970s and the oil embargo of 1973, the ability of the U.S. to guarantee Japan's mineral supplies was also opened to question.

This was not the end of the U.S.–Japanese alliance by any means. But it was certainly the beginning of the end. The creation of a tripolar instead of a bipolar world, the rising tension between the U.S. and Japan on economic matters, and the oil crisis all combined to start eroding the foundations of the relationship. In the long run, the two economic crises were probably the most dangerous of all. Thus, examining the economic relationship between the U.S. and Japan must preface any further political analysis.

 1. *Asahi Shimbun* staff, *The Pacific Rivals* (New York, 1971), p. 193.
 2. Frederick Shiels, *Tokyo and Washington* (Lexington, 1980), p. 74.
 3. Lindsey Parrott, "The Touchy Issue of Peace with Japan," in Lloyd Gardner, ed., *The Korean War* (New York, 1972), p. 63.
 4. MacArthur memo, March 21, 1947, in Akira Iriye, *The Cold War in Asia* (Englewood Cliffs, 1974), p. 149.
 5. These principles were contained in a memorandum from Foreign Minister Ashida to the War Department, September 10, 1947. See Martin Weinstein, *Japan's Postwar Defense Policy, 1947–1968* (New York, 1971), pp. 24–25.
 6. On the British view of the occupation, see Roger Buckley, *Occupation Diplomacy: Britain, the United States and Japan, 1945–1952* (Cambridge, 1982).
 7. William MacMahon Ball, *Japan: Enemy or Ally?* (New York, 1949), p. 183.
 8. Ibid., p. 185.
 9. Iriye, *Cold War in Asia*, p. 174.
10. George Kennan, *Memoirs* (Boston, 1967), p. 381.
11. Iriye, *Cold War in Asia*, p. 147.
12. John Denson, "Must We Rearm Japan?" *Colliers*, 126 (September 9, 1950), p. 69.
13. Weinstein, *Japan's Postwar Policy*, pp. 50–51.
14. Yutaka Kosai, *The Era of High Speed Growth* (Tokyo, 1986), p. 72.
15. Ibid., p. 66.
16. Ibid., p. 74.
17. Ibid., p. 78.
18. George C. Allen, *Japan's Economic Recovery* (London, 1960), pp. 97–100.
19. Ibid., pp. 103–105.
20. *Asahi Shimbun* staff, *Pacific Rivals*, p. 194.
21. Kosai, *High Speed Growth*, p. 78.
22. Shigeru Yoshida, "Japan and the Crisis in Asia," *Foreign Affairs*, 29:2 (January 1951), p. 180.

23. Frederick S. Dunn, *Peace Making and the Settlement with Japan* (Princeton, 1963) p. 105.
24. John W. Dower, *Empire and Aftermath* (Cambridge, 1979), p. 372.
25. Tadashi Aruga, "The Security Treaty Revision of 1960," in Akira Iriye and Warren Cohen, eds., *The United States and Japan in the Postwar World* (Lexington, 1989), p. 61.
26. Dunn, *Peace Making and the Settlement*, pp. 99–102.
27. In Shiels, *Tokyo and Washington*, p. 77.
28. Weinstein, *Japan's Postwar Policy*, p. 71.
29. Ibid., pp. 24–25.
30. Dower, *Empire and Aftermath*, p. 391.
31. Ibid., p. 391.
32. Iriye, *Cold War in Asia*, p. 147.
33. Tadashi Aruga, "Security Treaty Revision," in Iriye and Cohen, *U.S. and Japan*, p. 61. Also see Dower, *Empire and Aftermath*, p. 419.
34. *Asahi Shimbun* staff, *Pacific Rivals*, p. 207.
35. Martin Weinstein, "Defense Policy and the Self-Defense Forces," *Japan Interpreter*, 6:2 (Summer 1970), p. 167.
36. NSC 2/125, in Chihiro Hosoya, "Yoshida Letter to the Nixon Shock," in Iriye and Cohen, *U.S. and Japan*, p. 22.
37. Dower, *Empire and Aftermath*, p. 387.
38. James H. Buck, "The Japanese Self-Defense Forces," *Asian Survey*, 7:9 (September 1967), p. 605.
39. Dower, *Empire and Aftermath*, p. 467.
40. John K. Emmerson, *Arms, Yen and Power: The Japanese Dilemma* (New York, 1971), p. 78.
41. Ibid., p. 426.
42. Fred Greene, *Stresses in US–Japanese Relations* (Washington, D.C., 1975), p. 31.
43. James H. Buck, *The Modern Japanese Military System* (Beverly Hills, 1975), p. 242.
44. George Packard, *Protest in Tokyo* (Princeton, 1966) pp. 35–36.
45. Greene, *Stresses in U.S.–Japanese Relations*, p. 32.
46. Packard, *Protest in Tokyo*, p. 34.
47. The Bank of Japan, Economic Research and Statistics Dept., *Economic Statistics Annual: 1981*, pp. 227–228.
48. Emmerson, *Arms, Yen and Power*, p. 84.
49. *Asahi Shimbun* staff, *Pacific Rivals*, p. 227.
50. Robert E. Osgood, *The Weary and the Wary* (Baltimore, 1972), pp. 41–43.
51. Tang Tsou, Tetsuo Najita, and Hideo Otake, "Sino-Japanese Relations in the 1970s," in Morton Kaplan and Kinhide Mushakaji, eds., *Japan, America and the Future World Order* (New York, 1976), pp. 57–60.

6

Japan's Economic Miracle: Becoming Normal Again

Japan's recent economic success has left the world in awe and even terror. Books about the phenomenon abound: *Yen: Japan's New Financial Empire and Its Threat to America*; *The Japanese Conspiracy: The Plot to Dominate Industry Worldwide—And How to Deal With It*; and *How to Beat the Japanese at Their Own Game*.[1] It has become the conventional wisdom that Japanese economic power and its future growth will outstrip and overwhelm the United States. The question no longer seems to be whether this will take place, but why is it happening?

One needs to take such apocalyptic visions with more than a grain of salt. New economic powerhouses appear about once a decade. In the 1950s people believed that the Soviet Union's growth rate meant it would equal and surpass the U.S. by 1970 and that capitalism was doomed. In the mid-1960s economists believed they had discovered the way to abolish recessions and that the American millennium was upon us. And in the 1970s there was the belief that, due to the global mineral shortage, permanent power was now in the hands of Third World mineral producers and a new world order had been born.

The Japanese have put on a bravura performance. They will not go the way of the Soviets, nor is their success a matter of luck, as in the case of OPEC. They have banked on their skill, discipline, even

135

bravery, and have done magnificently. But magnificence is different from omnipotence, and Japan has its share of problems, many of them dangerous and difficult to solve. Indeed, much of the legend of Japan's recent performance is as much myth as it is reality. Thus, any discussion of Japan's economy must begin by considering just how successful Japan has been.

MEASURING JAPAN'S ECONOMIC SUCCESS

Some 123 million Japanese live in a rather small country, devoid of most natural resources, with a limited and backward agriculture. Unlike the United States, a vast, opulent country, Japan is an extremely ordinary, even a deprived nation. It is therefore extraordinary that Japan's economy is today the second largest in the world, trailing only the United States. In fact, in terms of per capita gross national product (GNP), Japan has slightly surpassed the United States. In 1945, the Japanese were literally starving and freezing. Less than a half-century later, Japan towers over all other nations in the magnitude of its achievements. It has become the world's largest lender, a creditor of first and last resort. Japan largely controls some fields of manufacturing, such as photographic equipment and consumer electronics, and vast swaths of other areas of industrial production. Japan has become this generation's standard of economic excellence, the nation to beat.

Japan's success is not something recent. For the past century, Japan's economic growth rate has towered over that of other nations. But Japan has really shown its greatest spurt of growth in the postwar period:

TABLE 6-1. Average Annual Rate of Growth (in constant prices).

	JAPAN	U.S.	U.K.	FRANCE	GERMANY
1947–50	9.7%	2.4%	1.5%	10.4%	—
1951–55	10.9	4.8	3.4	4.5	11.4%
1956–60	10.1	2.3	2.6	5.6	7.4
1961–65	11.3	5.1	3.4	6.5	5.3
1966–70	14.6	3.1	2.6	6.0	4.5
1971–75	4.7	2.3	2.3	3.7	5.2
1976–80	5.5	3.7	1.8	3.3	3.6
1981–85	4.2	2.7	1.9	1.5	1.2
1986–87	3.4	3.2	3.5	2.2	2.2

(Source: Economist: *One Hundred Years of Economic Statistics*)

The Japanese have consistently equaled or outperformed other industrialized countries, including Germany, a nation that shared the fate of being defeated and having to reconstruct its economy.[2]

Many are aware of the phenomenal growth of the Japanese economy; fewer are aware of the recent relative decline in Japan's performance. The last period of double-digit growth for the Japanese was the 1960s. Since then, the Japanese growth rate has moved closer to the general average of the industrialized countries. Japan ranked at the top of the Organization for Economic Cooperation and Development (OECD) heap during the period from 1977–1987. However, during the 1982–1987 period, Japan's growth rate fell to fifth place among the industrialized nations, behind Turkey, Norway, Canada, and the United States. Its 3.8 percent rate of growth was only 0.6 percent above the OECD average.[3] While Japan's growth rate improved in 1988 and 1989, it is still nowhere near the surging levels of the pre-1970 period. At the very time most of the world was singing Japan's praises, its actual performance was becoming substantially less impressive than before.

It is not difficult to understand the first spurt of growth after World War II. Japan ended the war with most of its labor force and substantial physical resources intact. What was disrupted was Japan's distribution systems. The simple act of reestablishing basic economic networks served to increase GNP dramatically.[4] Given the large pool of available skilled labor, return on investment was inevitably high, thus motivating large-scale investment. With the added impetus of demand generated by the Korean War, the ability to produce consistently high rates of return on capital propelled the economy forward.

Thus, for several decades after the war the Japanese economy grew at an extraordinary rate. Since the early 1970s—really since the 1973 oil crisis—Japan has grown much more slowly. It must be emphasized that in spite of this downturn, the Japanese economy did grow consistently even during global stagflation and recession, and that its performance remained impressive. But it was not quite as impressive as before.

For most economies, the decline in the underlying growth rate would be a normal and untroubling sign of a healthy, maturing economy. The U.S. has always been content with a relatively low but sustainable growth rate, as long as other economic indicators, such as inflation and corporate profits, did well. For Japan, however, the decline in economic growth is a much more serious problem, because the Japanese economy, unlike those of most other industrialized countries, is predicated on growth even at the expense of other economic values, such as corporate profits. Growth drives the Japanese economy and a decline in its growth can threaten the very fabric of

Japanese society. The key to this culture of growth is to be found in the nature of the central Japanese social and economic organization, the Japanese corporation.

THE JAPANESE CORPORATION

Many have breathlessly praised the Japanese corporation. As Ezra Vogel, dean of the "Japan as Number One" school of analysis, put it:

> Many of the reasons for Japan's success are well known: the high quality of Japanese manpower, the large number of trained engineers, the commitment of employees to a company, attention to manufacturing and especially to product engineering, the low cost of capital, high savings rates, availability of long term funds which permit long-term perspective, global strategy and government incentives to business.
>
> But these factors do not work in isolation. They are part of an overall system coordinated by key government and business leaders. There is no reason to expect that this system will be any less effective in the coming years. In fact, given the expanded capital base, the improved educational and research base, and the extended informational networks, Japanese competitiveness will certainly be even stronger in the future.[5]

The Japanese corporation is indeed the key to the Japanese economic system. It is also its major weakness. The Japanese corporation is, on the surface, a corporation like any other Western corporation. Like all corporations, it is a pool of capital placed there by investors seeking a return on their investment. The investor takes a risk by investing and hopes to produce a return on his investment commensurate with his risk. In addition, the investor expects to be liable for no more than his investment. The pooling of assets from otherwise uninvolved investors, to be managed by professional businessmen, allowed the growth of modern industrialism.

Beyond this, there are enormous differences between Japanese and Western corporations in their relationship with investors, management, and employees—the corporate triad. As a result, Japanese and American corporations behave in very different ways. The American investor expects to be rewarded for his risk-taking either by receiving a regular and rising dividend or by having the price of the stock rise as profits or expectations of profits rise. The stockholder therefore views the corporation as a means of generating return on capital and holds management responsible for this. To the extent that he holds stock in the company, he expects to control management, and legally and sometimes in reality the stockholder can force management to comply with his collective wishes.

For this reason, American management is extremely aware of the fluctuation of stock prices. Declines in stock prices can easily trigger a shareholder revolt in the form of a fight to replace management. The hostile takeover has become an art form in the American corporation. It has become the primary means for removing inefficient managers and restructuring operations so as to increase return on investment. Managers keep stockholders happy by maintaining and increasing dividends, protecting the bottom line, and generally protecting the price of the stock.

This concern with stock prices has met with much criticism. For example, the propensity to pay dividends cuts deeply into reinvestment, making the corporation excessively dependent on outside financing and particularly on new equity flowing into the company. It has also caused corporations to defer research and development (R&D). In addition, obsession with stock prices, which tend to react to short-term events, has caused American businessmen to ignore long-term planning in favor of actions with immediate payoffs.

At the same time, the American system makes capital mobility a reality. Dividends form a pool of capital available for reinvestment in other, newer companies. While the parent company might be deprived of capital, other less mature companies are maintained and created by the free-floating capital thus created. Moreover, solicitude to the investor permits a large and lively equity market to maintain itself, a market in which entrepreneurs can readily seek nonbank financing. This decentralized capital mobility depends on the continual payback of capital by existing corporations. Were these corporations to hold on to this capital, their propensity to reinvest in their own increasingly inefficient industries would retard total growth, choking off innovation.

Japan's system is substantially different. Japan's shareholders are paid a fixed percentage, based on par value of the stock, and while that amount is paid faithfully, it does not rise as profits rise. The rate of return on an investment is rarely more than 1 or 2 percent of market value.[6] This means that initial capitalization does not place a long-term limit on profitability, and Japanese corporations are able to reinvest in themselves more readily than their American counterparts. The price, of course, is that new corporations find it harder to raise equity, making them dependent on banks that frequently are bound to giant corporations.[7]

Unlike the American case, Japanese stockholders have almost no control over corporations. The board of directors does not operate, even in theory, as the shareholders' watchdog over management; it *is* the management. The board normally consists of the senior management of the Japanese corporation.[8] Additional members might be drawn from linked corporations or from banks with financial exposure in the corporation, but it is an insider's board, without stockholder input.

The key to the Japanese corporate system is its essential inwardness. In the large corporations, men—always men—enter the hierarchy after graduating from one of the selective universities. They rise in the corporation on the basis of seniority and a weeding process that limits the advancement of some. Should they reach the very pinnacles of power, becoming managing directors, they then control the fate of the corporation in which they have spent their lives.[9]

The decision-making process is internal and consensual. Directors consult all major constituencies in the company and try to find solutions that will satisfy all of their interests. These interests are primarily those of the administrative and technical strata of the corporations from which they themselves arose and the corporations that they are linked with, particularly their banks. And since the directors need primarily to satisfy the corporate culture and its members rather than some outside group, they can plan on a longer-term basis, ignoring questions of short-term profitability and equity growth.[10] Obviously, growth in sales is of greater immediate interest to their constituents than profitability, since growth assures the cash flow that supports pay raises and assures payment of interest on debts.

To a great extent, these corporations can control their fate. Since most of the profits they generate are plowed back into the corporation, they are less dependent on stock offerings to sustain growth than if the profits were paid out to shareholders. While this has changed to some extent in the last few years, on the whole it remains the case. It is difficult to raise capital in an equity market where the investor receives virtually no dividends, has no influence over the corporation's future, and where he will be treated not as the owner but as an irrelevant outsider. In a striking bull market, as we have seen in past years, where speculative fever fueled by surplus cash drives the price of stocks up, investors may gamble on equity growth, more as a lottery than as an investment. But for a prudent investment, stocks offer little future. This is doubly the case since outside takeovers are virtually impossible.

Japanese corporations tend to borrow the money they require for continued expansion. This tendency is reflected in Japan's extremely unfavorable capital-to-debt ratio compared to the United States'.[11] Japanese corporations do not raise most of their money in the stock markets. Instead of having investors, they deal with lenders, banks who have to be repaid on a regular basis rather than shareholders who are co-participants in the risk taking. In 1986, Japan's ratio of capital to capital plus liability was only 31.45 percent, compared to 44.04 percent for the U.S.; there was too much debt and not enough capital.[12] This means that Japanese corporations, facing substantial cash-flow problems posed by debt-repayment schedules, can best solve that problem through increasing cash flow via sales growth and more sales growth.

The greater indebtedness of the Japanese corporation is significant in several ways. First, in a dramatic economic downturn, both long- and short-term lines of credit could be reduced dramatically, causing severe deterioration in the Japanese corporation's financial position. The higher equity component in the American corporation's balance sheet gives it strength in downturns. Having relatively lower debt payments, American corporations can endure recessions, reduced sales, and slower growth much better than Japanese corporations, which have not yet had to cope with a major recession in the postwar period.

The problem of undercapitalization is also a recent one for Japanese banks. Because of the sudden decline of the Tokyo Stock Exchange in the first half of 1990, a three-month moratorium was placed on new issues. The International Bank of Settlements, which sets rules on capital-to-assets ratios, has said that all banks must have 8 percent ratios by 1993. Since 30 to 40 percent of Japan's loans are non-yen denominated, the rise of the yen has caused a substantial decline in their value. With the inability of Japan's banks to enter a declining market for capital, Japan's banks are so undercapitalized that they cannot meet international banking standards. The Moody's ratings of several major Japanese banks—called City Banks—including Mitsubishi, Sumitomo, and Yasuda, have been lowered, thus increasing the cost of raising cash on the international market.[13] Given the fact that Japan has a surplus savings rate and a substantial outflow of money to foreign markets, the decline in the Nikkei index (the equivalent of the Dow Jones) and the unwillingness of Japanese investors to invest in Japan is ominous, at least in the short run. While Japan will undoubtedly weather this storm, it does point to a fundamental weakness in Japan's economy, one that could be devastating in other circumstances.

American banks are prevented by debt-equity rules applicable in the United States from lending to Japanese companies.[14] One of the major complaints on the American side during the structural-impediment talks has been the inability of American banks to enter the Japanese market. Ironically, the impediment has been the apparent recklessness of Japanese lending practices, which are considered by Americans to be extremely dangerous.

To overstate the point a bit, the Japanese economy is a Ponzi scheme in which only continued growth generating larger cash flows can cover the debt payments faced by at least some corporations. It has continued to grow largely because the entire financial structure of the country favors growth over profits. In the current cycle, profits have risen to the point where some of the larger companies have managed to liquidate their outstanding debt and are now able to finance their growth through internally generated cash, something made possible by the disadvantageous position that investors occupy in the system. In the meantime, growth alone has inflated the capital base and therefore the value of equities, satisfying investors and further strengthening corporate positions. While profits have risen, the general profitability of Japan's corporations has lagged behind that of U.S. corporations. The pretax profitability, measured as profits against capital, of major Japanese corporations was 6.5 percent, compared to 12.3 percent in the U.S. After-tax profits also favored the Americans: 2.5 percent in Japan to 5.6 percent for American companies.[15]

At the heart of this system are Japan's thirteen "City Banks." All are part of *keiretsu*, the informal—but binding—system of corporate relationships that connect legally unconnected corporations to each other, creating vast conglomerates integrated horizontally and vertically. Grouped around each of the City Banks, and drawing from them their life blood—cheap money—are Japan's most important corporations, dependent on the financial relationships, as well as on suppliers and distributors linked to them via the *keiretsu*. While there are many intriguing aspects to these groupings, which are descendants of the banned prewar *zaibatsu*, none is more important than the banking link. Although there are other *keiretsu*, such as enterprise *keiretsu* and subcontractor *keiretsu*, the most important are financial *keiretsu*.[16]

Keiretsu is an extremely difficult concept to explain in Western terms. Westerners are used to speaking of legal, binding relationships. Japan's *keiretsu* are much more informal but nonetheless very real. Japanese corporations maintain relations with other corporations based on tradition, descent, and group loyalty. Much like a family, the precise rights and obligations that exist between these corporations are difficult to define in specific terms, but are extremely binding. Suffice it to say that a Japanese corporation linked to another corporation via a *keiretsu* might well accept less than optimal terms on a contract in order to protect the interests of the linked corporations, or the *keiretsu* as a whole. In the West, where the corporation's obligation is to the stockholders, such an action would be tantamount to fraud. In Japan, where the primary obligation of the corporation is to the corporation—broadly understood—such an action would be considered prudent.

The names of Japan's great City Banks are world famous, as well as historically noteworthy, as descendants of venerable *zaibatsu*. In descending order, these are Daiichi Kangyo, Fuji, Sumitomo, Mitsubishi, Sanwa, Mitsui, Bank of Tokyo, Tokai, Taiyo Kobe, Daiwa, Kyowa, Saitama, and Hokkaido Takushoku. Several, such as Mitsui, are descended directly from prewar *zaibatsu*. In 1950, these banks held fully 50 percent of the private banking assets of Japan.[17] While this has now fallen to about 25 percent of all assets, this is still an enormous amount to be controlled by only thirteen institutions. In 1988, financial *keiretsu* did 35.4 percent of the financing for firms listed on the Tokyo Stock Exchange. When one considers that this is a substantial decline from the 40.1 percent financing done in 1974, one realizes the extent to which outstanding long-term debt is still held and controlled by these institutions.[18]

This also helps explain the tendency of linked corporations to grow, as well as to explain some of the apparently reckless lending practices in Japan. By being linked to banks that are only formally separate entities, major Japanese corporations are not so much borrowing from banks as utilizing internally generated capital. These core banks, taking advantage of both Bank of Japan rediscount policies and the high savings rates of their own employees, allow the banks to transfer funds to daughter companies in a formal loan format that actually has far more leeway built into it than a normal loan. This places Japanese corporations at a great advantage over American firms limited by U.S. banking laws. It also makes the entire Japanese system extremely vulnerable in the event of a major economic malfunction. In fact, it is safe to say that the system as a whole is more vulnerable than any single part of it.

The success of these banks, and perhaps of the entire economy, is in the spread between the interest they pay and the interest they charge. In August 1990, interest on a three-month deposit stood at 3.63 percent while the prime rate was at 7.13 percent, a spread of 3.5 points, the widest in the industrialized world.[19] No matter which way it is measured, in absolute spread or ratio of prime to interest, the difference between the amount Japanese banks charge to lend money (the prime rate) and the amount they pay to depositors in interest is extraordinarily high compared to other industrialized countries. The spread between the prime rate and the payout on three-month deposits means that, in addition to an extremely high savings rate, Japanese financial institutions are able to enjoy dramatically successful rates of return on loans. This obviously enhances the powerful position they enjoy in the system. Their interests are also protected by Ministry of Finance regulatory policies that dictate rates.[20]

Yet these mighty banks depend on the smallest of events: the willingness of the ordinary Japanese saver to forego consumption in favor of savings—savings that frequently go into the vast postal system savings plan and wind up buttressing the banking system as a whole and the City Banks in particular.

SAVINGS, WAGES, AND THE GROWTH ECONOMY

In spite of declining growth, Japan remains oddly strong by other measures. Japan's rate of capital formation—the rate at which it creates the factories and equipment necessary for economic growth—has been consistently higher than the rest of the world and has remained high. In 1960 Japanese capital formation was nearly 30 percent of GNP, while the U.S. rate was less than 15 percent. Although growth has declined, capital formation has not. In 1987 the Japanese rate was 28.9 percent, the American 14.9 percent.[21] This is one of the strengths of the Japanese system. It is also one of the weaknesses, since the continued inability to transform capital growth into economic growth indicates serious structural deficiencies in the economy. We need to consider why Japan's capital formation has remained high without driving the growth rate.

The growth of real assets has been made possible by a phenomenon peculiar in many ways to Japan. In other countries, growth has been driven by domestic consumption, by rising standards of living, while in Japan it was originally spurred by investment. The general assumption in the West is that this has been achieved by imposed savings on wage earners in the form of low wages. However, this has not altogether been the case.

Aggregate salaries and wages have tended, since 1955, to grow more quickly in Japan than the economy as a whole, particularly in the early 1960s and 1970s. This has meant that wages constituted a higher proportion of GNP over time. Looked at another way, in 1967, of the total value added by labor, 31.7 percent went to wages as compared with 47.1 percent in the U.S. That 15.4 percent additional return on capital was a substantial contribution to capital formation and economic growth. Although the gap narrowed, it never quite closed. Japan's figure was 35.9 percent in 1985, while the United States dropped to 39.7 percent.[22]

In 1988, the average family in Japan had a monthly income of Y481,250. Of this amount, Y306,904 was regular wages, while

Y88,052 was bonuses for the head of the household, Y43,195 was the wife's income, and the rest was income from other family members, side businesses, and jobs. Expenditures totaled Y382,157, or 79.4 percent of income. Housing was only 3.3 percent of income, while food was 15.5 percent. Transportation, recreation, and clothing were the largest items in the average family's budget, at 5.8, 6.5, and 4.5 percent, respectively.[23] Since living costs in Japan are substantially higher than in America, except for housing,[24] Japanese frugality is quite amazing.

The average family saves Y60,676 a month, or about 12.6 percent of its income.[25] By the time a head of household retires, he averages savings that are 2.71 times his last year's disposable income.[26] From 1973 until 1978, the savings rate in Japan was consistently above 20 percent. Current rates are at about the mid-1960s level.

The overwhelming majority of this money is deposited in savings accounts, with a much smaller amount going into stocks and life insurance.[27] This money, in turn, is loaned out by banks to Japan's corporations in highly leveraged circumstances, fueling growth if not profitability. Since Japan's economy is driven by corporate debt, the abnormally high savings rate is essential.

Interestingly, the rate of savings by Japanese is more than the Japanese economy can absorb. Japan not only has a high savings rate, it has also managed to generate a *surplus* savings rate, in which more money is saved than can be invested in the Japanese economy. In 1985, 26.8 percent of GNP was saved while only 22.8 percent was invested domestically, leaving a surplus savings rate of 4 percent of GNP.[28] It should be noted that households are the only sector to have consistently generated surpluses, while all other sectors have operated at deficits.[29]

In most societies, surplus savings rates cannot be maintained because of declining interest rates. In the U.S., for example, surpluses of 3.2 percent of GNP in 1982 were rapidly replaced by a balance in 1985, and negative figures thereafter.[30] But the artificially low interest rates on retail bank accounts, enforced by Japan in order to protect the profitability of Japanese business loans, cannot fall much lower than they already are. Extremely high savings rates in the face of such low retail interest rates compound the puzzle. However, that imbalance explains Japan's emergence as an international creditor.

The Japanese propensity to save is partly cultural and this cultural aspect cannot be minimized. It is also partly rational. One of the key features of the Japanese economy is the weakness of the social security system and a general absence of systematic, private retirement plans. Until recently, the Japanese government provided no retirement benefits at all. Under a recent scheme, monthly benefits in Japan will equal about $370 after forty years of contributing at the maximum rate.[31] Maximum contributions for forty years would net an American worker about $975 per month plus 50 percent for a nonworking spouse.

The private handling of retirement is more generous but quite a bit less formal:

> The retirement at 65 of an employee who is given severance pay equal to two years' salary involves additional compensation on several levels: hiring his wife if she has not yet reached retirement age, or a son or daughter who is looking for a first job, and finally reclassifying the person who has retired either as a part-time worker in an affiliated company or with a subcontractor whose salaries are lower.[32]

The Japanese retiree, unlike his American counterpart, remains dependent on the benevolence of his company for a comfortable retirement. He must remain on good terms with the company—not that it would occur to him to part on anything other than good terms.

The Japanese salary-man lives in a tense relationship with his corporation. On one side, he is provided with certain very real benefits, not the least of which is lifetime employment.[33] He also is given social status, a clear function in society, and a system of workable values. In return he must mortgage his life to the company, living by its rules, its schedules, its expectations. For example, in Japan, about one-third of the salary is paid as a bonus rather than as salary; this one-third is, in effect, a gratuity rather than a contractual right. It is therefore a system of economic and psychological dependency that would be impossible for an American, but on which the Japanese thrive.[34]

Nowhere is this dependent relationship more evident than at retirement. The American worker parts ways with his company with a legally vested pension, his by right, not by charity. He is cast out, but he is also free. The Japanese retiree enters into a new phase of dependence on his corporation, because his savings and retirement benefits together cannot provide him with a comfortable retirement. The Japanese salary-man continues to need the corporation in order to survive.

Two years' salary cannot generate sufficient income to support a retirement. Japanese public pensions are completely inadequate as well. Therefore, the Japanese *must* save more than their American counterparts if they wish to avoid putting their wives to work or taking a lowly part-time position themselves. The bonus system helps in this, as most Japanese live on regular salary and save much of the bonus. But fear has a greater role; the insufficiency of retirement benefits clearly helps shape Japan's saving frenzy.

An average office department manager receives a pay of about ¥7 million (about $57,000) a year.[35] At retirement he would receive about Y15 million as a retirement bonus, plus about Y600,000 (about $5,000) annually from social security. If he wished to have an income of 70 percent of his working salary, he would need to generate an income of about Y5 million a year, less his social security, or Y4.4 million ($36,000) a year. A government long-term bond yields about 8 percent in Japan.[36] To generate the amount needed, the retiree would have to purchase bonds totalling Y55 million (a little over $350,000). Since he receives, on retirement, only Y15 million, he has a shortfall of Y40 million (over $250,000). Since the expectation is that the retiree will have about Y17.5 million ($120,000) in savings, his retirement income would be about Y3.2 million ($21,000), or a little over one-third of his previous income. He therefore remains tied to family and corporation for the difference.[37]

Thus, Japan's high savings rate should come as no surprise to anyone. If the United States had as inadequate a retirement plan as Japan does, it too would have an extremely high savings rate. In a way, it is surprising that the average Japanese worker has not saved more by the time he retires, given his vulnerability after retirement.

Thus, government retirement policy, traditional values of abstinence, and a minimal commitment to profits have gone a long way toward fueling the dramatic growth rate in Japan. But as the figures above indicate, the growth rate is slowing down. While the savings rate has been falling, the absolute pool of savings has been rising as wages and salaries have risen. But there, too, the rate of growth has slowed until it is no longer dramatically higher than the rest of the world's, although still higher than Japan can efficiently utilize.

Continued growth in the Japanese economy can come from only two sources. One is increased domestic consumption. This has been one of the American demands during the Structural Impediment Initiative talks in 1989 and 1990. The Japanese have committed themselves to raising domestic consumption. The problem with this strategy is obviously that it would cut dramatically into the nation's savings rate and thereby undermine the necessary expansion in the banking system's deposit base, limiting the ability to extend credit and curtailing growth. The only other option is from increased foreign demand: exports.

THE INTERNATIONALIZATION OF JAPAN'S ECONOMY

It has been clear for quite some time that the Japanese economy is maturing. The inability to maintain growth rates and profit margins in spite of massive investments indicates that a maturing economy and a chronic labor shortage have worked together to slow the Japanese miracle. The era of rapid growth, in which simply reconstructing damaged economic networks would yield tremendous returns, is clearly at an end. Yet failure to maintain that growth can mean serious stress for a financial system that is heavily leveraged and counting on growth to get it out of its bind. Failure to achieve this can be disastrous. The price of achieving this can be extremely high, not merely in an economic sense but in a political sense as well.

Internal forces have compelled the Japanese economy to internationalize. The consumption pattern of Japanese society will simply not sustain historical growth patterns. Japan's historical solution, an investment-fueled growth pattern, has run into serious problems, because Japan can no longer absorb the available capital—for several structural reasons, including a labor shortage. Unlike the United States, Japan cannot solve its labor shortage through immigration, because of cultural limits. Thus, a full employment position in Japan must limit domestic growth. If Japanese corporations are going to grow, they must look abroad for both markets and investment opportunity.

And indeed, the surge in overseas investment during the current cycle has been extraordinary. In 1984, Japanese annual overseas investment totaled a little over $10 billion. By 1988, the amount had soared to nearly $50 billion. The shifting of internal savings to foreign markets has had two major effects on Japan. First, it has allowed the Japanese corporation to maintain its growth rate and limit the decline of its profitability. Second, it has created a political dependency on the markets it has entered. The change in Japan's economic relationship to the United States is a case in point. As recently as 1982, the United States was a net creditor to Japan. In 1988, the net asset position had shifted to the point that the U.S. owed Japan $532.5 billion.[38]

Japan's need to protect its interest in countries in which it has invested grows in proportion to its financial exposure. One can see an emerging political trend in the following pattern:

TABLE 6-2. Japanese Overseas Investment as a Percentage of Total Investment.

	1984	1985	1986	1987	1988	CUMULATIVE
U.S.	33.1%	44.2%	45.5%	44.1%	46.2%	38.6%
Indonesia	3.7	3.3	1.1	1.6	1.2	5.3
Hong Kong	4.1	1.1	2.2	3.2	3.5	3.3

TABLE 6-2. Japanese Overseas Investment (continued)

	1984	1985	1986	1987	1988	CUMULATIVE
Singapore	2.2	2.8	1.4	1.5	1.6	2.0
Korea	1.1	1.1	2.0	1.9	1.0	1.7
China	1.1	0.8	1.0	3.7	0.6	1.1
Thailand	1.2	0.4	0.6	0.7	0.8	1.1
Malaysia	1.4	0.6	0.7	0.5	0.8	1.0
Taiwan	0.6	0.9	1.3	1.1	0.8	1.0
Philippines	0.5	0.5	0.1	0.2	0.3	0.6
Asia	16.0	11.7	10.4	14.6	11.8	17.3
Europe	19.1	15.8	15.5	19.7	19.4	16.2
Africa	3.2	1.4	1.4	0.8	1.4	2.5
Oceania	1.5	4.3	4.4	4.2	5.7	5.0
Middle East	2.7	0.4	0.2	0.2	0.6	1.8

(Source: Japan Economic Institute)

The U.S. has become Japan's main investment target. This has troubled many Americans, as it seems to imply a dependency relationship with Japan. While there is an element of truth to this, two points are missed. First, in investing in America, Japanese investors are implicitly showing their lack of faith in the Japanese economy and their relative faith in the American. Second, in a political sense, dependency is mutual. While the U.S. depends on Japan's money for its financial needs, Japan increases its dependency on the U.S. for the safety and stability of investments. In other words, Japan becomes even more politically dependent on the U.S. than before.

What is interesting, also, are the different mixes of investment. For example, in the United States the largest single Japanese investment target is real estate, followed by financial institutions and marketing firms. Only a little over 25 percent goes into manufacturing. This same pattern repeats itself in Europe, except that real estate there is of less interest to the Japanese.

It is in Oceania and Asia that we begin to see a real shift. In Oceania (essentially Australia), real estate and mining are neck-and-neck for first place, followed closely by banking. In Asia, manufacturing and mining is by far the largest category, followed by service.[39] In Europe, Japanese confidence in real estate is substantially lower and almost all investment has gone into banking. In Asia, the emphasis is on Japan's need to develop natural resources close to home. Thus, what might be called strategic investing—the search for foreign sources of labor to supplement Japan's shortage and for foreign minerals to fuel Japanese factories, the growing dependence on Indonesia in particular, as well as on the rest of Southeast Asia—serves as a focus of Japan's strategic interests.

Because Japan is a net money exporter, it is in a precarious position, much like the OPEC countries in their heyday. With wealth comes the need to find safe investments. Japan's dependency on the U.S. is, of course, mutual. The U.S. needs Japanese cash quite as much as Japan needs sound investments. But should there be a turn in Japan's fortunes, where Japan ceases to be in a position to service U.S. financial needs, the mutual need will shift. Japan understands, after 1941 and after the sequestration of Iranian assets in 1979, that political shifts leave investors vulnerable to powerful hosts.

The second politically significant point here is that Japan must find resources closer to home. But financial control of these resources is meaningless without political influence. And political influence in turn depends on the ability to frighten one's enemies. As Japanese investment in countries like Indonesia grows, Japan's need to protect those investments—with something stronger than the threat of no future investments—will grow as well. The process of foreign investment, therefore, brings foreign entanglements of the most dangerous sort. This is a reality that Japan has yet to confront, but one that is implicit in the Japanese need to invest overseas in order to maintain corporate growth. The same is true for the export side of its economy.

Foreign investment serves a number of functions for the Japanese. First, in the context of Japan's chronic labor shortage, it permits Japan to recruit foreign workers without needing to allow them to emigrate to Japan. This reduces internal social stress in a traditionally insular, indeed racist, society. Second, it gives Japan increased rates of return on capital, therefore permitting Japanese corporations to continue growing. Finally, in an age of increasing protectionist sentiment, Japan can use investments as a lever to prevent it from being frozen out of foreign markets, particularly the American.

This leads to the heart of the Japanese economic dilemma: its export policy. An export-driven economy has been a historical norm for Japan. The period between 1945 and 1970 was an aberration caused by World War II; Japan's current situation is merely the reassertion of a basic norm. The Japanese have always had an export-oriented economy. In 1930, Japan's exports equaled nearly 20 percent of its GNP, compared with 6 percent for the U.S. This fell in the immediate postwar period, during which Japan fueled its growth with domestic investments. However, by the 1970s this figure began to grow again, until by 1987 it had climbed to nearly 16 percent of

GNP, approaching prewar export dependency rates. American export dependency had grown as well, but only to about 11 percent.[40]

In general, the percentage exported by both the United States and Japan has grown. However, beginning in 1973, after the oil crisis, the Japanese began surpassing the United States, until their rate of dependency on exports rose to about 50 percent more than that of the United States. Perhaps of greater significance is the fact that Japan's broad exports in constant dollars relative to GNP are beginning to approach their pre-World War II levels.

Without exports, Japan's already declining growth rate would have fallen dramatically since 1980. On average, since 1980, exports have accounted for 37.4 percent of Japan's economic growth and as much as 50 percent in some years.[41] In an era where the economic growth rate had already significantly declined, it is clear that exports had to become the pivot of Japan's economic life.

This need to grow can go far in explaining otherwise apparently inexplicable patterns of Japanese behavior. Many Western businessmen, fighting to preserve profit margins, have experienced the dramatic entrance of Japanese corporations into their domestic markets. Apparently indifferent to profit margins, the Japanese cut prices in order to gain market share. Westerners have interpreted this obsession with market share as an attempt to seize monopolies, or as a pattern of "dumping" products at or below cost in order to drive competitors out of business.

The reality is far different, although the effect might be the same. Japanese behavior resembles nothing so much as that of a Western company facing a large quarterly interest payment to a bank, ordering its sales staff to clear out inventory, even at a loss, in order to generate cash. What is, or should be, a fairly rare occurrence in a Western corporation is standard operating procedure in Japan. The Japanese corporation has debt problems, not investor problems. It needs growth and cash flow much more than it needs profits. This is a normal pattern in all Japanese export markets.

It is fascinating to observe the persistence of patterns of Japanese trade over time. Japan has, for example, been returning to traditional patterns of export dependency. Consider the persistence in the targets of its exports, as shown in Table 6-3.

By measuring physical exports as a percentage of GNP, it is possible to measure the significance of each export relationship to Japan's economy as a whole. First, these figures show clearly that, measured in current yen as well as in constant yen, Japan has returned to its former dependency on imports. Indeed, it has now risen above prewar levels.

Even more striking is the persistence in its trading partners. The

TABLE 6-3. Japanese Exports by Country as a Percentage of GNP (current yen).

	1935	1940	1955	1965	1970	1975	1980	1988
Trade/GNP	7.88%	6.35%	3.84%	9.06%	10.87%	11.98%	13.06%	9.11%
U.S.	1.69	0.99	0.87	2.66	2.84	2.17	2.89	3.08
Europe	0.82	0.32	0.40	1.39	1.61	2.01	2.32	2.03
Korea	1.76	2.32	0.08	0.19	0.39	0.44	0.50	0.53
China	1.81	3.24	0.05	0.26	0.27	0.44	0.47	0.33
Formosa	0.69	0.74	0.01	0.23	0.34	0.36	0.47	0.49
Hong Kong	0.16	0.05	0.17	0.31	0.34	0.27	0.44	0.40
Canada	0.03	0.04	0.09	0.23	0.27	0.22	0.22	0.22
Mexico	0.02	0.02	0.01	0.04	0.04	0.07	0.11	0.06
S. America	0.23	0.21	0.28	0.27	0.29	0.86	0.71	0.26
Africa	0.58	0.22	0.39	0.88	0.68	0.97	0.62	0.17
Oceania	0.30	0.16	0.13	0.43	0.38	0.42	0.38	0.27
S&SE Asia	1.76	0.79	0.72	1.22	0.94	1.25	1.29	0.81
Persian Gulf	0.02	0.34	0.06	0.16	0.18	0.78	0.80	0.21

(Sources: *Japan Statistical Yearbook*; Bank of Japan, *Economic Statistics Annual*)

major shift in Japanese trading patterns has been the decline of trade with China, which has recovered relatively little, standing at only 18 percent of the prewar level (measured in terms of GNP significance). Although trade with Korea and Formosa declined tremendously in the aftermath of World War II, it has now rebounded, to 30 and 71 percent of prewar levels, respectively. Most of the shift has been to the United States and Europe, while trade with the rest of the world has remained relatively stable. However, the major trading nexus of Japan before the war was the U.S., Europe, Korea, Formosa, and China; it remains the same today.

Trade with the United States has obviously reached the saturation point, while expansion of trade with Europe is a dubious proposition in the face of 1992 and European unification. Moreover, export dependency on the U.S. in particular is politically risky, as forces might develop to limit unexpectedly Japanese access to the U.S. market. Thus, one can predict the direction of Japanese export policy in the coming years: China.

Japanese business leaders are already making this interest clear. As Isamu Yamashita, Chairman of the Board of Councilors of Mitsui Engineering and Shipbuilding, said:

Stability in China is essential to world peace, so that it is necessary to resume at the previous pace Japan's economic cooperation with that country, which has stagnated since the Tiananmen Square incident. Recent developments in the international community point to a gradual improvement in relations with China. Japan as an Asian friend of China should lead these developments.[42]

The coordinated effort on the part of Japan to break the general boycott of China following the brutal suppression of the democratic movement in Beijing is interesting in two ways. First, it shows the urgency with which the Japanese regard developing economic relations with China, even to the point of defying world opinion and the U.S. government. Second, it shows the integration of policy making and execution in Japan. The decision to emphasize good relations with China was made consensually and included figures from within and without the government. Having been made, it was pressed and defended by the entire elite. The so-called industrial policy of Japan is conceived and executed collectively by a small, self-aware elite. Much has been made of the particular institutions that make up Japan's industrial policy, such as the Ministry of International Trade and Industry (MITI). This is less important than the process of decision making in the Japanese elite and the willingness of the elite to make and execute decisions collectively.

The decision to emphasize China is not an imposed decision. It is vital to recognize that Japan's celebrated industrial policy is less a decision on how to proceed than a recognition of the direction that market forces are moving. There have been calls in the U.S. for the creation of an industrial policy at the federal level. Almost invariably, this call is from industries that have been thrown on the defensive and want the allocation by law of cheap capital in order to save their deteriorating position.

Japanese industrial policy has been ruthless on this score. While carefully nurturing new industries, MITI has obviously been diverting resources from older, declining industries.[43] Because of the interlocking nature of Japanese corporations, the diversions were planned and effects were minimized.

MITI had two advantages as the general staff of Japan. Unlike the Soviets, who had far greater direct control over their economy, MITI was not permitted to work in a vacuum. It had to remain acutely aware of the marketplace, both in Japan and overseas. However, unlike British or American society, the coherence of Japanese society, its natural solidarity and deference, and its small, mutually trusted elite have allowed MITI to make decisions that were carried out through informal influence as well as formal rules and structures. In a hypothetical case, a MITI official could call a member of the Keidanren (a super Chamber of Commerce) to discuss a problem cropping up in exports of two types of cassette recorders in Indonesia. An informal meeting of members of the Sony and Hitachi boards with the head of the Keidanren or an appropriate assistant would result in a solution, and thereby block inroads into the Indonesian market by General Electric.

Japan has had a remarkable run of luck in selecting the correct policy for the right time. One is reminded of the run of luck Japan enjoyed between Pearl Harbor and Midway, and how, with the error of Midway, the Japanese did not know how to recover. The current situation is similar, like that of a gambler who has played brilliantly. He risks staying at the table too long. Japan's problem is that it cannot get up from the table. It has moved so far so fast that disengaging from the aggressive tempo of the postwar economy is impossible. For Japan, economic life has become a high-risk gamble.

HANGING ON TO THE TIGER

The military metaphor is deeply rooted in Japan's historical reality. As Chalmers Johnson, a leading analyst of the Japanese economy, put it:

> In 1945, amid the ruins of Osaka, a group of businessmen lamented to an American observer that the militarists had "started the war twenty years too soon." Although the figure should probably be more like forty years than twenty, it is nonetheless true that from about 1941 to 1961 the Japanese economy remained on a war footing. The goal changed from military to economic victory, but the Japanese people could not have worked harder, saved more, or innovated more ruthlessly if they had been engaged in a war for national survival, as in fact they were. And just as a nation mobilized for economic development needs a military general staff, so a nation mobilized for economic development needs an economic general staff. The men of MCI, MM, and MITI have been preparing to play this role since the late 1920's.[44]

Much of what appears odd about Japan's economy derives from this war mentality. There is both a sense of commonality of purpose and of embattlement in Japanese economic life that makes one think of warriors quite as much as of businessmen.

The root cause of this behavior is a double desperation. Japan's economy is extremely fragile, far more fragile than most observers seem to think. The system of financial relationships that has been created depends on economic growth to maintain it. But economic growth within Japan is extremely difficult. The very factors that helped create the modern Japanese miracle—the willingness of its people to work hard, be frugal, and give their loyalty to their employer and the state—threatens the growth of Japan's economy.

In the first stages of recovery this sort of behavior was indispensable and gave rise to the extraordinary levels of capital formation the Japanese have achieved. While this is fine for an investment-driven boom, when the economy reaches a point where the labor force has been outstripped by investment, then consumption must drive growth. In Japan, a consumption boom is hard to generate because of the structure of compensation, the need of the banking system for continued high savings rates to maintain their liquidity, the weakness of the retirement system, and finally, the cultural norms of Japan itself.

The solution has been to transfer both investment and consumption overseas. Surplus savings are invested in foreign countries and export markets are developed there as well. For Japan, the solution to internal limits has been to exploit the rest of the world and to become increasingly dependent on the rest of the world for its growth.

This has placed Japan in an extremely difficult position. Fully one-third of its foreign exports go to the U.S., accounting for about 3 percent of its GNP, an enormous figure. The ripple effect on Japan of any politically motivated reduction of trade would be devastating. It would be far easier for the U.S. than for Japan to live without Japan's exports. Thus, Japan is in an untenable situation. Its dependence on the U.S. for absorbing exports makes Japan resemble nothing so much as a Third World country with a single major buyer for its goods. Obviously, there is a vast difference between Peru and Japan, for example, but they share one thing in common: both require the continued goodwill of the United States.

Since that cannot be assured, Japan has to begin the process of searching for alternate markets and investment opportunities. One solution might be to increase domestic consumption by means of public works projects to develop Japan's infrastructure, and by increasing consumer demand. MITI has targeted both as priorities during the 1990s. But there are acute problems with the latter in particular.

The Japanese banking system and Japan's financial system in general are built around high savings rates. MITI's new policies encourage Japanese to save less and buy more. Logically, they imply consumer borrowing will compete with commercial borrowing. Japan's economy simply cannot endure such dramatic declines in savings rates nor increases in consumer credit. Moreover, as long as the Japanese pension system remains as it is, ordinary Japanese cannot afford to increase spending. Japanese corporations would not be able to increase pensions in the short run without dramatic increases in labor costs and greatly increased borrowing from an overburdened banking industry.

Thus, Japan is facing the first great crisis in its postwar history. The Cold War relationship with the United States of ever-increasing purchases of Japanese goods by Americans will no longer continue unabated. The growth orientation of the Japanese economy demands that new markets be found to absorb Japanese goods. Attempts to shift demand to the domestic Japanese market are doomed by the fragility of the banking system. Thus, Japan is left with only one option: increased exports to countries other than the United States. This in turn will require a much more active and even aggressive foreign policy to open and sustain new markets.

This process is already underway where Japan can reasonably expect to be preeminent: the area of its old Greater East Asia Co-Prosperity Sphere. This is not as ironical as it might appear. Where else could Japan go if the U.S. became unreliable as a consumer? As Japan moves into this region as an increasingly aggressive exporter, it will discover that the most important export products will be in an area it has shunned thus far: arms sales. Thus, export policy will gradually merge with foreign policy into a logical and unavoidable whole.

Japan cannot become isolationist. It cannot survive economically unless it is deeply involved in the world. But as its relationship with the United States shows, involvement in a world that can be influenced but not controlled is an extremely risky proposition for any nation. No nation as dependent on foreign intercourse as Japan can afford not to engage in foreign policy, and there cannot be a foreign policy without both political intent and some quantity of military power. This becomes particularly true when we consider the import vulnerability of Japan.

Japan has again become a normal nation. It is powerful, creative, and in many ways to be envied. But it also has its weaknesses, as all normal nations do, and those weaknesses will cause it to act in certain ways. Its economy is maturing and the sustained growth of the post-war period is clearly coming to an end. This change will undoubtedly cause internal unrest and dissension, as it would in any country. However, since Japan's economy is more externally oriented than most, it will seek to correct the problems in its economy not so much by internal reform as by trying to take control of its external environment. This was Japan's solution during the 1930s, and it was not aberrant behavior on Japan's part. It followed logically from Japan's general condition, and that condition, controlled by geography more than by anything else, has not and cannot change.

1. Daniel Burstein, *Yen: Japan's New Financial Empire and its Threat to America* (New York, 1988); Marvin J. Wolf, *The Japanese Conspiracy: The Plot to Dominate Industry Worldwide—And How to Deal With It* (New York, 1983); Frederick W. Richmond and Michael Kahan, *How to Beat the Japanese at Their Own Game* (Englewood Cliffs, 1983).
2. Obviously, the view changes as the statistical perspective does. For example, in looking at GNP per capita (i.e., divided by the population) different perspectives give very different answers. According to the U.S. State Department, measuring in 1987 dollars, Japan's per capita GNP in 1987 was $19,254, greater than the U.S. figure of $18,403, and substantially higher than the Organization for Economic Cooperation and Development's average per capita GNP of $15,000. According to this, Japan passed the U.S. in per capita GNP for the first time in 1987, a major landmark in world economic history. The World Bank, on the other hand, tells a different story. Using 1980 dollars as a base, and converting 1987 dollars into preinflated 1980 dollars, Japan's per capita GNP stands at $15,760, compared to $18,530 for the U.S., and $14,670 for the industrialized countries. This indicates one of the grave dangers in making assertions based on financial rather than physical activity. How one measures is infinitely flexible and can tell you precisely what you want to hear. But the basic point, which is that Japan has outperformed the rest of the world, is unassailable.
3. United States Department of State, Intelligence Research Report IRR No. 156, *Economic Growth of OECD Countries, 1977–87*, March 31, 1987.
4. Yutaka Kosai and Yoshitaro Ogino, *The Contemporary Japanese Economy* (Armonk, 1984), p. 5.
5. Ezra F. Vogel, *Comeback* (New York, 1985), p. 23.
6. James G. Abegglen and George Stalk, *Kaisha: The Japanese Corporation* (New York, 1985), pp. 183–184. See also Clyde Prestowitz, *Trading Places* (New York, 1988), pp. 306–312, for a discussion of growth and finance.
7. Masahiko Aoki, "Shareholders' Non-Unanimity on Investment Financing: Banks vs. Individual Investors," in Masahiko Aoki, *The Economic Analysis of the Japanese Firm* (Amsterdam, 1984), pp. 193, 221.
8. Abegglen and Stalk, *Kaisha*, pp. 183–184, 185.
9. For an excellent description of the relationship between Japanese higher education and corporate employment, see Jean-Claude Courdy, *The Japanese: Everyday Life in the Empire of the Rising Sun* (New York, 1984), pp. 179–186.
10. Abegglen and Stalk, *Kaisha*, pp. 183–191.
11. See Masahiko Aoki, "Shareholders' Non-Unanimity," pp. 193–220.
12. JETRO, *Nippon: Business Facts and Figures, 1989* (Tokyo, 1989), Table 43, p. 100.

13. "Japan's Banking Uncertainties," *The Economist*, 30 June 1990, p. 75.
14. Abegglen and Stalk, *Kaisha*, p. 161.
15. *Japan Times Weekly*, February 12–18, 1990, p. 19.
16. Japan Economic Institute, *Keiretsu and Other Large Corporate Groups in Japan*, January 12, 1990, pp. 4–5.
17. Thomas Pepper, Merit E. Janow, and Jimmy W. Wheeler, *The Competition: Dealing With Japan* (New York, 1985), pp. 148–150.
18. Japan Economic Institute, *Keiretsu*, p. 10.
19.

Spread Between Prime Rate and Three-Month Deposits, August 1990

	PRIME	INTEREST	SPREAD	RATIO
Japan	7.13	3.63	3.50	1.96
U.S.	8.00	7.88	0.12	1.02
Germany	10.50	8.13	2.37	1.29
U.K.	16.00	15.00	1.00	1.07

(Source: *Economist*, August 4–10, 1990)

20. On regulatory reform, see Japanese Economic Institute, *Japan's Financial Reform Program: Stalled or Stoked?*, May 18, 1990.
21. See Raymond W. Goldsmith, *Comparative National Balance Sheets* (Chicago, 1985), pp. 1–3.
22. World Bank, *World Tables*, 1989, tables on Japan and the United States.
23. JETRO, *Nippon: Business Facts and Figures*, 1989, p. 136.
24. Ibid., pp. 138–141.
25. Ibid., p. 137.
26. Ibid. p. 146.
27. Ibid., p. 146.
28. *Japan Statistical Yearbook*.
29. Japan Economic Institute, *Japan as an International Creditor: New Economic and Political Realities*, November 3, 1989, p. 4.
30. Japan Economic Institute, *Japan as an International Creditor*, p. 3.
31. Japan Economic Institute, *Japan's Social Security and Pension Systems Face Need for New Reforms*, May 25, 1990, p. 6.
32. Jean-Claude Courday, *The Japanese: Everyday Life in the Empire of the Rising Sun* (New York: 1984), p. 169.
33. For the deeper cultural roots of this policy, see Makoto Sakurabayashi and Robert J. Ballon, "Labor–Management Relations in Modern Japan," in *Studies in Japanese Culture: Tradition and Experiment*, Monumenta Nipponica Monograph No. 23 (Tokyo, 1963), pp. 263–267.
34. See Tsuneo Ishikawa and Kazuo Ueda, "The Bonus Payment System and Japanese Personal Savings," in *The Economic Analysis of the Japanese Firm*, ed. Masahiko Aoki (Amsterdam, 1984).
35. JETRO, *Nippon: Business Facts and Figures*, p. 122.
36. Ibid., p. 20.
37. Waverly E. LeBard, Manager, Financial Services and Employee Benefits, The Feinerman Group, Harrisburg, Pennsylvania.
38. Japan Economic Institute, *Japan as an International Creditor*, p. 9.

39. Japan Economic Institute, *Japan's Foreign Direct Investment in Developing Countries*, August 11, 1989, p. 5.
40. Thelma Liesner, *One Hundred Years of Economic Statistics* (New York: Facts on File, 1989). Postwar figures are in constant dollars.
41.

Contribution of Exports to GNP Growth

YEAR	GNP GROWTH	EXPORTS CONTRIBUTED	GROWTH RATE W/O EXPORTS
1980	4.3%	3.4%	0.9%
1981	3.7	1.5	2.2
1982	3.1	0.3	2.8
1983	3.2	1.5	1.7
1984	5.1	1.3	3.8
1985	4.7	1.0	3.7

(Source: E. J. Lincoln, *Japan: Facing Economic Maturity*, 1988)

42. Isamu Yamashita, "Tackling Foreign and Domestic Problems Under the Leadership of the LDP," *Keidanren Review*, No. 121 (February 1990), p. 5.
43. For an economic analysis of MITI's and Japan's industrial policy in general, see Miyohei Shinohara, *Industrial Growth, Trade and Dynamic Patterns in the Japanese Economy* (Tokyo, 1982), pp. 21–56.
44. Chalmers Johnson, *MITI and the Japanese Miracle* (Stanford, 1982), p. 241. MCI = Ministry of Commerce and Industry; MM = Ministry of Munitions.

7

Japan's Nightmare: Imports and Dependency

Japan's trade problem is two-sided. It has been shown how Japan's growth economy is, historically, export driven. In this sense, Japan is becoming increasingly dependent on foreign countries for its survival. But there is a second, even more pressing aspect of Japan's foreign dependency: its imports.

For Japan, imports are not a financial problem, they are a political one. Japan is dependent on imports for almost all of its raw materials. The more it produces, the more raw materials it needs to import. For a growth-oriented economy, a lack of resources poses a serious and potentially disastrous economic problem. In order to import raw materials, Japan must have access to the country that supplies them, as well as secure sea-lanes for transporting the goods. Securing these resources and the sea-lanes is both a political and military problem, one that Japan has depended on the U.S. to solve. The issue is whether Japan can continue to rely on the United States, and if not, how it can go about securing these supplies itself.

Like any country, Japan imports many things. In 1989, Japan imported $209.7 billion worth of goods compared to exports of $273.9 billion, a strong balance of trade position. Financially, imports are reasonably balanced as well. Food makes up 15.2 percent of this total, crude oil about 10 percent, machinery 14 percent, and chemicals about 8 percent. But this financial balance covers a fundamental and dangerous weakness in the Japanese economy, something that can only be seen when Japan's imports are considered in physical terms.

Trade is basically something physical. It involves the movement of things from one place to another. This obvious point is often forgotten by observers who consider the financial results of trade rather than trade itself. Certainly the flow of money is significant, but that flow would have no meaning without the flow of goods. Indeed, at times the characteristics of the financial flow and the physical flow of trade might vary greatly. The flow of material, measured in terms of weights and ships, frequently provides a view of the world quite different from the one provided by the flow of money.

There are circumstances under which the flow of commodities is determined by forces other than the marketplace. When politics and war intrude, the use value of commodities tends to predominate over exchange value. During the 1930s, rubber went wherever there was money to buy it. But as politics began to intrude, the movement of rubber was determined by considerations other than those of the marketplace. Then money could sometimes not obtain rubber at any price and, because of this, battles were lost.

The tendency to measure trade in terms of money ignores a radically different and, in some ways, more essential dimension of trade, and of the trade of raw materials in particular. Though a nation might be financially secure, it might find, in an extreme situation, that no amount of money can secure what it requires because the physical means of transport are not available. In war, the physical and spatial characteristics of trade predominate, while in peacetime more abstract financial considerations take priority. Even in peacetime, considering trade as though it were dominated by the rules of war can clarify certain realities and vulnerabilities in a nation's condition.

It is in this context, and for this reason, that the physical and spatial characteristics of Japan's world trade ought to be considered. After all, Japan is a nation that has experienced great financial success in peace, while suffering physical strangulation prior to, and during, war. The issue that needs to be examined is the radical difference between Japan's financial and physical trade success, the geographic constraints conditioning this difference, and the implications should Japan once more find itself in the extreme condition of war, or even in some lesser condition of political constraint.

This question becomes all the more important in the context of today's dislocated international system. The apparent collapse of Soviet power has left much uncertainty about the future. Half-century-old verities—such as the unshakable nature of the U.S.–Japanese entente—seem to be eminently shakable in the international context

of glasnost. Japanese economic security, which has thus far rested
on the twin foundations of the U.S. nuclear umbrella and U.S. naval
supremacy, now becomes more indeterminate as the stable nexus of
U.S.–Soviet rivalry unravels.

In this context, Japan's comfortable assumptions about the security
of its import flow become less tenable, and considerations of its condition through more extreme, more physical, and spatial prisms becomes both valid and urgent. From the Japanese point of view, it
becomes more important to grasp the physical dimensions of its economic life and to face the enormity of the task of securing its raw
materials. For the U.S., it is important to measure policy responses
in terms of Japan's growing economic insecurity, an insecurity that
lurks just below the surface of its recent financial hubris. Beneath
the glory of Japan's economic miracle, there is a deep vulnerability
and insecurity, both real and psychological, that must be grasped in
all dealings with Japan.

TONS AND YEN: MEASURING JAPAN'S TRADE

Of late, the question of Japanese trade has become an obsessive matter. There has arisen a deep and growing concern about the financial
implications of Japan's balance-of-payments surplus. Indeed, the
emergence of a Japan that sells things worth more than what it buys
has come to be seen as the centerpiece of the contemporary social
and political order. Critics like James Fallows and Clyde Prestowitz
have replaced boosters like Ezra Vogel and William Ouchi. Where
the latter celebrated the Japanese success, the former have turned
to the question of how to cope with it.[1] There has been much discussion about the fairness of Prestowitz and Fallows' charges. What
is perhaps most important is that a leading Washington scholar/bu-
reaucrat and the editor of one of America's most prestigious mag-
azines should have joined those colloquially known as "Japan
bashers." While the American establishment was once solidly pro-
Japanese and anti-Japanese sentiment came from the scurrilous margins of public discourse, the growing respectability of the view that
Japan is a danger to America is symptomatic of a fundamental change
in relations between the two greatest economic powers in the world.

This growing fear of Japan in the heart of the U.S. policy-making
apparatus derives from an obsessive concern with financial realities
and a relative indifference to physical realities. Japan has come to be
seen as a flawless money-making machine when judged by its balance
of trade, which in 1989 declined to $64 billion from a 1987 high in
excess of $80 billion.[2]

Since the beginning of the current economic expansion, except for minor declines in growth rate since 1988, both the absolute and relative financial measures of Japanese economic power have risen steadily and dramatically. Looking only at these financial figures, Japan's economic success appears to be both irresistible and ineffable. It is neither preventable, nor fully understandable. Japan appears to be, and is frequently referred to as, a mystical force.

The danger in being so concerned with the financial aspects of the Japanese trade balance is that an equally important dimension of Japanese economic life—the physical—will be ignored. In order for the Japanese to have a trade surplus, they need to be able to manufacture the goods that they sell overseas. And in order to manufacture those goods, the Japanese need to have the sheer raw materials necessary for their manufacture. If those raw materials are not available, no amount of Confucian social cohesion, discipline, or managerial innovation will manufacture the cars and stereos necessary to produce Japan's powerful trading position.

Recently, this side of the Japanese economic equation has been neglected. Some attention was paid to the matter in the 1970s and early 1980s. However, even then the focus tended to be on Japan's importation of one commodity, oil, rather than on the broad spectrum of imports that made the Japanese economic miracle possible.[3] With the collapse of world commodity prices (and oil prices in particular) in the early and mid-1980s, attention turned away from the physical characteristics of Japanese trade to the financial.[4] By focusing solely on the financial, a sense of Japanese invulnerability arose. The deep and dangerous vulnerabilities of Japan's import flow tended to be ignored in the stable and prosperous atmosphere of the late 1980s.

In considering the physical characteristics of Japanese trade, two points are both obvious and crucial. The first is that Japan is a series of islands; the second is that those islands are devoid of a wide range of important commodities necessary to maintain not only the current export boom but also to sustain industrial life in general. This means that in order to secure the minerals necessary for its industrial machine, Japan must maintain a vast flow of seaborne material from nations and through waters it does not control.

As was shown in Table I-1 on page 9 in the Introduction, Japan's dependency on imports of minerals is enormous. Japan must import virtually all of its iron ore, copper, nickel, bauxite, manganese, molybdenum, titanium, and, most important, all of its oil and liquid natural gas. Overall, it imports 99.6 percent of all its mineral ores, and 96.3 percent of all its mineral fuels—less than 99 percent only because Japan has some coal.

Japan's food situation is only marginally better. It needs to import

85 percent of its wheat, 70 percent of its corn, 80 percent of its barley, and 97 percent of its oil seed. Because of national-security considerations and internal political pressures from rice farmers, Japan has become virtually self-sufficient in rice, the Japanese staple.[5] However, except for this single commodity, Japan's dependence on food imports is substantial and will likely grow as its standard of living rises and consumption shifts away from grains to meats.

One is therefore tempted to extend the analysis of Japanese mineral import vulnerability to foods. There is, however, a great difference between the two. First, and most important, substitution is much easier in foods than it is in minerals. Even where such substitution is possible, as in coal for oil, there are usually substantial capital costs and time delays built into conversion. Whatever the political costs, food substitution has no such built-in limitations. Thus, with self-sufficiency in rice and substitutability between corn, barley, and wheat, the functioning of Japan would not necessarily be threatened by a disruption of supply in one of these foods.

Second, although Japan is the world's largest importer of cereals, its imports totaled only 10 percent of the amount available on the world market, and only about 1 percent of total world production.[6] Thus, the wide range of available cereals and the relatively small impact Japan has on the highly diversified export market make Japan secure in a free-market environment. The same is not the case with minerals.

All nations are dependent on imports. All industrial nations are dependent on the import of minerals, and some nations are almost totally dependent on the import of some commodities. The United States, for example, needs to import over 90 percent of seven minerals (bauxite, chromium, cobalt, columbium, manganese, platinum, and tantalum).[7] Nevertheless, the U.S. is able to be a net exporter of some commodities (iron ore, coal) while being essentially self-sufficient in a host of others. The Japanese situation is radically different.

In 1987, the Japanese had to import over 97 percent (by weight) of all their metallic and fuel mineral ores. This applied to both large, bulk import commodities, such as iron ore, as well as the smaller, "strategic" materials, such as titanium. There is no other case of an industrialized nation so absolutely dependent on imports as Japan.[8] It follows, therefore, that there is no nation in the world that is so potentially vulnerable to disruptions in the supply of its raw materials. This is the fundamental political reality behind Japanese economic growth: without securing supplies of mineral commodities, Japan's industrial machine will almost instantly cease to function. It leads to a peculiar Japanese concern, summarized in the phrase "Comprehensive Security."[9]

There is a tremendous imbalance between Japan's physical imports and exports and its balance of payments. Japan's financial condition and its physical condition are wildly at odds. For this reason, Japan's economic security, as opposed to its economic well-being, cannot be measured simply in terms of its finances. In contrast to Japan's financial balance, its physical balance shows Japan as a great debtor. In 1988, Japan exported a little over 81 million tons while importing 667 million tons; more than eight times as many tons were imported as exported.[10] This means that for each pound of profit-making manufactured material it shipped out, Japan had to import over eight pounds of raw material with which to produce those exports. Of Japan's imports by weight in 1987, over 75 percent were raw mineral fuels and iron and nonferrous ores, the essential building blocks of an industrial society.

This situation becomes even more striking when we consider Japanese mineral imports in terms of the amount of the material available for trade in the world market. Of all the nickel ore exported in 1988, Japan imported 93 percent. It imported 57 percent of all the copper ore available, 30 percent of all the coal and iron, and substantial amounts of other minerals.[11]

Observers have come to take figures like this for granted, but in fact, they are stunning. The idea that a single industrial nation should consume over 93 percent of all nickel ore or 57 percent of all copper ore available in trade on the world market is important in two ways. First, it indicates the limits of Japanese growth. At least in nickel and copper—and probably in iron ore and coal—Japan should shortly reach a point of collision with other consumers. Second, the sheer physical process of transporting such vast amounts of material to a single country must become systemically stressful at some point. Table 7-1 gives some sense of the relationship between exported finished goods and imported raw materials.

Not only must Japan import over eight pounds for each pound it exports, but if it is to increase its trade surplus, it will have to increase its import tonnage by an equivalent amount. The inexorable consequences of this can be seen in Table 7-2 (on page 166), which illustrates tonnage increases with a trend line.

In a world of limitless resources and the absence of business cycles, this might not be a problem, but given any disruption, cyclical or political, in the supplies of material, Japan's economic condition must quickly and dramatically shift. The current status of stockpiles of some key materials might give the observer a sense of the relative nearness of such a crisis. In early 1989, Japanese stocks of copper were down to three weeks from ten in 1982; aluminum was down to five weeks from twelve, and nickel was also down to a five-week supply from seventeen weeks in 1982.[12]

TABLE 7-1. Japanese Inflow of Money/Import Tonnage.

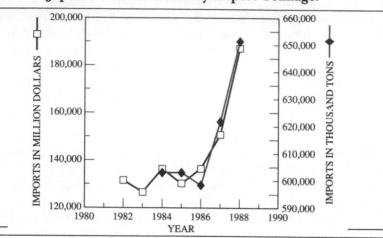

(Source: International Monetary Fund, *Direction of Trade Annual* and *Japan's Statistical Yearbook*)

TABLE 7-2. Japanese Imports in Tons.

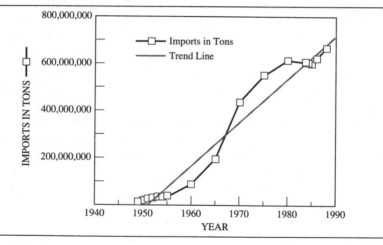

(Source: *Japan's Statistical Yearbook*)

The drawdown of current stocks in nonferrous metals is, of course, cyclical. However, if one considers Japan's relative level of copper consumption and considers that recent supply levels have fallen below the two-week mark (down from about 9.5 weeks at the beginning of 1982), then we can see how these cyclical limitations will effect both the price and quantity of Japanese imports and, therefore, Japan's ability to export manufactured goods at competitive prices, if at all. Put simply, the price of mineral imports must rise, and as they rise, the competitiveness of Japan's position must proportionately decline.

The effect of rising mineral prices on Japan's competitive position is not quickly and dramatically visible. For example, the United Nations Conference on Trade and Development (UNCTAD) index of mineral ores and metals, which stood at 71 in 1985, has surged to 117 in 1989.[13] While Japan's balance of trade began falling in 1988, the shift was not sufficient by itself to trouble the Japanese. The relatively low cost of nonfuel mineral imports explains this phenomenon. It also means that while Japan is marginally vulnerable to cyclical shifts in mineral supplies, any direct disruptions of these supplies are particularly troubling to the Japanese.

In 1987 the United States imported a total of 486.1 million tons, compared with 621.8 million tons by Japan. Given that the U.S. had a population of about 250 million, compared to Japan's 123 million, it can be seen that Japan's per capita import rate was more than five tons, compared with less than two tons for the U.S. In the same year, U.S. exports totaled 351.2 million tons, for a ratio of only 1.384:1. Not only does the United States import substantially less than Japan on both an absolute (78.2%) and per capita (40%) basis, but the structure of those imports differs greatly, pointing further to Japan's physical vulnerability.[14]

In the three energy categories of coal, POL (petroleum, oil, and lubricants), and LNG (liquid natural gas), Japan imports 356,909,096 metric tons, compared to U.S. imports of 310,300,000 tons. For Japan, this represents about 57 percent of its total import tonnage, whereas for the U.S., it represents about 62 percent. Superficially, these numbers appear to be quite similar.

This ignores three points. First, the U.S. percentage of energy dependence is higher because its imports of other raw materials is so low. Second, the U.S. imports only POL among the energy minerals, of which it nevertheless has substantial reserves of its own,[15] while Japan must import all three energy sources and is almost completely dependent on imports for its energy. Finally, all Japanese imports must be brought in over sea routes, while the U.S. can bring in much of its imports over land, from Canada and Mexico.

In short, U.S. energy imports can reasonably be classified as luxury items purchased with discretionary income. Their loss would be unfortunate, but not catastrophic. For Japan, the loss would be the end of their industrial empire.

Japan faces two dangers in imported minerals. The first is economic. Japan must be in a position to pay for the goods it imports, and their prices must be such that Japan can make a profit from purchasing and processing them into manufactured goods. In addition to the economic problem, there is another: physical threat.

The commodities that Japan purchases must be transported to Japan, usually by freighter and tanker. If, for some reason, Japan was not able to transport the goods to Japan, it would face an economic disaster. Two things could cause such a disaster: one would be if Japan began to import so much raw material that the world's fleets and harbors could not cope with the demand; the other would be the willingness of another country to interfere with the constant flow of vessels to Japan.

It is important to grasp the magnitude, in sheer bulk and weight, of Japan's imports to get a sense of its vulnerability. Japan has always imported more tons than it exported, even during the postwar depression year of 1950. There is another way to measure Japan's tonnage problem, which is to compare the quantity imported to the total tonnage capacity of the world's merchant fleet. This provides a measure of how much pressure a nation's imports are putting on the world's transportation system. In 1950 Japan's figure was only 0.119. By 1970, however, when Japan's ratio of tons imported to tons exported had soared to over 10 to 1, Japan's fleet utilization had risen to over 1.3. This meant that in order to keep Japan supplied with raw materials, every ship in the world had to make, on average, one and a third trips to Japan each year.

After the oil crisis of 1973 the ratio of tons imported began to decline steadily until, in 1985, the ratio had fallen to 6.4 to 1, barely above the 1950 ratio. However, during the same period fleet utilization dropped little, never falling much below 1.0, the level at which each ship would need to make one trip to Japan. This was in spite of an 84.1 percent increase in the size of the world merchant fleet from 1970 to 1987. In 1987, the world's cargo-ship capacity was just over 593 million tons, while Japan imported over 600 million tons.[16] By contrast, U.S. fleet utilization figures for imports in 1987 were 0.819:1 for a population more than twice the size of Japan's.

This, then, is the fundamental weakness of the Japanese economy. Japan places such an enormous pressure on the world's shipping system that any significant dislocation in that system for an extended period of time would pose serious dangers to Japan's economy. A war, for example, that immobilized a substantial part of the world's tanker or cargo fleet could, quite unintentionally, break the Japanese economy. More importantly, anyone wishing to do Japan harm would have only to interfere with the ability of just a few vessels to reach Japan for Japan to face grave difficulties. The world's largest consumer is always at the mercy of anyone who can interfere with its consumption.

DEPENDENCY AND VULNERABILITY: THE PHYSICAL AND THE FINANCIAL

Before considering shifts in the mineral markets and political disruptions, we need to consider Japan's dependency in the context of a "normal" free-trade environment where it can purchase raw materials freely, at world prices. The free market is quite different from politico-military conditions. In the former, money is king; in the latter, weapons that can stop shipping rule. Japan may be vulnerable to political or military disruptions, but we must also consider how vulnerable it is to disruptions due to the normal functioning of the free market.

Our analysis ought to begin with the big three Japanese imports: petroleum (259,970,000 metric tons), iron ore (112,034,000 m. tons) and coal (92,762,000 m. tons). These three, taken together, account for 69.6 percent of all Japanese imports by weight. Whenever Japan's import vulnerability is discussed, oil is the one commodity that comes to mind. Thus, we ought to begin by considering how vulnerable Japan is to an economic—as opposed to political—disruption in its oil supply.

Since 1930, Japan has been importing at least 65 percent of its crude oil. Indeed, since 1930 Japanese production of crude has little more than doubled while consumption has increased over 400 times. Thus, even in 1950, Japan imported 82 percent of its oil, and by 1965 this amount had reached 99 percent, or virtually all oil used.

There has also been a certain consistency in Japan's sources of oil. Japan has always had two groups of suppliers, one East Asian and one well outside East Asia. Japan's problem has historically been that its East Asian suppliers—Indonesia, Malaysia, and China—have never been able to supply Japan with more than 20 percent of its needs. Because of this, before World War II Japan imported the rest of its supplies from the United States. After the war it turned to the Persian Gulf for its needs.[17] Japan's history, indeed the history of the world, would have been quite different if Japan had not had to go far out of its region to secure its oil. However, because it did have to go farther afield, Japan's recent history has revolved around a deep-seated insecurity about oil.

Yet, in spite of the fact that Japan's imports of oil weigh and cost more than any other imports, and in spite of the fact that Japan depends more on oil than on other commodities, in economic terms the danger of oil disruption is not a particularly significant threat compared to the threat of disruption of other commodities.

There are two sides to every economic equation. There is the buyer's need to buy and the seller's need to sell. In order to discover not how dependent Japan might be on a relationship, but how vulnerable it might be to disruptions such as cartels, boycotts, and the like, the dependency of the seller on the relationship must be measured as well. It is obviously difficult to measure relative dependency and vulnerability in international commodity trade, but no sense can be made of Japan's economic situation unless some measure, however rough, is made.[18]

Japan receives something physical in its transactions, a commodity from which it can produce other things; the seller receives something financial in return: money. The monetary value of Japan's purchase of Australian bauxite is trivial compared to the value of the products, the cars and radios, that Japan manufactures. On the other hand, Japan might receive a small amount of a commodity from a small, poor country, but the money it pays for that commodity might represent a substantial part of the seller's income. In the former relationship Japan needs the seller, Australia, more than Australia needs Japan, because no matter how little it costs, Japan must have the commodity to function. In the other relationship, such as Papua New Guinea's sale of copper to Japan, the seller needs Japan a lot more than the other way around, because Japan gets only a small quantity of its copper from Papua New Guinea and has other places where it can buy the commodity, while the sale of copper to Japan represents a substantial part of Papua New Guinea's income.

Measuring this relationship is fairly simple:

1. Divide Japan's import of a commodity from a particular country (by weight) by the total weight of that commodity imported by Japan.
2. Divide Japan's payment for that commodity by that country's total export income.
3. Divide the result in step 1 by the result in step 2. Where the result is greater than 1.0, Japan is dependent; where it is less, the seller is dependent. This is a relative measure, and Japan's dependency can soar into the hundreds; note that such extreme cases should be disregarded, as this is a *very* rough measure of vulnerability.

There is one other measure that must be factored in: How easily can Japan replace its supplier if it runs into trouble with a current supplier? This can best be measured by market share: how much of the world's production is in the hands of the producer? The greater it is, the stronger the producer's position. Thus, in the fourth step:

4. Divide the seller's production by world production, and multiply the result found in Step 3 by that amount.

Thus, market share deflates Japan's vulnerability, sometimes substantially. The results are a set of figures from which a rough, relative vulnerability can be deduced. The following table gives a sense not only of Japan's suppliers and what they supply, but also a sense of the rough vulnerability of Japan to the economic pressure of each:

TABLE 7-3. Vulnerability Coefficients for Japanese Mineral Imports.

	BAUX	MOLY	ZINC	COP	TIT	CHRM	MNG	LEAD	IRON	COAL	OIL
Australia	240	—	15.9	0.71	159	—	23.4	41.5	0.77	13.4	—
Indonesia	3.59	—	—	0.10	—	—	—	—	—	—	0.02
Papua New Guinea	—	—	—	0.01	—	—	—	—	—	—	—
Philippines	—	—	—	0.01	—	—	—	—	—	—	—
Malaysia	—	—	—	—	64.1	—	—	—	—	—	—
People's Rep. China	—	—	—	—	—	—	—	18.1	—	—	0.09
Saudi Arabia	—	—	—	—	—	—	—	—	—	—	0.06
United Arab Emirates	—	—	—	—	—	—	—	—	—	—	0.01
Iran	—	—	—	—	—	—	—	—	—	—	0.02
India	—	—	—	—	10.7	—	9.98	—	0.28	—	—
Sri Lanka	—	—	—	—	0.94	—	—	—	—	—	—
South Africa	—	—	—	—	—	376	34.6	—	—	0.24	—
Madagascar	—	—	—	—	—	0.06	—	—	—	—	—
Peru	—	—	0.98	0.08	—	—	—	0.89	—	—	—
Chile	—	710	—	0.58	—	—	—	—	—	—	—
Brazil	—	—	—	—	—	—	—	—	1.42	—	—
Canada	—	223	109	11.9	—	—	—	136	—	0.25	—
U.S.	—	741	—	38.7	—	—	—	—	—	7.71	—

Japan is least vulnerable in copper from Papua New Guinea and oil from the United Arab Emirates, and most vulnerable to cutoffs of molybdenum from Chile and the U.S. Japan is in a good position with commodities that are widely available and are imported from relatively poor countries with low market share. Japan becomes highly vulnerable with imports from wealthy countries that have large market share for a relatively low-value commodity.

Large, wealthy countries do not need the relatively minor income that derives from mineral sales. They export other, more expensive things. Thus, they can afford to take risks in an attempt to boost the price of a commodity through market manipulation. This is particularly the case when they produce a large percentage of the world's supply of the commodity. Poor countries, with few industrial exports and with low market share, cannot take risks like that and are therefore at the mercy of the producer. This, then, turns into a political question as Japan plots its course in the export market.

GEOGRAPHY AND DEPENDENCY

While Japan may not be vulnerable to oil cutoffs (under present market conditions), it is vulnerable on a number of other fronts. Only eighteen nations supply the eleven key import minerals. We can divide Japan's mineral suppliers into three groups: Eastern Pacific Basin (U.S., Canada, Chile, Peru), Western Pacific Basin (Australia, Indonesia, Papua New Guinea, the Philippines, Malaysia, China), and the Indian Ocean Basin (Persian Gulf, India, Sri Lanka, South Africa, and Madagascar). There is only one supplier located elsewhere, Brazil, which supplies about 24 percent of Japan's iron ore.

TABLE 7-4. Matrix of Japan's Trade Import Vulnerability: Summary.

	WEIGHT (THOUSANDS OF TONS)	NUMBER OF MINERALS	VULNERABILITY
Southwest Pacific			
Australia	88,482	8	+6/−2
Indonesia	35,549	3	+1/−2
Malaysia	10,748	1	+1/ 0
People's Rep. China	20,560	2	+1/−1
Philippines	344	1	+0/−1
Papua New Guinea	264	1	+0/−1
Total	156,300	9	+9/−7
Indian Ocean Basin			
India	20,452	3	+2/−1
South Africa	7,082	3	+2/−1
Madagascar	582	1	0/−1
Sri Lanka	55	1	N1
Persian Gulf	176,519	1	+0/−1
Total	204,690	6	+4/−4
Eastern Pacific Rim			
Canada	27,697	5	+4/−3

TABLE 7-4. Japan's Trade Import Vulnerability (continued)

	WEIGHT (THOUSANDS OF TONS)	NUMBER OF MINERALS	VULNERABILITY
United States	11,918	3	+3/−0
Chile	6,519	2	+1/−1
Peru	343	3	+0/−3
Total	46,477	5	+8/−5
Atlantic Brazil	26,831	1	+1/ 0

(Vulnerability numbers represent the number of commodities with positive or negative values. The more pluses, the greater Japan's dependence; the more minuses, the greater Japan's strength. N1 indicates a neutral relationship in one commodity.)

Of the minerals under consideration here (over three-fourths of all Japanese tonnage), 47.13 percent comes from the Indian Ocean Basin, most from the Persian Gulf states in the form of crude and refined oil; 35.99 percent comes from the western Pacific, most from Australia, but rather evenly distributed otherwise; 10.7 percent comes from the eastern Pacific; and about 5 percent from Brazil.

Two striking facts emerge from this. The first is the already well-known importance of Australia to Japan's economic life.[19] The second—and not fully explored—is the emergence of the Indian Ocean Basin as a source for Japan's needs. Considering the relative vulnerability factors of the three regions, it is obvious that the Indian Ocean Basin is the most attractive for Japanese mineral trade, as well as being vital for its oil trade.[20]

Indeed, Australia, Indonesia, and Malaysia might be considered as much part of the Indian Ocean Basin as part of the Pacific Rim. For example, a substantial part of Australia's mineral industry is located in Western Australia. The bauxite deposits in the Darling Range outside of Perth, the iron ore deposits at Pinjara, and the bulk of Australia's titanium production must be shipped from western ports through the Indian Ocean. This is also true for the deposits located on the western coast of Sumatra in Indonesia.[21]

Of the thirteen nations on the Indian Ocean Rim (counting the Persian Gulf oil suppliers as one entity for this purpose), eight of them are important mineral fuel and metallic ore suppliers to Japan. This compares to ten Pacific nations out of twenty-three. Moreover, the absolute quantity of material shipped from the Indian Ocean, not including Western Australian iron ore or Sumatran oil shipments,

MAP 7-1. Geographic Sources of Japan's Mineral Imports – by Weight.

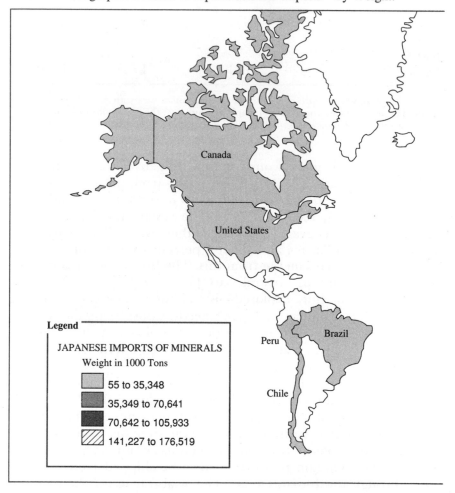

MAP 7-2. Geographic Sources of Japan's Mineral Imports – by Number.

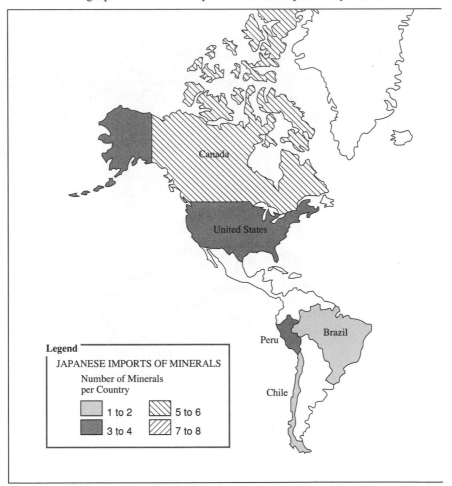

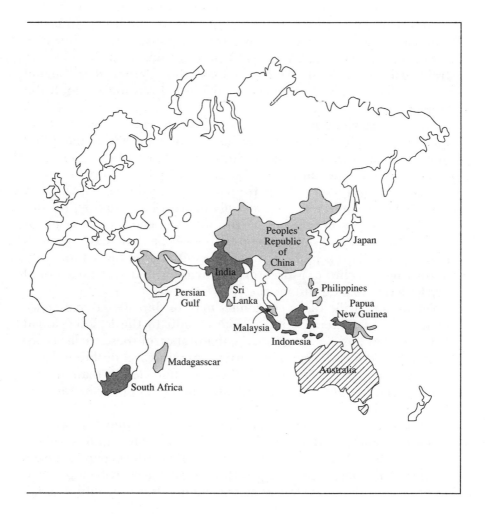

is about one-third greater than that shipped from the Pacific. Perhaps as important, Japan is less vulnerable in its dealings with the Indian Ocean nations collectively than it is with the other two regions.

It is striking to note the physical enclosure of the Indian Ocean. Sealed to the west, except for the Cape route and the Suez Canal, it offers equally limited access to the east. In order to enter the Pacific Ocean from the Indian, one must either pass south and east of Australia, or pass through one of the straits in the Indonesian archipelago. The shortest of these routes is through the Straits of Malacca and past Singapore. This is the only passage that is formally in international waters. About 140 to 150 ships pass through the straits daily. Forty-four percent of the ships larger than 30,000 tons are Japanese, as is 74 percent of the oil passing through the straits.[22]

All other passages go through Indonesian territory. The most important, through the Lombok Strait, requires an additional 1,500 miles passage down the coast of Sumatra, followed by a 2,000-mile navigation of the Java and Celebes seas, before passing into the Pacific south of the Philippines. Aside from political considerations, such an extended trip would increase not only the cost but also the pressure that Japan would be placing on the world's fleets. An increase of about 30 percent in distance requires an equivalent increase in vessels to haul goods. Given Japan's current fleet utilization rates, this might be difficult to achieve. Moreover, any trip around Australia would nearly double sailing distances.

Yet, as the Pacific Basin economies mature, Japanese dependence on imports of minerals will necessarily shift to the less-developed Indian Ocean Basin. Along with the maturation of these Pacific economies, their dependence on exporting minerals will decline relative to their total exports. Nowhere is this condition clearer than in Australia, which has become in many ways the key supplier of raw materials for Japan.

It is generally believed that Japan is dangerously dependent on oil imports from the Middle East and on imports from Saudi Arabia in particular. It is, therefore, interesting to compare the general statistics of Australia, a nation that frequently sees itself as heavily dependent on Japanese willingness to purchase its minerals, with Saudi Arabia's statistics.

Saudi Arabia and Australia have almost identical weight ratios in their trade with Japan. Australia ships about twice as much tonnage to Japan as does Saudi Arabia, indicating the relative physical importance of its material to the Japanese productive process. However, financially, Saudi Arabia enjoys a somewhat more favorable ratio of 1.48:1, as opposed to Australia's 1.27:1. Yet, in generating income,

TABLE 7-5. Saudi Arabian and Australian Japanese Trade Profiles.

	METRIC TONNAGE		VALUE, $THOUSANDS		WEIGHT RATIO	VALUE RATIO
	IMPORT	EXPORT	IMPORT	EXPORT		
Saudi Arabia	946,807	64,102,586	3,470,000	5,149,000	67.70	1.48
Australia	1,508,870	104,656,061	5,321,000	6,791,000	69.36	1.27

(Source: IMF *Direction of Trade*, JETRO *White Paper on Foreign Trade*)

minerals are far less important to Australia than oil is to Saudi Arabia. Oil exports to Japan accounted for nearly 20 percent of Saudi Arabia's total export revenues. The following table shows Australia's relative dependency:

TABLE 7-6. Australian Exports to Japan as a Percent of Trade.

	AUSTRALIAN EXPORTS FINANCIAL	JAPANESE IMPORTS PHYSICAL
Iron ore	2.90%	38.75%
Copper	0.14	4.86
Nickel	0.16	23.52
Bauxite	0.07	59.78
Zinc	0.09	45.07
Manganese	0.09	31.69
Coal	6.59	46.63
POL	0.18	—
LNG	0.0056	2.60

Given that exports represent roughly 17 percent of GNP for Australia, and that exports to Japan represent about 15.5 percent of total export earnings, it can be seen that Australian–Japanese trade is significant, but not crucial, to Australia. However, with the exception of iron ore and coal (the two minerals in which Australia is vulnerable), earnings from mineral exports are fairly insignificant. Since several imports are crucial to Japan, including bauxite and zinc, this leaves Japan vulnerable to Australian action.

Under normal circumstances, such action would be unlikely. However, a number of circumstances could arise, in the course of the regular functioning of a market, that would lead to a disruption of

MAP 7-3. Japan's Vulnerability in Mineral Imports.

Peoples'
Republic
of
China

Japan

Persian
Gulf

Sri
Lanka

Philippines

Papua
New Guinea

Malaysia

Indonesia

Madagasscar

Australia

South Africa

Australian exports. The first of these is labor unrest. Australia is notorious for the instability of its labor relations, particularly in mining. A large-scale strike in a key area, such as in bauxite, could leave Japan seriously short of supply. Given that, at present, Japan's stockpiles of a large number of metals have been drawn down to near exhaustion (due to the normal process of economic expansion), labor unrest in the next year or so could be particularly devastating.

A second, more distant threat is cartelization. There was an attempt to form cartels during the 1970s for several trade commodities, both mineral and agricultural. This was in response to the success of OPEC. However, all failed, due to the expansiveness of world commodity supplies as prices rose. Nevertheless, Japanese planners must take seriously the threat of cartelization, in which Australia would be a key participant as well as a key beneficiary.

PACIFIC OCEAN VS. INDIAN OCEAN

Maintaining the physical flow of material to Japan is the first priority of the Japanese state. It is a goal that transcends even financial considerations in its urgency. There are three avenues of approach Japan can take. The first is economic: relying on its financial power to purchase what it needs and deliver it. The second is political: creating a set of diplomatic arrangements to assure the delivery of raw materials in the event of the breakdown of financial relations. The third is military: assuring that Japan has the ability to secure what it needs without financial basis and without political support. While the latter is the goal to which most great powers aspire, because of the peculiarities of its history Japan must pursue its goals in the financial and, if necessary, political spheres. Confined to the financial and political, Japan necessarily faces dangers if it becomes too vulnerable and too dependent on any given supplier.

Therefore Japan must reduce its imports from Australia and find new suppliers more vulnerable to Japan and more eager to supply Japanese interests. This search has been underway for an extended period, particularly in iron ore. In 1975, Japan imported virtually all of Australia's iron ore production, for a total of 75.4 percent of its annual needs. In 1987, they imported only 38.75 percent of their iron ore from Australia (only about 70 percent of Australia's production). However, since the proportion of bauxite and coal imported from Australia grew steadily, the shift necessarily had a limited impact on Japan's search for economic security.

One of the results of this search for new supplies—in addition to an approach to Brazil[23]—was the opening of a new relationship with

India. This, along with expansion of trade with South Africa and new trade with Sri Lanka and Madagascar, represents a new chapter in Japanese trade policy.

Although in a fairly early stage, Japan's entry into the Indian Ocean Basin offers a promising long-term solution to its relative vulnerability arising from its concentrated trade with Australia. Aside from its Persian Gulf trade, shifting its demand to India, Sri Lanka, and Madagascar—and perhaps to sub-Saharan Africa Indian Ocean countries such as Kenya and Tanzania—would create a condition of substantial supplier dependency. This is due to the large quantities of material Japan is capable of purchasing as well as to the relative poverty of the region. What is a trivial amount for Australia is of enormous significance to Sri Lanka, or even India.

However, trade with the Indian Ocean Basin brings its own set of vulnerabilities, arising from its geographic configuration and subsequent military consequences. In particular, Japan's commercial entry into the Indian Ocean increases its dependence on the United States, a nation with which Japan is more and more at economic—and even political—odds. This is because the United States is still the guarantor of sea access in this region, as in other regions, of the world.

The key to Japan's mineral import policy is its ability to gain access to the Indian Ocean Basin. At the current time, Japanese access is guaranteed, due to friendly relations with the United States and the preeminent position of the United States Navy.

But the free-trade regime that followed World War II is approaching its half-century mark and the foundation of that regime is disappearing. It was an odd regime, with unfettered trade between brutally competitive economies. Free trade was the economic dimension of the vast political and military alliance the United States created in order to contain the Soviet Union. With the collapse of the Soviet Union, the rationale behind that alliance system dissolves as well. And with the dissolution of the West as a politically cohesive entity, the free-trade regime loses its political foundations. It can continue to function, but only to the moment when it runs afoul political divergences.

More than any other country's, Japan's postwar surge depended on this free-trade environment. Japan's growth was driven by exports and fueled by imports. Political impediments in the path of both threaten the very fabric of Japanese economic life and are not something the Japanese contemplate happily. It is in Japan's interest to prolong this period. For this reason, it is Japan's policy to appease U.S. demands for economic restructuring, at least up to the point where it will materially hurt Japan's economic well-being. However, since U.S. demands are essentially limitless, insisting that Japan permanently subordinate itself to American interests, it will become more and more difficult for Japan to accommodate American demands.

Under those circumstances, Japan's attention must shift away from the financial aspects of trade to the physical aspects. Financial considerations will draw Japan into the Indian Ocean, but the physical constraints of shipping will determine how long it will stay there. The fundamental issues of economic survival for Japan will, in due course, cease to be concerned with the financial arrangements with which it has been involved for the past forty years, but will be based instead on the physical arrangements of securing and delivering raw materials.

This is not an economic question. It is primarily a political question, and as with most political questions it is potentially a military question. The issue of Japan's relationship to Singapore, Malaysia, Indonesia, and Australia, today a matter of trade, aid, and investment, will become a grimmer question if there should be a political break between the U.S. and Japan.

It is for this reason that we must now turn away from Japan's economy and toward its political relations with other countries. Japan's vulnerabilities are partly economic, as with its high debt-to-equity ratio. But the economic problems are soluble economically. The threat of a physical disruption of mineral supplies is a political threat and requires a political and perhaps military solution. Until now, Japan has been compelled—and pleased—to confine itself to economic matters. With the end of the Cold War, this luxury must cease. And with that end, the question of Japan as a political actor on the world stage comes to the fore.

1. Clyde W. Prestowitz, *Trading Places: How We Are Giving Our Future to Japan and How to Reclaim It* (New York, 1988); James Fallows, "Containing Japan," *Atlantic Monthly*, May 1989.

2.

Japanese Balance of Payments, in $ Millions

	EXPORTS	IMPORTS	BALANCE	RATIO
1989	273,932	209,715	64,217	1.306
1988	264,856	187,378	77,478	1.413
1987	231,286	151,033	80,253	1.531
1986	210,757	136,176	74,581	1.548

Japanese Balance of Payments, in $ Millions (continued)

	EXPORTS	IMPORTS	BALANCE	RATIO
1985	177,164	130,448	46,716	1.358
1984	169,700	136,176	33,524	1.246
1983	146,955	126,437	20,518	1.162
1982	138,385	131,499	6,886	1.052

(Source: International Monetary Fund, *Direction of Trade Statistics Yearbook: 1990*)

3. An example of the concern during the 1970s can be seen in John Crawford and Saburo Okita, *Raw Materials and Pacific Economic Integration* (Vancouver, 1978). See in particular the article by Okita, "Japan's High Dependence on the Imports of Raw Material," which spends less than two pages on the problem of the import of minerals. Another work, along more strategic and military lines, is Charles Perry, *The West, Japan and Cape Route Imports: The Oil and Non-Fuel Mineral Trades* (Cambridge, 1982). This work focuses on the importance of the Cape route for the shipment of strategic minerals, and tends to place Japanese vulnerability on the same level as the rest of the West. A happy addition to this short list is the piece by Nobutoshi Akao, "Resources and Japan's Security," in Akao, *Japan's Economic Security* (New York, 1983). As the date reveals, this was another of the responses to what was seen as a particular crisis with general implications, rather than to the problem of Japan and its immutable nature.
4. Originally, it might be said that the Japanese turned to export orientation, during the 1940s, in order to avoid mineral pauperization: exports were led by the need for imports. See Michiya Matsukawa, *The Japanese Trade Surplus and Capital Outflow*, Occasional Paper No. 22, Group of Thirty (New York, 1987). On the reversal of this view recently, see pp. 4–5. See also Chapter 4 in the present book.
5. On the politics of grain imports, see Aurelia D. George, "The Japanese Farm Lobby and Agricultural Policy Making," *Pacific Affairs*, 54:3 (Fall 1981).
6. United Nations, *UNCTAD Commodity Yearbook*, 1989, p. 78.
7. R. Daniel McMichael, "Strategic Minerals: The Public Policy Process," in *Strategic Minerals and International Security*, ed. Uri Ra'anan and Charles M. Perry (Washington, D.C., 1985).
8. Both the Federal Republic of Germany and France have high levels of import dependency. However, this dependency is not across the board. The Federal Republic of Germany exports coal and imports only about 60% of its energy needs. France, more dependent generally, is still only completely dependent in iron ore, copper, and lead, and is an exporter of aluminum. Moreover, the shares of world market consumed by the FRG and France are all substantially lower than Japan's. In general, their market share is normally less than half of Japan's. Finally, France and the Federal Republic of Germany both import a large amount of their minerals from within continental Europe. They are far less dependent on the world merchant fleet and sea-lane

security than is Japan. For a systematic comparison, see Toshio Matsuoka, *Japan 1983: An International Comparison* (Keizai Koho Center, 1983).

9. Nobutoshi Akao, *Japan's Economic Security*, The Royal Institute for International Affairs (New York, 1983), p. 1: " 'Economic Security' is an expression used more often in Japan than in any other advanced industrialized country." See also Robert W. Barnett, *Beyond War: Japan's Concept of Comprehensive National Security* (Washington, D.C., 1984).

10.

Japanese Exports and Imports, in Metric Tons

	EXPORTS	IMPORTS	RATIO
1988	81,368,000	667,671,000	8.206
1987	84,320,000	621,757,000	7.374
1986	88,123,000	598,908,000	6.796
1985	94,307,000	603,684,000	6.401
1984	94,800,000	603,159,000	6.362
1980	83,853,000	612,992,000	7.310
1975	70,209,000	549,547,000	7.827
1970	42,008,000	435,924,000	10.377
1965	22,758,000	198,684,000	8.730
1960	14,039,000	89,540,000	6.378
1955	7,712,374	36,713,178	4.760
1954	5,717,132	33,526,063	5.864
1953	4,956,600	31,288,672	6.313
1952	5,055,562	23,738,302	4.695
1951	3,628,373	20,732,749	5.714
1950	2,259,169	12,767,211	5.651
1949	1,837,215	7,378,329	4.016
1939	12,497,000	21,649,000	1.732
1937	8,883,000	21,496,000	2.419
1935	8,908,000	18,104,000	2.032
1934	7,115,000	14,711,000	2.068

(Source: Statistics Bureau, Management and Coordination Agency, Government of Japan)

11.

Selected Mineral Ores: Japanese Imports as a Percentage of World Imports

	%	RANK
Copper	57.88	1
Zinc	20.79	2
Bauxite	5.28	5
Iron	29.79	1
Oil	17.52	2
Coal	30.58	2

Selected Mineral Ores (continued)

	%	RANK
Tungsten	5.23	5
Lead	18.88	2
Manganese	20.51	1
Nickel	93.15	1

(Sources: United Nations *International Trade Statistical Yearbook*, 1987; United Nations, *UNCTAD Commodity Year Book, 1989*; Japan Ministry of International Trade and Industry, *White Paper on International Trade: 1987*).

12. U.S. Department of the Interior, Bureau of Mines, *Minerals Yearbook*. Also, International Monetary Fund, *Primary Commodities, Market Developments and Outlook* (Washington, D.C., July 1989).
13. United Nations, *UNCTAD Commodity Yearbook* (New York, 1989), p. 376.
14.

Tonnage, in Millions, Imported by the U.S. in 1987

	TONNAGE (IN MILLIONS)	% OF TOTAL
Petroleum	91.7	18.9
Crude oil	216.7	44.6
Coal/Lignite	1.9	0.4
Nonmetallic ores	22.0	4.5
Iron concentrate	18.3	3.4
Farm products	6.5	1.3
Chemical	26.6	5.5
Food	13.4	2.8
Lumber	4.9	1.0
Primary metal	20.5	4.2
Scrap metal	0.7	0.1
Other	62.9	12.9
Total	486.1	—

(Source: United States Bureau of the Census, *Statistical Abstract of the United States*, Washington, D.C., 1989)

15. The United States was second only to the Soviet Union in crude oil production in 1987, and its 3 billion barrel production in 1987 was nearly 75% of the combined Persian Gulf total (including Iran and Iraq). See Bureau of Mines, Department of the Interior, preprint for the 1987 *Minerals in the World Economy*.
16. Sources: U.S. Department of Commerce, *Merchant Fleets of the World Annual*, and Government of Japan, Statistics Bureau, *Japan Statistical Yearbook*.
17. SCAP, *Japan's Natural Resources* and *Japan Statistical Yearbook*.

18. An excellent study on measuring resource dependence is to be found in Bruce Russett, "Dimensions of Resource Dependence: Some Elements of Rigor in Concept and Policy Analysis," *International Organization*, 38:3 (Summer 1984). Russett lists seven approaches: (1) imports as percentage of consumption, (2) market concentration, (3) imports as percentage of GNP, (4) supply alternatives, (5) elasticity of demand, (6) political measures of supply reliability, (7) symmetries between supplier and producer. It is this latter approach that is most attractive, since it measures an ongoing, dynamic relationship from both sides simultaneously and can incorporate all other variables as well. See also Joseph S. Nye and Robert O. Keohane, *Power and Interdependence: World Politics in Transition* (Boston, 1977).

19. See for example Rajaram Panda, *Pacific Partnership: Japan-Australia Resource Diplomacy* (Rohtak, 1982).

20. It is important here to distinguish between the Indian Ocean basin and South Asia. Although contrary to the view of some observers (Japan Economic Institute Report, *Japan and South Asia*, 15 December 1989), it would appear that South Asia, and particularly India and Sri Lanka, are growing in significance for Japan. The Indian Ocean Basin must be understood in a broader sense as including African and Southeast Asian countries west of Singapore.

21. On the location and types of Indonesian mines, see Bruce Lloyd, "Indonesia's Mineral Resources," *Resources Policy*, 1:6 (December 1975), p. 328.

22. Tsuneo Akaha, "Japan's Response to Threats of Shipping Disruptions in Southeast Asia and the Middle East," *Pacific Affairs*, 59:2 (Summer 1986), pp. 265–266.

23. The bulk of Brazil's exports go to West Germany. Assuming a boom in East European, or at least East German industrialization, the demand from that quarter can only increase, and it is therefore unlikely that the Japanese can depend on Brazil for long-term supplies.

PART III

THE ORIGINS OF THE SECOND U.S.- JAPANESE WAR

8

America's Reality: The Regionalization of Conflict

"Superpower" is a very real concept, but one that usually lacks definition, or is defined strictly in nuclear terms. If nuclear weapons were enough to create a superpower, then China or Israel would be one. Obviously, there is more to being a superpower than nuclear weapons. In order to be a superpower a nation must possess five capabilities:

1. A nuclear force large and secure enough to prevent the use of nuclear weapons by an enemy.
2. Absolute control of one's territory against internal disruption.
3. Completely secure borders, either with buffers of satellite nations, or by possessing overwhelming forces along unbuffered areas.
4. The ability to make massive and decisive intercontinental interventions even in the face of opposition by substantial secondary powers.
5. Sufficient resources for rapid and massive mobilization for extended intercontinental conflict using primarily internal resources.

As of 1990, there is only one true superpower in the world, the United States. The Soviet Union's claim to superpower status was always tenuous at best, given the weakness in its ability to project its forces intercontinentally, but for direct intervention the Soviets did manage to substitute surrogate operations—wars of national liberation that they supported. This was an adequate substitute until 1981, when President Reagan shifted the focus of the competition from the Third World conflicts to direct conventional and superstrategic (SDI—Strategic Defense Initiative) competition. The Soviets failed to meet this challenge, and lost their ability to compete for empire as well.

Because of internal decay and American pressure, the Soviet Union suddenly collapsed onto itself, barely able to hold on to the nations within its own borders. The Soviet Union had completely lost the ability to project forces, its internal cohesiveness was doubtful, and it was no longer clear that it could undertake a major mobilization for war. Even the security of its borders was in the air, depending on the behavior of Armenians or Lithuanians, rather than on Moscow's own strength. Only its nuclear capability was secure, and many speculated on what the breakup of the Soviet Union would mean in that regard.

The resulting American empire, like all empires at the moment of true emergence, appears ragged and malnourished. One could imagine that observers of Alexander the Great, noting the disarray of his forces and the undoubted disarray in the Macedonian economy, might have wondered what the prize was and who the winner was. If so, they vastly underestimated the importance of military power.

Just as it requires strategy to win an empire, it requires strategy to hold and exploit an empire. But if there is any constant in the history of nations, it is that military power, when founded on a stable society, transforms itself rapidly into political and economic power. Thus, the United States has won empire so suddenly that neither it nor anyone else quite realizes what has happened. It is clear that the Soviets have lost. However, no one is clear yet that the U.S. has won.

At this moment, it still appears that the real victors have been those who did not fight, but who were protected by the United States at little cost to themselves: Germany, the rest of Europe, and above all, Japan. In the short run this is true. The struggle left Japan the pampered child of history. But the struggle being over, the U.S. is now free to bring its massive military power to bear in solving its economic problems.

Japan was certainly aware of this possibility, for we saw it attempting to maintain the Cold War in Asia well after it had turned into a memory elsewhere. Other American officials, either understanding the regional consequences of the end to the Cold War or genuinely incapable of grasping the fact of victory, worked with the Japanese to maintain the illusion of a Soviet threat. This cannot work in the end. U.S. and Japanese relations will be redefined by the reality of American victory. It is in the process of redefinition that the next danger to humanity resides.

The confrontation between the U.S. and the Soviet Union was not a conflict between two nation-states, but between two continental states, for both America and the Soviet Union resemble continents more than ordinary nations. As continents, their conflicts had two basic characteristics. They were more strategic than economic in nature and they were intercontinental—nearly global—in scope. It has been assumed that nuclear weapons created global conflict, but they were merely an additional dimension to this basic development. Global conflict arose from the sheer size of the competitors. And, with the end of that competition, a new process will take place: the regionalization of conflict.

Since 1945, all conflict has been global. Wars in the Congo, the Middle East, Latin America, all affected the balance of power between the United States and the Soviet Union. Every conflict took its bearings, at least in part, from the U.S.–Soviet confrontation, and every conflict had implications on continents thousands of miles away. What happened in Cuba influenced events in Korea; events in Germany bore implications for Vietnam.

With the end of the Cold War, this single fabric of conflict has been shredded. Since there is no conceivable power capable of challenging the United States globally, formerly suppressed regional conflicts will reemerge—barring an American attempt to impose a global peace—and will carry regional rather than global implications.

One should not take comfort from this fact. The regionalization of conflicts might make them less globally apocalyptic, but might also make them far more brutal and unpredictable. During the Cold War the United States and the Soviet Union controlled most conflicts. Since all conflicts influenced the international balance, there was a tendency on the part of both sides, wishing as they did to avoid World War III, to contain these conflicts spatially or temporally. Vietnam was not permitted to spread throughout Asia. The various Arab–Israeli wars were forced to end quickly rather than drag on indefinitely.

The Iran–Iraq War was a precursor of future conflicts. Both superpowers were indifferent to the course of this regional conflict, so long as it did not culminate in a victor. The conflict never spread, but its brutality was noteworthy even for the twentieth century. Since neither side could win outright, the conflict continued, intensifying within strict geographical limits.

The Iraqi invasion of Kuwait illustrated the other possibility. In that conflict the United States sought to use its anti-Soviet alliance system, now including the Soviets as well, to impose a satisfactory set of regional relationships. In short, the U.S., rather than being indifferent to the outcome of the crisis, sought to use the alliance as an instrument of imperial will. Not incidentally, the reluctance of Japan to participate in the project showed Japan's understanding of the American intent, as well as an understanding that American interests and Japanese interests in the region potentially diverged.

The regionalization of world conflict leaves the U.S. with a set of options essentially divided between withdrawal and empire. It is not altogether clear which the U.S. will choose, except that it will undoubtedly follow the path of least resistance. The path of least resistance will obviously be determined by political and economic forces, and, in particular, by the manner in which they converge to shape the postwar world.

THE FREE-TRADE REGIME AND THE REEMERGENCE OF POLITICS

In a certain sense, the Cold War period has been a suspension of politics, at least among the non-Communist nations of the world. The struggle between the Communist and non-Communist world imposed a political truce on the latter, in which political competition among Western nations was, if not abolished, certainly limited or suspended. This was particularly true among formal members of the American alliance system. Yet while political competition was suspended, economic competition continued unabated. Indeed, unconstrained by political considerations, international economic competition became the centerpiece of relations among Western nations.

Many have become used to this world and have come to see political harmony and cutthroat economic competition as the natural order of things. For these, the end of the Cold War has caused a surge of optimism. The optimists have assumed that the decline of U.S.–Soviet tensions will mean a general decline in political conflict, as nations pursue economic ends and ignore politics, as the Western allies did during the Cold War. If this were so, then this would be a safer world, since without political conflict, war would be unthinkable. As Giovani Agnelli, chairman of Fiat, put it:

> Because 1992 has grown out of a recognition of the advantages of a free market, I believe that its success will depend on strengthening Europe's traditional economic and political alliances, rather than excluding the rest of the world.[1]

For Agnelli, the economic and political intimacy of the Cold War alliance will continue unabated, indeed, intensify. This is obviously the most important political question facing the world today: whether Agnelli's optimism, and the optimism of the Western industrial elites, about the future stability of the world order will be borne out.

The Western powers had an overriding fear of the Soviet Union, and that fear limited political competition. By limiting political competition, the intrusion of political power into international economic relations was also limited. The result was the establishment of an extensive free-trade regime among the non-Communist powers of the world. Built around the General Agreement on Tariffs and Trade (GATT), this regime had as its goal the creation of universal free trade.

Free trade is nonpolitical trade, trade which is beyond the intrusions of noneconomic considerations. In such a world, the rise and fall of national fortunes depends on variables such as productivity, savings rates, and the cost of raw materials. The power of nations to impose relative advantage by political or military means is banned.

When the dollar replaced all of the prewar hard currencies—the mark, yen, pound sterling—as the single, universally accepted currency, the U.S. suddenly gained tremendous power over the international economic system. The rise of the dollar did not represent the triumph of economic considerations over political ones. Rather, it announced the arrival of a nation so politically powerful that its currency would become the standard for the entire world. Because the U.S. had a powerful political agenda, creating a vast anti-Soviet alliance, the U.S. used this political power to create a free-trade bloc in the West under the umbrella of the dollar. To many, it appeared that within the bloc only economics mattered; that trade had supplanted politics and war. Thus, Germany and France, ancient enemies, suddenly felt as though their ancient rivalry had been abolished and that the only thing of importance was now trade.

All of this was an illusion, of course. The U.S., pursuing its political goal of containing the Soviet Union, had created a hothouse, an artificial environment, in which nations were forced to put aside their political disputes. Some did it easily, like France and Germany. For others, like Greece and Turkey, it was more difficult. But the U.S. ruthlessly stamped out regional conflicts in its alliance system, using as a stick the threat of the Soviet Union, and as a carrot the marvelous free-trade regime that allowed nations access to markets and resources on a more secure basis than ever before.

The free-trade regime was not a primarily economic event, but a political one. It was a means toward a political end: internal harmony in the alliance and the creation of healthy economies and societies within the alliance. The traditional disputes between nations had not disappeared. Rather, they had been suppressed by the United States. Within the confines of the alliance, broadly understood, and within the time frame of the Cold War, one could get the impression that this system was permanent and unchangeable. One could get the impression, as Agnelli has, that even withdrawing the reason for the alliance, the alliance will endure—and more important, the free-trade system will continue.

The United States, for example, has immediate trade problems with Japan concerning its penetration of the American market and impediments to American entry into the Japanese market. The assumption of free traders is that the American government, if it acts rationally, will always be interested in an economic solution to this problem.

Of course, the United States has other solutions to the problem of Japanese imports. It could, for example, simply ban them from the U.S., an act that would leave the Japanese with one-third of their exports unsold. Or, the U.S. could contrive to block Japanese access to oil; that would also solve the problem. The assumption that the U.S. would never do either rests on two propositions. One, that the ideology of free trade that dominates establishment thinking is deeply embedded in American public opinion, and the second, that the U.S. would never want to harm Japan. But the American public cares about short-term economic well-being more than it cares about free trade, and the American unwillingness to harm Japan depended on a Soviet threat more than any intrinsic concern for Japan.

Until the end of the Cold War, the U.S. could not rationally regionalize its market. GATT was the foundation on which the Western political system rested: without GATT the American alliance system would crumble. But the Cold War seems to be over and therefore the price the U.S. paid in recent years for the free-trade regime it created may no longer be worth paying. Both domestic and foreign political considerations will determine whether the United States continues to participate in a free-trade regime or proceeds to regionalize its own market, segmenting world trade with tariff and military barriers.

The creation of a European monetary system in 1992—essentially the creation of a mark bloc—is the first step in the direction of segmented markets. The North American free-trade zone is the second step. By creating an internal free-trade zone in North America, as well as reaching long-term agreements with Canada and Mexico on commodity flows, particularly oil, the United States takes a long step toward regionalizing oil markets. Regionalization occurs when the price of oil within one zone does not necessarily agree with prices outside that zone, as was the case in the U.S. prior to oil decontrol, when the price of oil domestically was much lower than it was on the world market. The ability to regionalize a market depends on political and military power. It will depend on one nation having the ability to coerce another nation to sell a commodity at a lower price, or force them to buy goods at a higher price. This was the essence of the old European imperial system. The question is whether this system will emerge again. Ultimately, this is a political, not an economic, question.

The end of the Cold War may well signal the end of the free-trade era and a cyclical return to segmented markets. In such a segmented and regionalized world, economic well-being will rest with those who hold political and military power. The ability to control the price of oil is the ability to divert vast resources to that country. The ability to close off one's markets to competitors might well bring great economic benefit, or at least social peace.

In self-defense, the Europeans have already acted to create their own currency bloc and to limit outsiders' access to European markets. Interestingly, one of the issues dividing the future Europeans is the role of the former colonies of Britain and France. The extension of the EC bloc to include former colonies will close the circle on the European imperium.

Japan too has developed a clear yen bloc, a group of nations organized around its currency. But Japan completely lacks the political power to order this bloc coherently. A true bloc will have a centrally imposed division of labor, something that does not exist with Asia's "Four Little Tigers," Korea, Taiwan, Hong Kong, and Singapore. As the U.S. closes off North America, questions such as the role of Australia and Indonesia caught between the two blocs will become critical, particularly to a Japan dependent on imports of raw materials from both countries.

This will pose the major strategic dilemma for Japan in the next decade. Japan has grown powerful in a free-trade environment and, lacking political and military power, it is clearly in its interest to maintain this environment for as long as possible. But its very success is what threatens the free-trade regime; and a unilateral act by the United States to abrogate the arrangement will be sufficient to bring it to a close.

Japan's dilemma today is how to prepare for this new environment without bringing it about or even hastening its approach. One way, obviously, is to pretend that the world has not changed, and that has certainly been the main thrust of Japanese policy thus far. But that is at best a temporary solution. Finding a more permanent solution is more difficult, because it must lead Japan into considering that all currency blocs are potentially empires, and that a Japanese empire requires military might, far more might than the last empire had.

We are facing an era in which the global system of free trade may well turn into a regional system of trading blocs. Along with that, the end of the Western alliance system will create a series of regional political and military powers. The processes of economic regionalization and of politico-military regionalization will inevitable intersect. The regional economic powers and the regional political powers will likely be the same. This convergence will constitute the shape of the next century.

THE RECONVERGENCE OF THE ECONOMIC AND STRATEGIC

The submergence of regional conflict began with the emergence of the European imperial system in the nineteenth century. Regional, indeed local conflicts, were utilized by imperial powers to gain advantage over each other. A conflict between two Chinese warlords or two African chiefs was used by European imperialists to increase their control in a region. Each local conflict took on a global significance as part of the struggle for empire. In this sense, the Cold War was merely an extension of the process of conflict globalization. Most local conflicts became part of the system of global confrontation between the U.S. and Soviet Union.

There was one essential difference between the European imperial system of 1815–1945 and the U.S.–Soviet competition of 1945–1990. The first conflict was conditioned by economic as well as strategic considerations; the second conflict was purely strategic, with economic considerations playing an insignificant role. Geography had much to do with the divorce of economy from strategy. The U.S. and the Soviet Union were and are generally self-contained and able to generate growth without extraordinary dependence on either exports of goods or imports of raw materials. As continents rather than mere nations, neither defined their basic needs in terms of foreign economic policy.

They were primarily concerned with physical security. The military threat posed by the Soviet Union to the United States was infinitely greater than any economic threat. On the other side, while the Soviets certainly desired good economic relations with the West, the military threat posed by the West was also the greater danger. Ultimately, the military confrontation was more important than the economic. Nuclear weapons, the most extreme manifestation of military threat, naturally emerged as the essence of U.S.–Soviet competition.

As American interest in policing areas of the eastern hemisphere subsides (except for areas of urgent interest to the U.S., such as the Persian Gulf), several regional powers will inevitably emerge. These regional powers—militarily and politically preeminent in a relatively circumscribed area—will impose a political order on a region. Thus, it can be expected that Nigeria will become a major controller of events in West Africa, India in South Asia, and Brazil in Latin America. In these and other cases, there will be local challenges to their hegemony, resulting in sharp, geographically contained conflicts.

One of the paradoxes of the new regional powers is that although they will be politically focused on their immediate area, their global needs will, in all likelihood, be much greater than that. Nigeria needs to sell its oil far beyond the range of its political influence. Thus, as regional powers emerge, their political power will not necessarily help with their economic problems unless they can reshape their spheres of economic vulnerability to coincide with their areas of political power. It is difficult to imagine Nigeria doing this, as its region cannot possibly absorb the oil it produces, nor provide it with the manufactured imports it needs. But a regional power like Germany or Japan, redirecting its economic energies into a smaller geographic frame, might well satisfy those needs in the area it controls. This would obviously reduce their individual areas of vulnerability and control.

One solution for a regional power is to contract the geographic sphere of its economic activity. In many cases, obviously, that is simply not possible. The second solution is to control the trade routes essential to a regional power's trade. During the Cold War, sea-lane control was left to the United States, which performed it effortlessly and without cost to the beneficiaries. All regional powers must now consider the extent to which the U.S. is likely to continue carrying out this task in the future and the price it is likely to exact if it does carry it out.

Ever since the rise of the European trading system, control of the sea-lanes has meant wealth and power. Small city-states like Venice became wealthy regional powers by controlling the sea-lanes. And other nations, like Portugal and Spain, sank into poverty when their navies and diplomacy proved incapable of maintaining control.

Thus, the U.S. faces a fundamental strategic choice. As regional powers emerge, it can try to force them into a subordinate relationship with the United States—in short, create an empire. Or, the U.S. can permit regionalization to happen and trust the balance of power to take care of itself.

On an economic level it has a more troubling choice. If it allows the free-trade regime to collapse, as it is tempted to do, the regional political powers will grow into regional economic blocs or into insecure trading countries with rapidly growing navies. Unless the U.S. is prepared to be a strictly hemispheric power, it will be challenged for control of the sea in some areas early in the twenty-first century. It is not clear that the U.S. can resist this challenge without recourse

MAP 8-1. World Sea-Lanes and U.S. Naval Power.

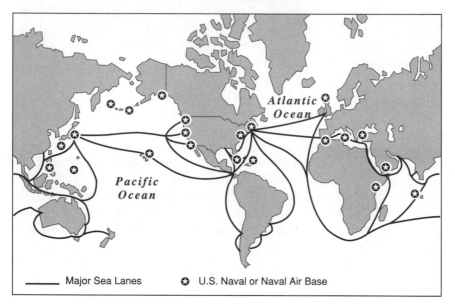

Major Sea Lanes   ✪ U.S. Naval or Naval Air Base

to empire. In other words, once the U.S. begins to resist the rise of regional naval powers, can its resistance be confined to sea control?

THE REEMERGENCE OF IMPERIALISM

The collapse of the European empire seemed to spell the end of imperialism. Although the U.S. and Soviet Union engaged in a violent contest for control of the fallen empires, each denied imperial intentions and they were both right, in the classic sense that imperialism was not simply a political relationship, but an economic one as well. The American interest in Vietnam and the Soviet interest in Afghanistan were strategic and political, but completely devoid of economic interests.

If our analysis is correct, then we are about to see the reemergence of an imperial contest, in the full politico-economic sense of the term. It will not be a European imperialism, or at least not strictly a European imperialism. It will be either a single giant American imperialism, or a series of regional imperialisms, or some combination of the two. In any event, the reemergence of imperialism is intellectually challenging to a world that is essentially liberal democratic. Since national self-determination is a principle of liberal democracy, it follows that liberal democrats naturally recoil at the thought of their regimes engaging in such behavior.

What reappears is a very old question: can industrial liberal democracies avoid becoming imperialistic, either regionally or globally? The events leading up to World War I reveal that liberal industrialism can move from economic to political and thence to military competition. World War I was a conflict between essentially like-minded nations, Russia excepted. Great Britain, France, and Germany were all industrial societies with more or less liberal democratic regimes. All were economic competitors.

Everyone understood, prior to 1914, that the world had become inextricably entangled financially and economically. Some took this to mean that war had become an impossibility, since it would shatter essential economic relations. Norman Angell, who published *The Great Illusion* in 1910, argued that due to the interrelatedness of capitalist nations, and since the financial structure of Europe would be shattered by such a war, a general European war was impossible. He wrote:

> Even if we could annihilate Germany we should annihilate such an important section of our debtors as to create hopeless panic in London. Such panic would so react on our own trade that it would be in no sort of condition to take the place which Germany had previously occupied in neutral markets, aside from the question that by such annihilation, a market equal to that of Canada and South Africa combined would be destroyed.[2]

By this reasoning, Angell proved that World War I could not take place.

His error was to assume that all men act to maximize their economic benefits and that all regimes act to satisfy the interests of their creditor class. In this way liberalism commits the same error as Marxism. Both assume that rational action means action that maximizes economic benefits. They ignore the idea that strategic interests might exist that are fundamentally more important than economic interests, and fundamentally different. Economics speaks to human *greed*, while politics speaks to *fear*. The fear of subjugation felt by a nation, or a large part of it, might well override their greed. Thus, Britain did go to war with Germany and ignored the economic consequences.

The predominant view today parallels Norman Angell's view, but does not have his excuse of innocence. The forces unleashed by the collapse of communism are not dissimilar to those which existed prior to World War I. Intense economic competition coupled with geopolitical insecurity caused World War I. The idea that the same forces can be kept in check in the twenty-first century by goodwill and careful negotiations is not really credible.

Edson W. Spencer, chairman of the Commission on U.S.–Japan

Relations for the Twenty-first Century, and former chairman of the Honeywell Corporation, epitomizes this Angellian illusion in his article in the March 1990 issue of *Foreign Policy*:

> A return to the protectionism of the 1930s also will not occur. None of the major trading areas or individual countries can afford a trade war in a world where the economies are so closely interrelated.[3]

Spencer's view is that the United States and Japan have much to gain by continued cooperation, that they cannot allow short-range disputes to impede efforts to work together in their mutual long-term interests. The peaceful resolution of disputes between nations requires compromise from all partners involved. He encourages leaders in Japan and the United States to redouble their efforts to bring about such compromises.[4]

Spencer's assumption is that wars can be avoided by careful planning and goodwill. This in turn assumes that wars are caused by carelessness. If a conflict between the United States and Japan can be solved by goodwill, then there will be no war, for there are few cases when senior leaders on both sides are more sincerely dedicated to Spencer's sentiments. However, wars arise from strategic realities rather than ill temper. As with World War I, economic relations can drive nations apart quite as much as they might bind them together. Which will occur depends on the nature of those economic relations and the strategic realities existent in the world.

The basic strategic reality today is that there is only one naval power in the world, the United States, and that the United States possesses the ability, should it choose to use it, to determine the flow of goods and, therefore, the wealth of nations. Thus far, the U.S. has used this power to strengthen its alliance system, but there is no intrinsic reason why this same power cannot be used, now that there is no other global power to contend with, to enrich America and impoverish America's enemies.

Should the United States abandon its role as guarantor of the sealanes, should it exact a price greater than regional powers can bear, or should regional powers grow wary of American intentions, then an imperial struggle of mammoth proportions might take place. The level of development in the world economy, the structure of interdependence, the penetration of the world economy to every corner of the globe—all indicate that a series of regional struggles for political and military hegemony would prove intense and brutal. This by no means proves that it would be impossible.

It must be remembered—as our world more and more resembles

the one prior to 1914, with like-minded regimes pursuing economic ends with increasingly military means—that sympathy and interdependence did not act as a brake on war then. The comfortable assumptions of perpetual peace assume that the U.S. will be willing to carry out a function that it is not in its interest to carry out, a function of carrying the burden of security without charge. Any other action by the U.S. would end in brutal competition.

In the pause between the Cold War and the new, as yet unnamed, age we are entering, the world holds its breath. How the United States will wear the mantle of ruler of the world's oceans—or whether it will discard it—will determine the shape of the next century. As yet, the surprise over the American victory has been so thorough that the awesome decisions confronting the United States have not yet been faced. Now the time has come for choosing its new role. Few nations in history have been handed such great power. Yet the U.S., rather than feeling that its century is dawning, seems to feel that its time is coming to an end, because of economic problems natural to the victor of a long and costly war. In the final analysis, charting the American response will require a close reading of the text of this historical moment.

THE SOVIET UNION'S NEW STRATEGIC ROLE

The starting point for understanding the new strategic environment is to consider the effect of the decline of the Soviet Union. Four general paths lie before the Soviet Union at this point. They lead to:

1. The emergence of a neo-Stalinist regime.
2. A weakened, introspective, but generally cohesive Soviet Union with a regional perspective on international affairs.
3. The peaceful breakup of the Soviet Union into multiple nations.
4. Civil war.

From a strategic viewpoint, the last three outcomes have the same effect. In any of these cases, the Soviets would lose their ability to project their power beyond their borders. The Soviets would lose their European buffers, their armed forces would either be slashed or detailed to internal-security duties, and the ability of the Soviets to influence events in the Third World would disappear. Indeed, it is interesting to contemplate the constellation of relationships that would emerge in the event of a breakup of the Soviet Union, where each or some of the republics became independent powers with diverging interests. A new ruble bloc might even emerge.

In practice, only the first outcome need concern us, for it is the one that foresees a return of the Soviet Union to its pre-1989 power. It is altogether possible that the Soviet Union will emerge with an anti-Gorbachev government of Brezhnevites combined with military elements. But it is not clear that this government can reverse the objective deterioration in the Soviet Union's politico-military position. The economic condition of the Soviet Union has deteriorated substantially since Gorbachev took power and it is no longer the case that limitations on the Soviet military are volitional.

Therefore, our strategic analysis must begin with the assumption that under any circumstances the Soviets will no longer be capable of controlling Eastern Europe militarily, threatening Western Europe with ground attack, posing an overland danger to the Persian Gulf, conducting a forward naval strategy with large-scale units operating in the North Atlantic and Mediterranean, carrying out massive covert operations in the Third World, or carrying out large-scale weapons development projects. The Soviets will be able to project power on a strictly regional basis, retaining, for example, a continued ability to intervene in one or two Eastern European countries simultaneously, protect the Soviet coastline, and selectively influence events in the Third World.

The decline of the Soviet Union is educational in one way: it teaches the general irrelevance of nuclear weapons in maintaining political and military hegemony and protecting political interests. The Soviets, in spite of their inability to keep pace with the American military buildup in the 1980s, retained a massive nuclear force. In a world where no one else had such a force, one might imagine that it would be a means to impose hegemony wherever a nation wished, assuming that nation was prepared to act with sufficient ruthlessness. But in a world in which several nations had sufficient nuclear forces to "tear off an arm," as de Gaulle put it, nuclear weapons cease to be relevant. The limits of nuclear weapons in the Soviet Union's politico-military crisis ought to be borne in mind by regional powers who are thinking about creating expensive nuclear forces instead of armies and navies.

The Soviet Union would still retain a large land army, able to deploy massive firepower in concert with sophisticated, if aged, aircraft. Its navy would still be able to carry out limited coastal duty, and its air defense forces generally protect its airspace. Its limitations would be in its ability to project its power beyond its borders or overawe its neighbors. The previous sense in Europe or the Middle East was that, save for an alliance with the U.S., the Soviet Union could not be resisted. The new sense is that a regional relationship—linking, for example, Poland, Czechoslovakia, and Hungary—might suffice to deter any Soviet return to Central Europe, particularly if it had the tacit support of Germany.

One must understand that the Soviet Union would not become inert. Unable to project its forces intercontinentally, it would still have to be reckoned with regionally, indeed in several regions simultaneously. Eastern Europe, Turkey, Iran, and China will all have to take the Soviet Union quite seriously. Not, as was previously the case, as an inexorable, irresistible force, but as a significant power able to inflict pain and provide benefits.

In short, the Soviet Union will behave as it did between 1922 and 1939. It will have to be reckoned with as an influential power along its borders, but the general effect of its power will be to cause nations to band together against it, rather than to submit to it. In the face of this general fear of Soviet intentions, the Soviet Union will find it impossible to act aggressively outside of very limited circumstances, and its strategic thinking will concern itself with internal security and protection against external aggression.

THE EUROPEAN BALANCE IN THE NEW ERA

The primary feature of the European balance of power has been the stable division of Europe between NATO and the Warsaw Pact countries. The dissolution of the Warsaw Pact has had two effects on Eastern Europe. First, effective Soviet military power has been moved east, behind the Bug River and Carpathian Mountains. Given conditions in the Baltic states, the Soviets might find themselves forced back to their pre-1940 borders. Unless the Soviets plan to use their occupation forces in Eastern Europe promptly, they will melt into irrelevance.

Second, the withdrawal of Soviet power has returned Eastern Europe to the status quo ante of 1939. In essence, the remnants of the Austro-Hungarian and Ottoman empires have reemerged as sovereign states. This Central European fragmentation was an unstable condition both before and after World War I. Torn apart by their own national conflicts, they were also divided by German and Russian ambitions. Indeed, the current situation looks more like a cyclic return of German preeminence over Russia than an unprecedented breakthrough.

Economically, Germany was the natural magnet for these countries. The Danube Valley nations (Austria, Hungary, Romania, Yugoslavia, and Bulgaria), along with Czechoslovakia and Poland, all have inadequate economies and require external sources of capital to increase development. Although they have the cheapest labor rates in Europe, the cost of capital generated internally is so high, owing to the relatively primitive level of capital formation, as to make competitive industrial output impossible. Only external investment can break the cycle of low return on capital. During the interwar period, the general weakness in the world economy slowed this process until the post-1935 German recovery caused German capital to flow into Eastern Europe. Naturally, along with capital came German political influence and domination.

Caught between Germany and the Soviet Union, these nations followed a shrewd policy during the interwar period. Rather than playing Germany off against the Soviet Union, a tightrope from which it was easy to fall, they steered clear of the Soviet Union. After all, the Soviets had nothing to offer economically. Instead, Eastern European nations, operating independently, sought to establish economic relationships with Germany while allying themselves politically with powers from outside Central Europe—Britain and France.

The decision of the Anglo-French powers to guarantee the territorial integrity of Eastern Europe in the face of German economic influence was a rational attempt to surround the Germans without having an alliance with the Russians. Allying with the Russians would have meant permitting the latter to dominate the area they eventually won after World War II. It would have tilted the balance of power heavily in favor of the Soviets. Alliances with Eastern European nations permitted the Anglo-French the illusion of surrounding the Germans without actually risking war with them, or risking accommodation with the Soviets.

The weakness of this strategy was that the Anglo-French were unable to bring military power to bear in defense of Eastern Europe except by directly attacking Germany, triggering a general war to achieve limited interests. Since the Anglo-French were loathe to do this, the Germans were able to poach in Eastern Europe at will, until they attacked Poland. Since the fall of Poland to Germany would have tilted the balance of power in Europe too far in Germany's favor, Britain and France had no choice but to declare war.

The recent reemergence of a united Germany, with nascent territorial claims, including the return of East Prussia by the Soviet Union, recreates the situation prior to World War II:

1. Germany is by far the most important economic power in Europe, and is the natural source of investment capital in the east, as well as a market for East European goods.
2. The Soviet Union wishes to keep this area a neutral zone, but its own emerging dependence on German capital, carefully nurtured by the Germans themselves, will prevent the Soviets from contesting Germany too directly for domination of the region.
3. The emerging struggles between Eastern European nations (Serbs and Croats, Hungarians and Romanians, Greeks and Turks,

Czechs and Slovaks) provides fertile soil for manipulation by the Germans to turn economic power into political power.

What makes the situation different today, of course, is the existence of Cold War institutions—NATO and the European Community— which are expected to contain and channel German national aspirations. However, it is not clear which is the dog and which the tail. Given the power of the German economy, these institutions might serve as the framework for a German-dominated European order. Using these instruments of free regional trade and security, Germany can effectively pursue the political goal it has sought since 1871: domination of Europe west of the Vistula.[5]

Neither the French nor the British are unaware of the implication of rising German power. The question of the Anglo-French response to growing German power is once again the pivotal question of the epoch. Given the fact that there are few ideological issues separating the Germans from the rest of Europe, the situation begins to resemble pre-1914 Europe more than anything else: a purely regional conflict of interest. Fears have been expressed that the politico-economic unification proposed for Europe in 1992 would be tantamount to a German empire and that the EC would become a framework for German domination, a new New Order. It is difficult to imagine a united Europe not dominated by Germany, and therefore difficult to imagine British and French agreement to a genuine surrender of sovereignty.

Assuming that Britain and France retained their sovereignty and wrecked 1992, one can easily imagine the French and British forced into alliance once again and competing with Germany for economic and political influence in Eastern Europe. Eastern European nations, seeking German investment and trade but fearing absorption by Germany, will maintain economic relations with Germany but develop political alliances with the Western Europeans.

The U.S. presence in Europe is, of course, the novel element in the equation. In previous reformulations of the German problem in Europe, the Americans were a distant presence who eventually intervened, but only after the balance of power had completely tilted in favor of German hegemony. This time the United States is already present in Europe as the guarantor of Western European independence and of the European balance of power. However, this presence is not ideal from the American standpoint. Far superior would be a situation in which the European balance of power was maintained by the dynamics of Europe itself. American withdrawal and a European stalemate is the optimal American solution. The American problem, of course, is whether Europe, on its own, can resist German domination.

The return of Europe to its pre-World War II configuration is possible. The idea that this time unity will be achieved by turning Cold War institutions into stable political and economic foundations for a pan-European regime fails to recognize that Soviet pressure was the foundation for these institutions, and that barring Soviet pressure the next fear on the European agenda will inevitably be fear of Germany. Moreover, since free trade favors countries with a large surplus of investible capital and countries with cheap labor forces, middle-tier countries like France or Britain will find themselves pressed in a free-trade regime. Their response—either alignment with the U.S. or tariff barriers—will only create traditional tensions in Western Europe, leading to regional conflict. Whether Europe unites or fragments is of fundamental importance to the U.S. A united Europe will pose a profound challenge to the U.S. In the short run, unification is likely. In the long run, holding such a melange of nationalisms together is problematic.

Thus, the strategic reality of Europe can be grasped by canceling out World War II and imagining the situation in the 1930s, save that Europe is in the midst of a great historical prosperity rather than a depression and that the Americans are still there. This means a great deal, but only as long as the prosperity remains intact, European politics do not return to their traditional desperation and the Americans do not leave. A prosperous Germany may concern other Europeans, but a hard-pressed Germany contemplating the unfairness of its territorial truncation ought to terrify them. As long as the Europeans are in a position to resist the Germans by themselves, it is a matter of no concern to the U.S.. Of course, their record on this is not good.

THE MIDDLE EAST AND THE STRATEGIC BALANCE

The traditional function of the Middle East in world politics has been to be a bridge between three continents and the eastern anchor of the Mediterranean. During the Cold War, the Middle East took on two other functions. First, it became a primary source of the raw materials that powered modern industrialism, and second, it became a crucial link in the chain containing Soviet expansionism. Had the Soviets broken out beyond Iran and Turkey, to the east coast of the Mediterranean and the Persian Gulf, both the world petroleum supply and U.S. control of the Mediterranean would have been damaged. The entire balance of power in Eurasia would have shifted.

Thus, the Middle East became a central arena for U.S.–Soviet competition during the Cold War. With an end to that competition, the function of the Middle East will change substantially. It will continue to be the crossroads of three continents, but of course the imperial forces seeking to control that crossroads will shift dramatically.

Geopolitically, the American interest in the region must decline, since its primary interest in the area has been to block Soviet control. Inasmuch as there is no other global power threatening to establish hegemony, and any regional power would either be counterbalanced by other regional powers or by forces immediately adjacent to the region, strict geopolitical reason would dictate an American withdrawal from the region, or at least substantial diminution of American interest.

Clearly, this has been something troubling American allies in the region. For Israel in particular, the end of the Cold War has ushered in a period of deep uncertainty. Israel's relationship to the U.S. has been the foundation of Israeli foreign policy since 1967. Israel must have a foreign sponsor to provide weapons and aid. With the end of the Cold War, the geopolitical interest the U.S. had in Israel as a counterweight to Soviet power clearly becomes irrelevant.

Economically, however, the region has a greater significance. It is the world's great producer and reserve of oil. The eastern portion of the Middle East, the Persian Gulf region, contains the bulk of the world's proven oil reserves. Since oil is the fuel that powers industrial society, control of these reserves gives any nation enormous power over the international economy, both in manipulating the supply of oil and because the profits that result from oil production make the producer a major, and occasionally controlling, force in the international economic system.

The United States therefore has a continuing interest in the region. In particular, if the U.S. were to take control of the region, its status as a political superpower would be supplemented by a vast economic power. In addition to controlling the world's oceans, the U.S. would be in control of the world's oil supply, since North American production, combined with that of the Persian Gulf, would be about 35 percent of world production and 65 percent of world oil reserves.[6] Controlling the Persian Gulf would open a period of enormous imperial power unprecedented in history, dwarfing even the Anglo-French imperial system.

Without oil, the Middle East would become an internal and regionalized dispute. Unlike the European conflicts, there are no clear recent historical road maps to follow in order to predict the future. The Middle East has been overwhelmed by imperial forces for centuries. It has been the fate of Arabic Islam to be subject to foreign domination since the rise of Turkish rule. Thus, one suspects that with the collapse of both European imperialism and the Cold War, a regional power would arise to impose some sort of order on the region.

With oil, the Persian Gulf becomes much more than a regional issue. It becomes the pivot of the world economy. For the U.S., domination of the region would open the door on unprecedented international power. On the other hand, allowing another regional power, such as Iraq or Iran, to seize control of the region and consolidate its own power would close the door on the possibility, unless the U.S. were prepared to wage a ground war in the region.

During the 1990 Iraqi invasion of Kuwait, the U.S. response was explicitly for one purpose: preventing Iraqi domination of the region's oil supply. However, it opened up quite another possibility. Success for the U.S. in retaking Kuwait, breaking the Saddam regime, and seizing control of Iraq would place the U.S. in control of a large amount of the world's oil reserves and production. No matter how benignly this power might be used, the U.S. would emerge in control of the international economic system.

Under those circumstances, any abrogation of the free-trade regime in petroleum products would be to the benefit of the U.S. This troubled American allies greatly. During the crisis, the U.S. attempted to use its anti-Soviet alliance system to fashion a response to the Iraqis. With the notable exception of the British, who after hesitation supplied two armored brigades, and the French, who provided forces not fully integrated with American forces, no other non-Arab ally provided ground forces. The Germans and the Japanese, in particular, sought to distance themselves from the military aspects of the operation.

It is interesting to note that this reluctance was covered by rhetorical support. It is one of the important signs of American power that only a handful of nations dared oppose the U.S. publicly, those few being pariahs like Cuba and Libya. The bulk of the international community supported the adventure but hung back from participation. The conventional interpretation was that these countries wanted to see American resolution, but were not prepared to assume the risks themselves.

In fact, another explanation is more reasonable. The success of the U.S. adventure would leave the U.S. effectively the world's greatest oil producer. It would be in a position to set production quotas and therefore prices, as well as control the movement of oil. A country like Japan, dependent on the countries within the Straits of Hormuz for over 60 percent of its oil imports, would find that its greatest economic competitor—the world's only large economy, and one increasingly bitter toward Japan—was in direct control of the Japanese supply of oil. While Japan was not in a position to resist that evolution in 1990, it made its fears about the situation quite clear through its reluctance to aid militarily the American Persian Gulf effort.

So, with the end of the Cold War, the geopolitical focus on the Middle East dissolves while the economic focus increases. The decline of Soviet power has increased American power to such an extent that the U.S. is suddenly in a position to impose its power on the region. A three-player game between Iraq, Iran, and the U.S. has ensued, with each seeking to minimize the possibility of a coalition involving the other two.

Hence, the political regionalization of the Middle East has run directly into the countervailing tendency of the globalization of the economy. Without oil, the fate of the region would become a matter of relative indifference; with oil, the dependency of the entire industrialized world focuses on the area. The leading political power, the U.S., suddenly finds itself in a position where its political power can be used to gain a hammerlock on the international economy.

The Persian Gulf will necessarily become a center of controversy between the U.S. and Japan. Japan's vulnerability to the flow of oil from the area means that increased U.S. power in the region must increase Japanese insecurity. The regionalization of conflict and the regional segmentation of economies will open an important door for the United States: the manipulation of Japan's oil supply could well end the challenge that Japanese exports pose to the U.S.

One of the causes of the breakup of the American alliance system will be the inequality of the relationship. Previously, U.S. power was balanced by Soviet power and the threat of switched alliances kept the U.S. in check. Without the Soviet Union, the ability of the U.S. to use its politico-military power to impose unfavorable trade relations on allies—such as Japan—will become the fear factor governing the functioning of the international economic and political system. The Persian Gulf and Middle East will be the center of that fear.

ASIA AFTER THE COLD WAR

In Europe, the post-Cold War world can already be seen. The re-unification of Germany, the collapse of the Warsaw Pact, the re-emergence of Eastern European nationalism are signposts to the future. In the Middle East the rise of Iraq's regional imperialism matching itself against America's global power are signs of a new era. In Asia—increasingly the world's center of gravity in terms of population and economic clout—the end of the Cold War has been felt only slightly. This is not because the Soviets remain an aggressive power in the region, but because neither of the two great Asian players, China and Japan, has yet chosen to move beyond its Cold War role. In a way, Japan's reluctance is understandable. The Cold War was a time of security for Japan; the post-Cold War world promises to increase insecurity. China, on the other hand, has been a less readable, more ambiguous player.

For China, the victory of the Communists over the Chinese Nationalists had two effects. First, for the first time since the nineteenth century, China was governed by a single state that controlled the full extent of Chinese territory. Second, ideological affinities caused newly united China to become an apparent extension of the Soviet Union. The perception that China was merely a puppet of the Soviets was reinforced during the Korean War, when Chinese troops were decimated in a conflict of which the Soviet Union was the only clear beneficiary.

The alliance with the Soviets collapsed because neither nation, regardless of ideology, could tolerate the presence of the other in Asia. The Soviets feared Chinese designs on vulnerable Siberia. The Chinese feared Soviet designs on Manchuria. The traditional beneficiary of this tension was Japan, which had used the Russo-Chinese split to secure its own security zone in the region, defeating both China and Russia in war, and then dominating northeastern China. After World War II, the U.S. replaced Japan in this role. It was now U.S., not Japanese, forces that occupied the southern Korean peninsula, invading via Japan. But the U.S. was less successful than Japan had been in this policy, in large part because the Americans first began their policy during the rare period of Sino-Soviet alliance, and because, during the entire period of the Cold War, the Chinese had a powerful central government.

The same forces that destroyed European communism are present in China, suppressed at Tiananmen Square. It is unclear how permanent that suppression is. It is also unclear whether the triumph of these forces would lead to the creation of a modern industrial democracy, unified and ruled from Beijing, or whether it would lead to the dissolution of the unitary Chinese state.

The ability of the Communists to impose a unitary state in China depended on the coinciding of a number of factors. First, the collapse of the British and other empires meant that the forces they had created abated; powerless vestiges like Hong Kong and Macao were merely symbols of European decline. Second, the destruction of Japanese power meant that the force pulling Manchuria away from China had collapsed. Finally, neither of the new imperial powers, the Soviet Union or the United States, had economic interests in China during the first part of the Cold War. Each had a politico-military interest instead. From 1948 until the mid-1960s, the Soviets supported a unified China as an anti-American force. After 1972, the United States supported a unified China as a counterweight to Soviet power. Thus, at no time were both imperial powers interested in dismembering China, and therefore, a united China survived.

The exclusively politico-military perspective has passed with the Cold War. The newly emergent regional powers, Japan chief among them, are trading states, driven by the traditional hunger for markets and resources. The United States as well has become much more vulnerable economically, even as its military power has soared. Thus, the reemergence of economic competition and the collapse of Soviet global power—but its retention as a powerful regional force with profound economic needs—suddenly leaves China vulnerable to the same forces that tore it apart in the nineteenth and early twentieth centuries. American, European, and Japanese foraging for markets must inevitably bring the great trading states to China again, looking to do business, and the political implications of their arrival are fraught with dangers for China.

Looking at the problem from Beijing's standpoint—since some parts of China might well benefit from freedom from central authority and linkage with a prosperous foreign power—China must choose among a limited set of options:

1. Remain neutral and withdrawn from Asian politics.
2. Form a new relationship with the Soviet Union.
3. Form a primary relationship with a noncontinental power, such as Japan.
4. Form a primary relationship with an intercontinental power, such as the United States.

It is difficult for China to remain isolated. If it fails to modernize its industry, China's military vulnerability might increase to a point where it would no longer even have the force to maintain internal controls. China cannot modernize without foreign economic relations. Moreover, in a world where export markets are at a premium, the outside pressure on China to enter into trade relations would be enormous. Thus, withdrawal from the international economic system, in the face of the unrest represented by the democratic movement, would be possible only with the absolute loyalty of the People's Liberation Army. But since the PLA has been the primary force pressing for modernization—precisely because it needs modernization in order to remain an effective military force—this option collapses because of its own internal illogic.

The creation of a new Sino-Soviet bloc could be attractive to both, since at this point neither needs to fear the aggressive designs of the other. The problem is that such a relationship might secure their long frontier, but would have no effect at all on the underlying problems of either country, which is economic and not geopolitical. A Sino-Soviet alliance would be an alliance of paupers who need to go begging to the same benefactors. That is not a stable foundation at all.

Thus, the Chinese must choose between their last two options: the Japanese or the Americans. Each choice has its advantage. The Japanese have more investment capital. The Americans are less likely to seek geopolitical advantage from the relationship. Japan's interest would be geopolitical in addition to economic; Japan would seek to secure its security zone, including Manchuria and Korea, and would inevitably focus its economic activity in that region in order to secure political as well as economic ends.

Since China could not resist the lure of Japanese economic relations, it would undoubtedly seek a counterweight in an American political and economic presence and would undoubtedly seek economic relations with a unified or fragmented Europe. One can easily imagine the creation of coastal free-trade zones in Shanghai and Canton and the continuation of British Hong Kong, as China sought to gain maximum advantage from such economic relations while playing the U.S. and Japan off against each other politically.

The problem would, of course, be containing the competition. U.S.–Japanese rivalry in particular would create centrifugal forces. Whether the Beijing government would be strong enough to control the forces struggling for regional supremacy in China is doubtful. China's failure to do this in the nineteenth century is not a good precedent for the Chinese. In some ways, the refragmentation of China is the most likely outcome. Regionalization of China would merely create another regional economic bloc, to be dominated by some major regional power. Obviously, the Japanese come to mind first.

In considering the Asian strategic picture, it is vital not to neglect India. Emerging from the comforting umbrella of its Soviet relationship and secure against Chinese encroachments, India is a likely claimant for regional power in South Asia, between Iran and Indochina. Perhaps its greatest promise is as a naval power in the Indian Ocean. In response to the massive U.S. intrusion into the Indian Ocean during the 1980s, India has been systematically and dramatically increasing its naval capacity, until it is today a substantial naval power. Its huge army and technologically sophisticated air force and aircraft-manufacturing facilities—constructed with Soviet assistance

—along with its nuclear capability, make India a power able to defend itself, and to project its power throughout the Indian Ocean basin. Thus, the emergence of India is likely. It may well become the key element of the Asian and perhaps Middle Eastern strategic environments.[7]

India's role becomes particularly significant because it has the potential to control the flow of material from the Persian Gulf and other Indian Ocean Rim countries to the Straits of Malacca. Particularly in the event that the U.S. should choose to withdraw from Diego Garcia and the Indian Ocean, India would suddenly emerge in control of the Hormuz–Malacca line, the key to Japanese import security.

Control of the Indian Ocean basin has an enormous effect on the economic life of the Pacific basin. As the level of industrialization in the Pacific basin increases, there will be a decline in the relative importance, to these countries, of mineral production and export of raw materials. The Indian Ocean will therefore become an alternative source of raw materials, and a doubly significant region. Should that happen, India's significance as a regional power might serve to attract a great deal of attention, some countries looking for alliance, others seeking to undermine Indian power.

Like China, India has a problem with centralization. Before the British, India was a divided mass of national, religious, and political groupings. All of those forces remain, and there is no assurance that India will be able to contain the varied claimants for independence. There are several foreign forces that would be pleased to aid in this process. Aside from Islamic forces, the United States, which is being challenged by India for control of the Indian Ocean, would not be displeased to see India collapse. China, as well, which fears Indian designs on Tibet, would be pleased to see it collapse.

The Soviets have been the most committed to a strong India as a counterweight to the U.S. The U.S. must anticipate a similar alignment with Japan, should Japan decide that the U.S. might interfere with its flow of supplies in the Indian Ocean. The Indian and Japanese economies fit in several ways: India exports several important commodities needed by Japan and could well serve as a lucrative market for Japanese exports and as a target of Japanese investment. Moreover, an Indian navy, financed by Japanese aid and investment, could become an important instrument in a Japanese alliance system, which would not have much reason to threaten Japanese interests. A Japanese navy east of Singapore and an Indian navy west of it might well become the naval configuration of the twenty-first century, one that the U.S. would be particularly hard-pressed to cope with.

The two other native challengers for Indian Ocean domination are South Africa and Australia. South Africa, however, with its land warfare problems, is unlikely to develop a blue-water navy capable of challenging India in the northern Indian Ocean. Nor does South Africa have trade or security problems that would warrant an extensive intrusion.

Australia, on the other hand, has both a naval tradition and some interest in patrolling the region. Australia has two concerns. One is the export of raw materials from its west coast through Indonesian waters or through the Straits of Malacca. To date, these have been secured areas. Australia has defined its interests in the region as reaching to the Cocos Islands in the Indian Ocean.[8] This would provide Australia with a north–south patrol area sufficient to guarantee movement of shipping to the Lombok and Malaccan straits, but no force-projection capability toward the northwest and the Persian Gulf. It is difficult to imagine the circumstances under which Australia, by itself, would have the need or ability to undertake the task of sea-lane control in the Indian Ocean.

Indonesia is a more direct threat to Australia. The immediate flash point between the two countries is New Guinea. Although nominally independent, New Guinea has been an effective protectorate of Australia. It is also an area rich in natural resources, which, at higher commodity prices, would be attractive to both Australia and Indonesia. Indeed, since independence, Indonesia has been quite aggressive in this area and a good deal of Australian strategic thinking has focused on the Indonesian problem.

The tension between Australia and Indonesia over New Guinea is part of a broader strategic opposition between the two countries. Indonesia's population is over 175 million; Australia's is about 16 million. If population were a sufficient factor, Indonesia might well be the most powerful nation in Southeast Asia. But obviously, population by itself is not sufficient. Far more important is naval capability, particularly for an archipelago such as Indonesia.

The potential Indonesian naval capability depends on its industrial capacity. With even a minor naval capability, Indonesia would be in a position to close off the southeast entrance to the Malaccan strait, an action that would effectively seal off the Indian Ocean from the Pacific. Indonesia's motive in this might be twofold. First, it would place Indonesia in a tremendously powerful political position vis-à-vis those Pacific powers that depend on imports from that region. Economically, such an action would raise the price of petroleum in the Pacific dramatically, thereby increasing the value of Sumatran oil.

In a circumstance where an outside navy, the American, both controls the waterways and has an interest in keeping those lanes open, Indonesia clearly lacks a naval force capable of carrying out the closure mission. But should Indonesia increase the size of its navy, or should the regionalization of conflicts cause the United States to become indifferent to the straits, or should the U.S. actually wish to see the straits closed in order to gain advantage against Japan or some other sea-lane-dependent Pacific power, then Indonesia would find itself in a powerful position.

There would be two ways to assure Indonesia's benign inclinations. The first would be political. For any nation interested in Indonesian trade, good relations would be imperative. In the face of the Soviet threat and in the wake of Sukarno's fall, Indonesia was firmly in the Western camp. However, since that term no longer has any substantial meaning, Indonesia's position as an international player must be redefined in terms of the new, regional issues dominating international affairs.

Aside from good relations with Indonesia, the other need for any Malaccan-dependent nation is a strong military presence in the region, primarily a naval presence. Obviously, the key to maintaining such a presence today, as always, is Singapore. Aside from being an extraordinarily useful port facility, Singapore is an economic power and a substantial regional military power. Its Israeli-trained armed forces are sufficient both to maintain internal security for Singapore and to deter aggression from its former countrymen in Malaysia.[9]

For any outside power that wishes to control the flow of material through Malacca, two elements must be the foundation of its foreign policy. The first: it must be able to position overwhelming naval force in Singapore, in order to discourage Indonesia or any other indigenous power from seeking to usurp control. Second, as a highly desirable, if not absolutely essential, supplement to a controlled naval presence, good relations with Indonesia are necessary. With these two elements, Malacca is secure; without them, it can be closed. With only one, it is a competition, a new Cold War.

The matter is complicated by fundamentally different interests among the regional players. Indonesia is interested in capital for modernization and regional influence on the order of its population. None of its neighbors, particularly Singapore and Australia, are eager to see this occur. Quite the contrary, both see a growth in Indonesian power as a threat to their security.

Thus, creating a coalition that includes both Indonesia and Singapore, let alone Australia, is difficult to imagine. A country like Japan, which also competes with Singapore for export markets, might be hard-pressed to forge a satisfactory relationship with them. Any growth in Indonesian power would force Australia to take steps not only to ensure the security of New Guinea and the Solomon Islands, and its access to Malacca and Lombok. Further, Indonesia is a competitor with Australia in the export of raw materials.

The United States has maintained good relations with Indonesia,

Singapore, and Australia because Suharto, unlike Sukarno, has consciously chosen to forego a more aggressive stand. The coalition exists because of the clumsiness of both the Soviets and the People's Republic of China in their attempts to sway and subvert Indonesia. A key element was the division of labor between the U.S., which maintained political influence, and Japan, which maintained economic influence. Should the U.S.–Japanese relationship deteriorate, it is obvious that the division of labor will also collapse. Indonesia's quiescence cannot be permanent. Neither the Soviet Union nor the People's Republic of China was, after 1965, in a position to manipulate Indonesia, to induce it to adopt a more or less aggressive position. But in any competition between the U.S. and Japan, both keenly interested in the Malaccan straits, the quickening of a more aggressive Indonesian stance could prove critical.

The reshuffling of Asian and Oceanic interests could well produce an alliance between three great regional powers: Japan, Indonesia, and India. The economic fit is clear, as is the strategic. Japan needs to secure the Straits of Malacca and Lombok, controlled by Indonesia. It also needs to secure the sea-lanes to Hormuz. A powerful Indian Navy, a strong Singapore, and a Japan whose military power is the equal of its economic power would be a powerful, mutually beneficial relationship. It would force an opposing coalition built around Australia and the U.S. The outcome would be a new Asian Cold War, with global implications and unlimited potential for war.

CONCLUSION

Thus, there are two processes under way. First, there is the reemergence of international economic issues as part of the political equation. The segregation of these issues in a strange, nonpolitical warp is at an end. Men fought over economic issues in the past and they will do so again. Economics is about how men make livings and how well they live. These are life-and-death issues quite as much as are political issues. The easy peace of the world's free-trade regime, which depended so much on the American alliance system, cannot continue. The logic of the alliance system is gone and with it the logic of free trade. Nations that are losers in trade wars will find too much political advantage in cutting themselves off from disadvantaged trade relationships. The emergence of regional trading blocs, on the order of Europe in 1992, is now a reality, and with it, the regionalization of economic life.

The second process, is the reemergence of regional political powers as independent forces. The continued willingness of the U.S. to resist these emergent forces, as in Kuwait, depends on the saliency of the threat to American interests. The Liberian civil war is a case in point. In the Belgian Congo in 1960, or in Angola in 1975, the U.S. was eager to intervene, fearing a Soviet victory. In 1990, while Liberia was being ripped apart in a civil war, the U.S. stood by and watched. The Soviets had no hand in the conflict.

The reemergence of economic issues and of regional powers poses a new challenge to the United States. If the U.S. chooses not to impose hegemony on the entire eastern hemisphere, not to get involved in every political crisis facing the world, then what will be the American role? What exactly are the new American interests? What exactly is the relationship of the world's only global superpower to an increasingly fragmented and unruly world?

1. Giovani Agnelli, "The Europe of 1992," *Foreign Affairs*, Fall 1989, p. 63.
2. Norman Angell, *The Great Illusion* (New York, 1910), p. 64.
3. Edson W. Spencer, "Japan as Competitor," *Foreign Policy*, March 1990, pp. 167–168.
4. Ibid.
5. For a thorough discussion of the incipient post-Cold War conflicts in Europe, see John Mearsheimer, "The End of the Cold War," *Atlantic Monthly*, August 1990.
6. United Nations, *UNCTAD Commodity Yearbook* (New York, 1989). U.S. Department of Energy, *World Oil* (Washington, D.C., 1989).
7. For a discussion of the emerging military power of India, see "Country Survey: India," *Jane's Defence Weekly*, May 26, 1990.
8. "Australia's Defence Capabilities: The Dibb Review," *Australian Foreign Affairs Review*, June 1986, p. 493.
9. On the Singapore Defense Forces, see H.M.F. Howarth, "Singapore's Armed Forces and Defense Industry," *International Defense Review*, 16:11 (1983), pp. 1565–1571.

9

America's Strategic Options: Coping With Empire

At the end of any great stuggle, the victor finds himself in an awkward position. His mind has been set on the struggle for so long and with such intensity that the collapse of his opponent leaves him startled and at a loss. Sometimes a victor is poised in such a way that he looks absurd to those whose memories include the victory, but not the struggle. At other times, the awkward pose of victory over one enemy is an invitation to attack by another. The victor can respond in different ways. Sometimes, he is so relieved to find the strife at an end that he imagines the world will now be a perfect place, without pain or danger. Sometimes he cannot accept that the conflict is over. He continues to insist that his fallen foe remains a danger, merely engaged in a devious ploy. Rarest of all, but most praiseworthy, is the victor who ends the war with his wits about him, understands that what is past is past, and prepares to meet new foes calmly, neither wishing for more conflict nor pretending that conflict has ceased for all time. The prudent victor ends by discarding those things necessary for the last victory and donning those things necessary for the next.

The end of the Cold War has left America at loose ends. America knew its place when the Soviets threatened to bury it. For over forty years the U.S. has, with reason, been obsessed with the Russian question. Now, the American strategy has worked. The painstaking crafting of the system of alliances that surrounded the Soviet Union did enclose the Soviets effectively. The Soviet's intrusions behind the frontline states, in the Third World, have failed because the Soviet system has failed. In the end, the Soviets had nothing to offer the world but equalized misery. America has won.

The current allocation of U.S. forces in the world shows the traditional disorder of the victor. The U.S. is still deployed to contain the Soviet Union, much as, at the end of World War II, the U.S. was still in a position to make war on Japan and Germany. The problem now, as in 1945, is to define American interests and the American mission.

FRIENDS AND ENEMIES, WAR AND PEACE IN THE NEW WORLD ORDER

It is said that a caged tiger, suddenly freed, will continue to pace as though the confining bars were still there. The United States, freed from its struggle with the Soviet Union, finds it almost impossible to put that struggle aside. Admiral William J. Crowe, while still chairman of the Joint Chiefs of Staff, said:

> Certainly, recent military initiatives by Gorbachev are encouraging. Yet I find more continuities than changes in the essential elements of Soviet military power. Moreover, we have yet to see a larger commitment of resources to consumer goods and services. Until this happens, the future of perestroika and glasnost remains cloudy.[1]

Crowe's position was not unreasonable. On paper, the Red Army has lost little of its strength. But the political realities in eastern Europe, then and now, make the force needed to threaten western Europe enormously greater. In order to attack western Europe, the Soviets would now have to secure a line of supply through the hostile territory of Poland and Czechoslovakia. Thus, a quantitative comparison of U.S. and Soviet forces without taking political realities into account will inflate Soviet power beyond recognition.

If we cannot admit that we have lost our enemy, it is even more difficult to imagine that we might lose our friends. The system of relationships the United States built up during the Cold War was predicated on that war. As the Cold War ends, the rationale for those relationships ends too. Yet, one of the ongoing premises has been that a stable, post–Cold War order can be constructed based on a system of alliances that fought the Cold War. It is as if you expected a skyscraper to continue standing after its foundation has crumbled, or that you thought that you could quickly invent a new foundation and slip it into place without anyone noticing.

MAP 9-1. Worldwide U.S. Force Deployment, 1987.

U.S./Western Hemisphere
1 Airborne Division
1 Air Assault Division
4 Armored Divisions
6 Mechanized Infantry Divisions
6 Infantry Divisions
4 Light Infantry Divisions
28 Combat
  Brigades

**Western Europe
(NATO)**
  2 Mechanized
    Divisions
  2 Armored Divisions
546 Fighter/Attack
    Aircraft

Mid–East Force
1 Command Ship
4 Surface
  Combatants

**Northeast Asia/
Western Pacific**
  2 Infantry
    Divisions
215 Fighter/Attack
    Aircraft
  1 Marine
    Amphibious
    Force

**Indian Ocean
Task Force**
1 Carrier Battle
  Group
  (Normally
  provided
  by Pacific
  Fleet)

**Pacific Command
East Pacific
(3rd Fleet)**
  4 Aircraft Carriers
  5 Helicopter
    Carriers
  1 Battleship
  21 Destroyers
  43 Frigates
  36 Attack
    Submarines
  20 Amphibious
    Ships
230 Fighter/Attack
    Aircraft

**Atlantic Command
North Atlantic
(2nd Fleet)**
  5 Aircraft Carriers
  5 Helicopter Carriers
  1 Battleship
  9 Cruisers
  35 Destroyers
  50 Frigates
  49 Attack Submarines
  18 Amphibious Ships
290 Fighter/Attack
    Aircraft

**Mediterranean
(6th Fleet)**
  2 Aircraft Carriers
  1 Helicopter
    Carrier
  3 Cruisers
  5 Destroyers
  6 Frigates
  6 Attack
    Submarines
  4 Amphibious
    Ships
115 Fighter/
    Attack Aircraft

**Pacific Command
West Pacific (7th Fleet)**
  2 Aircraft Carriers
  1 Helicopter Carrier
  5 Cruisers
  8 Destroyers
  7 Frigates
  8 Attack Submarines
  5 Amphibious Ships
115 Fighter/Attack Aircraft

(Source: compiled from numerous private and public sources)

A leading example of this thinking is the idea that NATO, invented to contain the Soviet Union, can serve as a framework for European security arrangements after the end of the Cold War. Behind this idea is the assumption that Germany's relationship with Europe— limited as it was by its division, occupation, and fear of the Soviet Union—will remain the same after unification and the collapse of Soviet power. Germany is very different after unification, and the idea that NATO will limit and gentle a unified Germany, unafraid of Russia, is more than a little farfetched. A British minister's view that the unification plan of 1992 was nothing but "a German plot" is the tip of the iceberg representing European fear of Germany and its now unleashed ambitions.[2]

Robert D. Hormats, an official of Goldman Sachs International and a former Assistant Secretary of State, typified this determinedly optimistic point of view in *Foreign Affairs*:

There is likely to be closer nuclear cooperation between Britain and France, as well as expanded coordination between their nuclear force planners and the commanders of conventional forces in West Germany. Over time this should give the Germans greater confidence in the credibility of these deterrents as a supplement to those of the United States. Improvements in intra-west European military cooperation will also demonstrate to Americans that Europeans are doing more for themselves. But at the end of this century there will still be no alternative to an American nuclear guarantee and troop presence in Europe.[3]

Who is being deterred? Why would Germany be comforted to see France and Britain cooperating on nuclear strategy and excluding Germany? Why is there no alternative to an American military presence? Whom are the troops guarding, and against what? Hormats' position is that the end of the Cold War need not have a significant effect on Cold War institutions and relationships. This comfortable, foreign-policy-establishment line is, of course, an inevitable failure of imagination and not a serious suggestion for the architecture of international relationships.

In America's relation to Japan, the same wishful thinking abounds on both sides. The U.S.–Japanese alliance was forged by the Soviet threat. American officials and Japanese have worked together to create the impression that the Soviet threat has not subsided in the Pacific. Admiral Huntington Hardesty, Commander in Chief, Pacific (CINCPAC), and General Louis Menetrey, Commander, U.S. Forces Korea, in testifying before the Senate Armed Services Committee in June 1989, discussed U.S. strategy in the Pacific without once discussing any possible danger other than the Soviet threat.[4] Only when questioned by Republican Senator John Warner did Admiral Hardesty consider other threats:

> *Senator Warner*: . . . what is the sentiment in the Pacific Rim for Japan increasing its military forces and its military budget?
>
> *Admiral Hardesty*: Well, there is some concern among our Pacific Rim neighbors that a significant increase in the Japanese self-defense budget would be bothersome to our neighbors. They have a memory of World War II obviously. They would not like to see Japan develop a power projection capability.
>   We have asked Japan in our security relationship to develop the capability to defend their sea lanes of communications out to a thousand miles and to provide for the defense of Japan. . . .[5]

Japan's neighbors are clearly aware of the threat it might again pose. The Americans, however, concerned about the Soviet threat, want Japan to assume more and more of the burden of defending the region. But why are the Americans concerned about a Soviet threat? It is a matter of the tiger and the cage. The bars are gone, but America is still pacing.

The Japanese are as tied to the past as are the Americans. Japan's *White Paper on Defense* for 1989 stated: "Soviet military power in the Far East has been continuously increasing and still poses a serious threat, not only to Japan but to other Far Eastern Countries." It further claimed that Gorbachev's statement of May 1989 that 120,000 troops, twelve divisions, eleven air force regiments, and sixteen warships would be withdrawn from the Far East was "vague and ambiguous."[6] It is odd that such a clear shift in policy by the Soviets would meet with *increased* suspicion and hostility, far greater than anything expressed by Prime Minister Yoshida during the early 1950s at the height of Stalinism and the Cold War.

Neither the U.S. nor Japan actually believes that there is any longer a possibility of a Soviet attack in the region. Rather, as long as both sides can pretend there is a Soviet threat, neither needs to fear that the other will begin reevaluating their relationship. Obviously this willful self-delusion cannot continue for very long. Reality will creep in and both sides will have to construct a new relationship. It is fear of the consequences of that new relationship that has caused both governments to proceed with the charade of the increased Soviet Far Eastern threat.

Extraordinarily, prudent observers have acted as if the U.S.–Japanese alliance can continue without the glue of the Soviet threat:

> In every dimension of Japan's strategic security—regional, global and nuclear—its alliance with the United States will play an important role. The test of any military alliance comes when a new contingency requires a common response. The Japanese-American alliance is potentially more flexible than NATO because, as a multilateral alliance, NATO requires consensus among many member states and must overcome the resistance of its own bureaucracy.[7]

One might think that, given the inertia of complex bureaucracies, NATO's bureaucracy would hold the alliance together even more firmly. The assurance that with the dissolution of the Soviet military threat U.S.–Japanese relations will continue without fundamental shifts is the issue that we must examine with care. If true, the world we are entering will be peaceful and secure. If not, the world will be full of new dangers and even terrors.

AMERICAN POWER AND EURASIA: THE POLITICO-MILITARY PROBLEM

It is useful to begin by recalling the four basic strategic interests of the United States, as described in Chapter 1:

1. That the U.S. Army should completely dominate North America.
2. That no power or group of powers should exist in the western hemisphere capable of challenging U.S. hegemony.
3. That the U.S. Navy should be able to keep eastern hemispheric powers out of the western hemisphere, by controlling the North Atlantic and eastern Pacific Oceans.
4. That no eastern hemispheric power should be able to challenge U.S. domination of the oceans, having their energies diverted by land threats.

The end of the Cold War finds the United States having achieved all four of its goals.

The most precarious and difficult goal of U.S. strategy is the fourth. The manipulation of the balance of power in Eurasia is difficult because U.S. forces shrink to relative insignificance when inserted onto the Eurasian mainland. During each of the two Asian wars fought since the Cold War began, the United States found itself in unsustainable wars of attrition. In Korea, the American confrontation with China's People's Liberation Army imposed casualty levels so high that the U.S. abandoned the goal of conquering the entire Korean Peninsula, in spite of the fact that its casualties were much lower than those of the PLA. In Vietnam, the U.S. strategy was to wear down the North Vietnamese Army by imposing unacceptable kill ratios using superior U.S. mobility and firepower. The United States found, however, that it could never achieve a politically disabling ratio. Quite the contrary, the U.S. Army found that even favorable ratios of 10:1 were not sustainable politically when it meant that 200–300 Americans were dying each week, even compared to 2,000–3,000 North Vietnamese Army dead.

Forces that are huge in the western hemisphere, or on the island peripheries of Eurasia, become insignificant on the mainland. This was the problem confronted by the U.S. in 1990, during the Iraqi invasion of Kuwait. Iraq, a nation of 16 million, of whom 3.5 million are Kurds, was able to field a land army of 600,000 men. Even assuming that each Iraqi soldier had a combat capability one-quarter that of American troops, mere equivalency would require the presence of 150,000 American ground troops, while superiority would require at least twice that number. The initial deployment of 70,000 ground troops posed a paradox: it required an enormous effort on the part of the United States, yet did not by itself pose a major threat to Iraq. Even later expansions were so burdened by support troops that U.S. ground forces alone could not guarantee decisive superiority over Iraqi defenders.

The United States has always understood the weakness of Eurasian intrusions, ever since MacArthur's famous warning against engaging in land wars on the mainland of Asia. It has tried to compensate for it by "force multipliers," technical aids that increase the lethality, mobility, and invulnerability of American troops. The most important force multiplier is air power. Operating both as direct ground support and as strategic support against enemy logistics and economic facilities, air power was designed to compensate for ground weakness at a relatively low manpower cost. As was seen in Vietnam, this strategy, while useful, was no compensation for ground forces able to sustain high casualty rates.

The unwillingness of the U.S. to sustain high casualty rates in Eurasia is extremely rational. The low population of North America compared to Eurasia makes it impossible to engage in extended attritional warfare in Eurasia, even on the most favorable terms. Further, the U.S. has to maintain large manpower pools for manufacturing and transporting material, owing to its distance from the battlefield. Even at full mobilization during World War II, the U.S. had to devote most of its forces to logistical support and defense of lines of supply.

Thus, U.S. strategy in Eurasia must be to shift the casualty burden to allies. In World War I, the U.S. shifted the primary burden to the Anglo-French. In World War II, the primary casualty burden was borne by the Soviet Union. In Vietnam, the ARVN forces bore the casualty burden. The U.S. contribution was minimal ground and naval forces to protect the lines of supply moving U.S.-manufactured materiel to the battlefield.

In this strategy, the key player is the United States Navy. The Navy performs a dual function. Defensively, its task is to deny other navies access to the oceans. Offensively, its purpose is to fight its way through so as to land ground forces in Eurasia in order to block the hegemonistic ambitions of any Eurasian power.

The key to fighting the European war was the carrier battle group. In post-World War II strategic thinking, the most important mission of the United States in the event of a European war would be to keep the sea- and air-lanes between the United States and Western Europe open against Soviet submarine and air threat. These lanes would permit the U.S. to rush men and materiel to Germany, reinforcing the four divisions the U.S. kept on duty there at all times and bolstering the air defenses as well. If the North Atlantic were closed and Western Europe cut off from the U.S., superior Soviet manpower would be expected to overwhelm the defenders. Thus, the Battle of Europe, like the Battle of Britain before it, would be fought in the North Atlantic.

The American expectation was that these sea-lanes would be threat-

MAP 9-2. Defending the GIUK (Greenland Iceland United Kingdom Gap).

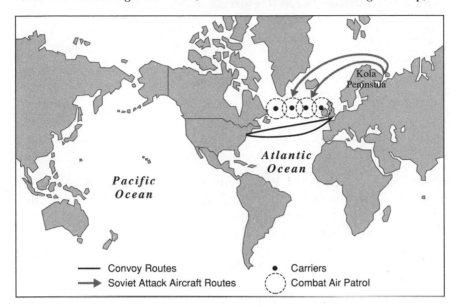

ened in two ways: submarines and aircraft. Both would come into the North Atlantic through the gap between Greenland, Iceland, and the United Kingdom (the GIUK gap) from the Soviet Union's Kola Peninsula. The aircraft would be particularly dangerous, since, firing long-range antiship missiles, they could play havoc with the convoys taking the shortest route to Western Europe without coming into range of the convoy's antiaircraft systems.

The first line of defense, obviously, would be fighter aircraft based in Iceland and in Norway. But the expectation was that Soviet air attack would make these bases unusable in short order. Indeed, it was conceivable that both the coast of Norway and Iceland would be occupied by Soviet forces. Thus, the ultimate defense against both air attacks and submarine attacks had to come from naval forces.

The distribution of U.S. Navy forces in the event of a general war with the Soviet Union would appear as indicated in Table 9-1.

In the Atlantic, the carrier battle groups would be deployed north of the line of convoys moving from eastern seaboard ports to Western Europe. Assuming that the F-14 aircraft on each carrier have an effective combat radius of 300 miles, four carrier battle groups would provide forward, overlapping coverage for about 2,000 miles, roughly the distance between Newfoundland and Europe. The five

TABLE 9-1. Wartime Force Requirements.[8]

	CARRIER GROUPS	BATTLESHIP GROUPS
Second Fleet, Atlantic	4	1
Sixth Fleet, Mediterranean	4	1
Seventh Fleet, Western Pacific Indian Ocean	5	2

carrier battle groups in the Pacific and Indian Ocean would provide coverage of the Sea of Japan, as well as provide three carrier battle groups to secure the sea routes for Persian Gulf oil. Similarly, the Sixth Fleet would help close the Bosphorous to Soviet traffic, as well as defend the Suez Canal. There is, of course, a secret surplus built into these figures, particularly in the Mediterranean. The reason for this surplus is simple: several of the Atlantic aircraft carriers would be sunk during intense combat operations, and there must be a reserve built into all naval calculations. Thirteen to fourteen carriers would be needed in order to defend the Atlantic, maintain control of the other oceans, and replace losses.

The development of the postwar navy around the carrier task force had another purpose: the projection of air power ashore in Eurasia. Throughout the Cold War, the U.S. used the aircraft carrier as a means of projecting American power ashore and as a means for gaining political leverage without great military exertion.

Aircraft carriers are formidable sea-lane control systems. Each aircraft carrier has:

TABLE 9-2. Aircraft Aboard U.S. Aircraft Carriers.

TYPE	MISSION	NUMBER
F-14	Air superiority	24
FA-18	Light attack	24
A-6	Medium attack	12
S-3	Antisubmarine	10
SH-3	Air search (helicopter)	8
RA-5C	Reconaissance	3
EA-6B	Electronic warfare	4
KA-6	Air refueling tanker	4
E-2	Early warning	4

(Source: *Jane's Fighting Ships*)

Of the ninety-three aircraft on board a carrier, only thirty-six, the A-6s and FA-18s, are suited to a ground-attack mode. Since each A-6 can carry 9 tons of weapons, and each FA-18 can carry 8.5 tons, the total ground attack tonnage a carrier can deliver is 312, assuming that all aircraft are launched simultaneously. Assuming no losses and two sorties a day, a carrier can deliver 614 tons of ordnance per day. An aircraft carrier battle group contains one cruiser, two destroyers, an attack submarine, and several support vessels. The number of men involved will approach 10,000. Including shore-stationed support personnel, the number assigned to a carrier battle group can add up to tens of thousands. The ability to deliver a little over 600 tons a day, under ideal circumstances, utilizing over 10,000 men in the effort, is not cost effective. When the U.S. chose to bomb Libya, two carrier task forces were insufficient for the mission; Air Force F-111 aircraft based in Britain had to supplement the strike.

During World War II attacks on Japan, B-29 bombers, stripped of armament, delivered seven tons of ordnance per sortie. Based on Tinian Island in the Marianas, and capable of long-range flight, they did not require the costly use of carriers to carry out their mission. A 300-flight sortie, involving fewer than 5,000 men in flight and ground crews, could deliver 2,100 tons of ordnance in a day. A present-day carrier, with about 6,600 men aboard, can deliver a maximum of 614 tons, less than one-third the World War II daily attack. The inescapable fact is that for strategic bombardment, there remains no substitute for ground-based aircraft. But for sea control, given the continued ability to counter the threat of incoming missiles, the aircraft carrier still reigns supreme.

The paradox of the carrier battle group parallels the paradox of American foreign and military policy in general. The aircraft carrier is a superb sea-control weapon, because at sea the absolute quantity of the threat is invariably less than the carrier can put aloft. Twenty-four F-14 aircraft could certainly match an incoming force of seventy-two Soviet Backfire bombers. As soon as this number of F-14s enters Eurasia, the quantity of force they bring to bear shrinks to insignificance.

Throughout the Cold War, the United States sought to solve the problem of its insufficiency in Eurasia. The United States has twenty-eight army divisions, including Reserve and National Guard units that can be fully mobilized in an emergency. This force is far greater than needed to control the western hemisphere, yet completely insufficient to operate in the eastern hemisphere without massive force multipliers. Air power has always been seen as the Army's force multiplier.

The United States could never construct any large-scale manpower-intensive units, since it has to maintain both a huge industrial base and a complex and extended logistical system in order to operate. The twenty-eight divisions fielded by the U.S. Army, were as large a force as the U.S. could afford, given its industrial and logistics needs. Air power, and indeed, tactical nuclear capability, were all designed to compensate, however imperfectly, for the basic manpower shortage experienced by the U.S.

Thus, the starting principle of all American strategic thinking was that, given the diversion of manpower necessary to control the sea, maintain the logistical system, and above all, mass produce war materiel, U.S. forces could never be sufficient to operate in the eastern hemisphere without force multipliers. All U.S. military research and development has focused on this problem, seeking to extract maximum efficiency from existing manpower by means of mobility of forces; timely coordination of command, control, communications, and intelligence (C^3I) activities; and concentrated firepower. The option of not projecting forces into the eastern hemisphere was not available to U.S. planners, as the assumption was that without the guarantee of U.S. action the alliance system would collapse.

There was another defect. Unlike other armies, such as that of Israel, the U.S. Army had to be able to fight in a wide range of environments, from arctic to equatorial desert to jungle. Mastering all those terrains and conditions was difficult. Designing weapon systems capable of fighting in all those environments was impossible. For example, the type of terrain determines the size and weight of the tank that can be used—ground-pressure characteristics, steepness of slope, and so on impose definite limitations. Since the U.S. had one primary mission, defending Western Europe, U.S. equipment tended to be designed for that purpose. The M-1 Abrams tank was designed to fight in the temperate, flat-to-hilly, forested terrain of the north German plain and the central hills of Germany. It was also *capable* of fighting in other terrain, but the type of armored fighting vehicle most suitable for the jungle would be far different from the M-1.

Thus, although the U.S. Army was intended to be a universal fighting machine, it was forced to be far more climate- and terrain-specific than it would have wanted to be. This is in no way a criticism of Army planners. They were given a difficult hand to play, and one might say that, on the whole, they played that hand as well as might be expected. The problem was the multiplicity of the American mission, coupled with the central importance of one specific mission that might never occur: the defense of Europe. Neglecting that would have been catastrophic. Being obsessed with that was reasonable but proved a constant irritation when equipment designed for Germany and men trained to fight there were suddenly deployed in jungles and deserts.

Thus, the U.S. created an extremely efficient Navy, an inherently inefficient Army, and an Air Force charged with compensating for the Army's inadequacy. The results were satisfactory. Ironically and unexpectedly, the process of creating force multipliers for the Army, the arms race that raged from 1950 until 1989, overwhelmed the Soviet economy. Even without that element, U.S. forces were sufficient to dissuade the Soviets from attempting any European adventure. They were also more than sufficient to maintain control of the seas. What they did not achieve was absolute control of Asia's periphery. From Korea to Indochina, U.S. land power proved not quite adequate to the task of suppressing political opposition, even when the force multiplier of the U.S. Air Force was added to the load. The Gulf War is the latest test.

Because of the weakness of its ground forces, the basic American military strategy during the Cold War sought to shift the primary manpower burden away from itself, to its European allies and particularly to the Germans. The U.S. contribution was a modest number of ground forces, substantial air forces, and an overwhelming naval presence to protect the flow of materiel from the United States. The Nixon Doctrine extended this principle of allied responsibility for absorbing casualties from Europe to the entire periphery of the Soviet Union.

The end of the Cold War left the United States only marginally capable of intervening unilaterally in Eurasia. During the Cold War, all interventions were intended to be in concert with allies. The structure of United States forces was intended to permit rapid deployment of U.S. material support into a region and a stiffening military element, primarily naval and air, with ground forces to be used only in extreme emergencies. The U.S. Rapid Deployment Force was intended to be used in conjunction with allied forces, not on its own.

According to the U.S. Department of Defense in 1987, the following forces would be available to the U.S. Central Command in the event of a crisis in the Persian Gulf:

1 Airborne division
1 Airmobile division
1 Mechanized division
1 Infantry division
1 Marine amphibious force (roughly three Marine brigades)
7 Tactical fighter wings (about 500 aircraft)
2 B-52 squadrons
3 Carrier battle groups
1 Surface action group
5 Maritime air patrol (P-3C Orion) squadrons[9]

In particular, it is instructive to consider the total size of this potential intervention relative to Eurasian forces already on the ground.

The main intervention force was to consist of four divisions, with the following major assets:

AIRBORNE DIVISION (82ND)

- 54 M551 Sheridan light tanks
- 84 TOW antitank guided munitions (ATGM) mounted on light, wheeled, unarmored vehicles
- 236 Dragon man-portable ATGM
- 63 Apache attack helicopters with TOW
- 54 105mm towed howitzer cannon

AIRMOBILE DIVISION (101ST)

- 162 TOW
- 243 Dragon ATGM
- 63 Apache attack helicopters with TOW
- 54 105mm SP self-propelled howitzer cannon
- 18 155mm towed howitzer cannon
- 90 UH-60 assault helicopters

MECHANIZED DIVISION (1ST, 4TH, 5TH, OR 24TH)

- 256 M-1 Abrams tanks
- 354 M-2 Bradley armored personnel carriers (APC)
- 170 Armor-mounted TOW
- 280 Dragon ATGM
- 54 155mm SP howitzer cannon
- 12 8-inch SP howitzer cannon

INFANTRY DIVISION (9TH)

- 54 M-1 Abrams tanks
- 59 M-2 Bradley IFV
- 170 TOW, soft-skinned and armor-mounted
- 260 Dragon ATGM
- 54 105mm towed howitzer cannon
- 18 155mm towed howitzer cannon
- 4 8-inch SP howitzer cannon

In addition, there would be one Marine Amphibious Force, consisting of three brigades armed with:

- 159 M-60 tanks
- 90 LAV-25 light armored vehicles

216 TOW, armor- and soft-skinned vehicle-mounted
 72 155mm towed howitzer cannon
 18 155mm SP howitzer cannon
327 Amphibious assault vehicles[10]

This force would comprise about 25 percent of the regular Army's total strength and about 33 percent of the Marine Corps'. Since the Army had committed one division to the defense of Korea and four divisions to Europe, the actual disposable force of the regular U.S. Army, measured in divisions, was eighteen at its highest level in 1988, many dependent on National Guard units. At full mobilization of the National Guard and U.S. Army Reserves, the maximum available force, not taking equipment and training problems into account, would be twenty-eight divisions. The total immediately available force was equivalent to about sixteen divisions, less five divisions committed in Europe and Korea. Thus, the four divisions committed to rapid deployment represents over one-third of the Army's deployable force.

Put simply, deploying the four Army divisions and one Marine division assigned to Central Command represents an extreme exertion on the part of the American military. Any greater exertion would probably require a general mobilization of Reserve and National Guard Units, and perhaps even a draft.

Thus, the immediate question is the impact of such a deployment in Eurasia. The total materiel the U.S. would put ashore under the Defense Department's plan would be:

310 M-1 Abrams heavy tanks
159 M-60 heavy tanks
 54 M-551 reconnaissance vehicles
802 TOW ATGM launchers
162 105mm howitzers
180 155mm howitzers
 16 8-inch howitzers

It is fairly obvious that the United States is incapable of putting a force ashore in Eurasia that would be numerically superior to enemy forces, except with full mobilization of reserves. Thus, the American strategy must be to put ashore materiel that would compensate for the manpower weakness.

Here, as with manpower considerations, the U.S. encounters an imbalance wherever it might go ashore. Consider three conceivable American interventions:

Case 1. A landing against Syrian forces in Lebanon.
Case 2. An intervention in the Persian Gulf against Iraq.
Case 3. An intervention against an Indian invasion of Pakistan.

When examining the ability of the United States to bring its force to bear in mainland Eurasia, the total number of weapons systems it plans to project must be compared to the number of weapons it will encounter. Using the three scenarios above, the numbers are:

TABLE 9-3. Comparison of Major Weapons in U.S. Rapid Deployment Scenarios.

	U.S.	SYRIA	IRAQ	INDIA
Newest heavy tanks	310	1,100	500	2,400
Older heavy tanks	159	3,000	4,500	700
Light tanks	54	—	250	—
Artillery tubes	358	2,700	2,400	NA

(Sources: International Institute for Strategic Studies; *Jane's Defense Weekly*; U.S. Department of Defense)

Taking all tanks together, the U.S. would be at an extreme disadvantage against Syria (8.38 to 1), Iraq (10.66 to 1), and India (6.61 to 1). Similar ratios would exist with artillery. Thus, the huge exertion of an American intervention in Eurasia, unless accompanied by a national commitment on the order of the Korean or Vietnam war, would still leave the U.S. at a tremendous disadvantage.

The U.S. would experience additional problems. First, the point of intervention would be relatively predictable. Any rapid deployment of forces would:

1. Initially, be an amphibious or airborne operation.
2. Require the availability of a port with sufficient off-loading capacity, close enough to the front to be useful but far enough removed to be secure.
3. Need sufficient airfields for dispersed basing, tanks for aviation fuel, and repair facilities.
4. Need airfields with runways long enough for landing C-5 aircraft as well as other jet transports.

With requirements as specific as these, any American intervention would be highly predictable and therefore dangerous for the U.S.

Time is a greater problem than predictability. During the Iraqi crisis, the U.S. Marines were able to move into the Persian Gulf with their older M-60 tanks in about ten days because of their use of prepositioned ships in the Indian Ocean, which were stocked with weapons and materiel for the initial phase of combat. Lightly armed airborne and airmobile divisions had advanced elements in place in about three days, while the full division was in Saudi Arabia in ten days. None of these forces, of course, were sufficient for holding Saudi Arabia. The transfer of advanced M-1 Abrams tanks to Saudi Arabia, part of the 24th Mechanized Division's equipment, did not begin until the end of August 1990, more than three weeks after the initial Marine deployment, and was not completed until October.

The key problem for the U.S. is its need to keep its projection forces in the U.S., in order to permit their availability for East Asian, South Asian, and European contingencies. The distance from the U.S. to the Persian Gulf via the Mediterranean and Suez Canal is 6,000 miles. At about 20 knots, by fast logistic ship, this trip would take about ten days; while at 33 knots, maximum speed, the trip could be done in about seven days. However, the ships can be deployed only with a minimum of ninety-six hours' warning. Therefore, the minimum transfer time, not including loading and unloading, would be about eleven days, and a more reasonable time is about two and a half weeks. The U.S. has eight fast logistic ships in its inventory, and they can together lift one mechanized division at a time.[11]

Since the bulk of armor in the projection force would be in the mechanized division, even the relatively small armored force being projected would not be available for at least three weeks after the first elements intervened. This three-week period of vulnerability is the minimum time, and does not make allowance for breakdowns or miscalculations.

Thus far, it is clear that the quantity of forces the U.S. can use to intervene on mainland Eurasia is dwarfed by the quantity of materiel held by native powers. It is also clear that this intervention is vulnerable, due to predictability and the length of time it takes to intervene. The final problem is the burden of supplying five division equivalents from a distance of 6,000–8,000 miles.

A standard rule of thumb in the U.S. Army is that each individual in combat must receive about 107 pounds of supplies a day. During the first thirty days this is multiplied by 2.4; for the next 120 days by 1.5, in order to build a supply reserve. Thus, each day during the first thirty days of an operation, every soldier must receive about 256.8 pounds of supplies, which declines to 160 pounds per day after that. During periods of combat, the basic amount must be increased by 20 pounds.[12]

Assume an intervention of 180 days, including all of the above forces. Assume that a total of eighteen days is spent in intense combat, and fifty-four days in sustained combat, all taking place after the initial build-up period. The total force would equal about 75,000 ground troops. The total consumption rate of this force would be about:

TABLE 9–4. Consumption Rate of 75,000-Man Ground Force.

	POUNDS PER MAN	TONS PER DAY	DURATION (180 DAYS)
Day 1–30	256.8	9,630	288,900
Day 30+	160.5	6,019	469,482
Combat	180.5	6,789	488,808

(Total consumption for the duration of intervention: 1,247,190 tons.)

Each day, therefore, 6,929 tons of materiel would have to be delivered without interruption. At the very least, without any combat at all, 1,191,750 tons of materiel would be consumed, or 6,621 tons per day. Somewhere between about 6,000 and 7,000 tons of materiel must be delivered without fail daily to U.S. forces.

It should be emphasized that this includes only U.S. ground forces, not the extensive requirements of aircraft fuel and munitions. For example, 100 A-10 aircraft used in attacking tanks would require about 5,520 tons of supply each day, while 100 F-15 fighters would require about 3,000 tons. Thus, assuming a mix of 100 A-10s, 100 F-15s, and 100 F-16s, the daily requirements would rise by about 11,500 tons.[13] Assuming that the U.S. engaged in sustained air operations for 180 days, the minimum requirement for force projection would rise to between 17,500 and 18,500 tons of supply per day. Assuming that fast logistic ships, transport aircraft, and vessels immediately available from the Ready Reserve Force were employed moving men and equipment, the problem facing the Navy would be supplying the quantity of materiel necessary to sustain troops and permit combat. How can the Navy move between 6,500 and 18,500 tons of supplies *per day*, since a trip from the East Coast of the U.S. via the Suez Canal to Southwest Asia would take, at 10 knots, about three weeks, one way?

Assuming a three-week trip with two days in port at either end, and no delays, the U.S. would need a minimum of 300,000 deadweight tons of shipping to merely sustain the projection force, 850,000 tons to do this and permit air operations, and one million tons to permit extensive combat operations. According to a National Defense University Study published in 1988, the U.S. Navy had set itself a goal of one million tons of sealift capacity. This figure would be enough to sustain projection forces at maintenance level and allow for air operations. However, less than half that goal was achieved, or even expected to be achieved, by 1990.[14]

This problem has been readily conceded by the Department of Defense. General H. Norman Schwarzkopf, Commander in Chief, Central Command, with responsibility for force projection to Southwest Asia, testified before Congress: "Currently, Central Command has only a 9,800-short-ton-per-day capability against a 21,000-short-ton-per-day goal."[15] Even this goal is modest. The 9,800-ton goal would satisfy the needs during the buildup phase, as long as combat was avoided. But a 21,000-ton-per-day supply would be only the minimal quantity of material needed in the above scenario.

This is not an easily soluble problem. The cost of such a logistical system would place the U.S. on a nearly perpetual war footing. The strategic goals being pursued do not clearly justify the expense and effort. Thus, the standing force projection capability is woefully short of what is required, even on the most optimistic basis.

It is evident that if a general war occurred, the Navy would have to go to civilian shipping to augment its force. Currently, the U.S. has about 25,576,000 deadweight tons of shipping available, divided among 675 ships.[16] Freighters and bulk cargo vessels suited for carrying dry cargo (as opposed to tankers), made up only 7,987,000 tons, or about 30 percent of the total. About 55 percent of Central Command tonnage requirements would be in dry cargo.[17] The 828,000 tons of minimal dry tonnage demanded would total more than 10 percent of the national fleet. The over one million deadweight tons capacity required for even modest combat operations described above would require nearly one-third the national dry shipping capacity, clearly putting the U.S. in an impossible economic position unless supported by stronger maritime allies, such as the Japanese. To make the problem even more difficult, General Schwarzkopf stated that less than 200 of the U.S.'s 675 ships were militarily useful.

Hence, it follows that the key to success is avoiding combat and having the insertion take place where there is an indigenous supply of petroleum. This was, essentially, the American strategy in 1990. Intense combat operations were a logistical impossibility *unless* Iraqi forces collapsed with such rapidity that American logistical problems would never show themselves. Moreover, by having Saudi refineries available, a great deal of the tanker tonnage problem, about 45 percent of all logistical needs, was solved.

The weakness of American ground forces obviously does not affect American power in the air or at sea. The power of the seven tactical air wings and the two B-52 squadrons scheduled for deployment can easily overwhelm any air force on earth, particularly when linked to the presence of three carrier task forces. In the air or at sea, the U.S. is an indomitable force. It is when these air and naval forces are projected onto the mainland that they tend to be less impressive.

The effectiveness of the American Air Force in multiplying U.S. ground strength depends on its effectiveness against enemy armor. The A-10 Thunderbolt, the mainstay of the American antitank force, was deemed obsolete at the time of the 1990 intervention, and was to be replaced by the more advanced F/A-18. The argument of the Air Force was that the A-10 was too slow and that its heat emissions were too visible for it to survive in modern battle conditions.

Whatever the truth of these claims, the A-10 was designed to kill advancing tanks. The distinction between attacking and defending tanks is not trivial. The Iraqis, for example, experienced in desert war, dig their tanks in to protect them from aircraft, and camouflage them as well. Tanks in defensive position are defended by antiaircraft missiles and guns, making an attack on them a formidable problem. Thus, the effectiveness of antitank air operations varies greatly depending on the deployment of the targets. The assumption in Europe was that the A-10 would be facing attacking Soviet tanks, exposed, moving in echelons, and weakly defended by antiaircraft systems. The equation shifts when the U.S. is the attacking force, and so too does the force-multiplier effect.

The U.S. Army was created after World War II to defend Europe. The key concept is *defense*. In defensive posture, U.S. ground forces, augmented by air power savaging exposed, attacking tanks, side by side with allies, had a chance of surviving. The U.S. could never have launched a ground attack against the Soviet Union, since the ratio of forces would have been so overwhelmingly unfavorable that U.S. forces would have been swamped.

Strategically, the American goal in Eurasia was simply to defend, to prevent victory by an emerging Eurasian hegemony. It was never to impose an American regime on the region. The U.S., to the extent it had any interest in this goal, pursued it through its alliance system.

U.S. strategy in the Cold War worked because the United States remained in a defensive posture and was never called on to use its extraordinarily strained projection capability in a genuinely critical case, as in defending Europe. The U.S. ended the Cold War with the ability to project overwhelming force to the shore's edge, but only limited and marginal power onto the shore. The need to control events in Eurasia, and the lack of resources with which to do this directly, led the U.S. to pursue a policy of indirection, in which surrogates were manipulated into performing American tasks.

This underscores the military context of American power. U.S. victory in the Cold War could lead some to assume that the U.S. has become militarily omnipotent. To achieve ground parity with a minor power like Iraq, the U.S. had to throw against it all U.S. land combat power. The U.S. cannot continually mobilize to this extent. It must either devise a strategy that makes it unnecessary to confront Eurasian land powers, or devise a more efficient means of Eurasian land combat. In either case, if the U.S. strategic triumph in the Cold War is one side of the picture, U.S. operational vulnerability is the other. It is in this context that we now consider America's strategic options.

AMERICA'S DECISION: STRATEGIC OPTIONS IN THE NEW ERA

The U.S would appear to have four basic strategic options:

1. *Permanent alliance.* Try to maintain the alliance system and the free-trade regime as a permanent system of international governance.
2. *Empire.* Transform its alliance system into an imperial system, using current military strength to impose hegemony over the former alliance system and the Soviet bloc.
3. *Hemispheric isolation.* Withdraw from the eastern hemisphere entirely, creating a political and economic bloc in the western hemisphere, and use the Navy in a purely defensive role.
4. *Oceanic hegemony.* Maintain American hegemony over the oceans, avoiding overt interventions in the eastern hemisphere unless a single power threatens hegemony, while using control of the oceans to manipulate world oceanic trade to prevent such a power from arising.

1. Permanent Alliance

The first political question of the new era for the United States is the fate of its alliance system. Since it was designed to resist Soviet aggression, the end of the Soviet threat means that this alliance will either be modified to serve new ends or will cease to exist. In the latter case, the U.S. must reconsider whether and how to achieve its fourth strategic goal: manipulating the balance of power in Eurasia.

The immediate response to the end of the Cold War by the Western foreign-policy establishment was that the alliance system could now serve as the framework for the permanent administration of the international system. They assumed that although the alliance had been created to stop the Soviet Union, it was not confined to this function. Moreover, they saw the free-trade regime that grew up in tandem with the Western alliance as a reasonable permanent basis for the international economic system.

Foreign Affairs, the journal of the Council on Foreign Relations and the most prestigious forum for the leaders of the Western alliance, abounds with analyses such as this by Robert Hormats:

> In this period of dramatic change, West Europeans and Americans will constantly need to remind themselves that, although their policies are likely to diverge increasingly on a greater number of issues, a fundamental and durable source of their international economic and political influence—and certainly of their security in what is still a highly uncertain, if improving, global environment—is their close relationship with one another. Societies on both sides of the Atlantic will need to keep that point in sharp focus lest the forces of change obscure it.[18]

Peter Tarnoff, President of the Council on Foreign Policy, wrote:

> As Americans wonder whether or not to maintain their substantial international commitments, it may seem paradoxical to learn that Bonn and Tokyo consider good relations with Washington to be indispensable, even as the Soviet threat recedes. During the present period of transition and uncertainty, and as both move to center stage, Japan and Germany are looking for support and counsel from the most reliable and experienced of their allies.[19]

There is something quite wistful in these arguments. For men like Hormats and Tarnoff, men who came to political maturity in a world in which collective security meant safety and prosperity, the end of the Cold War poses a severe intellectual test. The decline of the threat means the decline in the need for collective security. But that decline, in turn, means in their minds a decline in the importance of the United States. For the foreign-policy establishment, the postwar significance of the United States was as the leader of the Free World, the head of an unprecedented alliance system.

Tarnoff's rather charming vision of Japan and Germany looking for "support and counsel" from their more "experienced" ally (it is hard to imagine serious Japanese and Germans thinking of America as more politically experienced than they are) is a plea for their acceptance of America as first among equals even after the Cold War ends. The U.S., a wise and benevolent leader, will continue to guide the world's unruly flock to a better tomorrow. Grateful Germans and

Japanese, new to the ways of statecraft and unsure of their place in the world, will rely on the U.S. for wise guidance.

The real parallel in this vision is to be found in the British attempt to convert their lost empire into a commonwealth in which Britain, instead of being a rapacious exploiter, would provide wise and gentle counsel to the lesser peoples. Defeated imperialists frequently dream of retaining their power based on some imagined virtue or mutuality of interest. It is, of course, mysterious why the American foreign-policy establishment should, on the day of its greatest triumph, be reading Kipling's *Recessional* and wistfully praying for respect. Unlike Britain's conversion of its empire into a commonwealth, the United States stands at the height of triumph. Its strategic and naval capability are unchallenged, and there is nothing irredeemable in its economic position. American power is at its zenith. But it is a power without purpose; there is a malaise at the heart of American strategic policy, a lack of politico-military vision in the elite.

There is a very real nostalgia at work as the establishment that guided America and the alliance to its great triumph tries to perpetuate itself and the alliance, searching for a purpose beyond the Cold War. The purpose they have discovered is the old vision of the United Nations, of international solidarity and collective security. Wilson and Roosevelt both sought to solve the problem of American security by abolishing aggression through a centralized organization that would coordinate the international use of force in defense of national sovereignty. An attack on one nation would be regarded as an attack on all nations, and then the entire world would resist aggression.

The conversion of NATO into a system of collective security encompassing its former enemies is, of course, more than a little redundant. The United Nations was originally created to serve this function. During the Cold War, the U.N. became an arena for U.S.–Soviet competition. Now, it is finally possible—in the minds of those advocating this view of the alliance—to create an effective, functioning system of collective security.

Both the League of Nations and the United Nations (to this point in time) failed because there was no consensus among nations as to what the collective interest was, or what constituted aggression. Instead, the U.N. became an instrument of ideological warfare. Now the assumption is that the abolition of communism or of fundamental ideological division will make collective security a genuine possibility.

The strategic vision that prompts U.S. policy makers to think in terms of perpetuating the alliance system as a proto-U.N., or in tandem with the U.N., is the idea that the U.S. benefits from international stability. Throughout the Cold War, the U.S. saw itself on the defensive against the Soviet Union's attempt to overturn the international system. It became a fixed psychological perspective that international disorder aided the Soviets and harmed the Americans.

It is unclear whether the emerging world order will find the U.S. in the same position. For example, for political reasons the U.S. has entered into a series of economic relationships that are no longer clearly advantageous. The U.S., as an economic power on the defensive, might well find it advantageous to force adjustments or radical restructuring in that system. Obviously, such restructuring would come at the expense of its allies. Equally obvious, the use of political power to gain economic advantage would violate the governing spirit of an international system dedicated to stability and, therefore, to maintaining the status quo.

That is the central problem with this strategy. The framers of the continued alliance assume that maintaining the status quo will remain in the interests of the United States after the Cold War, just as it was in its interests during the Cold War. This is not likely to be the case. Indeed, the U.S. suspended pursuing matters of fundamental importance to itself because of the Cold War. These matters, mostly economic, will certainly need to be rectified after the Cold War.

The free-trade regime served the Cold War alliance well. Its cost to certain powers, particularly the U.S., is obvious. American defense spending has clearly had an impact on investment and productivity, which in turn have made the U.S. less competitive. Simply maintaining the free-trade system would perpetuate the inferiority of American productivity. Given America's post-Cold War political power, it would be naive to think that the U.S. would permit this.

Having borne the spending burden in the alliance, the U.S. clearly is in a mood to catch up economically. Moreover, the U.S. clearly wishes to catch up at the expense of its erstwhile allies, since their own comparative advantage was linked, to some extent, to America's defense-spending burden. The U.S. has already sought to use political pressure through various trade negotiations to interfere in the free-trade process with Japan. It will be even more emphatic as 1992's European integration looms.

Since free trade was a key element of the alliance system, U.S. pressure on that element, indeed, the general search for a post-Cold War rectification of inequities and the pressure toward regionalization and segmentation of economies, will create a situation that will have to erode the foundation of the alliance system. Maintaining the alliance system in the face of the decline of its economic dimension is as futile as trying to maintain the alliance in the face of the decline in mutual-security interests.

Some could argue that such revisions would be possible within the context of an ongoing alliance. Thus, for example, revising the trading relationship with Japan would not have to open a breach between the two countries, but could be contained within the alliance framework. Japan sends one-third of its exports to the U.S. American attempts to limit this in any fundamental way would have a profound and enduring impact on life in Japan. Japan would first resist, and then seek solutions that might threaten other American interests, such as an East Asian trading bloc. To argue that U.S.–Japanese trade disputes could be contained within an ongoing alliance relationship drastically underestimates the significance of economic issues. It is understandable why many make this mistake. During the 1970s and 1980s, profound economic disputes with Japan *were* contained in the alliance system, not because they were trivial but because the Soviet threat was so much greater that they paled by comparison. After the Cold War, they will reemerge and assume their proper proportions.

The vision of the alliance as a system of permanent collective security motivated the American intervention in Saudi Arabia against Iraq's attack on Kuwait. From the standpoint of President Bush, there could be absolutely no justification for an Iraqi attack on Kuwait. The right of Kuwait to exist, in perpetuity, without outside aggression, was self-evident, and the international community was obligated to ensure this right. Moreover, it was in everyone's interest to do so, as everyone benefited from inviolable borders. There was the added factor of protecting the prior system of oil production and distribution. From both perspectives, Bush evinced an essentially conservative perspective, beginning with the assumption that preserving the international political and economic system was a fundamental American interest.

The counterclaim, that Kuwait was an illegitimate British contrivance with no moral claim on sovereignty, was ignored. Bush also ignored the argument that most nations had little interest in maintaining the Kuwaiti regime, and that many nations were eager to see a disruption and reordering of the international oil distribution system.

At the very least, many nations had different interests concerning oil. Japan, which imported over 60 percent of its oil from inside the Straits of Hormuz, could not tolerate any action that threatened to disrupt the flow of oil for any period of time whatsoever. The U.S. could afford a more philosophic approach to the problem, since it depended on Persian Gulf oil to stabilize long-term prices, not for immediate consumption. Thus, the Japanese, who did not care in the least about the moral right of the Kuwaitis to be free, responded very differently to the crisis than did the Americans.

The Japanese, and many others, had another, deeper fear in the crisis. One of the possible outcomes of the Kuwait adventure was that a successful U.S. confrontation with Iraq would leave U.S. forces in control of the bulk of Persian Gulf oil. The assumption fueling internationalist American thinking was that America would never use this power to its own advantage. The U.S. intervened to prevent Iraqi domination of Persian Gulf oil, and it was understood that this control would be used to the disadvantage of the Western alliance system. The successful outcome of the operation would leave the U.S. in control of an even greater amount of oil. Yet the U.S. genuinely did not expect anyone to fear this control.

Thus, the idea of permanent alliance suffers from a profound and intractable defect: it assumes that the only conflict in the world was the one between the Soviets and the West, and that once that conflict is settled, the West will remain allied and comfortable, united in its common interests. The problem is that common interests will go the way of the Soviet Union, and all that will be left is the common conflict among nations, not rising to the ideological heights of U.S.–Soviet conflicts, but rather, falling to the depths of economic friction and power politics, as in 1914.

2. From Alliance to Empire

As the world's only superpower, the U.S. would appear to have another option: converting the alliance into a system of domination and exploitation. As the world's preeminent power, the U.S. could use its military power to reorder the world's economic and political relationships in ways that would give the U.S. overwhelming advantage. One gets a sense that much of the world is expecting just such a choice. It would be the traditional way of rewarding oneself after a great victory such as the U.S. has achieved.

Indeed, many have claimed that this was always the American goal. The charge that the U.S. used its system of alliances to create a system of imperial domination has been heard frequently, particularly from the Left, and particularly during the Vietnam War. There was certainly an element of truth to this charge. The United States was far more than first among equals. It was the overwhelmingly powerful entity that ordered its allies almost at will. Indeed, the U.S. tended to become enraged when one of its allies tried to break free from the pattern of domination. One need only recall American views of Gaullist France following France's withdrawal from the military structure of NATO and the expulsion of American troops from French soil.

Nevertheless, the U.S. was not—properly understood—an imperial power because, at root, its relationship with its allies was not exploitive. Quite the contrary, the U.S. did everything in its power not to exploit its major allies, even at great cost to itself. Although the U.S. frequently enjoyed portraying itself as engaged in selfless altruism, this policy had a shrewd, hard core of self-interest and calculation to it.

The easy assumption has been that the end of the Cold War has made political stability the norm and military security passé. In fact, the real consequence of the Cold War has been a decline in America's dependence on its former allies for its political and military security. This has opened up a wide range of political and military possibilities to U.S. action, from isolation to imposed empire.

There are two separate questions involved here. The first is how should the United States use its hard-won and enormous political and military power? The second is precisely how powerful is the United States at this historic juncture? These two questions were the core issues during the American intervention in the Kuwaiti crisis. Should the U.S. intervene on behalf of some principle of international morality, restoring the Al Sabah family to power in Kuwait, or should the U.S. intervene strictly on behalf of American oil interests? Indeed, should the U.S. use the intervention as an opportunity to seize control of the Persian Gulf oil fields and thereby become the largest oil producer in the world? Perhaps more important, just how powerful is the U.S.? The weakness of the U.S. in any ground intervention has already been shown. Were there compensatory political and military capabilities that would have allowed the U.S. to impose hegemony? Finally, would the efforts of empire be worthwhile, or would the exertion simply not be worth the benefits?

Certainly there are goals to be pursued. First, the U.S. could use imperial power to enhance its national security, the physical safety of North America. The problem with this argument is that there is not very much threatening North America, and should any of the distant threats grow larger, there are probably more efficient solutions for dealing with them than empire. Then, there are very real economic advantages involved in having the power to impose trade relations on the world. However, this turns into a cost-benefit analysis. Imperial power is extraordinarily costly, even granted the benefits. Would the profits of an imperial project cover the expenses? Thus, there is the question of whether the Americans can create a profitable empire. There is also the question of whether the U.S. can avoid having empire thrust on it. These questions must begin with a careful analysis of America's general military power.

At present, the U.S. spends a little over 6 percent of GNP in order to maintain a force structure shown in Map 9-1 on page 222. Imagine the following regional crisis. In the course of a holding operation in the Persian Gulf, which would tie up the five divisions assigned to Central Command, the United States faces a massive revolt by its European allies, who, unhappy with our policies in the region, wish to challenge U.S. power and at the very least be free of the burden of basing and paying for American troops in NATO. The problem: Could the U.S. wield sufficient force in Europe to prevent its expulsion while at the same time operating in the Persian Gulf?

For example, the United States currently has in Europe two mechanized and two armored divisions, nearly 1,400 tanks in place, along with 546 first-line air superiority and attack aircraft. Compared with the four American divisions in Europe, West Germany has six armored and four mechanized divisions, each with three brigades and additional independent brigades.

A comparison of German and American weapons in place in Germany reveals the following:

TABLE 9-5. U.S. and German Weapons Available in Germany.

	TANKS	IFV/APC	ARTILLERY	ATGM
U.S.	1,391	1,298	282	722
Germany	2,288	3,348	780	1,944

(IFV = Infantry Fighting Vehicle; APC = Armored Personnel Carrier; ATGM = Antitank Guided Missile)

The function of American forces in Europe was to supplement European forces in resisting a Soviet attack. The hope was that this would be sufficient force to fight the Red Army to a stalemate. The American force was never conceived of as an autonomous force able to unilaterally impose its will on Europe.

Were the United States to shift its policy and attempt to impose on the Germans some sort of imperial relationship, it would face an impossible military situation. Its forces would be outnumbered, surrounded, and need to hold open a 3,000-mile supply line through hostile ports and enemy-controlled road nets. Moreover, reinforcement from CONUS, the continental United States, would have to be drawn from the reserves. Given the limitations inherent in shipping, the possibility that the U.S. could fight a successful battle to dominate Germany, and make it economically profitable, is extremely doubtful.

It is impossible to estimate the precise number of divisions the U.S.

would have to raise in order to assert control over the eastern hemisphere, but it would be so far beyond its ability to achieve that further speculation is pointless. One might, however, recall that at full mobilization during World War II, the U.S. did not have sufficient manpower to engage in combat in both the Atlantic and Pacific theaters without the aid of its allies.

Many might wonder how Germany, with its relatively low defense budget, manages to have such substantial forces available. There are several answers. First, Germany can concentrate its forces while the Americans are forced to divide theirs. Second, the U.S. has devoted a tremendous amount of its budget to strategic forces, particularly nuclear weapons and delivery systems, which take up about 8 percent of defense costs. But most important is the enormous cost of force projection. The U.S. must move its forces into Germany via an extended supply line, defend that supply line, and transport materials along that supply line.

The limitation on American activities in the eastern hemisphere can be seen in the U.S. defense budget breakdown:

TABLE 9-6. Defense Budget by Service, FY1990.

	DOLLARS (BILLIONS)	PERCENT OF DEFENSE BUDGET
Army	78.8	26.8%
Navy	97.8	33.4
Air Force	97.7	33.3
Agencies	19.0	6.5
Total	293.3	100.0

(Source: Committee on Armed Services, U.S. House of Representatives)

Only about 25 percent of the U.S. budget is spent on the development and maintenance of ground forces. Two-thirds is spent on air and naval power. Indeed, given the fact that naval strategy is built around the aircraft carrier battle group, it is not an exaggeration to claim that strategic forces and air power make up the bulk of U.S. defense expenditures, with a relatively small amount available to ground forces for eastern hemispheric deployment. This is conditioned by the need to project forces over vast intercontinental distances. It shifts the ratio of forces toward those elements that make the movement of forces possible and safe, and away from the forces themselves.

Thus, direct military control of the eastern hemisphere is simply impossible. For the U.S., as for any other nation with an imperial dream, even those situated in Eurasia proper, the dream is much larger than the forces available. The United States would be swamped. Further, any attempt to rectify this imbalance would be futile, and far less than cost effective.

Successful empires, one should recall, do not normally seize control by main force. In retrospect, it becomes clear that the forces of the Roman and British empires were vastly insufficient for the task at hand. They succeeded, in general, in taking their empire through three means:

1. The successful manipulation of conflicts among enemies, siding with various factions to create local coalitions.
2. Using their land forces as a strategic asset to intervene in local conflicts where their presence represented the margin of victory, or where their presence was of psychological significance.
3. Using their naval forces to move their troops rapidly from central staging areas to areas of conflict; in addition, using their naval forces to confine conflict to land masses, making efficient broad coalition formations impossible, and making sea-borne operations against the center impractical.

The British in particular compensated for their notorious weakness on the ground with efficient utilization of their control of the sea.

Empire, in the sense of the direct Soviet or German occupation of subject nations, is not an option for the U.S., at least outside of a limited area of the western hemisphere. One should recall, of course, that neither of these were successful empires. In the German case, they simply ran out of manpower. In the Soviet case, they had sufficient manpower, but the cost of holding and defending their empire broke their economy.

The difference between the German/Soviet experience and the British experience was that, in many cases, the British presence was welcomed by at least some factions in the colonial entity. The German experience is instructive. In attempting to impose empire by main force, the Germans were welcomed by few, quite marginal groups. The masses were at best neutrally hostile. The British usually intervened on behalf of some class, ethnic group, or faction, and while not universally welcomed, they were not universally despised. At least for some sectors of society, the British arrival was a genuine boon.

The imposition of direct political rule was, therefore, something of an afterthought, having created mutually beneficial economic and political arrangements prior to annexation. Using their navy to control the access of the colonies to other markets and relationships, the British were then able to enter into relationships that were beneficial. The key was, of course, the Royal Navy. The Royal Navy was able to control maritime intercourse to an extent that created a sense of inevitability in relationships.

The problem for the United States is not naval. The U.S. Navy is far more powerful than the Royal Navy ever was. The British had to look over their shoulders at the French, German, Italian, and Japanese navies, which together could be quite a match for Britain. The U.S., on the other hand, has no such problem.

The problem for the United States—in the British approach—is in the granting of mutually beneficial economic relations. As was the case with Britain, it is not always clear that relationships with the U.S. are more beneficial than, for example, multiple economic relationships or relationships with Japan or Germany. The British effectively barred such relationships. Such a decision by the U.S. to bar relationships with Japan and Germany would be a signal of imperial ambition that would invariably trigger a response. Since the U.S. lacks the ability to impose itself on these countries, it would have to sit offshore, awaiting the creation of the challenging navies. In the meantime, in a struggle for markets, the U.S. might find itself with maritime markets but barred from the more important Euro-Japanese market.

The British were able to rely on the continental balance of power to keep the European challenge to its naval hegemony at bay. If the U.S. is to emulate Britain on a global scale, it must create a similar balance in Eurasia. To attempt naval hegemony without an assured balance of power would be to irritate some very dangerous adversaries prematurely. This is the key weakness of any American attempt to emulate the British.

Thus, using the alliance system as a springboard to empire will simply not be possible, nor would it be clearly desirable. It is necessary to define with some precision what it is that the U.S. would seek to achieve from empire in order to devise a means for an imperial project. Paradoxically, the best way to do this is to consider the views of those who would seek to abandon the notion of foreign adventure altogether, limiting American political activity to North America or, at most, to the western hemisphere.

3. Retreat to Hemispheric Empire

There is good reason to wonder at not only the ability of the U.S. to dominate Eurasia, but the rationality of any such attempt. Given the collapse of the Soviet Union, an argument could be made for withdrawing from eastern hemispheric affairs altogether, forgoing the vast expense of maintaining a navy and the threats to peace that such aggressive patrolling implies. Assuming that the peace and security of the U.S. is the primary goal of American strategic policy, and accepting the proposition that war diminishes both, reasonable men now argue that the avoidance of conflict is the only rational course, since the benefits to be won in a war clearly are outweighed by the dangers.

There were those who made this argument prior to the end of the Cold War. Their calculations were simple. Nothing could be more damaging to American interests than fighting a nuclear war. Continued political competition with the Soviet Union in Eurasia might risk a confrontation that would lead to nuclear war. Since there was no interest in the eastern hemisphere worth pursuing at that risk, the most rational strategy for the United States was the withdrawal from the eastern hemisphere and placement of the U.S. Navy in a posture defending the coasts of North America, albeit to a substantial distance.[20]

The weakness of this argument during the Cold War was that it assumed that the Soviet Union could be contained without direct U.S. intervention, or that Soviet domination in Eurasia would result in minimal consequences to the U.S. In other words, this view held that the fourth U.S. strategic goal, maintenance of the balance of power in Eurasia, had minimal meaning, and that even the third interest, the domination of the North Atlantic and Pacific, was insignificant, since the Soviets had little interest beyond the shore. However, the same analysis that led to U.S. intervention against Germany twice in the twentieth century remained valid against the Soviet Union. Soviet domination of Eurasia would inevitably mean a Soviet challenge on the oceans and, given the relative power of the hemispheres, the U.S. in the long run might well fall prey to the Soviets.

This analysis proved generally persuasive during the Cold War, even after the Vietnam experience. However, the situation has changed fundamentally. The weakened condition of the Soviet Union makes it extremely unlikely that an American withdrawal would lead to Soviet domination of Europe. Moreover, the current balance of forces in Europe leads one to the conclusion that the most likely outcome of an American withdrawal would be a resurgence of the international system that first appeared after the Napoleonic wars, with France, Germany, Russia, and England struggling for dominion. Old Austro-Hungarian fragments might find it necessary to reconstruct their past federation and contend as a fifth power. Furthermore, China, not strong enough to dominate Asia, not weak enough to collapse, would further act both to contain the Soviet Union and to counteract the power of Japan.

Thus, this theory argues that now is the time to abandon the 6-percent-of-GNP defense budgets we have incurred, maintain our strategic nuclear deterrence, maintain a naval force capable of defending against the minimal threats posed to our coastline, and spend the savings on plant modernization, social welfare, and education. In short, instead of competing militarily, we ought to compete economically. At the very least, U.S. expenditures for European defense, in the context of 1992 and growing German strength and nationalism, no longer make very much sense.[21]

This is an extremely seductive argument. It faces squarely the reality that the least desirable outcome for the U.S. of any foreign policy would be one that would cause us to fight a land war in Eurasia. Particularly unattractive would be the possibility of being in such a war from the beginning, rather than as a final intervening force tipping the balance in favor of whichever side we choose. Vietnam and Korea, examples of early intervention, were not happy experiences, while World Wars I and II ended satisfactorily.

The problem with this plan is that it is too extreme. It assumes, reasonably, that we are safe for an extended period of time from the threat of Eurasian hegemony. Moreover, there would be plenty of warning before another power could attempt to lay claim to Eurasian hegemony. But, frequently, reasonable assumptions—particularly about political matters and in the measurement of time—are in error. No reasonable person would have predicted the rapidity of the fall of Soviet Communism, nor the rapidity of the reemergence of an imperialist Germany after World War I, nor the rapidity of most events since the Russian Revolution and World War I.

The assumption that no Eurasian hegemonist could emerge in the near future is probably valid. It is not at all certain, however, and acting with certainty on matters that are only probable is an invitation to catastrophe in political life. Moreover, even if political change in Eurasia is slower than we might imagine, the construction of military forces, particularly naval forces, is slower yet. Construction time for a carrier battle group, even assuming that facilities were available for simultaneous construction, approaches ten years between design and commissioning.

Withdrawal to a coastal posture means that the U.S. would be prepared to survive primarily as a continental power. That is certainly possible, assuming that the few critical metals not found in North America could be obtained through the open market. However, the shape of the American economy would change dramatically. While the U.S. is far less dependent on exports or imports than the Japanese or Germans, becoming a completely autarkic, self-contained economy would be difficult.

It has been shown how strangely Eurasian politics can evolve. The past century has revealed some of the most exotic growths in a history filled with exotica. Moreover, the pace at which a willful regime can create a hegemonic menace has been rapid. The oceans are a great defense, but they did not defend Germany or Japan against the U.S. in World War II, nor Korea, Vietnam, or Iraq. Navies can sail in either direction. Were politics to cease in the eastern hemisphere, the U.S. could entertain the possibility of resting behind a thin maritime shield. But that is unlikely to happen. History will go on.

In preparing for the unexpected, it is clear that while the U.S. can pull its forces out of Eurasia, it must do so in such a way that its power can still be felt on the periphery of events, and in such a way that, if necessary, U.S. forces can be reinserted. There is therefore a middle position between American global imperialism and isolating the U.S. from Eurasia altogether. This might be called the Blue Water Strategy, or perhaps more appropriately, the Miserly Empire. It is a strategy of holding open all options, defending the main interests of the U.S., and being in a position to control the fate of nations cheaply, should the U.S. choose to do so. This is the fourth and most desirable post-Cold War strategy: global maritime power.

4. Global Maritime Empire

The oceans are the area of the globe under indisputable U.S. control. At the end of 1989, the U.S. Navy was overwhelmingly powerful. The key measure of modern naval strength is the aircraft carrier. While some have argued that the carrier is doomed by the advent of the antiship missile, this has not been proven. Certainly, the aircraft carrier will become obsolete one day, as all weapons do. But the aircraft carrier's ability to control a quarter-million square miles of an ocean's surface, so that four or five carriers and their escorts can completely control the North Atlantic, makes them the contemporary measure of a nation's maritime power.

The U.S. currently has fourteen aircraft carriers. There are only thirteen other aircraft carriers in the entire world, many obsolete, all inferior to American carriers. (See Table 9-7.)

The distinction between catapult-launched and very short takeoff and landing (VSTOL) aircraft is extremely important. A VSTOL aircraft normally has much shorter range, carries a much smaller payload, and is less effective in aerial combat than a catapult-launched aircraft. A VSTOL aircraft carrier cannot engage a catapult-type

TABLE 9-7. Aircraft Carrier Capability.

COUNTRY	LAUNCH TYPE	NO. OF AIRCRAFT PER CARRIER	YEAR LAID DOWN
Argentina	Catapult	18	1942
Brazil	Catapult	20	1942
Britain (3)	VSTOL	5	1973–1978
France (2)	Catapult	40	1955, 1957
India	VSTOL	22	1943
Spain	VSTOL	20	1979
USSR (4)	VSTOL	32	1970–78
U.S. (14)	Catapult	70–95	1952–86

(Source: *Jane's Fighting Ships*)

aircraft carrier, all other things being equal, and hope to survive. All U.S. carriers are catapult-launch platforms.

Nimitz class carriers, of which the U.S. has six, each carry over 90 aircraft; the two Enterprise class carriers also carry 90 aircraft; four Kennedy class carry 85; four Forrestal class, 70; two Midway class, 75. Only the French have catapult carriers launched after World War II, and those carry about half the number of aircraft of an American carrier.

The overwhelming power of the U.S. Navy is both very obvious and politically and militarily essential. This overwhelming power extends to battleships, where the U.S. Navy has the only two afloat, as well as to other weapons systems where the numerical value might be less overwhelming, but the qualitative difference is absolute. The difference between an American Aegis cruiser or destroyer armed with surface-to-surface missiles and a conventional gun-carrying destroyer is so great that only the names make them comparable.

Quantification in such matters is always dangerous, but James F. Dunnigan, an eminent military analyst and war gamer, studied the aggregate combat power of all of the world's naval fleets. His conclusion was that the combat power of the American fleet was slightly over 50 percent of the world's total naval combat power. The next most powerful navy, the Soviet, was less than half as strong, totaling only 21 percent of the U.S. Navy's combat power. That means that the rest of the world, taken together, contains only about 29 percent of available combat power.[22]

Thus, even during 1983, when this study was completed, and prior to the buildup to a 600-ship navy, U.S. combat power was equal to the total found in the rest of the world. Since the rest of the world is unlikely ever to act as a single force, it follows that the U.S. Navy is invincible, at least for the time being. What clearly cannot be said for the U.S. Army can easily be said for the Navy: it goes where it wants and brushes aside whatever opposes it.

Naval power is the strong suit of the United States, and is the one it must play to. The U.S. must pursue an intermediate strategy, for it cannot maintain an ongoing, unallied presence in the eastern hemisphere. The Western alliance system cannot survive the collapse of the Soviet Union, and the United States cannot simply retreat into the western hemisphere, indifferent to events in the east. That intermediate strategy is one of maritime domination, and one might add that it is itself a low-cost means of imperial control.

One use of the sea is as a means of defense and attack. A second, more important use is for peaceful trade. The sea is still, today, the chief highway of trade. An enormous proportion of international trade travels by sea, particularly the trade in primary commodities such as energy, industrial minerals, and food. Control of the sea gives a nation control of that trade. By controlling the primary commodities trade, a nation has control of the economic life of the planet, or of any individual country it might wish to control.

During the war with Iraq, the United States found itself in a paradoxical situation. On the ground the Americans were reluctant to engage the Iraqis in direct combat in spite of the fact that the bulk of the Army's combat power had been deployed in the Persian Gulf. The full U.S. Army could not, by itself, guarantee success over the Iraqi Army. The initial American strategy was to try to avoid ground combat for as long as possible. Yet, at the same time, the U.S. Navy was able to guarantee complete domination of the Persian Gulf and surrounding waters. Thus, the U.S. controlled Iraq's trade far more easily than it controlled Iraq militarily.

The use of trade to achieve political ends is a rather old tactic for the United States. Prior to World War II, the U.S. used trade embargoes against both Japan and Germany. After the war, trade sanctions of diverse forms were used at various times against North Korea, North Vietnam, Cuba, Iran, the Soviet Union, South Africa, Nicaragua, and other countries. On occasion, embargoes are called for economic reasons, as in 1973, when the United States suspended the sale of soybeans to Japan in order to lower the domestic cost of meat. What makes trade sanctions attractive to the U.S. is their capacity to inflict substantial damage on an adversary without putting a great deal at risk.

There are, of course, possible miscalculations. The suspension of grain sales to the Soviet Union after its invasion of Afghanistan caused far more harm to the United States than it did to the Soviets. This is because it is necessary to have cooperation among economic competitors in order to make an embargo successful. As the U.S. discovered in several cases, including that of Iraq, this is frequently impossible to achieve.

The most successful embargoes by the U.S. occurred when it could physically control a nation's access to the sea. For most countries, this goal can never be achieved. For the U.S., it is attainable worldwide and at will. The blockade of Cuba in 1962 is a case in point. On the obverse side, the U.S. showed in its 1988 reflagging of Kuwaiti tankers that it could break any local embargo as well.

In the postwar period the U.S. has hardly used this power at all. Control of trade for parochial benefit is anathema to the United States ideologically and, more important, because of the free-trade component of its alliance system. The American Revolution was fought in large part in opposition to Britain's use of its navy to impose favorable trade relations on its colonies. The Boston Tea Party was about just that sort of attempt to use American trade dependency to profit the Crown.

Memories of the Smoot-Hawley tariffs and their calamitous effect on the world economy still cause reasonable fears among analysts. The thought of another collapse of world trade and its effect on economies, like the American, that depend on trade for substantial portions of their GNP is frightening in the extreme. This fear has warned Americans against the temptation of imposing trade barriers, even when they appeared to be an attractive political, if not economic, option.

The problems facing the United States originated in the American decision to build fourteen carrier battle groups. The constant expenditure of money on defense, the diversion of the finest minds into military research and development, the absorption of investment capital to build tank production lines—all resulted in the relative uncompetitiveness of the United States. It also gave the U.S. control not of the world by any means, but of the world's oceans.

The task facing the U.S. today is twofold. First, it must secure the safety of North America, a constant need. Second, it must convert its massive defense establishment into something productive. The conventional understanding of this is to demobilize the armed forces, store the weapons and the ships, and rebuild a civilian industry. There is another version.

Converting from defense to economic growth does not have to mean abandoning the military. Rather, it can mean utilizing it in a different way, adopting a different national strategy. Domination of the oceans can be used for economic gain. Control of the oceans is control of trade, of the flow of minerals, oil, automobiles, and tape recorders. The price, destination, even the origin of those goods is in the hands of the navy that rules the oceans.

Using military power for economic ends is an old story. The history of Europe's borders is the history of war for profit. An empire can be quite blatant about it. Nations that wish to trade must pay fees or tariffs or taxes to the protecting force. It can be dressed up and called "burden sharing," or dues to an alliance, or contributions to peacekeeping. How the diplomats frame the reality is unimportant. The power of the U.S. to impose tolls on trade and punish traders that cut into U.S. markets is a starkly real power.

The power is there, but the thought of using it is quite alien to the American mind. Brute interference in free trade is anathema to American moral principles and the American psyche itself. But ideologies change, particularly in the face of anger. The deep-seated resentment by America of the economic price it has paid in fighting the Cold War is very real. The American feeling of betrayal, of allies having taken advantage of America's good nature, might not be a reasonable view of things, but it is a very real view. And that sort of anger can easily wash away ideological or psychological limits.

It is not clear how the Americans will use this power. As the British showed, power can be projected on shore. Building a land-based maritime empire is a tricky business. It requires subtlety to maximize limited land power, the ability to avoid friendships while pursuing interests, and mastery of the fine art of duplicity. Whether America can learn to emulate perfidious Albion is not clear. Ultimately, the British could not make it pay and their empire collapsed, rather quickly as empires go.

It is easier to imagine a rather unsubtle attempt by the U.S. to parlay its naval power into control over world shipping, covered with suitable ideological justifications. But whichever route the Americans take, the maritime land empire or the pure blue-water strategy, one thing is certain: It is utterly inconceivable that the United States will not use its vast naval power to try to gain economic advantage. The stakes are too high and the power too great for any other outcome. Surcharges on oil passing through the Straits of Hormuz or Malacca, economic boycotts backed up by naval interference against nations pursuing policies opposed by the U.S., demands of trade concessions in return for continued naval protection, are all ideas that have been bandied about in Congress and on the op-ed pages of American newspapers.

The vast military power accumulated by the U.S. during the Cold War will not dissipate by itself. Nor will the United States lay aside this extraordinarily expensive power without something to show for it. It would not be rational to retreat to a continental or hemispheric defense, as that would incur dangers the U.S. has no reason to face. Nor would it be rational to try to go ashore in the eastern hemisphere, given the limits of our land power. But the vast maritime power, the control of the oceans that is one of the essential goals of U.S. strategy, coupled with a manipulation, if not domination, of Eurasia, is a coolly rational approach to the future.

America's dilemma is that it does not wish to rule the world, but only to protect its continent. The tragedy of the American condition, not dissimilar to the tragedy of other great empires, is that the simple goal of protecting itself has led America to accumulate a vast military power, one so huge that large parts of the world have come to depend on it for their basic security. The United States cannot lay that power aside without unleashing chaos in the world, chaos that would inevitably endanger the physical security of the United States. Thus, quite without choosing to, the act of self-defense has thrust enormous power on the United States, power so great that establishing a new international order, virtually an empire, becomes a real practical possibility.

The issue is what America will do with this power. Whatever it chooses, the choice will make enemies for the United States. The nations most dependent on the sea for their livelihoods will seek to protect themselves from the United States. No nation is more dependent on distant maritime trade routes than Japan. The inevitable process whereby the United States converts its military power to economic advantage will force Japan, out of self-defense, to take action. That action, as we shall see, will set both nations on a collision course.

1. U.S. Senate, Committee on Armed Services, *Hearings on International Security Environment (Strategy)*, April 14, 1989, p. 410.
2. *New York Times*, July 13, 1990, p. 1.
3. Robert D. Hormats, "Redefining Europe and the Atlantic Link," *Foreign Affairs*, Fall 1989, p. 89.
4. U.S. Senate, Committee on Armed Services, *Hearings*, June 1, 1989, pp. 599–656.
5. Ibid., p. 659.
6. Kensuke Ebata, "Japan Warns on Soviet Build-Up," *Jane's Defense Weekly*, September 23, 1989, p. 544.
7. Fred Charles Ikle and Terumasa Nakanishi, "Japan's Grand Strategy," *Foreign Affairs*, Summer 1990, p. 92.
8. James D. Watkins, *The Maritime Strategy* (Annapolis, 1986), p. 36.

9. Department of Defense, *Annual Report, FY 1987* (Washington, D.C., 1987), p. 272.

10. Combined Arms and Services Staff School, *E709: Organization of the Army in the Field* (Fort Leavenworth, November 1985). Navy League of the United States, *Seapower Facts and Figures*, 1987. Association of the U.S. Army, *The 1989–90 Green Book*.

11. Navy League of the United States, *Seapower Facts and Figures*, p. 186.

12. Combined Arms and Services Staff School, *E210: Basic Logistical Principles* (Fort Leavenworth, 1985), p. 154.

13. James F. Dunnigan, *How to Make War* (New York, 1982), p. 322.

14. Robert P. Haffa, Jr., *Planning U.S. Forces* (Washington, D.C., 1988), p. 124.

15. U.S. Senate, Committee on Armed Services, *Hearings*, June 1, 1989, p. 757.

16. Maritime Administration, U.S. Commerce Department; figures are as of January 1, 1989.

17. Combined Arms and Services Staff School, *E210: Basic Logistical Principles*, p. 154.

18. Hormats, "Redefining Europe," *Foreign Affairs*, Fall 1990, p. 73.

19. Peter Tarnoff, "America's New Special Relationships," *Foreign Affairs*, Summer 1990, p. 73.

20. A very moderate expression of this point of view can be found in The Boston Study Group, *Winding Down: The Price of Defense* (San Francisco, 1982), pp. 298–309.

21. On this last point, and on the general view of burden sharing, see U.S. House of Representatives, *Hearings Before the Defense Burden Sharing Panel*, September 27, 1988.

22. Dunnigan, *How to Make War*, p. 425. Note that this study was completed prior to the massive buildup of U.S. naval forces during the latter part of the Reagan Presidency.

10

Japan's Reality: Regional Power, Global Needs

Japan's politics has been governed by its geography. It has had but one of two choices: to be a seafaring nation or an isolated one. The history of Japan is the history of alternation between these two modes. After World War II and the disastrous end of Japan's last seafaring adventure, it might have been thought that Japan would return to its isolation once again. That is what some Americans planned for Japan and what many Japanese expected to be their fate. However, Japan was prevented by its conqueror from isolating itself. The United States required that Japan become a great industrial power, and it was impossible to be an industrial power and remain isolated. This was because Japan had neither the resources nor the domestic market to fuel an industrial society.

Yet, to some degree, Japan remained an isolated country. From 1945 until 1989, in many ways Japan did not have to engage in the affairs of the world beyond its islands. The United States secured for Japan the resources it required and provided access to the foreign markets it needed. In a strange way, Japan remained an unworldly nation—in the world, but not fully of it. Japan was freed from the burdens of statecraft by the overwhelming presence of the United States. The normal elements of a modern nation-state—armies and risks, navies and dangers—were borne by its ally. Japan was free to pursue its ends without risks as long as it was willing to subordinate itself to the United States.

Thus, Japan has had a freedom of action that few nations have enjoyed. It has been free to choose the extent to which it wished to be a nation-state, and the extent to which it would engage in political life. This freedom is not unnatural to Japan. Since the mid-nineteenth century, Japan has experienced preindustrial feudalism, theocracy, fascism, and liberal democracy. It has won and lost a vast empire, and recouped a vast fortune. Japan is a nation that is, in its soul, freer than most because as a nation it has donned and doffed so many cloaks that adopting roles comes easily to it.

Japan's plasticity is aided by the fact that Japan is fabulously wealthy. By most world standards, save those of the freakish oil principalities, Japan is rich. Because it is richer than most nations, Japan is free to make fundamental decisions about its future in ways that nations such as Bangladesh, for example, cannot.

Japan has not had to control its political-economic environment, for it has lived in a hothouse; for the past forty years, Japan has depended on the United States to control that environment for Japan's benefit. As the international system adjusts to the end of the Cold War, the issue facing Japan—the issue that will determine what kind of nation Japan will choose to be—is whether the United States will continue in this role, or whether Japan will be forced, regardless of its wishes, to take control of its own environment. The key to divining the future in this matter is to consider the significance for Japan of the regionalization of the international system.

The regionalization of the world, the end of the international alliance system, leaves Japan alone to face a different and far bleaker world. Isolation, which is the protection of the United States, becomes Japan's prison. This was not always the case. During the Tokugawa period, Japan indulged in its isolation. But industrialism has made that luxurious solitude impossible. Japan is simply too needy in too many things to survive as an industrialized nation in isolation. Moreover, the defenses that once comforted Japan, the treacherous waters of the Sea of Japan, the isolation of Kamchatka, the vastness of the Pacific, have all been overcome by technology. Japan is no longer immune to the wars of the Asian mainland, nor the fears of the rest of the Pacific Rim.

Thus, Japan alone, forced to fend for itself, must of necessity—and quite contrary to the very real wishes of its people—become an imperial power. This should not surprise anyone. When Japan was last alone in the world as an industrial power, it was forced by the world and by circumstance to launch the political and military adventure that began with the attack on Port Arthur and concluded aboard the battleship *Missouri*. For the past forty-five years, circumstances have shielded Japan from the necessity of making its own way again. As can be seen, the old epoch is coming to an end and a new epoch, a more dangerous and, for Japan, precarious one, is beginning.

There are two forces that will compel Japan to pursue an imperial policy in the coming generation. One is economic. It has been shown how Japan's economy is driven by exports and fed by imports. In a world of free trade, Japan's access to minerals and markets would be unimpeded, and the only limit on Japan's well-being would be its own creativity and efficiency.

However, it is no longer certain that the postwar free-trade regime will continue unimpeded. Japan, in considering its position, must be open to the possibility that access to certain resources and markets will be blocked by political and military powers that cannot be controlled by economic and financial means. Japan must prepare to control its environment under those circumstances, and an imperial foreign policy, however disguised, is its only solution. By some means, Japan must secure for itself the resources necessary for its prosperity as well as access to the markets in which it must sell its exports.

The other force is geopolitical. Japan's position in the northwestern Pacific, the configuration of forces surrounding it, the physical imperatives for its safety—all force Japan to act in certain ways. This has been considered in Chapter 1, but it is useful to review Japan's geopolitical and geostrategic position in a contemporary context.

FROM GEOPOLITICS TO A JAPANESE STRATEGY

As we noted in Chapter 1, Japan has five fundamental geopolitical interests and imperatives that it must pursue:

1. To keep the home islands under the control of a central government and a unified army.
2. To maintain control of the seas around Japan's islands with a coastal navy in order to avoid invasion.
3. To dominate land masses threatening this localized sea control (Korea, Liaotung, Taiwan).
4. To be the dominant naval power in the northwest Pacific as far south as Taiwan, and as far southeast as Iwo Jima.
5. To secure and maintain control of access to Japan's mineral sources in either mainland China or Southeast Asia by dominating the entire western Pacific and excluding all foreign navies.

In 1945, Japan was compelled to abandon all five of its interests. Defeat had placed Japan in an extraordinary—and, for it, unprecedented—position. Japan no longer even controlled its home islands. The central government was broken, and power was completely in the hands of the Americans.

It has been shown in Chapter 4 how this situation was turned to Japan's advantage. The occupying forces, preoccupied with affairs elsewhere, permitted the continuity of the prewar government and its bureaucracy and in due course transferred more and more administrative responsibility to it, until, de jure, the United States returned sovereignty to the Japanese government and, with it, centralized control.

The basis of Japanese politico-military strategy is summarized in the following paragraph from *Defense of Japan: 1989*, the annual summary of Japan's defense policy issued by the Japan Defense Agency:

> It is impossible for Japan to establish its own defense system capable of coping with any conceivable developments ranging from all-out warfare, involving the use of nuclear weapons, to aggression in every conceivable form using conventional arms. Therefore, Japan makes it a policy to ensure its own security by not only possessing an appropriate scale of defense capability, but also maintaining security arrangements with the U.S.[1]

Defense of Japan does not explain precisely why it is impossible for Japan to develop a broad-spectrum military capability. Quite clearly, the reason has nothing to do with technical ability. The population of Japan, while smaller than that of the U.S. and Soviet Union, is still enormous, over 120 million people. Its economy is the second largest in the world and in 1989 its defense budget was the third largest. Its technological capabilities are second to none and its ability to produce a broad range of weapons, from small arms to nuclear delivery systems, is certainly the equal of any other country in the world, except the U.S. and Soviet Union. Moreover, no reasonable person could doubt that if they chose to do so, the Japanese could rapidly equal or surpass the technical achievements of the Soviet Union, if not of the U.S.

Thus, the explanation for this passage has to be political and not technical. One might think that the limit on Japan is American fear of the growth of Japanese power. But, in fact, the United States has been urging Japan quite forcefully to increase its military forces. While the official American position is rather modest, urging enhancements in the Japanese territorial defense capability,[2] unofficial sentiment in the U.S. is much stronger. Sentiment outside the government has gone so far as to demand that Japan undertake the burden of its own defense completely. Thus, one would expect that a large-scale expansion of Japan's defense capabilities would be welcomed by most Americans.

The "impossibility" of assuming complete responsibility for the defense of Japan has much more to do with Japan's own interests than it does with technical capability or American response. The purpose of a complex grand strategy is to achieve the first and simplest goal. For Japan, this means the unity and sovereignty of the home islands. All of the other ends are enhancements, intended to secure the primary interest. Thus, the long-range naval goals of principles 2, 4, and 5, as well as the land-mass goals in principle 3, are intended as a means of achieving and guaranteeing the first principle.

Ever since the late 1940s, the United States has guaranteed Japan's territorial integrity, its freedom from invasion, and its access to raw materials and markets. These guarantees were not based on capricious variables, such as moral values or visions of justice, but on brute necessity. The United States badly needed Japan and these guarantees were things the U.S. was eager to give and eager to have Japan accept. Thus, Japanese strategy prior to the end of the Cold War depended on the United States to achieve the five principles of grand strategy for Japan. Put simply, Japan did not need to occupy Korea and Taiwan if the U.S. did it for her.

With the end of the Cold War, Japan is faced with the difficult task of redefining its national strategy in order to secure these ends for itself. The United States may continue to make these guarantees, but it cannot be relied on to do so. Quite the contrary. With the growing intensity of anti-Japanese sentiment in the U.S. and the growing divergence of Japanese and American economic interests, U.S. maritime control, previously the guarantor of Japan's interests, might well become the noose that strangles Japan. Thus, Japan will have to seek ways of doing the impossible and assume the burden of national defense that the U.S. first took from her, and which Japan has, to date, fought valiantly against reassuming.

In a way, Japan has moved slowly and carefully up the scale of strategic principles. As early as 1981, Japanese Prime Minister Suzuki floated the idea of Japan defending her sea-lanes up to a distance of 1,000 miles, and controlling the three straits through the Japanese archipelago. Such an idea, in its most extreme form, would give Japan control of the sea as far south as the Philippines and as far east as Guam, as well as the entire Sea of Japan.[3]

It is vital to understand that the expansion of Japan's area of sea-lane control is not unilateral. Quite the contrary, it is something that the U.S. has supported for years. The most recent Department of Defense study on Pacific strategy states that the U.S. will:

> . . . continue to encourage Japan to increase its territorial defense capabilities and enhance its ability to defend its sea lanes out to a distance of 1,000 nautical miles, while at the same time discouraging any destabilizing development of a power projection capability.[4]

There is an obvious contradiction in this position. The United States wants Japan to develop a blue-water navy able to control the sea-lanes in an area roughly the size of its post-1905 area of control. (See Map 10-1.) As a static deployment, this would increase Japan's politico-military capability enormously. While putatively intended to stop Soviet passage through Japan's straits, it goes far beyond anything required for that. Essentially, it transfers to Japan responsibilities for waters as far north as the Aleutians (an area never mentioned in the 1,000-mile range discussion), the waters around Taiwan, including the entire East China Sea, and the Pacific out to an arc reaching the Bonins and the Marianas and passing just west of Guam. Most important, it returns control of the Sea of Japan, as well as the waters around the Korean Peninsula, to Japan.

While not quite on the level of a treaty, the mutual understanding that Japan's area of naval responsibility extends 1,000 miles cannot help but be expanded into the idea that Japan's area of naval *control* extends that far. Under any circumstance, the hope that Japan will return to the sea control it enjoyed prior to World War I, but that this will not be used for force projection, is rational only to the extent that the U.S. is prepared to project its own forces on behalf of Japan. In transferring military power to Japan's hands, political power must follow unless the U.S. is willing to use its political power on behalf of Japan.

In reality, of course, the 1,000-mile expansion is not an alternative to Japanese force projection, but is itself force projection. Japanese warships are now authorized by the predominant naval power to patrol the Chinese coast, control the waters between Taiwan and the mainland, ferry convoys north from the Philippines, patrol the Korean coast, and probe eastward into Micronesia and northeast toward the tip of the Aleutian bayonet. In short, Japan is being encouraged by the United States to become the predominant naval power in the northwest Pacific, a return to the position it held between 1905 and 1944.

The American assumption in all of this is that Japan will permit

MAP 10-1. Extent of Japanese Patrol Area After Extension
1,000 Miles South and East.

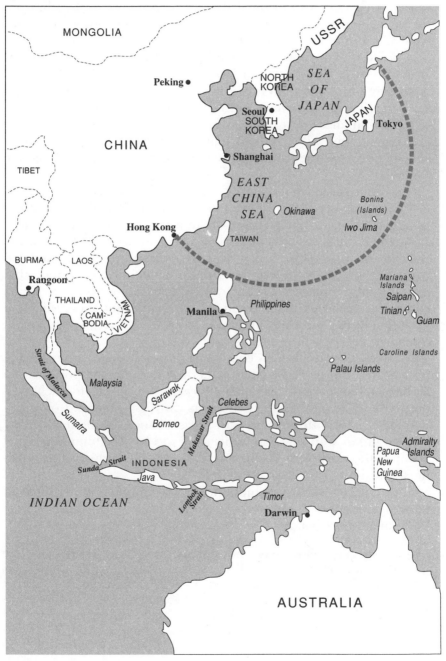

its navy to be used as an adjunct of the U.S. Navy—that it will be, in effect, a unit of the U.S. Navy and an instrument of U.S. military policy. One might recall similar dreams on the part of British, who, during the period of the Anglo-Japanese Treaty, encouraged Japan's expansion in the region. The British expectation was that the Japanese would remain a permanent adjunct to British policy. Japan was content to play that role until 1918, when it found its needs as an expanding industrial power clashing with British needs. One should recall that it was the British, not the Japanese, who broke their alliance. The Japanese were quite content to expand under British guidance indefinitely. The fate of Britain in the Pacific ought to serve as a useful guide to American policy makers bent on increasing Japanese power.

The American encouragement of Japanese military growth is utterly incompatible with a desire that this not be transformed into a force-projection capability. Even though the Japanese Navy is not, at this time, in a position to exploit and fully control the area for which it is responsible, Japan as a nation is obviously capable of producing naval forces able to carry out that mission. Once that mission is accomplished, aside from being in a position to exclude, or at least regulate, U.S. forces in the region, the Japanese will be in a position to expand their influence on to the shore, or farther out to sea.

In effect, the decision to encourage Japan to take responsibility for sea-lanes out to 1,000 miles is the first and most important step of the postwar period for Japan's foreign policy. Having achieved the first and second strategic interests during the period of U.S.–Japanese alliance, the closing act of this alliance will be to formally provide Japan with the fourth principle, to be the dominant naval power in the northwest Pacific as far south as Taiwan and as far to the southeast as Iwo Jima.

Left undiscussed, as yet undreamed, and infinitely more difficult is domination of the Asian land mass facing Japan, particularly Korea. As Hisahiko Okazaki put it:

Japanese geo-politics have not changed over the centuries. The strategic importance of the Korean Peninsula remains as it always has been. If any change has taken place, it is that the main thrust of the Russian advance towards the Pacific coast was shifted from the East China Sea to the Northeastern Pacific, having been blocked by the Sino-Soviet conflict and by the presence of strong U.S.-Korean forces in the southern part of the Korean Peninsula.[5]

But what if the Soviets are no longer capable of moving toward the sea and the U.S. leaves the Korean Peninsula? Then Japanese foreign policy will encounter the deep and abiding anger of Koreans toward the Japanese, the growing strength of Korea as an independent nation, and the unwillingness of Korea to coordinate its economic life with that of Japan. However, should the U.S. find it desirable to withdraw from Korea and should South Korea feel threatened by a continental power, then it might well, out of sheer, reluctant necessity, turn to the Japanese for support. Once before, during the Korean War, there was some talk of Japan supplementing U.S. ground troops in Korea. Were those troops to be withdrawn, the opportunity for Japan to intervene in Korea or to manipulate the North–South relationship would grow tremendously. This ability would be greatly increased, of course, if the Korean economy ran into substantial trouble and the Japanese intervened financially to stabilize it.

The Korean Peninsula was a historical problem to Japan. In the hands of either of the great Asian powers, China or Russia, Korea could well be the bayonet pointing at the heart of Japan, as it was described in the late nineteenth century. Korea in its current configuration, divided, balanced between China and the Soviet Union, with its south occupied by the Americans, is merely a geographic oddity. In the event of an American withdrawal, or of increased aggressiveness by either China or the Soviet Union, or of hostility between the U.S. and Japan, Korea would be something that Japan would have to deal with—in all likelihood, as it did in 1895.

The end of the Cold War leaves Japan the dominant regional naval power, and probably the dominant regional land power, *if* the U.S. should choose to withdraw from the region. U.S. withdrawal from Korea is certainly likely over the next decade, inasmuch as the Soviet threat to the peninsula has ceased being meaningful. If the U.S. should choose to abandon the mainland of Eurasia altogether, then Japan's task would be to serve as the regional replacement. It could not do this without expelling the U.S. Navy from the region.

This is therefore the basic difference between regionalization in northeast Asia and regionalization elsewhere in Eurasia. Japan, the key player in the region, cannot assert itself without naval power. It must become a major presence in the western Pacific as it emerges from American domination. Therefore, the strategy that the U.S. will use in the rest of Eurasia to avoid confrontation with regional powers—avoiding the land and dominating the oceans—will in fact trigger confrontation with Japan. Japan's act of taking control of the region will inevitably require confronting American domination of the northwest Pacific. Regionalization secures the U.S. from confrontation everywhere but in the Pacific, for there the U.S. must confront Japan, continuing as the dominant power or ceding control of part of the Pacific, a fundamental violation of U.S. interests.

Moreover, Japan's geopolitical interest in physically securing the area around it produces an economic problem. Japan is simply incapable of flourishing and growing economically within the constraints of Northeast Asia. Even should Japan be able to reach some accommodation with the Soviet Union for the utilization of Siberia for imports and for the use of the Soviet market for exports, the former would neither be accessible enough nor secure enough to satisfy the Japanese economy, while the latter would not be large enough to replace Japan's European and American exports. Siberia might be *part* of Japan's strategy, but as Japan discovered in the 1930s and 1970s, it could never be much more than a small part.

Thus, Japan's regional security zone and its economic interests do not neatly overlap. In precisely the same manner as in the 1930s, Japanese economic interests compel Japan to go beyond the boundaries of this limited region. But the problem, now as then, is that while Japan might well be able to generate sufficient military power to control its geopolitical region, it must make a much greater assertion of power, a much riskier one, to assure its control over an adequate economic sphere. In the first U.S.–Japanese war, Japanese armed forces proved inadequate to this task. Japan's problem is that while this might remain the case, U.S. hostility to Japanese interests might well leave Japan with no choice but to take this wild gamble again. Japan's strategic dilemma is this divergence between a limited geopolitical security zone and a much vaster, almost global economic interest. The only solution would be to deglobalize its economy and contract it to a sphere closer in size and location to Japan's security zone. In the 1930s and 1940s, the name of this area was Japan's Greater East Asia Co-Prosperity Sphere, much larger than the northwest Pacific, but substantially smaller than the world.

Therefore, in thinking about the future of Japanese strategy, it is necessary to supplement geostrategic thinking with economic analysis. For Japan, the defense of the nation and the protection of economic growth are intimately bound up, perhaps more so than for most nations. During the pre-World War II period, Japan's foreign policy was very much dictated by its trade and investment patterns. Indeed, during the period 1920–1940, the geopolitical and the economic were interlocked. There is every reason to think that this will be the case in the coming era. Thus, it is vital to consider the political implications of the trade patterns previously discussed.

JAPAN'S EXPORT-DRIVEN ECONOMY AND FOREIGN POLICY

Chapters 3, 6, and 7 considered the nature of the Japanese economy and its odd dependence on both imports and exports for its fundamental economic well-being. This dependency has obvious political consequences that intimately affect Japan's emerging strategy.

There are three important variables to consider in Japan's economic relations with the outside world: exports, imports, and investments. Each is in some way connected with the other, but they also stand apart. By looking at these three, understanding where the Japanese buy their raw materials, where they sell their goods, and where they invest their money, we can begin to see where some of their political interests lie. Then, by overlaying the economic map onto the geopolitical map, the structure of Japan's political imperatives can be revealed.

A good place to begin drawing the politico-economic map of Japan is by considering exports. It has been shown, in Chapter 6, that Japan's indispensable growth is increasingly maintained by exports. Anything that threatens to disrupt its stable export pattern is dangerous to Japan. This is nothing new. Indeed, it simply recreates Japan's pre-World War II pattern.

During both the prewar and postwar periods, Japan's export of goods cycled between the 9- and 15-percent-of-GNP bands, with a slightly higher bias in the prewar period.[6] While exports seem to have fallen below this level, the explanation has more to do with the strong yen and the shift toward exports of services than any real change in Japan's export dependency. In 1989, exports of goods and services together totalled 15.4 percent of GNP.[7] For the U.S., this figure was only 9.4 percent.[8]

Thus, Japan's dependency on exports is among the greatest in the world. Only Germany is more dependent. But Germany's export dependency is in fundamental ways different and less dangerous than Japan's. The bulk of German exports go to neighboring EC member countries, with whom it is intimately linked politically. Indeed, as 1992 looms, trade with these countries will be more like domestic trade than foreign trade. Secondly—and this is a point that is critical geopolitically—Germany's exports can be shipped by land, without the need for an extensive, over-the-horizon foreign policy. About two-thirds of Germany's trade is with EC members and countries like Switzerland that share borders with Germany.[9]

Japan's position is the exact opposite of Germany's. Japan must reach extremely distant trading partners in order to sell its goods. And in having this dependency, Japan incurs potentially severe political costs, as shown in Table 10-1.

All of Japan's trading partners are overseas, naturally, but historically they have been at great distances. In 1935, the three major export destinations were, in roughly equal amounts, Korea (then part of the Japanese empire), China (including Manchukuo), and the United States. Together, these accounted for over half of Japan's

TABLE 10-1. Japanese Exports by Country as Percent of Total Trade.

	1935	1989	CHANGE IN SHARE
Korea	17.94%	6.02%	−11.92
Taiwan	7.00	5.60	−1.40
China	18.45	3.09	−15.36
Hong Kong	1.60	4.19	+2.59
Malaysia	1.64	4.86	+3.22
Indonesia	4.59	1.20	−3.39
India	8.86	0.73	−8.13
Philippines	1.54	0.87	−0.67
Thailand	1.28	2.48	+1.20
Iran	0.00	0.34	+0.34
Europe	8.31	21.89	+13.58
U.S.	17.20	33.86	+16.66
Canada	0.26	2.47	+2.21
Mexico	0.16	0.69	+0.53
S. America	2.34	2.93	+0.59
Africa	5.91	1.67	−4.24
Oceania	3.05	3.33	+0.28

exports. In 1989, over half of Japan's exports went to the United States and Europe. The rest of what was to become the Greater East Asia Co-Prosperity Sphere purchased about 18 percent of the goods that Japan sold in 1935, and about 19 percent in 1989.

Thus, there has been a remarkable stability in Japan's export patterns, with one enormous exception. In 1935, Japan's empire was in Korea, China, and Formosa. Trade with that region declined from 43.9 percent of Japan's export trade to 14.71 percent in 1989, a drop of 29.19 points. American and European trade increased from 25.51 to 55.75 percent, a rise of 30.24 points. Thus, what has happened in the postwar period is that Japan's lost exports to China, Korea, and Taiwan have shifted to the U.S. and Europe, a change of vast political significance.

This enormous dependency on the West is a grave problem for Japan. Europe's integration in 1992 will probably close Japan off from some of that market. More important, Japan's sale of one-third of its export goods to the United States, a figure that represents only about 20 percent of total U.S. imports, makes Japan utterly dependent on American willingness to maintain the relationship unchanged.

It is extremely doubtful that Japan can afford to increase exports to the U.S., as that would serve to increase Japanese exposure there tremendously. The economic factors that made the U.S. so open to Japanese exports are cyclical in nature, and in due course the relative competitiveness of the Japanese and American economies will rotate. That is one threat. The political limits on Japanese imports in the U.S. are another and more immediate threat.

It has become a standard part of political life to hear Americans blast Japanese exports to the U.S. A fairly typical statement along these lines was made by Rep. Toby Roth, Republican from Wisconsin:

> We are on the brink. According to one poll, almost half of the American public believe that the United States is not doing enough to restrict the sale of Japan's goods in our country. American voters name trade barriers against the farmer as the foremost reason for our problem in agriculture. And there are good reasons for these perceptions. A pound of steak, for example, costs $30 in Tokyo— six times what it costs here. . . .
>
> The alarm clock sounded many months ago. But we've just been pushing the snooze button. The American public is fed up and wants to see results. Our world leadership is at stake as is our ability to provide for our people the standard of living and opportunities to which they aspire.
>
> In any event, things are going to change, one way or the other.[10]

The examples of such polemics are endless, and they are quite serious.

The possibility of further expansion of exports to the U.S. is politically nil. Japan has, in effect, acknowledged this in the agreements encouraging U.S. exports to Japan. As a political matter, it is already extremely dangerous for Japan to depend on the U.S. to take one-third of its exports. Since exports to the U.S. already total a little over 3 percent of Japan's GNP, the political threat to Japan is enormous. It cannot go forward by expanding trade and it cannot retreat without alternatives lest its entire growth structure, and therefore debt structure, unravels.

This means that Japan must open up new markets for exports. Given events in Europe, that continent is not an inviting target. Between Europe's obsession with developing Eastern Europe and the coming of integration in 1992, the Europeans are hardly open to penetration by the Japanese. This leaves Japan's traditional markets, particularly China, which has been neglected by the Japanese since 1950.

It should be recalled that Japan was prevented from establishing relations with the Communist Chinese by John Foster Dulles, but prior to that, some revival in trade had gone on. Japan was compensated by the U.S. for breaking with China in two ways. First, it was encouraged to develop and exploit Southeast Asia, and particularly Indochina. Second, the U.S. threw its market open to the Japanese.

It is interesting that the former Greater East Asia Co-Prosperity Sphere (aside from China, Korea, and Formosa) has remained an extremely steady market for Japanese goods, absorbing just under 20 percent of Japan's exports. For the past sixty years, the Japanese have not managed to exceed this level in Southeast Asia. Given the successes of the industrializing Four Little Tigers—Korea, Taiwan, Hong Kong, and Singapore—and the competition they represent, it is doubtful that Japan has much room for maneuver there, except in countries like Indonesia, Malaysia, and the Philippines.

Japan therefore has only one practical target for increased exports in East Asia: China. This is Japan's historical market. Indeed, for Japan, World War II began as a struggle to secure the Chinese market, or at least the market in northeastern China, against European and American intrusion. Sales of processed foods such as ground flour, textiles, and manufactured products accounted for over 18 percent of all Japanese exports in 1935. It is obvious that from the export side, at least, China will loom large in Japanese strategic thinking.

India must also be noted in this context. In 1935, over 8 percent of Japan's exports went to India. India was a consumer of Japanese textiles and, to a lesser extent, machinery.[11] At the end of the war India was developing its own textile industry and attempting to become self-sufficient in light manufacturing. Nevertheless, the Indian market is today over $21 billion, with Japan holding fourth place behind Iran, the U.S., and Germany.[12] But while Japanese–Indian trade has surged since 1985, and Japanese exports to India have increased by 60 percent, these exports constituted only about 1 percent of Japan's total exports.

In 1988, Japan exported about $90 billion worth of goods to the U.S. and about $47 billion to the EC. In the event of a political rupture, Japan would have to retarget about $137 billion worth of exports. In 1988, India's total imports were $20.6 billion and China's were $61 billion. If Japan were to take over all of the Chinese and Indian markets they do not now control, the increase would make up for less than half the exports Japan sent to the U.S. and Europe. If we expand this market to include the other nonindustrialized countries of Asia (Bangladesh, Brunei, Indonesia, Cambodia, Malaysia, Myanmar, Nepal, Pakistan, the Philippines, Thailand, and Vietnam), it would increase by about $82 billion, to total about $141 billion, or roughly the amount of Japan's trade with Europe and America. It should be noted that the bulk of these exports would be to Indonesia, Malaysia, Thailand, and the Philippines.

Since Japanese exports to China, India, Indonesia, Malaysia, Thailand, and the Philippines are already at about $25 billion, growth potential would be about $116 billion. Assuming that export growth to these countries could be stimulated by Japanese investment, then Japan could substitute markets in Asia for the U.S. and EC if it achieved two goals. First, it would need to develop an export mix suitable to those markets, and second, and far more important, it would need to force out of those markets all other exporters, including the United States and Europe, but also including the newly industrialized Asian countries: Korea, Singapore, Hong Kong, and Taiwan.

Since these countries—China, India, Indonesia, Malaysia, Thailand, and the Philippines—are the natural targets of Asia's Little Tigers, and since the U.S. also needs the Asian market for its own export growth, Japan would immediately clash with regional and global powers. Indeed, one of the reasons Japan might be forced to impose a regional empire might have nothing to do with national security. It might have to do with the fact that Japan would find it impossible to live in the constricted region imposed on it by the U.S. and the EC, or to tolerate Korea and Taiwan's aggressive marketing.

Thus, the regionalization of the world economy would pose terrific problems for Japan. Japan could only respond by regionalizing its own economy and attempting to dominate the East and Southeast Asian regions, up to and including India. The willingness of these nations to enter into exclusive relations with Japan is, of course, one issue. After all, in 1935, China's unwillingness to cede Japan exclusive trading rights in vast areas of China helped to trigger war. Second, Japan would have to bring the newly industrialized countries (NICs) of Asia under some sort of control, or at least arrive at some sort of understanding. Finally, the U.S. would have to accept that the price for accepting the exclusion of Japan from the western hemisphere markets would be its own exclusion from a Japanese–Asian trading zone. Given the likelihood of the newly industrialized countries resisting Japan's new order and America resisting exclusion from Asia, the makings of this alliance emerges as a pattern for conflict as well. Ultimately, these become political and military issues, rather than purely economic ones.

Japan's freedom to maneuver will depend to a great extent on the ability of potential markets, such as China and India, to grow. This growth, in turn, depends on their ability to export. From Japan's point of view, the most desirable imports from these countries would be raw materials, and in particular oil and other mineral products. India and China could supply some of the raw materials that Japan currently must import from Australia and the Persian Gulf. In addition, since China and India are poor countries, they are likely to become increasingly dependent on Japan, and less likely to attempt to manipulate the short-term mineral markets for long-term gain (see the discussion of vulnerability in Chapter 7). Unlike OPEC members, they lack the deep pockets necessary for such maneuvers and are in fact more dependent on maintaining their export relationship with Japan than OPEC members would be.

MINERAL IMPORTS AND JAPAN'S STRATEGY

Japan's regional control cannot rest solely on an export policy. For Japan, imports of raw materials are essential for the survival of its economy and the nation as a whole. Thus, any foreign policy adopted by Japan must include a mineral component: some plan for guaranteeing Japanese access to raw materials that it simply does not have in Japan.

The structure of Japan's imports, ranked by tonnage, including data for a number of minerals imported by Japan, and the vulnerability of those imports to disruption was discussed in Chapter 7. (See Table 7-4 on page 172.) Two areas are important to Japan: the Persian Gulf for its oil supply and Australia for a wide range of minerals. Indeed, these two nations between them supply over 60 percent of the total tonnage of raw materials imported by Japan annually. The Persian Gulf is obviously vital for oil. Japan imports about 63.5 percent of all its crude oil from inside the Straits of Hormuz, and over 70 percent of its crude from around the Persian Gulf in general.[13] The importance of Australia is, of course, somewhat different. It is not so much the large quantity of a single commodity that is important, but the wide array of products supplied by Australia, including coal, iron, lead, manganese, titanium, copper, zinc, bauxite ores, as well as intermediate fabrications.

Japan's dependency on imports is not new. It has been established in Chapter 3 that Japan's hunger for imports contributed to the first U.S.–Japanese war.[14] In particular, American domination of the Japanese oil import market in 1940 placed Japan at the political mercy of the United States. But it is extremely important to remember that there were two dimensions to U.S. control over Japanese imports. One was its own ability to interfere with U.S. minerals going to Japan. The other, more dangerous one, was the ability of the U.S. to use political and military power to prevent third parties from shipping oil to Japan. The former power was a vast inconvenience to Japan. The latter, if used effectively, was a deadly threat.

Prior to World War II, 80 percent of Japan's oil came from the U.S. In 1988, a slightly smaller portion, a little over 70 percent, came from the Persian Gulf, a region over which American politico-military control is again vast, although clearly unstable. Another important change is the rise of Australia as a major supplier of a wide spectrum of mineral ores. Beneath this top tier, the constellation of suppliers very much resembles prewar suppliers. Prior to the war, Japan's most important suppliers were the Netherlands East Indies, Malaya, the Philippines, China, Canada, and Micronesia. Only South Africa, Sri Lanka, Papua New Guinea, and Latin America appear on the 1988 list but were not on the 1939 list. And only Korea has ceased to be a mineral supplier, dropping off the list altogether.

Japan's task before 1941 was to change suppliers from the politically uncertain United States to more reliable (i.e., politically controllable) suppliers and to do this without at any point rupturing the flow of supplies. Japan's inability to do so caused it to act as it did at Pearl Harbor. Today, the political and military reliability of the Persian Gulf and Australia are the twin issues in Japanese mineral policy. And in both cases, as before World War II, the hidden key is the United States, which is the chief military actor in both regions.

The American intervention in the Persian Gulf in 1990 has radically intensified this question. The American occupation of Saudi Arabia vastly increased U.S. influence over Saudi oil policy, as well as the policies of the other, lesser Persian Gulf states. Implicit in the new relationship, the steel beneath the velvet, is the fact that if it wished, the U.S. could assume complete control of the entire region. The mere possibility that the U.S. could wind up controlling Iraqi, Kuwaiti, and Saudi oil fields, either directly or by proxy, poses grave problems for Japan's import policy. The U.S. is Japan's major economic competitor. The idea that in the 1990s, as in 1940, the U.S. would have direct control over oil imports is of deep concern. However, one must bear in mind that this has been the reality for the past forty-five years. U.S. control over Japan's sea-lanes placed the U.S. in effective control of Japan's mineral imports, without the need to rely on direct control.

Oil is, of course, vital and the Persian Gulf crisis focuses attention on its importance. However, other minerals are equally indispensable to Japan and, as has been shown, exports are equally vital. Thus, we need to look at a total matrix of Japan's dependency, imports and exports taken together. Consider the rank each nation holds as an importer of Japanese goods, and as an exporter of raw materials to Japan. (See Table 10-2.)

TABLE 10-2. Top Importers From Japan and Top Exporters of Minerals to Japan.

	IMPORT RANK	MINERAL EXPORT RANK
U.S.	1	8
Europe	2	—
Korea	3	—
Taiwan	4	—
Malaysia	5	9
Hong Kong	6	—
Oceania	7	2
China	8	6
S. America	9	4
Thailand	10	—
Canada	11	5
Persian Gulf	12	1
Africa	13	10
Indonesia	14	3
Philippines	15	12
India	16	7
Mexico	17	—
Madagascar	—	11
Papua New Guinea	—	13
Sri Lanka	—	14

An obvious problem that Japan has with its import needs is that its major importers are not also Japan's major mineral suppliers. Of Japan's top five customers, three supply almost no minerals to Japan, while the other two, the United States and Malaysia, rank only eighth and ninth, respectively, as suppliers.

Japan's major suppliers and major customers are different. The Persian Gulf and Australia are major suppliers, while the United States and Europe are major consumers. The neat, symbiotic relationship that would be desirable for Japan's security, in which Japan's suppliers and customers were the same, does not exist. Japan's most important customers are not dependent on Japanese purchases in order to maintain their economies, at least not on the level of mineral resources. The United States and Europe could cut their purchases from Japan without concern that mineral exports to Japan would be cut. At the same time, important suppliers like Australia are not, as was seen in Chapter 7, particularly dependent on mineral exports to Japan for their economic well-being either.

Japan's inability to hold its major customers with reciprocal dependency in mineral sales means that Japan is both vulnerable to trade barriers and to mineral embargoes. However, there might be some basis for a solution. The key is the general overlap of customers and mineral suppliers—of Japan's twenty most important customers, only six do not supply Japan with some minerals. If Japan could shift trading patterns, it might be able to establish some reciprocity.

Beneath the top tier of trading partners there is a group of countries that are both consumers of Japanese goods and exporters of raw materials to Japan: Malaysia, China, the Pacific Rim nations of Latin America, Canada, Africa (particularly South Africa), Indonesia, the Philippines, and India. Four of these countries are in Asia and were formerly, in whole or in part, included in the Greater East Asia Co-Prosperity Sphere: Malaysia, China, Indonesia, and the Philippines. India is part of Asia and was only a prospective part of the old Japanese empire. The others, in Latin America, are far outside the current political horizon of Japan.

Note that Malaysia, China, Indonesia, the Philippines, and India all are prominent components of a Japanese export policy designed to overcome Japan's expulsion from the American and European markets. This is extremely important, as developing these countries as customers will require developing them as exporters not competing with Japan for third markets. Mineral production and refining obviously fits neatly with Japan's possible strategic export policy. Thus, the appearance of these export targets on the mineral import market list is an extremely hopeful sign for those designing an export policy for Japan.

One obvious strategy that Japan could pursue is to strengthen economic ties to these countries, particularly Indonesia, the Philippines, Malaysia, and India, in order to increase their ability to produce and export needed raw materials and, thus, increase their ability to consume Japanese exports. The creation of this yen bloc is the basic Japanese dream in this century. It motivated Japan's foreign policy during the 1930s, and as dependence on the United States becomes less and less comfortable, it will increasingly motivate Japanese behavior in the future.

There is an obvious problem with this strategy. Just as there is an extremely tight fit between Japan's export needs and the size of the markets it would focus on, the fit between Japan's resource needs and the supply available in East and Southeast Asia may not be right. There might simply not be enough oil and other minerals there to carry out this strategy. If that were the case, then even the supra-regional strategy for Japan would be insufficient and Japan would be compelled to pursue a broader, indeed, global strategy. Another consequence might be to cut so deeply into the producer's economic needs as to make a friendly alliance impossible, necessitating a more direct and brutal relationship.

NOBUTOSHI AKAO AND THE PROBLEM OF ECONOMIC SECURITY

In thinking about Japan's predicament, there are two measures that must be taken into account. One is an objective measure, an evaluation of Japan's position from the standpoint of the objective forces that shape Japan's experience of the world. In a certain sense, this objective measure is the most important. Whatever the subjective consciousness of the Japanese might be at this moment, the future of that consciousness will be shaped by these objective forces.

Nevertheless, it is intriguing to consider the second measure: the extent to which officials of the Japanese foreign-policy establishment share this view. In general, Japanese officials are circumspect on all matters of foreign policy and particularly those aspects that might compel Japan to take more active roles in the international arena. The general passivity of Japanese foreign policy has led to a foreign-policy cadre hesitant to pose Japanese needs in any consistent—let alone persistent—manner.

An interesting and important insight into the thinking of Japanese officials on the problem of mineral vulnerability is to be found in the writings of Nobutoshi Akao. His work was done under the auspices of the Royal Institute of International Affairs in London, as part of a study group on Japan's resource condition in the face of the Arab oil embargo and the general scarcity of raw materials during the late 1970s. Akao edited the final product, *Japan's Economic Security*, wrote the introduction, and contributed a chapter entitled "Resources and Japan's Security."

What makes Akao important is that at the time of the publication of his work, he was chief economic counsellor at Japan's embassy in Washington. Even more important, Akao was appointed head of the Japanese Foreign Ministry's United Nations Bureau on October 15, 1990.[15] In that position he was directly charged with the deployment of any Japanese forces that might be sent under U.N. auspices to the Persian Gulf. In a sense, the crisis over Kuwait was the one that he had been preparing for during his study group when he wrote, for publication in 1983:

> Because keeping the Straits of Hormuz open is so vitally important to Japan, the possibility of some form of contribution to the US-proposed Rapid Deployment Force in the Gulf and Indian Ocean could come up for consideration in the future.[16]

Obviously, many Westerners and many Japanese have commented on Japan's dependence on Hormuz for its economic existence, and some have speculated on some sort of Japanese military action to keep the straits open. What makes Akao important is that his role as a senior Japanese Foreign Ministry official makes his pronouncements particularly authoritative. Even though they were not published as official Japanese views on the matter, their author is certainly both in an excellent position to observe these policies and has, not incidentally, been placed in the position of executing the policy about which he speculated in the early 1980s. Thus, a close look at his insights would be particularly valuable.

Akao argues that the postwar arrangement with the United States

> . . . enabled Japan to concentrate almost exclusively on economic activities. As a nation poorly endowed with indigenous resources (except human resources), it was left with no alternative but to develop as a trading nation, importing raw materials and exporting manufactured goods. To guarantee its development in this direction, there was the IMF-GATT system, which aimed at the expansion of world trade on a free, multilateral and non-discriminatory basis. Japan enjoyed the full benefits of free trade.[17]

Japan existed as a passive partner to the United States, urged by the Americans to take a more active role but generally left to develop as a trading state. During this entire period, the U.S. kept the threat of a disruption of raw material supplies at bay. But 1973 changed all that:

> In post-war Japan, incidents such as the U.S. embargo on soybean exports and the oil crisis of 1973 painfully exposed Japan's economic vulnerability. Even before the oil crisis, however, the importance and seriousness of the resource problem had been recognized. . . .[18]

The conclusion to be drawn is that:

> The foregoing shows that raw material problems cannot be treated solely in the context of domestic economic and industrial policies; they have far-reaching implications for Japan's security and foreign policy. In order to ensure stable supplies of important raw materials it will be essential for Japan to maintain close, friendly and interdependent relations with their producers. The solution of many problems, especially those in the energy field, must be tackled by the major industrialized countries together, through close cooperation and coordination of policies and not by competing for even scarcer resources.[19]

Akao fully understands the geography of Japanese vulnerability:

> The possibility of a closure of important passageways such as the Straits of Hormuz and the Malacca Straits is a constant cause of concern: over 70% of oil bound for Japan passes through the Straits of Hormuz; about one-third of Japan's total export and import goods, including about 80% of its oil imports, passes through the Malacca Straits. An alternative to the Malacca Straits is the Lombok Straits, but the Lombok route means rerouting by an additional thousand miles. Furthermore, whereas the former are de facto international straits surrounded by Malaysia, Singapore and Indonesia, the latter are within the territorial waters claimed by Indonesia, and would subject Japan's lifeline to the policy influence of one country.[20]

Akao clearly understands the general problem facing Japan, but his understanding is rooted in the context of the early 1980s, a time of a very real and even intensifying Cold War between the United States and the Soviet Union. Akao's notion of cooperation between the advanced industrialized nations is really a vision of cooperation among the anti-Soviet capitalist liberal democracies, the same powers that created the IMF-GATT system as part of their anti-Soviet struggle. Akao proposed that Japan participate in an American Rapid Deployment Force to hold open the Straits of Hormuz. Today Akao is a key player in that nascent Japanese participation. But the international reality has changed dramatically since Akao so discerningly sketched the Japanese perception. Now, the Soviets are almost part of the alliance system that was created to destroy them. This is a reality that Akao, no matter how brilliant or perceptive he is, could not have imagined in 1983.

Akao's analysis is useful in gauging the Japanese foreign-policy elite's perception of its problems. Its solutions, however, are limited by the apparent permanence of the circumstances in which it was written:

> It is out of the question to try to expand an empire in order to control overseas resources, as Japan tried in vain to do in the 1930s and early 1940s. The only choice left in this regard has been to develop (1) long-term purchase contracts with overseas suppliers, often accompanied by the provision of loans for the development of resources to be imported, and (2) so-called "autonomous development" schemes, by which Japanese firms make direct investment for the development and import of resources.[21]

The failure of Japanese imperialism during the 1940s caused Akao to argue that the only defense Japan could develop would be an economic defense. Implicit in his thinking is the notion that the security of those investments would be guaranteed either by the hope of further investment or by American power.

A world in which Japan is not in a position to make further investments and in which the U.S. is not inclined to safeguard Japanese investments in mineral-producing countries raises the question of whether Akao's casual dismissal of an imperial solution would continue to hold.

Akao's published work was a study of the forces threatening Japanese economic security. In this study, he focused on Japan's well-known mineral vulnerability and linked that vulnerability to the sorts of political crises that might threaten Japan's access to minerals, in particular to oil. It is altogether appropriate that the man who literally wrote the book on Japanese resource dependency should be placed in charge of a possible deployment that is ultimately concerned with securing the resources on which Japan depends.

Whether or not the Japanese Diet ever approves this particular deployment, Nobutoshi Akao is significant as one of the most insightful and forthright of Japan's postwar foreign-policy thinkers. His caveat that empire is "out of the question" is a reasonable point of view within the context in which he was working: the Cold War. But the agenda that Akao set for Japan—securing its mineral lines of supply—must remain Japan's permanent strategy. And if empire is out of the question, then the matter of a more subtle approach to securing those resources is still of the essence.

FOREIGN INVESTMENT AND AID: FRIENDLY IMPERIALISM

Akao does focus our attention on the one currently active dimension of Japanese foreign policy: investments. In Chapter 6 it was shown that the Japanese economy, particularly since the decline in growth during the 1980s, has become a money-exporting economy. Japan's high savings rate and the inability of a maturing Japanese economy to absorb those savings internally has forced Japan to engage in massive foreign investments. Moreover, Japanese promotion of growth rates through aggressive export policies has generated an economic and political need to make foreign investments. Resentment at aggressive trade policies is frequently assuaged by transferring production to the target country. Since one of the reasons for Japan's domestic investment constraints is a massive labor shortage, which the Japanese will not solve through immigration, making foreign investments increases the Japanese labor supply without requiring immigration.

Thus, in looking at Japanese foreign investments, we are looking at Japan's first response to the crisis of economic success. And since foreign investment is, if not managed, certainly broadly directed by the Ministry of International Trade and Industry (MITI), we can glimpse the thinking going on in the Japanese establishment about foreign policy. In the case of most free market societies with free currency flows, this would not necessarily indicate conscious decision making. However, in the case of Japan, MITI is quite conscious in planning and directing Japan's overseas activities, including its foreign investment. In addition, discussion of the manner in which Japan routinely creates savings surpluses that must be invested overseas has shown that Japan's room for maneuver in this area is substantial.

It is useful therefore to consider Japan's recent investment patterns, as well as its foreign-aid policies, for some insight into Japanese thinking on the subject. Of all Japanese overseas investment holdings, 42.9 percent are in North America, 17.7 percent are in Europe, 15.9 percent in Asia, 14.5 percent in Latin America, 5.5 percent in Oceania, and the rest in Africa and the Middle East.[22]

Obviously, Japan's investments have gone where its exports go; North America and Europe are the targets of most Japanese investment. That is a safe and prudent course. It is also necessary, particularly to the U.S. as it struggles with its enormous federal budget deficit. The ability to demonstrate that production takes place in the U.S. is a safeguard against anti-Japanese sentiment. In addition, the North American investment environment, apart from long-term political dangers, is the safest and most lucrative in the world. It is a safe solution to Japan's labor shortage.

Breaking things down a little further and expressing Japanese investment in dollars reveals the enormous importance of the U.S. in Japan's investment strategy. Japan has over $104 billion invested in the U.S., while only $15.8 billion is invested in Britain and about $12.4 billion in Australia. What is particularly interesting is Indonesia's appearance on this list as the fourth-largest target of investment ($10.4 billion), as well as Hong Kong in sixth place and Singapore in eighth place ($8.1 billion and $5.7 billion, respectively).[23]

It is worth noting that there are other targets of investing, but they are primarily transit points for rather ambiguous investments. Among these are Panama ($14.6 billion), the Cayman Islands ($6.7 billion), the Bahamas ($3.3 billion), Bermuda ($1.2 billion), and Liberia ($4.3 billion). Panama and Liberia are obviously flags of convenience for Japanese merchantmen, while the others are investment blinds, the purpose of which we will leave unexamined.

The level of its investment in the U.S. is an obvious problem for Japan. On one hand, ongoing investment in the U.S. both makes economic sense and is a smart political ploy, since it serves as insurance in the event that Japanese-produced imports are banned from the market. But with the U.S., freezing and expropriating foreign assets for political reasons is a tradition. The ability of the U.S. to manufacture a justification for seizing or sequestering some or all of such funds is legendary.

Japan's vulnerability to seizure of assets must limit its political activity against U.S. interests. It should also shortly set in motion a policy of redirected investments, particularly into the region mentioned in our discussion of Japanese imports and exports. This has not yet become visible, and from a strategic viewpoint Japan's investment policy appears purposeless.[24] But it has been understandable. The cumulative breakdown of Japanese investment shows a country that has been emerging from American domination and has taken its first few steps toward freedom. But it is now only the early 1990s. All this will become much clearer by the year 2000.

Equally as interesting as where the Japanese have invested their money is what they have invested it in. In North America, the bulk of the investments has gone into real estate, followed by banking, merchandising, and services. Primarily, the Japanese have searched for places to park their money, instruments for investing money, and infrastructure for their exports. In Europe, nearly half of their investments have gone into banking, with the remainder fairly well scattered.[25]

Japanese investments in Asia have been far different. There, Japan's number-one target is mining and manufacturing. There has evidently been tension between Japan's investment plans and the desires of the host governments. For example, in Indonesia the Suharto government has wanted to see investment in manufacturing, while Japanese investment has been primarily in oil and gas development. Japan has consciously set itself the goal of developing Indonesian oil and gas as a close-at-hand alternative to Persian Gulf oil.[26]

Japanese investment policy is clearly bifurcated. The bulk of Japan's investment goes to the United States and other developed countries. About two-thirds of Japanese assets are in North America, Europe, and Oceania. Fully 25 percent of Japan's Asian investment goes to Indonesia, ahead of Hong Kong and all of the other newly industrialized countries. Indonesia is significant in two ways. First, it is a potential supplier of large numbers of minerals to Japan. Second, its strategic position, controlling Pacific access to the Indian Ocean, is of great significance to the Japanese. This is reflected in their investment policy and also in their aid policy.

This emphasis on Indonesia can also be seen in Japanese Official Development Aid (ODA). Japanese aid is significant on an international scale. In 1990, Japan became the number-one aid donor in the world, disbursing nearly $9 billion dollars' worth of aid (19.3 percent of the world's total), compared to $7.6 billion for the U.S. It is in the area of ODA that Japan's strategic interests can be seen most clearly:

TABLE 10-3. Ten Recipients of Japanese Foreign Aid, 1988, 1987.

1988		1987	
COUNTRY	% OF TOTAL	COUNTRY	% OF TOTAL
Indonesia	10.8	Indonesia	8.6
China	7.4	China	7.1
Philippines	5.9	Philippines	6.4
Thailand	3.9	India	4.7
Bangladesh	3.7	Thailand	4.6
Pakistan	3.3	Bangladesh	4.2
Burma	2.8	Burma	3.1
Sri Lanka	2.2	Malaysia	2.9
India	2.0	Korea	2.3
Egypt	1.9	Pakistan	2.2

(Source: Japan Economic Institute)

The importance of Indonesia, China, and the Philippines in Japanese aid efforts is clear, as is the decline in Korea's neediness and Japan's interest. An interesting shift in the pattern is the apparent decline of India on the list of recipients. However, this really represents a shift from direct aid to more complex forms of lending. Where India received about $200 million dollars in direct aid, Prime Minister Kaifu, on a recent visit to India, pledged credits equaling nearly $700 million. Indonesia was targeted to receive more than $2 billion during the 1990 fiscal year in total grants and loans.[27] Loans give an added sense of Japan's targets: 17.7 percent of Japanese development loans in 1988 went to Indonesia, 14.5 percent to China, 11.6 percent to the Philippines, and 9 percent to India.

As with Japan's investment, it is instructive to look at what Japan is aiding. In 1988, the single largest grant area was development of energy resources (13.2%), followed by transportation development (12.4%), mining and industrial development (9.4%), with a heavy emphasis on mining, and agriculture (9.2%). Debt relief, food aid, emergency aid together equaled only 3.4 percent, education was 4.7

percent, health was 2 percent, and so on.[28] In short, the Japanese have been extremely generous, but their generosity has centered on things that they expect to profit from themselves. They have behaved fully rationally in the targets of their aid, and in their funding areas.

Investment is one key to political domination. But, as America discovered in Cuba in 1960, investment can itself be a form of vulnerability, unless the investor can make the recipient respect the property rights of the investor. One way is to make the relationship continually beneficial to the recipient. Dependence on the investor's technical abilities to maintain factories and mines is one such lever. Another is the promise of greater investment down the road. A third is an ongoing, reciprocal trade relationship.

Ideally, this is the kind of relationship Japan wants to have with the nations it is interested in. However, as has been seen, there are countervailing tendencies in Japan's relationship with these countries, which might well turn these relationships more exploitative than symbiotic. This is particularly the case, as will be seen, in the matter of oil production and allocation. In the event of shifts in Japan's—or the international—economic environment, Japan might find itself incapable of maintaining a mutually satisfying relationship with countries like Indonesia and India.

On a recent trip to South Asia, an extraordinary thing occurred. President Ghulam Ishaq Khan of Pakistan said, "A power vacuum is emerging in Southwest Asia and this should be filled by countries such as Japan."[29] Indian Prime Minister Singh, on the same trip, was quoted as saying that Japan should exercise "strong leadership" in the region.[30]

The idea that India and Pakistan should both regard Japan as a friend and a champion and that both should welcome Japanese power in the region was not only an extraordinary event, but perhaps a turning point in their regional affairs. The Indians clearly were interested in a Japanese counterweight to the Americans, while the Pakistanis were concerned with a power vacuum developing in the region. While the Iraqi intervention shifted the equation, putting off the day of reckoning somewhat, it is quite clear that the Japanese have an open door in South Asia.

The problem is whether everyone is operating under false pretenses. Clearly, neither India nor Pakistan expects to feel the force of Japanese power. Nor do the Japanese expect to be harsh. A Japanese Foreign Ministry official was quoted as saying, after the meeting, that "South Asian countries traditionally have attached more importance to military power than economic might in the international order, but under the new international order that is emerging . . . military power has a more limited impact on international affairs."[31]

From the official Japanese perspective, Kaifu's visit was not an exercise in power politics. Rather, it was an attempt to wield influence through strictly economic power. In a sense, the issue here is whether the South Asians or the Japanese have a tighter grip on reality. The South Asian position seems to be that Japan will shortly have political and military power to match its economic power, and they are courting the Japanese with an eye toward that day.

The Japanese position is that what power they do wield will be economic and moral, rather than politico-military in any traditional sense. Both may be disappointed. The Indians and Pakistanis may be proven right about the future of Japan's power, but quite disappointed in how it is used. Japan, on the other hand, may be proven quite wrong in its assessment of its strengths. One would like to think that the Japanese will be pleased with the uses of power, but there it is necessary to stop, for as in most modern political affairs, they are as likely to be as disappointed as their victims.

THE POLITICAL REALITY OF JAPANESE INVESTMENT

Japan's essential strategic problem is the clash between its economic and political interests, and the tension between its regional security needs and its broader economic interests. This is a struggle confronted by most nations, but it is particularly lethal in Japan's case because its wealth is as great as its vulnerability. As World War II showed, miscalculation in Japan's case, either way, can have catastrophic consequences.

Japan, like all nations, must think about its physical security, and that means Japan has to begin thinking about matters close to home. Securing the waters around Japan, the Korean Peninsula, and the near coast of Asia are all matters that would concern an ordinary nation first.

But Japan is no ordinary nation. It is the world's second-largest economy, and that economy is located on a series of islands too small to sustain it. If the Japanese economy is to compete with vast entities such as the United States and Europe, it must secure the markets and resources that are readily at hand, as have the other two. Japan has to go quite a distance before it can secure either markets or resources, and it must do so through waters controlled by the world's greatest economic power, Japan's old and dangerous nemesis, the United States.

This compulsion to think intercontinentally clashes with Japan's regional security needs in a number of ways. First, Japan cannot neglect the economic question. This means that it must plunge into intercontinental ventures before it has secured its own backyard. Second, the nearest nations, particularly Korea and Taiwan, are direct competitors of Japan. Their economies compete with Japan's, which means that the possibility of bribing or seducing them is minimal. Finally, America's global interests and the regional interests of Korea and/or Taiwan might well mesh more efficiently than Japan's would with either of those neighboring countries. That would pose a particularly deadly threat to Japan.

The American question is the most important and the darkest for Japan. Japan's first and best hope is to maintain its present relationship with the United States. But any prudent nation will prepare for the worst, and it would certainly not be absurd to anticipate some sort of rupture between Japan and the U.S. before the end of the century, if not sooner. Thus, Japan's strategy must begin by measuring its environment for alternatives to the United States.

Which countries are of most interest to Japan can be seen if we consider trading partners and investment targets. (See Map 10-2.) Indonesia, China, Malaysia, the Philippines, Singapore—in short, the entire Greater East Asia Co-Prosperity Sphere except Korea and Taiwan—represent the great alternative for Japan. Unfortunately, Japan remembers the inadequacy of this empire last time. It could neither provide the markets and raw materials required by Japan, nor could it be easily defended.

Obviously, Japan hopes to avoid a military confrontation altogether; indeed the thought of such a confrontation would strike most Japanese as preposterous and horrendous. Avoiding such a confrontation requires one of two things. The U.S. should be willing to remain in the strategic relationship it has had with Japan and preserve Japan's free-trade environment regardless of cost to the U.S. Or Japan should use its economic power to create a system of relationships that will assure its economic needs without recourse to politics or, particularly, to war.

The problem with this last option is that being very rich and quite weak is normally an invitation to catastrophe. This is one of the lessons the Kuwaitis have taught the world. For Japan to have the kind of vast, transoceanic empire that the second-largest economy in the world must have in order to maintain its economic prosperity, it must be able to control the disorder inherent in such a system of relationships. Japan's hope is that wealth alone will be sufficient inducement to Indonesians, for example, not to disrupt the internal functioning of Japanese imports, exports, and investments. But in a country as fractious as Indonesia, expecting government and dissidents to operate according to Japan's notion of economic well-being is unrealistic.

MAP 10–2. Top 5 Trading Partners With Japan; Investment Targets; Aid Recipients.

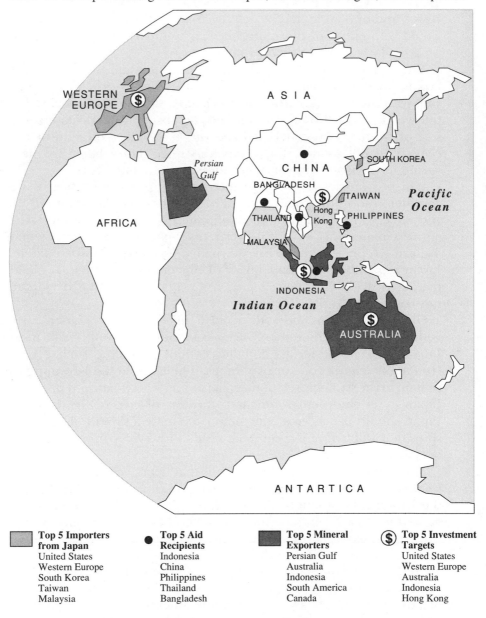

	Top 5 Importers from Japan		Top 5 Aid Recipients		Top 5 Mineral Exporters		Top 5 Investment Targets
	United States		Indonesia		Persian Gulf		United States
	Western Europe		China		Australia		Western Europe
	South Korea		Philippines		Indonesia		Australia
	Taiwan		Thailand		South America		Indonesia
	Malaysia		Bangladesh		Canada		Hong Kong

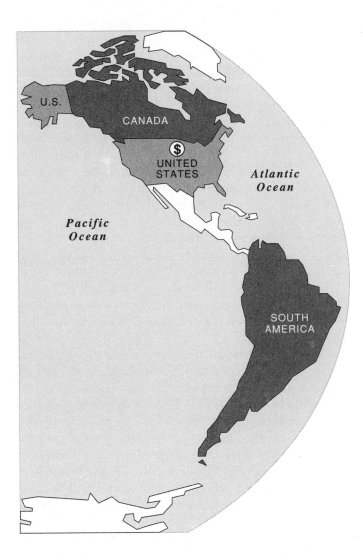

In a way, Japan is confronting the same problem as the U.S. The end of the Cold War has created a power vacuum in vast areas of the world. This vacuum appears to be primarily economic, but in essence it is political. A need for order is the foundation of economic growth. Japan would like to engage in economic intercourse with these countries without becoming involved in ordering their internal and external affairs. As the U.S. found at the end of World War II, and in Japan in particular, political consequences are frequently the unintended result of other pursuits.

The empire that was thrust on the U.S. at the end of World War II was never an easy burden to bear. To this day, the U.S. cannot admit publicly or even to itself that it is an imperial power with imperial responsibilities. The U.S. has always hidden its imperialism behind the veil of its alliance system. This was natural, since the U.S. began its history in rebellion against imperialism and still holds national self-determination to be the highest moral principle, even as it must violate that principle with regularity if it is to defend its fundamental interests and those of its empire.

Japan also finds empire anathema to its pacific spirit. One ought to take this at least as seriously as we take the American ambivalence, although one might suspect that Japanese pacifism is less deeply rooted in the culture and psyche of Japan than anticolonialism is in the American psyche. In both cases, circumstances have compelled them to act as they do.

As the United States cuts Japan adrift, Japan's vast economic resources will inevitably create a system of dependencies in the Pacific and Indian Ocean basins. Such a complex and vulnerable set of relationships, which are also so essential for Japan's well-being, cannot endure without being protected. First, it needs to be protected from the chaos that is endemic to the region. Second, it needs to be protected from regional conflicts that can disrupt the flow of goods in both directions and destroy valuable investments. Finally it needs to be protected from other imperial powers that inevitably will become frightened by the growth of Japanese power and influence in the region.

The natural antagonist to this growth in Japanese power is the United States. It was, after all, the United States that sought to break the Japanese empire in the 1930s and finally succeeded in defeating it in war. It is also the United States that is the world's largest economic power and is therefore dependent, although to a lesser degree, on trade with the region that will naturally fall under Japan's sway.

The U.S. will be frightened for geopolitical reasons as well. The growth of Japanese power in the Pacific will inevitably cause the U.S. to feel that one of its fundamental interests, domination of the Pacific, is being threatened. Just as in the 1930s, when the U.S. reckoned that the growth of Japanese power would first force the U.S. out of the western Pacific and then threaten the Pacific as a whole, so, too, in the twenty-first century the growth of Japanese power will be construed by the U.S. as a direct challenge to American hegemony in the region. This will certainly be true, although not at all Japan's intention.

Japan will attempt to reassure the Americans; the Americans will engage in minor economic and political competition with Japan and, just as it did from 1920 until 1941, the cycle of well-founded mistrust, fed by paranoia on both sides, will create an untenable condition in the region. But before this situation can be analyzed fully, it is necessary to stop and examine with some precision Japan's geopolitical and economic options. We need to understand precisely the choices facing the Japanese, and, as with the Americans, divine the course they will most likely pursue.

1. Japan Defense Agency (JDA), *Defense of Japan, 1989*, p. 85. *Defense of Japan* is a critical document, indispensable for understanding Japan's defense policy. An annual issued by the JDA, the Japanese equivalent of a defense ministry, it is translated into English by the *Japan Times*. Each year, the JDA summarizes its analysis of the international politico-military situation, and discusses in some detail Japan's response to it. In many ways it is a reticent document. It is "official" not only in the sense that it is a product of a government agency, but also in the more subtle sense that it does not deviate from the publicly stated understanding and policies of the Japanese government, and does not engage in heterodox analysis, as several documents published by the U.S. Department of Defense do. Within these limits, however, it is a candid document that gives the careful reader real insights into the thinking and actions of the Japanese defense community.

2. See U.S. Department of Defense, *A Strategic Framework for the Asian Pacific Rim: Looking Toward the 21st Century* (Washington, D.C., 1990), p. 18.

3. Malcolm McIntosh, *Japan Rearmed* (New York, 1986), p. 88.

4. Department of Defense, *Strategic Framework*, p. 18.

5. Hisahiko Okazaki, *A Grand Strategy for Japanese Defense* (Washington, D.C., 1986), p. 132.

6.

Japan's Physical Exports as a Percentage of GNP

1930	10.57%
1931	9.18
1932	10.85
1933	13.01

Japan's Physical Exports as a Percentage of GNP (continued)

1934	13.83
1935	14.96
1936	15.13
1937	13.57
1938	10.04
1939	10.80
1940	9.28
1971	9.86
1972	8.79
1973	8.42
1974	11.53
1975	11.76
1976	12.85
1977	12.39
1978	9.58
1979	9.88
1980	11.66
1981	12.72
1982	12.57
1983	12.17
1984	13.20
1985	12.83
1986	10.28
1987	9.21
1988	8.93
1989	7.02

(Sources: Bank of Japan; Japan Bureau of Statistics)

7. Japan Economic Institute, *Japanese Economy at Cruising Speed in 1989*, Washington, D.C., p. 8.
8. U.S. Bureau of the Census, *Statistical Abstracts of the United States* (Washington, D.C., 1989), p. 421. This figure is for 1988.
9. International Monetary Fund, *Direction of Trade Statistics* (Washington, D.C., 1990), p. 186. It is interesting, of course, to speculate on the effect on Germany should 1992 fail, and should its neighbors and co-Europeanists begin erecting tariff barriers as a result of the falling-out. The pressure on Germany to force open these tariff barriers, or find more distant, over-the-horizon trading partners, might well become intense.
10. U.S. House of Representatives, Subcommittees on Asian and Pacific Affairs and on International Economic Policy and Trade of the Committee on Foreign Affairs, *Hearings*, April 23, 1987, Washington, D.C., p. 8.
11. Mitsubishi Economic Research Bureau, *Japanese Trade and Industry: Present and Future* (London, 1936), p. 559.
12. International Monetary Fund, *Direction of Trade Statistics*, pp. 222–223.
13. Petroleum Association of Japan, *Japanese Oil Statistics Today*, No. 155 (Tokyo, May 1990).

14. For an interesting discussion of the connection between Japanese resource imports and its foreign-policy options, see Yashuhiro Murota, "Options for a Resource-Poor Country—Japan," in *Mineral Resources in the Pacific Area*, ed. Lawrence B. Krause and Hugh Patrick (San Francisco, 1977).
15. Reuters News Service, October 16, 1990.
16. Nobutoshi Akao, *Japan's Economic Security* (New York, 1983), p. 19.
17. Ibid., p. 2.
18. Ibid., p. 7,
19. Ibid., p. 9.
20. Ibid., p. 19.
21. Ibid., p. 21.
22. Source: Japan Ministry of Finance.
23. Source: Japan Economic Institute.
24. See Taggart Murphy, "Power Without Purpose: The Crisis of Japan's Global Financial Dominance," *Harvard Business Review*, March–April 1989.
25. Japan Economic Institute, "Japan's FY 1989 Foreign Direct Investment," No. 23B, June 15, 1990, p. 3.
26. Japan Economic Institute, "Japan's Foreign Direct Investment in Developing Countries," August 11, 1989, p. 11.
27. Japan Economic Institute, "Kaifu's South Asia Initiative," No. 19B, 11 May 1990.
28. Japan Economic Institute: "Japan's Foreign Aid Policy: 1989 Update," October 27, 1989., p. 9.
29. *Japan Times*, May 14–20, 1990, p. 1.
30. Ibid., p. 1.
31. Japan Economic Institute, "Kaifu's South Asia Initiative," p. 2.

11

Japan's Strategic Options: Return to Empire

There is something inherently unstable in Japan's strategic position. The grand strategic goals of the United States build on each other neatly, one flowing into the other, each adding strength to the next. In Japan's case, the goals pull in different directions. Japan's need for physical security requires that it take control of its regional environment, the northwestern Pacific, which is an extremely difficult, if not impossible, task. Japan's need for raw materials demands that it adopt a much broader policy, reaching far beyond the confines of the northwestern Pacific. This, too, is an extremely difficult task. Compounding this difficulty is the fact that regional domination requires economic security, which in turn requires a broader strategic interest. A broader strategic interest in turn demands that Japan be completely secure within its region. The regional and broader strategies presuppose the success of each other, in an endless circular logic. By its strategic requirements, Japan is trapped in contradictory and mutually exclusive demands that push it beyond the limits of its power. Once before, this situation resulted in the catastrophe of a U.S.–Japanese war.

For Japan, accepting the domination of the United States solved this insoluble problem. By turning regional security and broader Pacific security issues over to the Americans, who had the power to impose an acceptable order on the Pacific as a whole and on the northwestern Pacific in particular, Japan did not have to face the contradictions in its strategic position, nor the limits of its power. The result was a golden age for Japan, one that will be remembered for centuries.

What made this golden age possible, apart from the alliance with the United States, was America's fear of the Soviet Union. This fear tempered America's behavior toward Japan. The United States was willing to be not only the guarantor of Japanese security and economic well-being, but also an open free market for Japanese goods. The only price was the passive availability of Japan's geography for strategic uses. Certainly, if war had broken out, Japan would have been in grave danger. But war never did break out and the price Japan paid, compared to what it received, remained extremely low.

The Cold War is over and the question facing Japan is whether the U.S.–Japanese relationship forged during the Cold War can survive its demise. It must be understood that, for Japan, continuing this relationship is of vital importance. No one has been more sincere than the Japanese in hoping that nothing will happen to destroy the friendship between the two nations. The problem is whether or not American and Japanese interests will continue to mesh without the American fear of the Soviet Union.

There are three facts with which any analysis of Japan in the post-Cold War period must begin:

1. The United States Navy is the indisputable master of all the oceans.
2. Japan sends one-third of its exports to the U.S., and the U.S. deeply resents this fact.
3. Japan imports almost all its critical raw materials by sea.

These three facts constitute an extraordinarily explosive mixture. At this moment in history, America has the military capability to break Japan at will simply by blocking its imports and exports. It also has the power to ensure the safety and profitability of Japan's trade. Which tack the U.S. takes will depend to a great extent on how it deals with the second fact, that Japanese exports to the U.S. are understood to be damaging vast swaths of less-efficient American industries.

Japan must calculate its future path in light of its vulnerability to American economic and military action. Whatever resentments the Americans had toward Japan over the last twenty years or so, their hand was always stayed by a greater fear of the Soviet Union. With that fear effectively gone, Japan's question is whether it can continue to depend on the U.S. for its economic and political security. Indeed, it must ask whether American power will be turned on Japan. Japanese statesmen may hope for a continuation of the golden age, but as prudent planners they must prepare for a grimmer age.

As the twentieth century draws to a close, Japan has three basic strategic choices:

1. Permanent subordination to the United States.
2. Replace the United States as the dominant power in the northwest Pacific and Northeast Asia.
3. Domination of the western Pacific at least as far as the Singapore–Indonesia–Papua New Guinea line.

It is not a neat choice for Japan, for the second and third choices, far from being mutually exclusive, ultimately rest on each other. Yet Japan must begin with one of these three policies and not necessarily with the one most Japanese would prefer.

JAPAN AS AMERICA'S JUNIOR PARTNER

There is a story told in which a Japanese is asked whether the United States is Japan's friend or elder brother. The Japanese answers, "Elder brother; you can pick your friends." There is much truth in this bittersweet response. For forty-five years America has been ever-present in Japanese life. The American presence has been benevolent, but overwhelming and unavoidable. The Japanese might have been willing to have America as a friend, but they never really had a choice. America was an older brother.

The relationship between the United States and Japan has, on the whole, been mutually satisfying. The U.S. increased its national security and blocked the Soviets. The Japanese grew prosperous and were protected. The relationship was pleasant, if not wholly dignified, even though America could at times be overbearing and inconsiderate. Japan was not, however, entirely a free country. It could not choose its friends and enemies; that was done by the Americans. But it could choose where to buy and sell; that was guaranteed by the Americans. Junior partnership carried its indignities, but it was also a safe and rewarding environment. On the whole, it was one that the Japanese wanted to maintain.

For Japan, the desirable strategy remains the one it pursued for the last forty years. Alliance with America, in which the United States carried the burden of defense and Japan provided geographic opportunities, gave Japan the best of both worlds. Being a protected part of the American alliance system, Japan had full access to the free-trade regime. On the other hand, it was not expected to share the risks of war, except that in the event of a general conflagration, U.S. bases in Japan were sure to be attacked. Short of such a cataclysm, Japan was freed from the burdens that were placed on all other American allies.

The Japan Defense Agency (JDA), which had the job of turning this into a working strategy, lists four governing principles in its Basic Policy for National Defense:

1. To support the activities of the United Nations and promote international cooperation, thereby contributing to the realization of world peace.
2. To promote public welfare and enhance the people's love for the country, thereby establishing the sound basis essential to Japan's security.
3. To develop progressively the effective defense capabilities necessary for self-defense, with regard to the nation's resources and the domestic situation.
4. To deal with external aggression on the basis of the Japan–U.S. security arrangements, pending the effective functioning of the United Nations in the future in deterring and repelling such aggression.[1]

Leaving aside the pieties in clauses 1 and 2 , the heart of Japan's defense policy has been to allow the United States to take care of it. The JDA quite frankly admits that it does not plan to stretch Japan's resources beyond the limits of the "domestic situation"—or public opinion—and that the U.N. is utterly ineffective. Thus, pending shifts in public opinion and the effectiveness of the U.N., Japan's policy is to allow the United States to protect it.

For Americans, the main threat came from the Soviets. The Japanese considered this a dubious proposition, since, as was mentioned in Chapter 5, they deemed a Soviet attack to be unlikely. From the Japanese point of view, the real purpose of the U.S.–Japanese alliance was quite different. It was to secure Japan's lines of supply in the Pacific and Indian Oceans and permit it access to export markets, particularly those in the United States. These were two very different understandings of the purpose of the alliance.

From the American point of view, every ship, plane, or gun produced by Japan is an addition to the American arsenal. The American assumption has been that, at the very least, increased Japanese power would secure the region around Japan and free the U.S. to deploy forces elsewhere, in more dangerous areas. At most, it was assumed that in the event of a general conflict with the Soviet Union, the Japanese, under the terms of the alliance agreements, would permit

Japan's forces—essentially under U.S. command—to augment America's capabilities.

Thus, the United States pressured Japan to increase spending under the rubric of "burden sharing," with veiled threats that the failure of Japan to increase its cooperation would lead to lessened American interest in Japanese security. The Japanese understood full well that such talk was nonsense, that the U.S. was utterly dependent on Japan's geography far more than on its military. Thus, Japan produced only as much force as it felt was needed to placate the Americans.

During the last years of the Cold War, U.S.–Japanese relations became a struggle between the trade problem and the defense problem. Of the two, the trade issue has become the more immediate concern. In a Louis Harris poll conducted for *Business Week* in July 1989, the level of public antagonism toward Japan became manifest:

1. 69% felt that the problem of the trade imbalance was serious.
2. 79% felt that Japan should be required to permit certain quantities of U.S. products into Japan.
3. 61% favored higher tarrifs on goods from Japan.
4. 69% favored quotas on goods from Japan.
5. 68% regarded the economic threat from Japan to be greater than the Soviet military threat.[2]

It is clear that Japan would be crippled by a break with the United States, but it is far from clear that the reverse would be true. Moreover, as was seen in World War I, the threat of financial damage does not necessarily prevent conflict.

The thought that its golden age is drawing to a close is frightening for Japan. It is natural, therefore, for Japan to make every effort to pretend that the Cold War is not over. Yozo Ishikawa, Director General of the JDA, argued in April 1990, long after the Soviet decline had set in, that:

> The Soviet Union recently announced unilateral troop reductions in the Far East and has already carried out partial reductions in this area. However, qualitative reinforcement continues, most notably through modernization of arms and additional deployment of naval and air force units.[3]

Ishikawa's concerns about the Soviets are ironic when we recall that Prime Minister Yoshida, at the height of the Cold War in 1954, dismissed out of hand the idea of a Soviet attack on Japan. The idea that the threat was greater in 1990 obviously cannot be taken seriously, nor is it intended to be.

The long-term solution for those seeking to preserve the alliance is the argument that the end of the Cold War does not have to change the U.S.–Japanese relationship fundamentally. Ishikawa and Kaifu are both engaged in an attempt to keep the blessings of the Cold War after it is over. The first, and obviously doomed, tack is to buy time by pretending that the Soviet threat continues to grow. If that is the case, then the Americans will continue to tolerate Japan's economic success at the minor price of increased Japanese defense spending.

This sentiment is not unique to Japan. The American foreign-policy establishment is at least as wedded to continuing the Cold War alliance system as are the Japanese, but with much less reason, unless they mean to convert it into an instrument of empire. Throughout 1989 and 1990, Secretary of Defense Dick Cheney was firm in his public conviction that the Cold War was continuing in Asia. Neither side wanted to face the wrenching future.

The benefits of the alliance system for the Japanese are obvious, and the alternatives are grim. A break with the U.S. would close off the essential markets that fuel Japanese growth. The 33 percent of exports that Japan sends to the U.S. could not easily be sold elsewhere. Japan's economy would not merely stop growing; it would contract —and contract dramatically.

If Japan could maintain the relationship indefinitely, it would be happy to do so. Unfortunately for Japan, the key element of the alliance is missing: the United States no longer fears the Soviet Union. Indeed, there is very little that the U.S. need fear in the world at this moment except, perhaps, the Japanese economy. Junior partnership to the U.S. once proved lucrative because the U.S. was prevented from turning that relationship into something exploitive. Junior partnership to an America unafraid of the world is a different matter altogether. In this relationship, American power is not held in check; it can be used to force substantial economic concessions from Japan.

Certainly, the Japanese and American foreign-policy establishments both hope that this resentment can be contained. But the pain caused by Japanese exports to the U.S. is very real and will be particularly noticed during recessionary periods, when xenophobia will combine with unemployment. This may not be a pretty picture, but it is a real one, and the idea that the passions set loose in the U.S. will be constrained by fruitful conversations between delegations of technicians is patently absurd. It is also something sensed in Japan. A majority of Japanese, when asked if the U.S. would defend Japan if it were attacked, answered that no help would be forthcoming.[4]

This is not a matter of mass anger and distrust competing with elite perspectives. The American agenda is to repair its economy, and to do it as painlessly as possible. The temptation to do it at Japan's expense is nearly irresistible.

Since it is at least possible that the U.S. will use its political and military power to extract more and more painful trade concessions from the Japanese until, like Eastern Europe facing Soviet demands in the 1950s, Japan is broken, Japan must think carefully before subordinating itself to the U.S. A statesman can never go wrong by planning for the worst. Certainly, any Japanese politician who assumed the best about the United States would be guilty of professional malpractice.

Japan cannot assume that its relationship with the U.S. will continue to guarantee its interests. It must plan alternative export markets and new investment strategies that do not leave such a vast overexposure in the U.S. Japan must have noticed the American penchant for freezing the funds of those with whom it is having political disputes.

Most important perhaps, Japan must prepare for the task of securing its own raw materials. Given Japan's absolute dependence on imports for its very survival as a modern industrial society, Japan cannot continue to rely on the United States or its system of alliances to secure those raw materials. There is simply too much potential advantage for the U.S. to hold Japan hostage to the delivery of those raw materials for Japan to trust America's good intentions. No nation should place its national survival in the hands of another nation, no matter how good-natured that nation might be. And, as Japan knows full well, counting on America's good nature is precarious, especially when there are real issues on the table.

Devising such a strategy is not easy. First and foremost, it will force Japan to face the limits of its mutual defense treaties with the U.S. and to accept the need for larger and more expensive military forces. Japan would sincerely like to avoid this expense. It was a happier time when the U.S. footed the bill. But there are no easy choices for Japan after the Cold War. Its golden age is passing, and the future will be complex, dangerous, and costly. Japan must return to history and live in the place assigned it on earth, living by its own wits and its own powers, a free and therefore endangered nation.

THE DOMINATION OF NORTHEAST ASIA

Japan has never been successfully invaded. Even the United States did not attempt this, and it is still debatable whether an invasion would have worked. In part, Japan has been protected by the waters surrounding it. It has also been protected by the chaos that was the normal condition on the threatening Asian shore. But on occasion, as after 1905, Japan secured itself against that chaos, against the possibility of a single power emerging out of the chaos, by taking control of its physical environment and seizing the far Asian shore. The tragedy for Japan was that this seizure was not enough, for it left much unsettled. Yet, in another sense it was too much, for the price of protecting its Asian shore was enormous and sapped Japan's vital strength.

The actual beginning of the geopolitical problem for Japan will be a naval problem. The immediate surrounding spaces are water, and therefore Japan's first need must be to become a regional naval power. However, this cannot be the end of the picture. Just as the U.S., in order to protect its naval security, seeks to manipulate events in Eurasia, so, too, Japan, on a much smaller scale, needs to dominate the land adjacent to its immediate oceans. The traditional solution has been to dominate the Korean Peninsula and then to deal with either defeating or neutralizing the two great powers of Northeastern Asia, China, and Russia.

The decision by the U.S. to urge Japanese maritime responsibility out to a 1,000-mile radius effectively reestablishes the maritime component of regional security. But it does nothing for what Prime Minister Yamagata had defined, back in the 1890s, as Japan's "line of interest," the land masses surrounding Japan's maritime interests. Japan's ability to dominate this line of interest depends as much on the Chinese and the Soviets as on the Americans. Chinese and Soviet responses to growing Japanese regional power will, in turn, depend on the status of Sino-Soviet relations. Put differently, the withdrawal of the U.S. from the Asian mainland will be the preface to Japan's emergence as a regional power. In that case, the three-player game between the U.S., the Chinese, and the Soviets will be replaced by a three-player game between Japan, China, and the Soviets, with the U.S. playing the wild card.

In Chapter 2 it was shown how Japan once assured its security zone by defeating China and Russia in successive wars. This made Japan a great regional power. But for important reasons that are still valid, regional preeminence has not been sufficient for Japan. The reasons have partly to do with the United States. As early as 1905 and the U.S. intervention at the Treaty of Portsmouth negotiations, the U.S. has been a limiting factor in Japan's regional authority. This extraregional power kept intruding on Japan's attempt to establish regional security.

Throughout the first period of empire, the Japanese had to look over their shoulder at the intentions of the United States. Even more important was the unfolding of the great struggle between China and Russia on the mainland. The unending conflict between the two powers, ranging from Mongolia east to the Pacific, both secured Japan's Asian flank and threatened the stability of the region. Above all, Japan could not afford the triumph of one over the other. Thus, the traditional mission of Japan was to balance the two Asian land powers and hold the coast on the Sea of Japan against penetration.

In the postwar period, the great danger to Japan was the alliance between China and the Soviet Union, which occurred after Japan was expelled from Asia by the United States. The U.S., which replaced the Japanese as the non-mainland power, initially failed to maintain the balance of power in the region, and that failure threatened disaster for Japan. The disaster was averted, of course, because the alliance was a fraud. At root, Russia and China could not make peace.

In a way, the Sino-Soviet split was the real end of the Cold War as an ideological conflict. The split between the Soviets and China demonstrated that ideology was not enough of a bond to hold nations together. The split was almost purely geopolitical, Mao's broadsides against Soviet revisionism notwithstanding. China's territorial claims were a challenge to the Soviet's ability to control Siberia, which was not only underpopulated but also was distant and tenuously connected to European Russia.

This geopolitical tension between overpopulated China searching for land and underpopulated Russia seeking to protect what it already owned is a permanent feature of the Asian landscape. It cannot be suppressed unless one or the other nations were to disintegrate. China cannot convince the Soviets that it does not have designs on Siberia and the Soviets cannot convince China that they are not planning to preempt China by attacking first and destroying Chinese power in Manchuria and Inner Mongolia. If the two nations were able to overcome their fears, they would, together, be an awesome power. During the 1948–1968 period, when China and the Soviets appeared to be inseparable, U.S. Asian policy was the desperate search for a counterweight to this coalition. After the battles in 1968 on the Ussuri River, the Sino-Soviet split was certain, and U.S. policy shifted to the much easier task of assuring that the split remained unmended.

During this period Japan was assured that the U.S. would bear the burden of containing the Sino-Soviet alliance in the region and that Japan would remain secure under the American strategic umbrella. After the split, Japan was also assured that the U.S. would play the predominant role in maintaining the balance of power between the two great Asian powers.

There were three elements to U.S. policy:

1. U.S. strategic nuclear capability.
2. U.S. control of Chinese and Soviet coastal waters.

3. The ability to substantially aid either side should the other gain the upper hand.

It was the latter element, the probability that the U.S. would come to the aid of China, if not with nuclear weapons then with naval and material support, that undoubtedly deterred a Soviet attack on China in the late 1960s and 1970s. The stakes were high for the U.S. inasmuch as the end of a Chinese threat on the Soviets' eastern border would free over one hundred Soviet divisions for European or Middle Eastern service. But the risks were high as well. As disagreeable as Korea and Vietnam were to the U.S., the risk of being dragged into a war in mainland China was not something any policy planner could countenance.

While it was a rational choice in the 1960s and 1970s, in 1990 the weakening of the Soviet Union and deep economic and political problems inside China means that the threat of war—and hence, of single-power hegemony—has declined enormously. Unless some overarching economic reason for continued American manipulation of the Sino-Soviet split becomes apparent, this would be an excellent time to withdraw from direct exposure in the balancing act, if possible.

Most American policy makers have not yet thought of the matter in these terms, since low-risk situations rarely breed innovative policies. However, it would be far more useful to have another third party, one with a direct and unavoidable interest in the region, play the role of flywheel to the regional balance of power. The historical choice for such a task is, of course, Japan.

Japan, on the other hand, would much rather that the U.S. bear this burden. However, Japan cannot afford the emergence of a single, overwhelming Asian power either; indeed, Japan can afford it far less than the U.S. In any rational American calculation, the likelihood is that Japan will assume the role of balancer of Asian power out of necessity. Thus, while the U.S. certainly wants to see the Northeast Asian balance of power maintained, it is unlikely that Japan would fail to fill any vacuum left by the U.S. and thereby would incur the risks of such a policy. It is certainly something that the Japanese are reluctant to do, but given the possible alternatives, they would have no choice.

What makes the problem particularly acute is the possibility of the emergence of a new Soviet-Chinese alliance. In the early 1970s, when China threw in its lot with the U.S., it was understood that the two weaker great powers were pooling their power to control the stronger, growing power. China saw itself as the balance between the two great superpowers—just as the U.S. saw itself as the balance between the two Communist powers. If this line of thinking continues to hold for China, then it is reasonable to expect that it will be interested in some alliance with the Soviets to limit and even bring down the emerging power, the United States.

Both the Soviets and the Chinese are limited in their room for maneuver by economic considerations. The condition of the Soviet Union, in particular, but China as well, is such that neither can afford to engage in geopolitical maneuvers at the expense of economic interests. Thus, both could be dissuaded from forming coalitions by suitable economic incentives. Obviously, Japan is ideally suited to offer these incentives, and to bear the burden of inefficient investments. One can see, therefore, how the general balance of power intersects economic interests and the manner in which both, if combined, can expose Japan to danger and cost in Northeast Asia.

The U.S. has not yet advanced its strategic thinking to this point. It is still thinking in terms of the Cold War, and continues to insist that it is interested in maintaining a strong force in the region. Undersecretary of Defense Paul Wolfowitz, the emerging architect of American Pacific thinking, has said about continued American exposure in the region:

> We do not bear this role and retain these forward forces only because we are concerned over the vacuum which would be created if we were no longer there, although that is a source of concern. Nor are we merely motivated by altruism. Simply, we must play this role because our military presence set the stage for our economic involvement in this region. With a total two-way transPacific trade exceeding 300 billion dollars annually, 50% more than our transAtlantic trade, it is in our own best interest to help preserve peace and stability.[5]

According to Wolfowitz, what might keep the U.S. in the region is what brought the United States to East Asia in the first place: trade. Maintaining trade markets and securing sea-lanes has been a traditional concern in the region, predating the U.S. strategic role.

THE ECONOMIC LIMITS OF A NORTHEAST ASIAN STRATEGY

The problem is that while this might well keep America in the region, it will not necessarily keep it on the side of Japan, for the issue is not the magnitude of trade but its profitability. In 1989, the total U.S. deficit was $128.3 billion. Its trade deficit with the region was:

TABLE 11-1. U.S. Trade Balance in the Northwest Pacific, 1989.

NATION	TRADE BALANCE ($BILLIONS)	PERCENT OF DEFICIT
Japan	−52.5	40.9
China	−5.8	4.5
Hong Kong	−3.9	3.0
South Korea	−7.1	5.5
Taiwan	−14.3	11.1
Total	−83.6	65.1

(Source: International Monetary Fund)

These five countries account for 65 percent of the total trade deficit the U.S. incurred in 1989. If Wolfowitz is serious in arguing that protection of U.S. trade is a prime interest for U.S. forces in the region, then we must assume that he regards a financial hemorrhage on the order of $83 billion a year as something vital to our national security. It would have been useful had the Department of Defense expanded its thinking to include an explanation of why losing this trade would damage the national interest.

The trade argument militates either for withdrawal from the region, concentrating on more profitable markets and sources, or for the use of U.S. military power to correct our trade weakness. Certainly, there are potentially more profitable areas in the world than Asia on which to concentrate U.S. trade efforts—such as Europe, Latin America, and the former Communist world. The idea of committing troops to protect this ongoing national calamity is more than a little farfetched.

It is possible for Japan to assume the U.S. role in the region, but not without a substantial redefinition of its role in the world, and indeed of its own self-image. The easiest and least stressful strategy would be the creation of a regional common market, a sort of yen bloc. We have seen the outlines of this market in Chapter 10.

The problem with the common market idea is not Korea, China, or the Soviet Union. It is Japan. These markets, taken together, are not sufficient for Japan's vast and growing export trade. The total market of these three major countries was $164 billion. U.S. sales in the region totaled $55 billion, while Japanese exports to the U.S. totaled $97 billion. Unless the Japanese supplanted America's $55 billion in sales in this region (including Hong Kong), Japan could not possibly have a chance of successfully replacing a closed U.S. market.

This was precisely the same dilemma that confronted Japan in the 1930s when it tried to create a similar trading zone. Japan was caught between two imperatives. On one hand, it needed to ensure is security in the region. On the other hand, it needed an arena for its economic growth. In 1930 this region proved insufficient as a source of raw materials or as a market for Japanese exports. No matter what political means Japan used to stimulate trade in the area, including the exclusion of other exporters from the region, it could not produce sufficient growth in demand to fuel indefinitely the Japanese economy.

As a result, Japan was forced to alienate the U.S. by the actions that circumstances forced upon it. First, it blocked American access to larger and larger parts of China, violating the free-trade accords that had been the post-1920 foundation of Pacific trade. Then in an effort to secure a large enough market for its needs, Japan was forced to expand its sphere of control in, and eventually to go to war with, China, against American wishes. Finally, since the bloc it had created could not possibly provide Japan with the resources it needed to develop and protect itself, Japan was forced into a dependency on the U.S. anyway, not only for imports of oil and other raw materials, but as an export market itself. When the U.S. tried to use this power to restrain Japan in China, Japan sought an alternative to its relationship with the United States in Southeast Asia and the result was the first Pacific war.

It was not economics that interested Japan in Northeastern Asia in the first instance, but national security. In the post-Cold War environment, as the U.S. becomes a less reliable partner with very different interests from Japan, the Japanese are going to be compelled to take a stronger hand in Northeastern Asia. They cannot be indifferent to events there. Particularly in the event of a collapse of the Soviet Union, the possibility of China emerging as the single major power in the region must, in the long run, be unacceptable to Japan.

Japan will not be drawn into the region, at first, in the same manner as the U.S. For Japan, it will be trade and investment, the carrot and not the stick, with which it will seek to stabilize the Soviet Far Eastern position and develop firm relations with China. This trade relationship cannot help but antagonize the U.S., as it did in the 1930s. The Chinese economy is small, particularly its capacity to increase its imports. To the extent that Japan becomes a more and more important player in China, it will necessarily exclude the United States. Indeed, in the Soviet Union as well, the similarity of the products offered by the U.S. and Japan will mean that an aggressive export and import policy in the region will leave the U.S. in a weak position. Given the fact that Japan's surplus savings rate permits it to engage in far more extensive foreign investment than the U.S., Japan's advantage in entering into complex trade/investment agreements will give it an enormous advantage over the U.S. Since both the Soviets and China will be eager to court the Japanese for geostrategic as well as economic reasons, Japan is likely to win this competition.

Japan's actions are already becoming more candidly political. For example, the decision by Prime Minister Kaifu to renew aid to China in spite of the Tiananmen Square massacre was explained by the Japan Economic Institute's *Report* this way:

> Tokyo's insistence that China not remain isolated arises from several sources. A lack of foreign aid or foreign investment could cripple China's efforts to modernize its economy, creating domestic discontent and more instability. An economically sound and politically stable China is a keystone of Japanese foreign policy in Asia. A friendly China also is seen as a counterweight to the Soviet Union. China's purported influence with North Korea and the Khmer Rouge rebels in Cambodia—areas where Tokyo is now becoming more active—are two more reasons for Japan to patch up things with Beijing.[6]

The China move must be understood as essentially political. A strong and secure China is Japan's counterweight against the Soviet Union. The Soviet Union, in turn, will be courted—with proper attention to continued Soviet occupation of Japanese territory in the form of a few minor islands—to act as a counterweight to the Chinese. Since the Japanese military capability is at present insufficient to attract or frighten either party, what Japan will have to offer is trade and investment.

Clearly, Japan has a military option. It could easily create a military force rivaling any other. After all, a nation with 123 million people and the second-largest economy in the world can construct a military force able to match any in the region. Thus, in looking back on Japan's earlier period of empire building at the turn of the century, it is evident that Japan was willing and able to use military force to subdue its enemies. Most of its great battles were naval battles, as in the defeat of the Chinese Navy in 1895 or the Russian Navy in 1905–1906. Japan was rather cautious on land then, as it is today.

The Sino-Soviet dispute will pull Japan onto the mainland. The first issue is the Sino-Soviet balance. At this moment, both nations appear to be sickly; the Soviets appear to be on the brink of collapse, while the Chinese, after Tiananmen Square, seem to have merely papered over their deep problems. Should either power collapse internally, Japan would immediately be faced with a tremendous dilemma. Should the other power, the Soviets or the Chinese, seek to take advantage, the outcome would be a single-power-dominated Asia. Should both collapse simultaneously, the resulting chaos could spill over into the Korean Peninsula or suddenly coalesce into a threatening power on the shore.

Japan must have two capabilities as it moves into the next century. One it already has—the economic power to manipulate political events in Northeast Asia. It must, however, also have sufficient resources available to stabilize collapsing regimes or bribe emergent ones. The U.S. played the Sino-Soviet balance as a military problem with two stable regimes. Japan will have to play the same game as an economic problem with two desperately needy and unstable regimes.

Japan's problem is that with all the wealth in the world, it may not be able to stabilize the situation on the mainland. That will leave only a military option. Obviously, it is Japan's quite sincere desire that the U.S. carry out this function, and toward that end it will supply the U.S. with bases in Japan in perpetuity. But while the Sino-Soviet balance in Asia is a long-term matter for the U.S., and the Americans can now afford to play a waiting game (since post-1992 Europe may well balance any Soviet power and Japan will deal with China), Japan has no such luxury.

Japan must therefore be in a position to assert control at least over the areas that threaten it most directly: the Korean Peninsula, Kamchatka, and the northeastern Chinese coast. In other words, if all hell breaks loose in Northeast Asia, Japan must be in a position to reassert its old line of interest, its fourth geopolitical goal, the domination of Northeast Asia as a region.

Obviously, Japan is appalled by the thought. For one thing, it has absolutely no desire to engage in military action. Its view is that it will buy and sell and not put its faith in generals. Further, the cost of such an enterprise would be huge. Japan's defense budget would soar, as would taxes, and investment and productivity would decline. Any such insertion would require an army, which manpower-poor Japan would be hard-pressed to raise. But the Japanese remember quite clearly another reason. Japan lost the first U.S.–Japanese war because it got bogged down in China, with over one million men committed there. If it must become an imperial power, the last place to begin that adventure is in China, a bottomless pit that never pays off as much as expected.

Thus, an intervention in China may be the last thing that the Japanese want. Unfortunately, if the U.S. leaves Japan in the lurch and the Soviets and Chinese continue their erratic course, it may be precisely what they get. Japan could leave the Soviets and Chinese to stew in their own juices, but then there is a real possibility of chaos coalescing into real, unified, powerful danger. Japan cannot simply hope that things will turn out. A powerful and hungry Asia is a threat Japan cannot endure. Mao's Asia was gentled by the Soviets. Stalin's Asia was gentled by the U.S. The next threat will leave Japan only with itself. And therefore, like any prudent power, it may decide it needs to act before the threat emerges.

This will leave Japan with terrible problems, such as Korea. Korean memories of Japanese brutality are still raw, as are the rest of Asia's. Moreover, the Korean Army, both North and South, is tough and well trained, a match even for the Japanese. But both Koreas, or a unified Korea, will be as deeply concerned as Japan is with events in China or Russia. One might think that mutual strategic interest would, this time around, make a joint imperialism possible. This would, of course, be a tremendous test of Japanese racism, for Japanese contempt for Korea runs as deep today as it ever did.

Japan's strategy, therefore, must be to think its way beyond its strategic relationship with the United States and to calculate its actions in the event that the evolution of events in Northeastern Asia leads to a rupture of U.S.–Japanese relations. Japan must devise a strategy that is prepared to cope with such a rupture without precipitating it. It must also seek a solution so that should rupture come, it does not come in as calamitous a form as last time. But the Japanese strategy should also be one that can deal with the worst the Americans can throw at them. It is obvious that the Japanese are now in an extraordinarily difficult position. This problem is compounded by the economic inadequacy of a purely Northeast Asia strategy.

JAPAN'S RETURN TO GREATER ASIA

There are two defects to Japan's adopting a purely regional strategy. First, at this historical juncture the return of Japan to the Northeast Asian mainland, while possible, would be fraught with enormous risks and serious opposition. Unless the Soviet Union and China both undergo serious internal disruption, creating a power vacuum in the region that Japan can exploit, or unless Korea becomes desperate for outside support, Japan will have to force its way onto the mainland—a difficult, dangerous, and perhaps impossible task.

There is a second defect to the regional strategy as well, a defect the Japanese encountered during their first empire. Northeast Asia has neither the ability to absorb Japanese exports nor the resources to run Japan's industry. If Japan is to secure its economic well-being in any imperial enterprise, the very least that it will require is an arena large enough and rich enough for its needs.

Any analysis of such a strategy must begin with oil. Although Japan has severely restricted its imports of oil, it must still import about 50 percent of its energy in that form. Japan cannot cut its oil consumption any further without cutting into its very economic muscle and bone. The Japanese already have set their thermostats in the minimal comfort zone, already have extremely high gasoline prices, and already have industrial conservation programs in place. There is nothing more to conserve. All other savings will come at the expense of economic growth.

In 1989, Japan imported 208,691,000 kiloliters (kL) of oil. Of that, 148,969,000 kL, or 71.3 percent, came from inside the Straits of Hormuz and from Oman and North Yemen just outside the straits. Southeast Asia was the second most important source, supplying 34,908,000 kL, or 16.7 percent, of Japan's oil. This source included Indonesia, Brunei, and Malaysia, with Indonesia being the most important.

Thus, 88 percent of Japan's oil imports either came from the Malay Peninsula and the Indonesian archipelago, or had to pass through one of the three straits, Malacca–Singapore, Sunda, or Lombok, in order to reach Japan:

MAP 11-1. Mineral and Oil Flow to Japan.

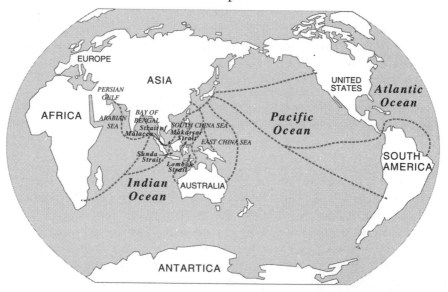

The problem here is physical and political. The door to the Indian Ocean basin is not in Japanese hands, nor in the hands of the Persian Gulf and Indian Ocean nations. Rather, it is in the hands of the three countries that are closest to the three straits—Indonesia, Malaysia, and Singapore—as well as in the hands of any naval power strong enough to close those straits or force them open. The last is a short list: the United States. In one of history's more important coincidences, two of the nations in a position to close the straits, Indonesia and Malaysia, are, together with Brunei, the only major non-Persian Gulf sources of oil for Japan. Thus, those two nations must be a focus of any broad Japanese foreign policy.

Japan's problem, obviously, is the vulnerability of the various straits to foreign closure. Given the relative naval weakness of Singapore, Malaysia, and Indonesia, Japan could find Malacca or Lombok closed even if it had favorable relations with the surrounding governments. Thus, the first step in formulating a broad-based strategic policy for Japan would be to estimate the extent to which Japan could shift its reliance on oil away from Persian Gulf crude to petroleum available in the Pacific Basin and accessible without passing through ocean choke points.

TABLE 11-2. Japanese Oil Consumption and Southeast Asian Supply.

	RESERVES (KILOBAR- RELS)	PRODUC- TION (KILOBAR- RELS)	NUMBER OF YEARS OF RESERVES	% EX- PORTED	% EX- PORTED TO JAPAN	% TOTAL JAPAN IMPORTS
Indonesia	9,550,000	519,808	18.4	59.6	26.4	11.5
Malaysia & Brunei	4,097,000	239,649	17.1	81.9	38.1	5.7
China	18,200,000	956,665	19.0	21.8	8.3	6.9
World	672,296,529	20,507,104	32.8	—	—	—

(Sources: United Nations Council on Trade and Development; Japan External Trade Organization; Petroleum Association of Japan; U.S. Department of Energy. For consistency, figures are for 1986. Reserve figures are as of January 1, 1985.)

Southeast Asia's two major oil producers are Malaysia and Indonesia, each with reserves totaling about eighteen years at current production. However, together they have only 2 percent of the world's proven reserves. Both are heavy exporters at 60 and 80 percent of production, respectively. This means that it is unlikely that production could be diverted from domestic uses without substantial damage to the domestic economy. Moreover, at the current rate of usage it would probably be imprudent to increase production without first increasing reserves through new finds. However, imports of oil by Japan could be increased, since Japan currently imports only about one-quarter and one-third of their total production, respectively.

Even if Japan were to purchase all of Malaysia, Brunei, and Indonesia's export oil, it would amount to only about 38 percent of its needs. Outside of massive increases in production capacity and in proven reserves, this region alone could not provide Japan with enough oil to keep going.

The only other major producer east of Singapore is China. Its reserves are substantially larger (about 2.7 percent of world reserves) and its production is proportionately larger as well. But its needs are huge, and China can export only about 21 percent of its annual production, making it no larger an exporter than Brunei and Malaysia. However, Japan imports only about 8 percent of China's exported crude. Were Japan to appropriate all of China's exportable crude, that would satisfy about 18 percent of Japan's crude-oil needs. Combined with the exports of Southeast Asia, this would bring Japan's imports to about 56 percent of the amount required.

To achieve oil sufficiency without going west of Singapore, Japan would have to nearly double its imports from east of Singapore. One promising possibility is Latin America, particularly Mexico. However, given Mexico's political subordination to the United States and its ties within the North American market, the very process of regionalization and market segmentation that threatens Japan's well-being would make Mexico the least likely source of petroleum. Put simply, if Mexican crude were available to Japan on the open market, then Japan would not need to be concerned about its resource security.

Thus, the only possibility of sufficiency east of Singapore would be a ruthless diversion toward Japan of Chinese, Indonesian, and Malaysian crude from other buyers, and even a good deal of their domestic consumption. Since these other buyers would be regional economic competitors like South Korea, Taiwan, Hong Kong, and Singapore, the Four Little Tigers that are beginning to press Japan economically, there is a certain attractiveness in this strategy for Japan. Just as the U.S. could curtail Japanese economic health by interfering with its supply of oil, Japan could curtail the economic health of these other countries by diverting all East Asian oil to Japan.

As attractive as this option might be, it suffers from a fatal defect. Japan is not only an importer of raw materials, but also an exporter of manufactured goods. The regionalization and segmentation of the world market would make Japan heavily dependent on this region for sale of its products. By diverting their petroleum imports, Japan would devastate the East Asian industrialized economy. Not only would the Four Little Tigers become scenes of economic desolation, but the diversion of oil from China and Indonesia beyond what they normally export (something essential if self-sufficiency is to be reached) would abort the modernization of both countries and end hopes that they could substitute for European and American markets lost through regionalization.

This is precisely the problem that Japan encountered in its attempt to create the Greater East Asia Co-Prosperity Sphere in the late 1930s and during World War II. On paper, the Netherlands East Indies, China, Korea, Formosa, and Indochina had sufficient resources to maintain the Japanese economy. However, they did not have sufficient resources to both maintain the Japanese economy and their own. The Greater East Asia Co-Prosperity Sphere (GEAC) became an economic shambles as the Japanese tried to force increased production out of its empire while diverting the ingredients essential for increased production out of the region. The brutality of the Japanese occupation was in large measure an attempt to compel a population to achieve economic ends that were clearly unattainable. The Japanese were not naturally brutal. Rather, they were trying to achieve ends that could not be achieved.

A very similar picture emerges when considering some critical metallic ores:

TABLE 11-3. The Ability of the Former GEAC to Satisfy Japanese Mineral Needs, 1987.

	BAUXITE	COPPER	IRON ORE	MANGANESE	NICKEL
GEAC exports	48.46%	54.80%	0.00%	0.32%	70.23%
GEAC exp + China	78.38	54.80	0.00	1.27	70.23
GEAC production	59.77	71.65	0.18	0.63	177.35
GEAC prod + China	206.66	120.35	71.06	105.02	220.66
GEAC + India prod	208.20	78.37	47.58	111.67	177.35

GEAC = Indonesia, Malaysia, Myanmar, Philippines, Papua New Guinea, Thailand, New Caledonia
(Source: United Nations Conference on Trade and Development)

The Greater East Asia Co-Prosperity Sphere is a useful concept for measuring Japan's potential to achieve mineral self-sufficiency through political domination. The issue is whether these former targets (New Caledonia was targeted but never seized) of Japanese expansionism could supply Japan's needs if they came under Japanese domination again.

The limits of this empire in the case of oil have already been seen. The same is very much true in the case of minerals. Even if China's exports were added to this group, full self-sufficiency would be impossible. Only if Japan seized all of China's production for its own use, leaving nothing for China, would Japan be able to reach self-sufficiency (except in iron ore). However, if Japan were to seize 100 percent of China's production, Chinese domestic modernization would collapse, Chinese industry would cease to function, and China would be devastated. Clearly, if Japan had visions of creating a vast market in China for its exports, this strategy would be disastrously counterproductive.

However, when India is added to this group, something very much like self-sufficiency is achieved. Indeed, a bloc consisting of Japan, India, and China would come very close to achieving a rough self-sufficiency in bauxite, copper, manganese, and nickel. If Japan were to institute a vigorous investment program designed to increase mineral production, it is quite possible that this bloc would achieve a very comfortable sufficiency. Thus, as was the case with exports, India's inclusion in a Japanese bloc would solve many of Japan's problems.

RETURN TO EMPIRE

A Japanese trading bloc based east of Singapore could not possibly work unless Japan had access to substantial amounts of raw materials from outside the trading bloc. North America and Europe can constitute a coherent economic whole; one can imagine them regionalizing their economies and prospering. They have sufficient resources and well-trained labor to survive, even without massive trade. The East Asia region is different, and the key to the difference is the underdevelopment of China. Because of this, an industrialized economy like Japan's must have geographically diverse, rather than concentrated, relationships. And with this diversity and dispersion comes political vulnerability.

The forces that drive Japan beyond its own region are also forces that compel Japan to reenter politics. Long-term relations cannot be defined strictly in economic terms. The volatility of world mineral markets is such that a purely economic relationship with a supplier could have catastrophic results, as Japan has learned repeatedly in the Persian Gulf. Even long-term economic contracts with nations like Australia have proved to be unenforceable.[7]

Political power, always based in some way on military capability, is necessary to tie a trading bloc together or secure investments. Simply the act of moving petroleum from nations that want to sell it to nations that want to buy it has proven itself to be a herculean political and military task. We have seen how broad and diverse Japan's markets and suppliers are. Japan, like any modern state, must have a degree of control over these relationships that goes beyond mere market controls. Third parties can always interfere with those market controls, by subtle means or by direct means of invasion. Thus, the broader Japan's needs, the more Japan will have to engage in politics.

Nowhere is this political aspect clearer than in the case of India. It was shown in Chapter 10 how India fits into Japan's export strategy in a regionalized world. Indeed, if Japan were forced to fall back on the resources of Asia—in a world in which the U.S. had created a western hemisphere trading bloc, and the Europeans a pan-European system, including much of sub-Saharan Africa—then Japan would have to enter into a relationship with India on two bases: India as a customer, and India as a supplier of raw materials.

After Pearl Harbor, several Japanese military figures argued that a purely Pacific/Asian strategy was doomed. They argued that only by moving into the Indian Ocean, expelling the British, and utilizing Indian resources could Japan hope to secure the resources necessary to retain its Pacific empire. The project was rejected on the thoroughly sound basis that Japan was simply too overextended to carry out the plan. Japan lacked the force to conquer India.[8]

As long as India remains a unified country, it will be fair to say that Japan cannot secure that much military power today either. But whereas in 1942 India was subject to British power, it is now an independent country. As such, it is free to enter into a mutually satisfactory arrangement with Japan. From the Japanese point of view, such an arrangement might be based on these premises:

1. That Japan be given favored treatment in access to Indian raw materials in return for mutually beneficial Japanese investments in Indian industry.
2. That India favor Japanese products in world trade.
3. That the Indian Navy, augmented by Japanese technical assistance, guarantee the flow of raw materials between Hormuz and Singapore.

The Indians, in turn, would receive the following:

1. Substantial investments and coproduction agreements with the Japanese, with Japanese offshore production facilities targeted toward India.
2. Transfer of Japanese technology to India, particularly in the manufacture of mid-technology products being phased out in Japan and suited for India's low-wage environment.
3. Japan would underwrite the cost and technical development of the Indian Navy, in return for which Indian land power would be available for mutually satisfactory uses in Asia.

The Japan–India relationship is a logical outgrowth of Japan's growing dependence on the Indian Ocean basin for minerals and for the transport of minerals. An economic and military alliance would not only satisfy Japan's needs, it would permit India to develop its economic infrastructure with the help of a nation with which it has mutual political interests.

One issue would be whether a compact between India and Japan would be large enough to admit third parties, particularly Indonesia and China. Including other Pacific nations in the relationship would be essential to Japan, since India, by itself, cannot be Japan's solution. The problem is that India has not always had cordial relations with some of these powers. China is a particular problem, inasmuch as it has had an antagonism toward India dating to the 1962 war between the two countries. China would certainly feel threatened by an entente between Japan and India and, if sufficiently threatened, might well seek alternative relationships with either the Soviet Union or the United States.

The Soviet Union, as the Chinese discovered in the 1950s, has precious little to offer China economically. The United States, on the other hand, would have much to offer. However, the U.S. is far away and its interest in Asian affairs has been variable. It is not clear how much interest the U.S. would have in an Asian adventure after it adopts its blue-water strategy and sets about regionalizing its economic relationships. China might find itself with nowhere to go but Japan, on the best terms it could obtain. But the same issue that dominated the 1930s could well recur: Japan's encroachments on China might well trigger U.S. economic and political pressure designed to stop the encroachments, beginning the disastrous cycle one more time.

One must therefore consider precisely how deep the animosity between India and China is. Strategically, the question of the High Himalayas is hardly critical. Neither country is capable of waging serious war in that terrain. A more fundamental problem is that China and India are competitors. Indeed, one might include Indonesia and Malaysia on the list of industrializing countries with vast overpopulation and desperate need for investment capital and, therefore, along with India and China, competitors for Japan's investment yen.

Thus, the question is posed neatly: Can Japan supply sufficient investment capital, trade incentives, and high prices for raw materials to China, India, *and* Indonesia? If not, then each, particularly China and Indonesia, would need to seek a third party, probably the United States, as a source for markets and capital. It is, of course, unclear whether the U.S., caught up in its own regional relationships with

Latin America, could absorb the mineral produce of these countries, or invest heavily enough in them to make a difference. Thus, there may be no counterweight to Japan.

It is clear that Japan and India have sufficient mutual interests to ensure a lasting and mutually profitable relationship. It is not clear that Japan has sufficient resources to be equally generous with China, Indonesia, Malaysia, and Singapore. Moreover, an Indo-Japanese relationship has a neatly fitting military dimension to it that these others would not. India can do a great service for Japan in the Indian Ocean, and the growth of Indian power need not frighten Japan. Should Indonesia, however, develop too powerful a navy, it could well place Japan in an impossible position, forcing it to bargain for its imports through the Indonesian straits.

Thus, where the Indian relationship could be an essentially political relationship, Japan's relationship with China, Indonesia, and the rest of the Pacific nations must in some sense be a military relationship. Japan does not have enough to offer them economically to bribe them into submission (particularly China and Indonesia). Therefore, Japan must make its dominance a matter of military, as well as economic, inevitability.

Political and military power are as important to alliance politics as is economic advantage. Fear must supplement desire. In the case of Indonesia, in particular, economic incentives must be supplemented by political and military threats. These need not be as direct as the occupation of 1942–1945. Indeed, such an occupation would be a sign of the failure of Japan's policy, rather than an element of it. At the same time, Indonesia, Malaysia, the Philippines, and the Solomon Islands all require an ordering hand, particularly against internal instability.

All of these nations are subject to internal dissolution through ethnic and social conflict. One of the primary attractions to alliance for the central governments of these countries is access to supplementary military power, from weapons, to advice, to intervention, to putting down insurrection and civil war. Japan's all-important function for them would be as a source of internal stability and of regional stability as it polices its alliance.

The fact emerges that Japan must return to its imperial ways. While an alliance with India is both the best Japan can achieve and in all likelihood quite sufficient, mere alliance is less than adequate in the Pacific. Japan's physical security interests dictate a more direct domination of that region. Moreover, the cost of the Indian alliance will be so high that Japan will probably lack sufficient capital to entice its Pacific allies into accommodation. Nevertheless, the less-developed countries of the Greater East Asia Co-Prosperity Sphere are essential

MAP 11-2. Division of the Pacific Basin Between U.S. and Japanese
Spheres of Influence, Year 2000.

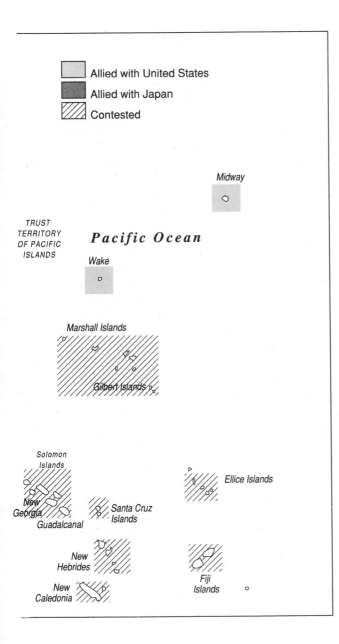

for Japan's economic well-being. Indeed, Japan must force these nations into an exclusive relationship with Japan, one that some will be reluctant to enter into. Military pressure, if not direct use of force, is the essential ingredient of empire. And one must understand that if Japan breaks with the United States, it will have to enter—not willingly, but out of reluctant necessity—into imperial relationships with these countries.

There can be no Japanese strategy, ultimately, that does not guarantee access to the Persian Gulf. Japan's problem is the security of the long, vulnerable line to the Persian Gulf. From 1945 to 1990, security for that long line was the responsibility of the United States. The U.S. carried out the responsibility vigorously, protecting the two choke points, Hormuz and Malacca, as well as the long passage north through the South China Sea to Japan. Even during the Vietnam War, when a naval war was going on in the South China Sea, no one tried to cut that vital line of supply to Japan. Unless it remains protected, Japan has no hope of a more complex political and economic strategy.

Precisely how long will the United States be willing to guarantee the flow of oil to Japan? At what point will this guarantee turn into control of Japan's economic and political life? Whether it stays in the Indian Ocean or withdraws, the U.S. poses a deep problem for Japan. If it stays, will the U.S., in the course of normal politico-economic relations, use its naval power to manipulate Japan's economic condition? And if it leaves, what other regional power will emerge that will threaten Japan?

The United States has other assets in this duel. The American relationship with Australia is particularly troubling for Japan. Until the mid-1950s, the Australians refused to sell raw materials to Japan. As was shown in Chapter 7, the benefits to the Australian economy of the sale of raw materials to Japan are minimal. Australia and Japan are both industrial powers, selling the same sorts of products and using the same sorts of technology. Australia is a very real possibility as a countervailing force to Japan among the Association of Southeast Asian Nations (ASEAN), particularly acting in conjunction with the United States in joint development projects and joint military operations.

The outline of a Pacific struggle emerges. On one hand, Japan will seek to create an alliance of Indonesia, Singapore, Papua New Guinea, the Philippines, Malaysia, Thailand, Myanmar, India, and, of course, China. On the other side, a U.S. seeking to maintain control of the Pacific and Indian Oceans (following its blue-water strategy) would seek an alliance including Korea, China, Taiwan, Indonesia, Australia, the Philippines, and Singapore.

Too many entries on this list overlap. Singapore, for example, will be the site of a deadly and complex struggle for influence and control, as will China and Indonesia. A large number of nations accustomed to good political relations with the United States and good economic relations with Japan will suddenly find the two incompatible. A long, weary Cold War will begin to sweep Asia and the Pacific.

CONCLUSION: JAPAN ENTERS THE POLITICO-MILITARY AGE

The prospect of consistent American concern for Japanese needs obviously dims as American dependency on Japanese geography declines. Add to this the possibility of growing hostility, rather than indifference, on the part of the United States, and Japan obviously has two choices. First, it can continue its dependency on the United States and hope for the best. Second, it can attempt to make its own arrangements for securing its supply lines. At issue for the Japanese is which is the more dangerous route, a question that can only be answered by defining the undefinable: What does hoping for the best mean?

As was discussed in Chapter 9, the most likely long-term American strategy is the blue-water strategy. But the meaning of American sea-lane control is unclear. Since World War II, this power has been used to buttress the free-trade system and facilitate maritime commerce. Even if the U.S. remains a benign force, its continued commitment to police the sea-lanes on behalf of economic competitors is not at all clear. While it is hard to imagine, no reasonable person could dismiss out of hand the possibility that the U.S. would use its naval power to interdict the flow of Japanese supplies. In the postwar world, the United States used its navy against several political competitors, but never against an economic one. However, in the new era, when economic competition is no longer necessarily cordoned off from political competition by fear of the Soviet Union, economic and political competition might well cease to be distinguishable.

In any event, prudent statesmen, while hoping for the best, prepare for the worst. In this case, growing competition with the United States requires the Japanese to prepare for four lines of action:

1. Anticipate the disruption of the flow of petroleum from the Persian Gulf either at the source or at some point along the supply route, and make plans to cope.
2. Make certain that the actions necessary for securing petroleum lines of supply do not interfere with Japan's access to suitably large and sophisticated export markets.
3. Assure the continued inflow of other mineral ores from secure sources.

4. Protect the territorial security of Japan against possible threats from mainland Asia.

For a nation accustomed to having all four of these missions secured by the United States, the assumption of responsibility will be a wrenching shift for the Japanese consciousness.

To some extent, we see this adjustment taking place already, in all its ambiguities. For example, in response to the publication of the U.S. Department of Defense report *A Strategic Framework for the Pacific Rim*, which called for an increase in Japanese self-reliance, Yozo Ishikawa, Director General of the Japan Defense Agency, said, "Japan has made it clear that it never intends to be a military power, and that policy has not changed."9

Just a week later, an intriguing meeting took place. Ishikawa was touring Malaysia, Thailand, and Australia, the first JDA Director General to visit the area. The obvious object of the talks was the future of maritime security in the region after the Cold War. J.N. Mak, senior analyst at a Malaysian government defense institute, put the matter in perspective:

> You can see that things are changing [in Southeast Asia]. Many people argue that the Japanese will play a bigger role, especially the Maritime Self-Defense Force, because nobody else will look after [Japan's] interests.

Another Malaysian analyst added that the Association of South East Asian Nations would have to build some sort of security relationship with the Japanese. On May 4, 1990, therefore, the de facto Japanese Minister of Defense met with his Malaysian counterpart, Ahmad Rithauddeen, to discuss the future of Japan in the area.10

The public and private roles of Japan will now begin to diverge. Since the Japanese are sincerely committed to maintaining the status quo, they will publicly remain faithful to their alliance with the United States, as indeed, they hope the Americans will. But there is already an expectation in Southeast Asia, particularly in Malaysia, Singapore, and Indonesia, that the role of the United States must change in some way. There is also the recognition that the alternative to the United States is Japan. It is the only other power capable of controlling the sea-lanes.

Imagine for a moment a world in which Japan decides it will have to take control of its destiny. The question that arises is what sorts of alliances will Japan have to develop in order to implement the four-point program?

Beginning with the problem of the line of supply to Hormuz, the

Japanese will have to proceed in three stages, simply due to the time constraints involved in constructing a navy:

1. Enter into a long-term relationship with India. Simultaneously enter into relationships with Indonesia and, if at all possible, Singapore. Continue to work closely with China, including offering guarantees to soothe Chinese fears of India. Try to expand influence in Micronesia, Melanesia, and Polynesia in order to control American routes to the western Pacific.
2. Having constructed the first part of a naval force, negotiate basing privileges in Singapore, and if possible, at Subic Bay in the Philippines. Offer assistance to India toward developing a suitable navy.
3. A powerful India could, in the very long run, become a threat to Japan quite as much as the United States is. On completing the first phase of naval deployments, move into the Indian Ocean Basin and try to control the entire line from Hormuz to Singapore to Japan.

It need not be mentioned that the U.S., with its own blue-water strategy, will observe the growth of the Japanese Navy in the western Pacific and its movement into the Indian Ocean with less than pleasure. The fear that the U.S. entertained during the 1930s, that it would be forced out of the western Pacific and eventually have its West Coast exposed to Japanese attack, will inevitably revive.

American responses would undoubtedly include:

1. The closing of Micronesia and Polynesia to Japanese warships and attempts to limit enormous Japanese interest in the area.
2. Attempts to create an anti-Japanese coalition in the region. Particularly susceptible to this would be the Koreans and Taiwanese, whose economies clash with the Japanese, and who could be enticed through fear of the Japanese and greed for the U.S. market. Finally, Australia, with its primordial fear of Indonesian expansion, would be frightened by the Japanese-Indonesian alliance and basing of a Japanese fleet in Java into seeking to block Japanese expansion.
3. The U.S. would seek an alliance with China in order to limit Japan's economic room for maneuver and search for levers with which to control Japanese trade flow.

Japan's greatest vulnerability would be close to home, in the areas it took for granted during the first war: Korea and Taiwan. Paradoxically, Japan's interests and the interests of the ASEAN countries, particularly Indonesia, are probably closer now than ever. Under any circumstances, a long, unpleasant Cold War between the U.S. and Japan will break out throughout the Indian and Pacific basins. Whether a Cold War will become hot will be the next point to consider.

It must be emphatically pointed out that it is not Japan's intention to rearm, nor, if it rebuilt a blue-water navy capable of extending beyond 1,000 miles, would it do this in order to seek conflict with the U.S. Nothing is further from Japan's mind than rebuilding its old empire. Quite the contrary, the Japanese would like nothing better than to maintain the current relationship.

Unfortunately, the bill for the Cold War has fallen due. Just as Iraq, after its war with Iran, presented its bill to Kuwait and the rest of the Persian Gulf, so, too, the United States, after the Cold War, is adding up the bill for its allies, and in particular Japan. The price, permanent subordination to the United States and a willingness to suffer economic damage on American demand, is too high a price for Japan—or any sovereign state—to pay. On the other hand, for the United States to continue protecting Japan's global interests free of charge after the Soviets have collapsed is too high a price for Americans to pay.

Thus, America and Japan now reach a parting of the ways. It is extremely unlikely that these two powers, with so many reasons to dislike and distrust each other, with so few interests in common and so many interests opposed, can reach an amiable divorce. It is, therefore, time to consider just how unfriendly the divorce will be.

1. Japan Defense Agency, *Defense of Japan, 1989* (Tokyo, 1989), p. 82.
2. *Business Week*, August 7, 1989, p. 51.
3. *Japan Times Weekly*, June 4–10, 1990, p. 8.
4. Tokyo Broadcasting System polls, 1985–1989, cited in Japan Economic Institute, "American and Japanese Polls on the Bilateral Relationship: Trends and Implications." March 2, 1990, p. 17.
5. U.S. Department of Defense: *A Strategic Framework for the Asian Pacific Rim: Looking Toward the 21st Century* (April 1990), p. 8.
6. Japan Economic Institute, "Tokyo Prepares to Resume China Aid," July 27, 1990, p. 9.
7. Raymond Vernon, *Two Hungry Giants: The United States and Japan and the Quest for Oil and Ores* (Cambridge, 1983), p. 101.
8. H.P. Willmott, *Empires in Balance* (Annapolis, 1982), pp. 440–441.
9. *Japan Times Weekly*, April 30–May 6, 1990, p. 3.
10. *Japan Times Weekly*, May 7–13, 1990, p. 5.

PART IV

JAPAN'S
SECOND
PACIFIC WAR

12

Can Japan Rearm?
Japan's Moral Dilemma

Any discussion of Japan's military future must begin with a consideration of Japan's cultural and constitutional rejection of war. There are those who would argue that a second U.S.–Japanese war is impossible because Japan has genuinely renounced war, and that the renunciation must be taken seriously. This is not a frivolous idea. Japan's renunciation of war—indeed, the general argument that war has become obsolete—must be dealt with in order to consider the future of Japan's war-making capability.

There has been a great deal of speculation that military force has ceased to have meaning in the modern world. This view has been expressed from two different directions: first, from those who argue that nuclear weapons have made war irrational and unthinkable as an instrument of national policy and, second, from those who argue that economic relations have become so interconnected and delicate that disrupting them through war would be catastrophic to all concerned. For obvious reasons, this kind of thinking is particularly prevalent in Japan. After all, Japan is the only nation that has been subjected to atomic attack, and Japan's economy is in fact so interconnected with other nations that war might well prove catastrophic.

ARTICLE 9 AND THE FUTURE OF WAR

Japan's postwar political culture has therefore been opposed to war. Article 9 of the Japanese constitution forbids the use of war as an instrument of national policy, and this prohibition is taken by many to be an expression of sincere revulsion at the thought of war:

> Aspiring sincerely to an international peace based on justice and order, the Japanese people forever renounce war as a sovereign right of the nation and the threat or use of force as a means of settling international disputes.
>
> In order to accomplish the aim of the preceding paragraph, land, sea and air forces, as well as other war potential, will never be maintained. The right of belligerency of the State will not be recognized.

Thus, any discussion of Japan's future military strategy must begin with the question of whether Japan will in fact permit itself to have a military strategy at all.

Given Article 9, one would expect that Japan would have no armed forces at all. The fact, however, is that Japan today spends more money on defense than any other country except the United States and the Soviet Union. To some degree this is an illusion, since the soaring yen has inflated the defense budget, just as it has inflated the amount of money Japan gives in aid. Still, Japan's 1991 fiscal year budget, although trimmed in the face of declining tensions, will increase by 5.8 percent. This may be the lowest increase in thirty years, but it comes at a time when most other defense budgets are being slashed. The Y1.7 trillion budget translates into about $33 billion.[1] It is on the same order as the Chinese, French, British, or German defense budgets, yet no one questions whether the Germans or the British are rearming. It is therefore ironic that the question of Japan's rearming should be consistently posed as if it were a prospect rather than an accomplished fact.

Much of this has to do with outsiders' perceptions of Japan. The pacifism of the constitution, the genuine reluctance of the Japanese government to engage in foreign military adventures, and the perceived hostility of the Japanese people to rearmament all work together to obscure a simple fact: Japan has already rearmed. Indeed, by spending only 1 percent of GNP on defense, a quasi-legal limit,[2] Japan has managed to achieve a sizable military capability. This indicates the extent to which Japan has the potential to arm itself, if exertion were really necessary.

Since Japan currently fields twelve maneuver divisions, 650 combat aircraft, sixty antisubmarine warfare (ASW) ships, sixteen submarines, and so on, it is rather bizarre to read the Article 9 stipulation that Japan may never maintain land, sea, or air forces. One would think that any Japanese judge would rule all this highly unconstitutional. It is interesting that there is only one case on record in which the Japanese Supreme Court ruled on the legitimacy of Article 9. The Sunakawa case in 1959 concerned trespassers on a U.S. Air Force base at Tachikawa. A district court had ruled that the trespassers were not guilty, because the agreement that brought the U.S. Air Force to Tachikawa was unconstitutional under Article 9. The Supreme Court then reversed the Tokyo District Court, ruling that:

> Naturally, the above (Article 9) in no way denies the inherent right of self-defense, which our country possesses as a sovereign nation, and the pacifism of our Constitution has never provided for either defenselessness or non-resistance.

The Supreme Court has never made a general ruling on the legitimacy of the Japanese Self-Defense Forces (JSDF), and confined the Sunakawa case to the right of the Japanese government to enter into treaties for mutual defense.[3] How the court could rule that Article 9 permits self-defense when it specifically bans the creation of an armed force is a matter best left to lawyers and theologians.[4]

The important point is that the Sunakawa case undermined Article 9 without destroying it. This was of fundamental importance to Japan. The existence of Article 9 permitted Japan to resist American pressures to rearm and join the U.S. in its anti-Soviet crusade. As was evident during the 1990 Iraqi invasion of Kuwait, Article 9 permitted Japan to refuse to participate in American risk taking without causing a rupture in U.S.–Japanese relations. On the other hand, Sunakawa allowed Japan to control the extent of rearmament on any basis that pleased it. Article 9 and the Sunakawa decision gave the Japanese government the best of both worlds: an American-designed constitutional ability to say "no," and the power to say "yes" at the moment of their choosing.

COMPREHENSIVE SECURITY: PACIFISM AS NATIONAL POLICY

Yashuhiro Nakasone, Japan's Prime Minister in the late 1980s, wrote in 1978:

> Our basic principle is self-defense. We therefore have no intention of possessing offensive and aggressive weapons that would present

an unwarranted threat to foreign countries. However we will maintain the minimum weaponry necessary for the defense of the land and people. We will also conduct controlled defense, which means that an attack on Japan will invariably be met by a counterattack. To provide for such minimum defense is an international responsibility. What precisely constitutes the minimum varies, of course, with the developments and changes in the international situation. . . . Of course I am quite sure that at this stage Japan will not possess ICBM's, aircraft carriers and other materiel that is clearly offensive in nature, and we will abide by this principle.[5]

Thus, Japan's defensive policy became a shifting, indeterminate set of possibilities guided more by the international situation than by a fixed set of principles, by Japan's needs broadly defined, and by the pressures brought to bear by its senior partner, the United States.

During the mid-1970s, Japan's postwar foreign policy was named a policy of "Comprehensive Security." It was intended to be a strategy suited to Japan's unique position as a powerful economic entity that had substantial economic and political interests, but had renounced war. Masashi Nishihara of Japan's Defense Academy pointed out that Comprehensive Security had many sides for many audiences. To Japan's pacifists it was intended to show that although Japan had become a great economic power, it did not intend to become a great military power. It could also be seen as an attempt to placate American concerns about Japan's willingness to share the burden of defense.[6] In other words, Comprehensive Security was less a strategy than a political device to permit Japan to placate both its own pacifists and the Americans, who were pulling the country in different directions.

This domestic aspect of Comprehensive Security was rather neatly summed up by a Japanese economist in 1981:

Japan will lose its ability to deal with crises and its cohesion if it loses its sense of vulnerability—which is why we continue harping on the subject of our reliance on outside sources of supply beyond our control. If we should rearm and become a world military power, we would indefinitely reduce our effectiveness and limit the ways in which the government can—often cynically—manage business and manipulate a national consensus.[7]

Comprehensive Security taught the Japanese that they were vulnerable, and was therefore useful in creating a national consensus for a military buildup. At the same time, it built itself around the principles of Article 9, which permitted Japan to resist American pressure to rearm. It therefore had multiple political uses.

In fact, Comprehensive Security was a working strategy for taking maximum advantage of America's dependency on Japan and extracting maximum economic benefit from it. As has been discussed, Japan's strategic interests are more than military: they are primarily economic. Therefore, a military policy that would disrupt Japanese economic relationships would be disastrous for Japan.

Thus, Comprehensive Security is not, as some argue, a new moral and political principle. It is simply a shrewd and rational appreciation of the situation and an attempt to maximize Japan's advantage in those circumstance. As circumstances change, Japan's response must change.

This is the central point: there are no constitutional limits on Japanese action. Article 9 is a dead letter and has been ever since the U.S. forced Japan to reconstitute its armed forces. No legal fiction can hide the fact that Japan has a large and growing military establishment and nothing can cover up the fact that Japan will use that armed force as it sees fit.

Indeed, one cannot fault Japan for this. Article 9 was an American invention forced on the Japanese. Of their own accord the Japanese would never have written that clause into their constitution. It does not flow from the character of Japanese culture, and therefore it is not morally binding on Japan. It has never been used as a moral principle. Rather, it has been used as a moral shield, a protection against American adventurism. It has not seriously limited Japan's rearmament, and cannot be used to predict Japan's behavior in the future.

Japan's military behavior will be determined, as it is for any other country, by its needs, fears, and greed. The moral garment the United States created for Japan has worn quite thin. Particularly with the reunification of Germany, the end of Allied occupation, and the creation of a unified German military, the idea that Japan's sins require it to do further penance is insupportable.

PACIFISM AND MILITARISM

There are those who hold that pacifism has entered the Japanese character in certain special ways as a result of the experiences of war and particularly the experience of Hiroshima and Nagasaki. Thus, this argument goes, the Japanese will not rearm and engage in aggressive politico-military behavior because they have learned that war decreases, rather than increases, national security, and that risking war is not a rational way to pursue national policy.

There are two arguments being presented here, one moral and one prudential. The moral argument holds that Japan has come to an understanding of war unavailable to those who have not gone through Japan's agony, and that Japan, purged to its core of aggressiveness, can no longer be expected to behave like other nations. The prudential argument parallels the moral one. It holds that Japan has learned that it cannot win a war and that the risks of waging a war in the nuclear age so outweigh the possible benefits that Japan would be foolish to engage in war.

The starting point of both arguments is Hiroshima. This is also the starting point for a discussion of the meaning of nuclear weapons, morally and prudentially, in the waging of war. There are two separate areas here. First, what did Hiroshima mean psychologically to Japan; how permanent is its effect and how profound? Second, what is the military significance of nuclear weapons? Does their existence mean that statecraft has been permanently transformed and that war is no longer a rational instrument of national policy?

It is interesting to compare the numbers killed by the atomic bombs at Hiroshima and Nagasaki with the fire bombing of Tokyo. An estimated 130,000 people died at Hiroshima and 35,000 at Nagasaki; in the great bombing raid on Tokyo on March 9, 1945, over 100,000 Japanese died in a single night action and sixteen square miles of Tokyo were obliterated.[8] Aerial bombardments had become routine over Japan and many cities had suffered much worse devastation. The main difference was that a single aircraft dropping a single weapon had accomplished as much as raids by 300 bombers. Such devastation would require much less exertion, although only by one measure. The effort required to build 300 bombers was substantially less than the effort that went into the Manhattan Project that built the atomic bomb. If the goal was to devastate Japan's population centers from the air, conventional bombardment with incendiary devices was the simpler and cheaper method. There was a technical difference; was there a moral or psychological one?

The focus on Japan's moral regeneration and transformation has centered on the atomic bomb. The basic view has been that having experienced nuclear bombardment, Japan has confronted the horror of war in a unique and unprecedented manner and has therefore permanently recoiled from war. The epiphany of atomic bombardment is critical to those who feel that Japan has fundamentally reformed. Japan was one of the most militaristic cultures in modern history. The individual's role in going to war transcended mere political consideration—it was a religious act, and death in war sanctified and justified life. The warrior was deeply celebrated as a religious figure.

At first, all this boiled down to a single question: could Japan be trusted to abandon militarism? Over time, it turned into a political question. When Japan refused to undertake a military role in its alliance with the United States, it justified this by way of Article 9 and a deep moral aversion to war. When outsiders wondered about the sincerity of the conversion experience, pointing out that other countries had been defeated, devastated, and occupied in war without abandoning war as an inherent power of the state, the Japanese were forced to point out the uniqueness of their experience with war: atomic bombardment. For this reason we must consider whether atomic bombardment did in fact make the Japanese experience in war different from that of other nations, such as Germany. This is a very practical question. In predicting Japan's future military behavior, the question of whether Japan has actually permanently abandoned war is the central issue.

Atomic warfare was a natural outgrowth of the concept of aerial bombardment. In 1921, Giulio Douhet, commander of Italy's first aviation unit, wrote *Command of the Air,*[9] a document that deeply influenced all future thinking on air power, including that of America's Billy Mitchell and Germany's Hermann Goering. The importance of this work cannot be overestimated, for it put forth the proposition that wars could now be won from the air, through aerial bombardment.

Modern war is industrial war containing two components, factories and workers. The ability to systematically destroy these targets would end an enemy nation's war-making capability. Therefore, by seizing command of the air and eliminating enemy air power, an air force had the ability to bombard at will both enemy troop concentrations and its production and logistical systems, thereby destroying the real engines of war. Billy Mitchell's famous experiments against battleships sought to demonstrate that the ability to dominate the land from the air could be extended to the surface of oceans as well.

The great aerial campaigns of World War II, Germany's bombardment of Britain, the Anglo-American counter-bombardment of Germany, and the American bombardment of Japan all shared certain characteristics in common:

1. An attempt to destroy the enemy's war-making capability before it was deployed on the battlefields, right in the factories and warehouses.
2. An attempt to make life in the capital and other key cities unbearable, thereby undermining the enemy regime's political support and sapping the continued will to resist.

The instrument for this destruction was the strategic bomber carrying various explosive and incendiary devices. The operational principle was the bomber force of several hundred, or even thousand, aircraft attacking in massed waves and destroying enemy concentrations. Massed bombardment, whether in its American form of daylight precision bombardment or the British doctrine of nighttime area bombardment, boiled down to the same practical end: blowing up enemy cities in order to compel the enemy to surrender.

Many German and Japanese cities, Coventry in England, and several parts of London all were devastated by these attacks. What made the German campaign different was its lack of sufficient bombers with which to concentrate on given areas, as well as the limited range and bomb loads of those aircraft. Later in the war, the Germans spent considerable effort and resources in perfecting the V-1 and V-2 rockets, which followed the same principle without the expense of air crews but with the added expense of unrecoverable vehicles. The U.S. concentrated on manned aerial bombardment, command of the sky, and concentrated bombardment.

Atomic bombs may have been technologically novel, but strategically they were merely a refinement. Atomic bombardment changed the time frame of devastation from hours to seconds and the number of delivery vehicles from hundreds to one. It also changed the cost of developing and delivering the weapons from a few million to billions of dollars and required massive manpower and material diversions to achieve. The yield, in terms of casualties, was smaller than with conventional bombs (due to the wider distribution of conventional bombs during a given raid). Its major virtue was that, wedded to unstoppable missile systems, it became in the long run a low-cost method of destroying industrial concentrations substantially removed from the battlefield (because of the risk of radiation on the battlefield).

Although not a single strategic bombardment campaign in history (the Battle of Britain, Germany in 1943–1945, Japan in 1944–1945, North Vietnam) has ever succeeded in bringing a regime to its knees by itself, the myth of the air campaign persists.[10] As was seen in Chapter 3, Japan was not defeated by aerial bombardment. It was defeated by unlimited submarine warfare, which strangled Japan's factories long before air power tried to knock them out.

Thus, the experience of atomic bombing was not quantitatively or qualitatively different from the experience of incendiary bombardment. When Hiroshima was destroyed, there was substantial argument within the Japanese government over whether or not the American claim that an atomic bomb had been used was true. Even a team that went directly to Hiroshima after the bombing could not agree on whether the damage was caused by a new type of weapon.[11]

In retrospect, it seems amazing that days after the bombing the

Japanese were still debating whether Japan had been atomic-bombed. However, the damage in Hiroshima was generally consistent with damage caused in other cities by conventional bombardment. What was new was not the experience of aerial bombardment but the delivery system—one plane—something about which the Japanese were not really clear for quite a while. Moreover, it is arguable that the motive for surrender had far more to do with the entry of the Soviet Union into the war than with the danger of atomic bombardment. Hiroshima was terrible, but no more terrible than Tokyo or Nagoya or any of the other cities devastated by aerial bombardment.

Retrospectively, Hiroshima became an important explanatory device for the Japanese. It was important first in explaining the Japanese defeat. It is one thing to gamble; it is another to gamble and fail. Japan had gambled and failed. That the Japanese military command had failed to take steps to defend its merchant fleet against submarine attack and had failed in its decision to maintain huge forces in China rather than shifting them early toward battle fronts were substantial indictments of the regime and the Imperial High Command. Implicitly it would have been a criticism of the Emperor, who had permitted the war to begin but had failed to execute it properly. By blaming their surrender on atomic war, the High Command could argue that they had prepared for any eventuality, but not for one this unprecedented and barbaric.

Second, Hiroshima—and Nagasaki—allowed the Emperor to save face in his capitulation. The Emperor's Imperial Rescript of August 14, 1945, reveals this reasoning clearly:

> Despite the best that has been done by everyone—the gallant fighting of the military and naval forces, the diligence and assiduity of Our servants of the State and the devoted service of Our one hundred million people, the war situation has developed not necessarily to Japan's advantage, while the general trends of the world have all turned against her interest. Moreover, the enemy has begun to employ a new and most cruel bomb, the power of which to do damage is indeed incalculable, taking the toll of many innocent lives. Should we continue to fight, it would not only result in an ultimate collapse and obliteration of the Japanese nation, but also it would lead to the total extinction of human civilization.[12]

The need to surrender had become manifestly evident weeks before the Soviet intervention or Hiroshima. As early as July 12, 1945, the Japanese ambassador to the Soviet Union was instructed to seek an immediate end to the war.[13] The failure of the Soviets, for their own reasons, to transmit these feelers properly to the Americans had much to do with the American perception that the Japanese intended to fight to the end. But in fact, Japan's key leaders realized that the war was lost.

Japan knew it was defeated well before Hiroshima. The destruction of Hiroshima simply made the surrender more palatable. It also shifted the moral burden. Japan's capitulation was in part the result of America's immoral and unscrupulous use of a brutal new weapon. But by surrendering, the Japanese were showing their moral decency in sparing Japan—and indeed, the Americans and the rest of the world—the burden of ongoing war.

Hiroshima allowed Japan to play the martyr on the stage of world public opinion. From the Imperial Rescript onward, the claim would emerge that Japan was the victim of a hideous action, an act of wanton slaughter beyond the bounds of civilized behavior. Through this, the terrible barbarity of Japan's war in China, its treatment of civilians in occupied territories, its brutalization of prisoners of war, not to mention the decision to start the war in the first place, all paled by comparison. By turning Hiroshima into an event of unprecedented immorality, Japan was able to emerge as the war's victim, rather than as the war's perpetrator.

Japan subsequently expanded on this theme by appropriating Article 9 as a Japanese response to Hiroshima. Article 9 had been an American invention, imposed on the Japanese by an America fearful of a resurgence of Japanese imperialism. It became part of the postwar myth of Hiroshima that Japan, devastated by the first atomic bombing in history, understood the futility of war better than any other nation. This understanding was made manifest in the Japanese constitution, in which Japan made this insight a matter of fundamental national policy.

Myth becomes reality in politics. The idea that Japan, the victim of war, has learned the futility of war has become an important principle in Japanese political life, expressed in support for Article 9 of the constitution and in opposition to an expanded role for the Japanese military. The Gensuikyo, the Anti-Atomic and Hydrogen Bomb Council, which developed during the 1950s after U.S. hydrogen bomb tests poisoned some Japanese fishermen, became an instrument of left-wing opposition to American policies. In equating its antinuclear position with anti-Americanism, Gensuikyo became an instrument very much in the control of the Japanese Communist Party.[14]

The merger of anti-Americanism and antinuclear sentiment was extremely useful to the ruling Liberal Democratic Party (LDP). The threat of leftist unrest, particularly after the 1960 riots, allowed the LDP to keep American demands for a more active military role at arm's length. While the LDP was building up Japanese forces to the precise level that it wanted, calibrating Japan's military exposure to Japan's political interests, it could use the threat of left-wing unrest as a hedge against being forced over the line.

Thus, both the Japanese Left and the Right endorsed Article 9 and the doctrine of pacifism, but both did it for primarily political reasons. The Left used pacifism as a means of turning antiwar sentiment into anti-American sentiment. The Right used pacifism as a means of increasing its room for maneuver against American pressure by invoking antiwar sentiment as a limiting and destabilizing element.

There was certainly sincere antiwar sentiment in Japan. Japanese were appalled by what had happened in the war, but one might speculate that this was all the more traumatic because of the defeat and the occupation. The sincerity of antiwar sentiment was reinforced by the fact that it worked so well. Refusing to rearm, or to rearm to the extent that the United States wanted, made good political and economic sense. Even the radical opposition played an indispensable role in this. The threat of the Left made the Americans, fearful of a left-wing coup in Japan, less likely to press their cause.

The real question has always been whether Japanese antiwar sentiment is any more than a prudent policy for dealing with the Americans. It is generally assumed that pacifist and antiwar sentiment is fairly widespread in Japan. Actually, polls show little evidence for this. The following are the results from a poll taken in 1988 concerning Japanese reaction to aggression against Japan: only 10.2 percent would have no part in resisting aggression, while 39.5 percent said they would support the Self-Defense Forces in some way; 18.9 percent said they would put up nonmilitary resistance, and 7 percent said they would engage in some sort of paramilitary resistance. Thus, we have about 29.1 percent of the population not willing to engage in violent military action, while about 46.5 percent are prepared to take or support violent action. When men alone were considered, the ratio of nonviolent to violent became 22.3 to 60.2 percent. The current arrangements were supported by 67.4 percent of the public, only 5.9 percent wanted to abrogate the alliance with America and rearm, while just 7.2 percent wanted to eliminate the Self-Defense Forces.[15]

Since the current posture of Japan is anything but pacifistic and since sentiment to eliminate the Self-Defense Forces is marginal, it would appear that there is no fundamental psychological block limiting Japan's actions. The current psychological configuration has permitted the construction of a military machine larger than those of most other countries. Prudential considerations have prevented the use of these weapons, but prudence is not the same as moral constraint.

A shift in Japan's international reality, as described in Chapter 10, will not force the Japanese leadership and public to consider whether Japan should rearm, since Japan *has* rearmed, but it will force a consideration of how or whether these weapons ought to be used. Nothing in Japanese history or in current public opinion indicates that there is a deep, permanent block to the use of military force in the Japanese national interest. All that was seen during the Cold War was an aversion to the use of force on behalf of another country's interests. That is not pacifism, it is merely common sense.

Japan was once more than a country prudently pursuing its natural interest. There was a period during which war was a genuine exercise in moral excellence, the pinnacle of a man's possible activities. The tradition of Bushido—the feudal-military code that valued personal honor and "right action" more than life—was defined by a leading practitioner as rectitude, properly understood:

> Rectitude is the power of deciding upon a certain course of conduct in accordance with reason without wavering—to die when it is right to die, to strike when to strike is right.[16]

There are many who have argued that this sort of militarism is just beneath the surface in Japan. It has been pointed out that within the Self-Defense Forces, many of the old virtues are still celebrated. For example, at the Japanese Navy officer training school, there are displays of mementos of kamikaze pilots, certainly a celebration of the most extreme form of Bushido.[17] Others have argued that the modern Japanese corporation, with its extremes of conformity, self-sacrifice, and celebration of the group over the individual is a modern form of Japanese militarism.[18]

It is easier to imagine a revival of militarism in Japan than it is to imagine a genuine pacifism. Obviously, the question of the extent to which Japan is Shinto and the extent to which Shinto Buddhism contains pacifist tendencies is beyond the scope of our discussion. We do know this: Japan was once convincingly militaristic, and Asia shook before its dedicated, disciplined, *believing* armies. Japan has never been persuasively pacifist. As a nation, its deeds never conformed to its words. Japan's pacifism has always been more an instrument of foreign policy than a genuine moral principle.

But at the same time, the question of whether or not Japan is going to see a revival of militarism is irrelevant in the extreme. Japan need only behave like a normal nation, pursuing a rational foreign policy, for it to engage in war. War is not an instrument only or primarily of maniacal killers, of men willing to die on command and kill as a matter of honor. War is an instrument of men and nations who would, by far, rather not be soldiers and go to war.

As a normal nation, Japan's capacity for war is great enough. There is little evidence that Japan's experience during World War II taught it very much more than the virtues of winning and the vices of defeat. It is unclear whether or not militarism as a moral and cultural form is dead in Japan, but it is also genuinely unimportant. Japan as a normal nation will wage war as necessary, not as a matter of pleasure but as a matter of need. That alone is enough to give Japan the energy for creating a war machine necessary for coping with America.

THE FUTURE OF WAR

Many have argued that war was made obsolete by nuclear weapons. If so, history has not heard of war's obsolescence. Quite the contrary, the history of the world since 1945 has been a history of war. What has been most striking is that even though several nuclear powers— the United States, the Soviet Union, Great Britain, France, Israel— have all fought wars, not once have nuclear weapons been used. Indeed, the United States and the Soviet Union were each defeated in major wars, and permitted themselves to be defeated without re-course to nuclear weapons.

There is something odd about a weapon that is said to be absolutely powerful, yet is never used as an instrument of statecraft. One is left with one of two suspicions: that nuclear weapons are too powerful to use or that they are not powerful enough. To be more precise, they are so powerful that they have very little practical use.

Consider the case of Vietnam. Assume that the United States had been prepared to use nuclear weapons in order to win. What precisely would they have attacked? They could have bombed Hanoi and Hai-phong, but both cities were fairly well flattened with conventional devices. Moreover, destroying them would not have affected the fighting in the South. Using nuclear weapons in the South would have been ridiculous: there were no concentrations of forces that were large enough to warrant an attack, nor any far enough away from American forces to permit the use of nuclear weapons. The Soviets faced the same problem in Afghanistan. The circumstances under which nuclear weapons have targets that are large enough, far enough away, and not manageable by conventional weapons are few indeed. In the forty-five years since nuclear weapons have ex-isted, no nuclear power has found such a target.

The primary function of nuclear weapons is as an instrument of terror. Nuclear weapons threaten to bring enormous destruction, so that one nation will be expected to capitulate to the demands of another. There is a serious problem with this reasoning as well. In World War II, the Soviet Union suffered over 20 million dead at the hands of the Nazis. Had they known at the beginning of the war that they would incur such casualties, it would still not have made sense to capitulate. Even 10 percent of the population dead would not be worth the price of submitting to Hitler. It is doubtful that even 20 or 30 percent dead would have been sufficient to persuade the Soviets to surrender.

There were two reasons for this. First, Stalin himself was prepared to spend his nation's blood. The assumption in all aerial bombardments of civilian targets is that the government cares about the suffering of the people. Usually, it cares only about the country's war-making capability. Second, submission would have meant slavery, and faced with Hitler, death was a rational and preferable alternative. Thus, the terror of nuclear weapons is mitigated by the terror of capitulation.

As an instrument of war making, the problem is to find a mission for nuclear weapons that cannot be accomplished with conventional weapons. One can imagine some industrial complexes that could not be destroyed with conventional bombardment, but under any circumstance, the problem of fallout makes the proximity of the target to the front a seriously limiting factor. The Soviets could hardly use nuclear weapons in Afghanistan when wind could have blown dangerous radiation over Iran, Pakistan, India, or even the Soviet Union.

Even these considerations become insignificant when the opponent is another nuclear power. Charles de Gaulle realized early on that it was not necessary for France to match Soviet nuclear power. It was sufficient that France be in a position to "tear an arm off" the Soviet Union to stop it. The utility of nuclear weapons disappears when the nuclear power's enemy can inflict massive casualties. They simply cancel each other out.

Thus, far from abolishing war, nuclear weapons have had almost no impact on it. War has been limited by the mutual interests of the Soviets and the Americans, and where these interests collided, there was war. The constancy of wars against Israel and the willingness of the Syrians and Egyptians to attack Israel, even in the face of overwhelming evidence that Israel was nuclear-capable, shows the limits of nuclear weapons and the ubiquity of war.

Another argument often given against the future of war is the notion that economic interdependence limits the likelihood of war. The dependence of the U.S. and Japan on each other economically, the fact that disruptions in trade relations would cause tremendous problems, is taken as evidence that war would be avoided at all costs.

There are two problems with this idea. The first is that the argument has no idea of the long run and the short run. It may be true that very painful short-run dislocations would occur in the event of war. But this does not take into account the fact that, in the long run, war might be economically beneficial. Thus, Iraq incurred short-term economic pains in order to pursue long-term economic benefits in Kuwait. Additionally, this argument forgets that interdependence does not necessarily mean mutual pleasure. The fact that the U.S. is dependent on Japanese imports does not mean that maintaining that flow of goods is a matter for which it is worth avoiding war.

The second problem with this idea is that it is both old and historically discredited. The classic example is World War I, when several people argued that war had been made obsolete by the interdependence of economies. The disruptions caused by the war were indeed horrendous. Nevertheless, none of the combatants hesitated to jump into the fray.

For the U.S. and Japan, it is precisely the discomfort of interdependence that drove them to war the first time around. The dependence of Japan on the U.S. tempted the Americans to use that dependency for political advantage. All interdependence is unbalanced. No two nations have precise equality in a system of economic relationships. Because of that, when the imbalance is sufficiently extreme, the desperation of the inferior nation and its need to rectify the imbalance can lead to war when the means of waging war are present.

The means of waging war must always be weighed against the costs of doing business. This is a fundamental equation that has not been abolished by nuclear weapons and has only been intensified by the growth of economic interdependence. For Japan, business is dependent on the availability of markets and resources. The cost of war is, under those circumstances, part of the cost of doing business.

The task here is not to prove the inevitability of war, but merely its possibility. The idea that war has ceased to serve a function in the nuclear age simply does not bear up to historical scrutiny. War *has* continued to serve a function in the nuclear age, and one suspects that with the end of the Cold War this function can only increase. Suffice it to say that, in the words of Plato, only the dead have seen the end of war. Our task is to consider the very real future of war in the context of the U.S.–Japanese relationship, and to consider it concretely, in very practical terms. To begin with, we must consider the substantial armed forces developed by Japan in recent years, in spite of Article 9 and Hiroshima.

1. Japan Economic Institute, "Growth in Defense Spending Trimmed," August 3, 1990, p. 4.
2. In November 1976, the Miki cabinet issued the following policy statement: "Each fiscal year's defense-related expenditures, required for the buildup of defense capability, will be limited to not more than one percent of the estimated gross national product for each fiscal year for the time being." See Robert F. Reed, *The U.S.–Japan Alliance: Sharing the Burden of Defense* (Washington, D.C., 1983), p. 24.
3. Reed, *The U.S.–Japan Alliance*, pp. 17–19.
4. On the general question of Article 9 and the JSDF, see Theodore McNelly, "The Constitutionality of Japan's Defense Establishment," in *The Modern Japanese Military System*, ed. James H. Buck (Beverly Hills, 1975), pp. 99–112.
5. Yasuhiro Nakasone, "Toward Comprehensive Security," *Japan Echo*, 5:4 (1978), p. 38.
6. In Robert W. Barnett, *Beyond War: Japan's Concept of Comprehensive National Security* (Washington, D.C., 1984), pp. 24–25.
7. J.W.M. Chapman, R. Drifte, and I.T.M. Gow, *Japan's Quest for Comprehensive Security* (New York, 1982), p. 92.
8. The official U.S. Air Force estimate is 80,000 dead; the generally accepted figure is 100,000. See John Costello, *The Pacific War: 1941–1945* (New York, 1982), p. 532.
9. Giulio Douhet, *Command of the Air* (New York, 1942).
10. An important new National Defense University study of the role of air warfare persists in making the assertion that "war can be won from the air." The importance of this book in shaping American thinking during the Kuwait affair was extremely large. See John A. Warden III, *The Air Campaign: Planning for Combat* (Washington, D.C., 1988), p. 39.
11. Robert J.C. Butow, *Japan's Decision to Surrender* (Stanford, 1954), pp. 151–152.
12. Ibid., p. 248.
13. Ibid., p. 124.
14. John K. Emmerson and Leonard A. Humphreys, *Will Japan Rearm?* (Washington, D.C., 1973), pp. 14–15.
15. Office of the Japanese Prime Minister, Foreign Press Center, Japan, *Public Opinion Survey on the Self-Defense Force and Defense Problems*, August 1988, pp. 8–9.
16. Inazo Nitobe, *Bushido: The Soul of Japan* (Rutland, Vt., 1969), p. 23.
17. Albert Axelbank, *Black Star Over Japan* (New York, 1973), p. 49.
18. See, for example, Jared Taylor, *Shadows of the Rising Sun* (New York, 1983), for a discussion of the Japanese corporation that causes one to think in terms of Bushido rectitude.

13

The Japanese Self-Defense Forces

In a political sense Japan has not been a fully autonomous nation for the last forty-five years. In many ways, it has been a protectorate of the United States, a precious and protected imperial possession. Its armed forces have behaved more like those of a protectorate than those of a sovereign state. Just as British India had an army that served British more than Indian interests, so Japan's military has tended to behave more as an adjunct to American power than for its own purposes.

Since the American domination of Japan has been mutually satisfying there have been no Japanese mutinies, rebellions, or plots. Protectorate status has suited the Japanese well and they have taken full advantage of it. However, the days of the protectorate are drawing to a close, much as are the days of the alliance, and with that the emergence of a genuinely Japanese armed force in its first stages can now be perceived.

For many years Japan's Self-Defense Forces have been laying the groundwork for this new era. Japan has a small army—although it is larger than most people imagine—but more important, Japan's military industrial capability is much greater than is generally assumed. Japan has already created some of the most advanced weapons in the world and knows how to mass-produce them. Japan's emergence as a great military power in the future depends more on

343

its will than its ability. In order to have a world-class military force in a few short years, Japan merely has to decide that it needs one.

Given Japan's relationship with the U.S., its military has had a much odder growth than those of most nations. In order to understand Japan's military force, it is necessary to begin by analyzing the American presence in Japan and on the surrounding waters.

AMERICAN FORCES IN JAPAN

The two pillars of Japanese defense policy are the Japanese Self-Defense Forces and the alliance with the United States. In many ways Japan's alliance with the U.S. is the more important element, inasmuch as U.S. power in the region is still overwhelming. Concurrently, the Japanese Self-Defense Forces are growing steadily and have become a formidable force in their own right. The critical turning point in Pacific affairs will occur when the power of Japanese forces in the region surpasses that of American forces. This has not yet happened. However, given the commitment of the U.S. to cut forces in the aftermath of the Cold War and the continued growth of the Japanese budget when the budgets of other nations have entered a decline, the continued superiority of U.S. forces in the area is not at all assured.

U.S. forces in Japan currently include: 2,100 army personnel who are primarily engaged in administrative duties—except for a special forces unit in Okinawa; two tactical fighter wings equipped with F-15s and F-16s; the Third Marine Division and the First Marine Air Wing, with F-18s and Harriers. The U.S. Navy maintains the *Midway*, a carrier battle group with Japanese home ports. The bulk of U.S. forces, except for naval vessels, is to be found in Okinawa.

Thus, the U.S. presence on the home islands is relatively light and almost devoid of ground forces. The primary presence is in port facilities for elements of the U.S. Seventh Fleet and air bases for U.S. tactical fighter planes. The largest ground-force presence is the Marine division on Okinawa, whose primary purpose is as a rapid-deployment force in the Far East and the Indian Ocean. Japanese ground forces, which number nearly 200,000, could easily overwhelm American forces, including those on Okinawa. It is obvious that the presence of U.S. forces on the home islands in no way limits Japan's sovereignty or freedom of maneuver. The U.S. can no longer impose a regime on Japan nor can it resist Japanese demands for withdrawal, should such demands be made. It is important to understand that the U.S. no longer occupies Japan and that the American presence there is dependent on mutual agreement.

The U.S. permitted this situation in order to economize its forces, and has relied on the Japanese being interested enough in their own security to permit the continued basing of U.S. forces in Japan. Japan's armed forces developed in the shadow of the alliance with the United States, since they were originally designed to fulfill American needs in that region. First, the U.S. wanted Japan to have sufficient ground forces to protect itself against attack without requiring immediate American assistance. Second, the U.S. wanted an air force capable of protecting Japanese airspace from Soviet intrusion. Finally, the U.S. wanted the assistance of the Japanese Navy in controlling the Soviet threat in the region, particularly the threat to regional shipping posed by Soviet submarines.

Japanese military deployments were developed in the face of a perceived Soviet threat, as can be seen in Table 13-1, published by the Japan Defense Agency, which displays Soviet deployment.

Noteworthy in the Soviet deployment is the concentration of air power and submarine forces but the relative paucity of amphibious forces. For example, the Soviets are shown to have one naval infantry division (marines) at Vladivostok, while all other divisions are landbound. The Soviets potentially could pose a maritime threat and certainly could pose an air threat, but their ability to threaten Japanese national security is minimal. Indeed, the 1989 edition of *Defense of Japan* was the last to list the Soviets as a possible threat. By the 1990 edition, the Soviet threat was no longer the primary consideration in justifying Japan's Self-Defense Forces; instability on the Asian mainland was.

JAPAN'S DEFENSE STRUCTURE

In the context of the U.S.–Japanese alliance, the function of the Japanese Self-Defense Forces has been to secure the physical area around Japan, to assist the United States Navy and Air Force in securing a broader defense perimeter, including patrolling a 1,000-mile zone south and east of Japan, and to serve as a base for U.S. operations in the region.

Japan's armed forces are properly designed for this task, and a casual glance at their capabilities would find Japan confined to this role. But beneath the surface, the Japanese defense structure is more flexible and capable than would be necessary if this were the only task in mind. This is evident in the types of technologies used, the methods of procuring material and weapons, and the emphasis on developing new weapons systems that might not be immediately necessary.

Over the past year or so, the Japanese have come to recognize that they must possess an independent military force if they are to function in the post-Cold War world. This recognition has come from all sectors of the Japanese political order. A former foreign ministry official, Motofumi Asai, said:

At a time when the Soviet Union can no longer afford to maintain its military aggressiveness, should the U.S. continue its Cold War strategy of maintaining world order by the deterrent of its military strength? Japan should re-examine its adherence to the security treaty with the U.S.[1]

TABLE 13-1. Soviet Military Deployments in Areas Close to Japan.

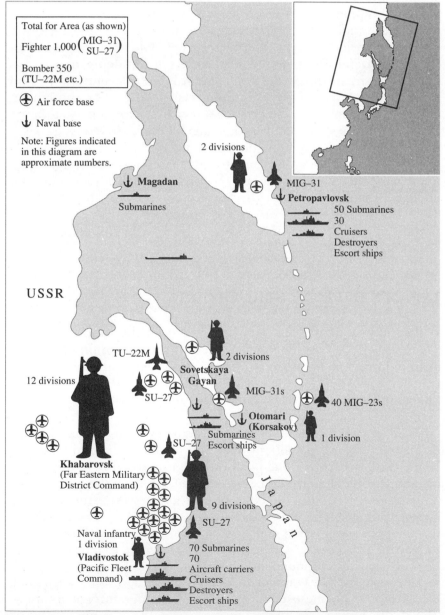

Source: *Defense of Japan*

Masao Kunihiro, a Socialist and former advisor to Prime Minister Takeo Miki, said that with the end of the Cold War the U.S. might come to regard the Security Treaty as a device of the United States for keeping Japan under economic control and that therefore, "We should have a cooler attitude toward the security alliance with the U.S. and start preparing for the next stage."[2]

Even a prominent establishment figure like Masashi Nishihara, professor at the National Defense Academy, said:

A nation's defense policy should be changed in accordance with the international situation of the times. . . . Rather than adhering to the old document, the agency should adopt a new defense program outline that takes recent East-West developments into consideration.[3]

The issue of Japan's defense orientation has already created furor in Japan. In March 1988, there was heated debate over the future of Japan's defense capability, started when then Prime Minister Noboru Takeshita told defense cadets that Japan would have to possess "defense capabilities commensurate with our national power."[4] Given the self-imposed limits on military power discussed in the last chapter—and when viewed in economic terms—the willingness of a Japanese prime minister to call publicly for a military power equal to Japan's vast national power can only be seen as a break with the past. Indeed, it could only be understood as placing Japan on the threshold of becoming a great Pacific, if not a global, power.

There is a popular notion that Japan either has no armed forces or that it maintains, at best, a skeleton force incapable of defending Japan or serving as an instrument of national policy. While it is true that Japan's armed forces are much smaller than they could be, given Japan's manpower and industrial potential, Japan's current forces are both substantial and completely suited for the tasks at hand. Moreover, the current forces are large enough and sophisticated enough that in an emergency they could rapidly be expanded into a world-class military force.

It should come as no great surprise that Japan is capable of manufacturing the materials necessary for a modern military force. The world's second-largest economy, with one of the most efficient work forces in the world and a tradition of technical innovation and precision, is obviously capable of providing the wherewithal for a modern military. Anyone familiar with the sophistication of Japanese products could have no doubt about Japan's ability to create a military-industrial base. Indeed, the discipline that is found in the Japanese factory is a virtue that is easily transferrable to the battlefield. Japan has not had a strong military tradition for forty-five years, but there are still many Japanese alive who recall Imperial glory. The fact is that despite the problems—and chief among these is the shortage of manpower to man the factories and guns—the decision to become a great military power is not a technical but a political one.

Nineteen ninety was a turning point for Japan in two ways. First, it was the year in which the Cold War ended; second, it was the year in which Japan's largest postwar rebuilding plan, its 1976 National Defense Program Outline, was completed. Under the plan, the Japanese Self-Defense Forces were rounded out to thirteen full divisions plus six brigades, sixty-two antisubmarine warfare vessels, sixteen submarines, 214 naval combat aircraft, and an air defense force with 415 planes.[5]

Japan therefore must simultaneously devise a new plan for military development and adjust its foreign policy to the collapse of communism and the Soviet Union. The old plan was forged during the Cold War, as the force structure of the Japanese Self-Defense Forces reflects. Japan's areas of expansion were those areas in which the U.S. required supplemental help; the areas neglected were generally those in which the U.S. was secure or in which there was no significant Soviet threat.

In developing their forces, the Japanese frequently went beyond the role of supplementing the United States, toward capabilities that would prove themselves useful to Japan in its own right. As Marine General Henry C. Stackpole, a divisional commander on Okinawa, said in an interview quoted in the *Washington Post*:

> Japan will beef up "what is already a very, very potent military," if United States forces withdraw. No one wants a rearmed resurgent Japan, so we are a cap on the bottle, if you will.[6]

The sense that Japan is in a position to rapidly expand its military force and is restrained only by the American presence is not based solely on the views of American military leaders in Japan. It can also be gleaned from looking at the weapons-procurement policies pursued by the Japanese.

The Japanese have the wherewithal in place to rapidly expand their forces should the need arise. This does not mean that militarism is reemerging in Japan or that the Japanese elite is plotting for war. Quite the contrary, the Japanese power structure dreads the thought of remilitarization or of conflict. Nevertheless, a prudent nation must prepare for the worst case while hoping for the best.

The administrative structure of the Japanese armed forces is designed to minimize their significance while in no way limiting their utility. The Japanese Self-Defense Forces (JSDF) are not controlled by a defense ministry but by an agency in the Office of the Prime Minister, a slight which tends to convince people that the Japanese Defense Agency (JDA) is less than a full partner in the regime. This impression is an illusion. The Director General of the JDA is a minister of state who sits in the Cabinet and functions as a full-fledged minister.

The structure of the Japanese Defense Agency is that of a completely normal defense ministry. The Director General of the JDA serves also as Minister of State for Defense: in the former capacity he reports to the Prime Minister, while in the latter he reports to the Cabinet. The Prime Minister and Cabinet are served by the Security Council of Japan, a recent invention dating from 1986 that replaces the National Defense Council. The Prime Minister presides over the Security Council along with Director General JDA, the Foreign Minister, the Finance Minister, the Chairman of the Public Safety Commission, and the Director General of the Economic Planning Agency.[7]

It is interesting to note the bias in favor of economic as opposed to strictly military functionaries, a reasonable perspective given the Japanese position on comprehensive security. A staff system exists with the Chairman of the Joint Staff Council reporting to the Director General JDA but without any operational authority over the Self-Defense Forces. Thus, a very normal command structure exists, parallel to those in other countries.

Most important, of course, the Japanese Defense Agency controls a substantial budget both in terms of share of the general budget and in comparison to other countries. The size of the defense budget of the Japanese Defense Agency influences the impression one gets of the size of the Japanese Self-Defense Forces. In 1990 Japan spent Y4,159 billion, about $33 billion, on defense—an amount that gave Japan the third-largest defense budget in the world, behind the Soviet Union and the U.S. Moreover, the Japanese defense budget has been growing at a rapid rate, rising an average of 6.4 percent each year and continuing to rise during the latter part of the 1980s, when the declining Soviet threat caused other nations to decrease spending.[8]

WEAPONS AND DEFENSE

The process of Japanese defense procurement is of particular interest. All defense requests developed by the Japanese Self-Defense Forces must be approved by two government ministries: the Ministry of Finance and the Ministry of International Trade and Industry. The Ministry of Finance evaluates the requests against other budgetary needs and tends to be a fairly severe hurdle for defense planners; the Ministry of International Trade and Industry, known as MITI, is more interesting.

Americans are used to hearing about MITI in the context of Japan's trade policy, and admire the coordination and aggressiveness it brings to bear on trade problems. However, under a 1953 law MITI also has the power to regulate and control the manufacture of all aircraft, weapons, and munitions. Private firms must give MITI data on all aspects of their production, including information on proprietary technology. MITI therefore has tremendous control over details of procurement and thus over the defense budget.[9]

This is an extremely novel approach to procurement. In a way it is appropriate, since MITI had its origins as a munitions ministry in prewar Japan. However, the idea of coordinating defense procurement with a wide range of other political and economic considerations is extremely shrewd. Defense planners, who tend to care most about maximizing budgets and procuring appropriate weapons systems, frequently lack an overview of the significance of overdependence on a given supplier or, more frequently, any sense of the impact of procurement practices on import and export practices.

MITI is in a unique position to evaluate this. It is also in a unique position to evaluate the relative strengths and weaknesses of the Japanese defense industrial base. Finally, it is in a unique position to evaluate political threats to Japanese munitions sources and to take appropriate steps to protect Japan from cutoffs.

Thus, with this law and the manner in which it is implemented, MITI becomes the most important player not only in industrial planning for the civilian economy but also for the development of Japan's defense industries. In the United States there is rarely coordination between the Defense, Commerce, and Treasury departments, and one can tend to ignore the possibility of broad strategic implications in U.S. procurement policy, but the same is not true in Japan. The concentration of power and data in MITI means that there is a central coordinating power acting with substantial intelligence on defense matters. This warrants an extremely close look at Japanese procurement policies.

MITI has emphasized self-reliance in procuring military hardware. In part this is motivated by national pride and in part by resentment of the United States and its overbearing attitudes.[10] Mostly, it is simply the result of rational strategic thought. Japan wants to build self-dependence in military procurement because there might come a time when it must be wholly self-dependent. And Japan is prepared to spend substantial amounts of money on developing this self-reliance.

Maintenance of domestic production capability, even when foreign purchase would be more economical, has been a hallmark of Japanese defense policy since the late 1950s. Almost all of Japan's warships and over 80 percent of all other materiel is manufactured domestically, sometimes at a higher cost than importing it.[11] In 1979, Japan produced 85.2 percent of its military needs domestically. In 1987, this figure had risen to 91.1 percent,[12] an extremely high proportion, indicating that only those weapons that could not be produced in Japan under any circumstances were being imported.

Japan has four options in securing a weapons system: domestic production, co-development and production, production under license from a foreign defense contractor, and outright purchase. In those cases where Japan simply lacks the capability to produce a system itself, it will seek to purchase a production license that would allow for technology transfer, rather than purchase the weapon on an outright basis. Advanced weapons systems such as the F-15 fighter and the Patriot missile were all obtained under license. In many cases licensing has led to domestic development of the next-generation system. In all cases Japanese procurement invariably moves from outright purchases to other methods where technology transfers can be achieved.

The Japanese military-industrial complex even now has fairly large chips to play with. Japanese defense spending has been substantial in absolute numbers, but not as a measure of gross national product. It has been Japanese policy since the late 1970s to bring defense spending to 1 percent of gross national product and to hold it there. It came to 0.9 percent of GNP in 1980 and reached about 1 percent in 1984, a level roughly held ever since. The sheer size of the Japanese economy has permitted the dollar amount of the Japanese defense budget to edge past the budgets of America's NATO allies without going above the 1 percent limit. The budgets of NATO countries rest between 3 and 6 percent of gross national product, giving a measure of how much Japan's defense budget could grow without becoming disproportionate to Japan's economy. A defense budget of only 4 percent GNP would give Japan a $130 billion defense—an important measure of Japan's potential military power.

Japanese military research and development (R&D) has been increasing, but in 1989 it was still only 2.35 percent of the total defense budget—or about $750 million—far less than expenditures in other countries. These figures are deceptive, however. The Japan Defense Agency's policy in this area is that:

Japan has a great industrial might which enables it to push ahead with high-tech research and development on its own. High technology, dual purpose high technology in particular, has been intensively applied in the development and production of defense equipment today, and the nation's technological might forms a powerful bedrock in the furtherance of equipment research and development. Therefore, the Defense Agency will positively utilize the private sector's technology on the basis of its excellent technology in the field of microelectronics and new materials including ceramics and composite materials. Particularly in the area of basic research, the Defense Agency, heavily relying on the private sector will positively utilize its technologies. Furthermore, the Defense Agency, while carrying out research to enable these private-sector technologies to apply to future advanced defense equipment, will build up the results of such research into a system that will be able to meet the operational requirements of Japan. In this way, the Defense Agency will attain the effective improvement of superior equipment capable of matching the technical standards of foreign countries.[13]

What makes this approach practicable is the integration of Japanese defense production in corporations primarily engaged in nondefense activities and the role of MITI as a general integrator of industrial and military-industrial efforts.

Japan's top defense contractors derive much less of their total revenue from defense production than do their American counterparts. For example, where McDonnell-Douglas got 53.1 percent and General Dynamics 68.3 percent of their revenues from defense-related contracts, Mitsubishi Heavy Industries, the largest Japanese defense contractor, got only 21.3 percent of its revenues from defense.[14]

While the business done by Mitsubishi Heavy Industries is substantially less than the defense business of major U.S. contractors ($2.8 billion vs. $8 billion for McDonnell-Douglas), so is the dependency of Mitsubishi on defense spending to maintain its R&D capability. The ability of Mitsubishi to draw on civilian-oriented R&D is a tremendous advantage to its defense work. Where American defense R&D tends to support civilian research, the opposite is true in Japan.

This tendency is further supported by MITI, which selects various technologies to emphasize their dual utility, civilian and military. Consider the following civilian-oriented projects funded by MITI for the 1990 fiscal year:

1. Systems for unmanned space experiments: satellite technology
2. Superconductors
3. Artificial intelligence for computers
4. Fuel cell power generation
5. Laser and ion beam processing
6. Hypersonic aircraft propulsion
7. High-performance materials for use in aerospace
8. Advanced optical fiber systems

(Source: *Business Week*)

Obviously, all of these selected from the largest MITI projects are applicable to civilian uses, but each of them would also be quickly convertible and completely applicable to military needs. In the United States each of these would be funded through the Defense Advanced Research Projects Agency (DARPA). The military-track research would frequently outpace civilian-track research and would eventually spill over. The opposite is true in Japan. This means that U.S.

defense R&D is frequently inflated as corporations shift R&D costs for basic research onto Department of Defense contracts. In Japan the opposite occurs, as MITI shifts potentially useful military research onto civilian-sector projects.

Perhaps nowhere is the dual use of technology emphasized as much as in space exploration. Japan has been extremely active in space, quietly building up an enormous expertise. For example, in January 1990, Japan became only the third nation in history to launch a satellite into lunar orbit.[15] Japan's space ambitions are far greater than this, however. In May 1990, Japan's National Space Development ment Agency unveiled a plan for a lunar space station, as a prelude to a direct landing on the moon in the next century.[16] Japan has also taken a leading role in the U.S. effort to construct a lunar base habitable by humans in the next century.

The key to future Japanese ambitions in space is a new, completely Japanese-designed and -built booster rocket, the H-2. Intended to be deployed in 1993, the H-2 will be able to place a satellite directly into geosynchronous orbit, a stationary position necessary for communications and earth observation satellites. The H-2 will give Japan parity in boosters with the United States and the Soviet Union, since its capabilities are the equivalent of the advanced Titan 34D used by the United States. The Japanese have prepared a huge launch facility at Tanegashima, an island about fifty miles off the southern end of Kyushu. Its facilities rival those of the most advanced American facilities. The Japanese have not, however, emulated American openness in their civilian space program. During a tour of Tanegashima, the Japanese prohibited photography of the H-2's engines or of a Japanese communications satellite that was to be launched on an older H-1 rocket.[17]

The dual importance of the H-2 should be obvious. In addition to being a mainstay of Japan's studiedly understated civilian space program, the H-2 is the equivalent of the Titan systems that are the mainstay of the American nuclear deterrent. The acquisition of the H-2 rocket gives Japan a strategic capability, which, if coupled with an easily attained nuclear capability, would permit Japan to develop a deterrent to superpower nuclear pressure.

There can be little doubt that Japan could manufacture nuclear devices if it chose to do so. Since it already has a reprocessing plant, Japan's civilian reactors have the potential to produce weapons-grade plutonium in a relatively short period of time.[18] Any argument over Japan's ability to go nuclear is senseless because nuclear weapon technology is thirty-five to forty-five years old and has already been mastered by the Chinese, the Indians, the Israelis, and recently by the Brazilians, hardly a world technical power. If India can master nuclear technology, is there anyone who doubts Japan's ability to do so?

While possessing nuclear weapons is of minimal importance, not having them can be significant. Japan's space program clearly gives the Japanese the opportunity to cancel out the nuclear threat posed by any other nation.

In addition, the various technologies now being pursued by Japan—including the unmanned Space Flier, a shuttle being pushed by MITI; various planned space stations; and, above all, the increasingly sophisticated communications and observation satellites being lofted—will also give Japan the opportunity to develop space-based spy satellites, military communications systems, and possibly even space-based weapons. While Japan does not have any public plans in this direction, every action taken in space permits it to pick up a military option should it choose to do so.

The strategy of dual use was summed up in a government explanation of a resolution entitled "The Utilization of Satellites for 'Peaceful Purposes' by Self-Defense Forces, as Defined by Diet Resolution":

> Clearly, the wording "for peaceful purposes only," used in the resolution signified disapproval of direct use by the Self-Defense Forces of any satellite as a lethal or destructive weapon. The government interprets the Diet resolution as prohibiting the Self-Defense Forces from exploiting any satellite unless it is commonly used.
>
> Accordingly, the government considers that the Self-Defense Forces may be permitted to use any satellite which is in common use and any other satellite which is capable of similar function.[19]

In other words, as long as a satellite is capable of common, that is, civilian use, it may be used—even exclusively—for military purposes. This may prohibit the use of orbiting nuclear weapons, but not much else; it also permits all civilian satellite programs to have built into them a conscious military function.

The dual-use approach to technology is highly rational and is in fact the practice in the U.S., where spin-offs from military research are the rule. The Japanese reversal is not practically different, but it has a political consequence. Japan appears to be doing much less military research than is actually the case; although Japan's advanced research is substantial, it is hidden.

The same can be said about military exports. Officially, Japan does not export military hardware and it has been scrupulous about not exporting lethal weaponry. However, the use of contemporary technology is frequently not very clear-cut. The famous example is Toshiba's decision to sell milling equipment to the Soviet Union that would permit them to improve the survivability of Soviet submarines. Toshiba's position—that the equipment had numerous nonmilitary uses—was true, but its single military use made the equipment price-less to the Soviets. There are numerous examples of Japanese sales of helicopters, vehicles, floating docks, and computers that have wound up as part of a military system.[20]

The fact that Japan has not exported weapons has substantially increased the cost of weapons development in Japan. The U.S., for example, uses foreign sales—particularly to Japan, which pays cash and purchases almost all its imported weapons in the United States —to factor down the cost of its weapons production runs. Japan, already suffering the cost of relatively low production runs, forgoes substantial opportunities by refusing to sell weapons overseas.

Japan's motives are understandable: weapons sales and political entanglement go hand in hand. Particularly in the non-Communist Far East, where the U.S. is the dominant weapons dealer, an ag-gressive export policy would cause friction with the U.S., as well as political complications in the region.

It is not clear that Japan will be able to afford the luxury of avoiding arms exports in the future. As other export markets close or become more competitive, exporting arms could be the only strategy to main-tain export growth and therefore economic growth. Moreover, as Japan seeks to increase its exports in Asia, a willingness to supply weapons could well be a quid pro quo for access to local markets. Countries like Indonesia or Thailand, which do not have substantial domestic defense industries, must have a reliable source of arms. Whoever is permitted to dominate the regional market will be re-quired to provide suitable weapons to maintain these regimes and protect these nations.

Export hunger will compel Japan to increase arms exports. It will also force Japan to become a more prolific producer of these weapons. Inasmuch as this will dovetail with Japan's own growing military needs, an explosion of Japanese military production and exports during the mid-1990s can reasonably be expected. But the explosion that will take place then should not cloud the already substantial achievements of the Japanese in weapons design and production.

The tendency to underestimate Japanese weapons-production ca-pability is matched by the tendency to underestimate the size of the Japanese military. It is generally assumed that Japan's armed forces are substantially smaller, in terms of manpower, than those of other countries. Certainly, Japan's total armed force of not quite 250,000 is smaller than the total armed forces of most other countries both in absolute terms and relative to population: Japan's total armed forces are only 0.2 percent of its population (see Table 13-2).

The most important difference between Japan's armed forces and the rest of the world's is the almost complete lack of a reserve. This

TABLE 13-2. Manpower of Armed Forces as Percentage of Population, 1988.

NATION	STANDING ARMY	RESERVES ADDED
Japan	0.22%	0.23%
France	0.98	1.68
Germany	0.81	2.07
Britain	0.57	1.13
U.S.	0.89	1.36
Australia	0.43	0.59
China	0.29	0.72
India	0.16	0.19
Indonesia	0.17	0.64

(Source: Strategic Institute of Military Studies)

has been noted carefully by the Japan Defense Agency, whose publication, *Defense of Japan*, included an expanded section on reserve forces in 1989. *Defense of Japan* also contains an extensive section on the Swiss conscription and reserve system, without recommending it for Japan; it is included in the publication without comment.[21]

When comparing standard forces, the Japanese military is smaller than that of most European land powers, but all these major powers have less than 1 percent of their population under arms. In spite of its larger political commitments, Britain, like Japan an island off the shore of a continent, devotes only 0.57 percent of its population to standing forces. It is interesting that while Japan's standing forces are smaller than those in Europe, they are completely in keeping with Asian forces. Indeed, the Japanese Self-Defense Forces' total percentage of citizens under arms is higher than in either India or Indonesia.

In short, Japan has more than a skeleton armed force; it is reasonable in size compared to the armed forces of other countries and reasonable compared to its current political needs and fears. In terms of absolute numbers, the quarter-million military would be sufficient to concentrate and destroy any force seeking to land on Japanese soil. It might also be enough for some minor expeditions around the periphery of Asia, for example, aiding the Philippines or Indonesia in putting down a minor insurgency. It would also be sufficient to enforce Japan's decision to deny further basing rights to American forces in Japan. For the time being, that is as large as it needs to be.

THE JAPANESE GROUND SELF-DEFENSE FORCE

The Ground Self-Defense Force (GSDF) is the largest of Japan's three services, with about 60 percent of JSDF's manpower, compared to the U.S. Army, which has only about 36 percent of U.S. military manpower. The Ground Self-Defense Force, however, is not where present and future procurements are taking place. Just over 50 percent of Japan's future procurement is committed to aircraft, 22 percent to missiles, and 17 percent to new vessel construction. Only 9 percent is going to ground-weapons procurement.

Thus, while the GSDF is the largest service in terms of personnel, the procurement yen is not being spent on ground weaponry, nor will it be in the future; and ground equipment procurement will lag far behind naval, air, and missile development. In a way, this represents a major transition in Japanese defense history from the days in which the primary focus of the Japan Self-Defense Forces was the physical security of Japan against attack to a modern and more complex defense posture.

The Ground Self-Defense Force is divided into five regional commands or armies, each of which has several divisions and other units attached to it. The GSDF currently has twelve infantry divisions and one armored division: the Seventh Armored Division is currently stationed in Hokkaido along with three other divisions, the Second, Fifth, and Eleventh Infantry divisions. The Northern Army in Hokkaido is already the largest of Japan's five armies, and even more armor is on its way to Hokkaido. In plans being drafted for Japan's next five-year midterm plan, the GSDF is planning to shift more armor to the region by supplementing the Seventh and the other three divisions, turning the Second and Fifth Infantry divisions into armored forces.[22]

The concentration on Hokkaido is reasonably explained by fear of Soviet invasion. Should a general war break out, it would be expected that the Soviets, hoping to pass through La Perouse Straits, would try to seize northern Hokkaido. It is interesting that the Japanese were rather indifferent to this threat at its height but have chosen to become much more sensitive as the threat declines.

There are two possible explanations for this behavior, assuming we exclude the possibility of a currently increased Soviet threat. The first possibility has to do with the northern territories that were seized by the Soviets in 1945 and which the Japanese have been demanding be returned to them. Partly, this odd display of Japanese territoriality has to do with Japanese interest in maintaining the Cold War atmosphere for the sake of their American alliance and partly it stems from genuine Japanese nationalism. In either case, as the Soviet Union weakens, Japan might be presented with wholly unexpected possibilities on these islands and in the region in general. A complete collapse of central Soviet authority can no longer be ruled out, even though it may not be likely. Japan could find itself the major power in the region amid a sea of Soviet instability. Not only would Japan have the opportunity to reclaim its islands, but it might find itself in a position where it would need to impose some sort of order in maritime Russia. As distant as that possibility might be, the buildup in Hokkaido might be an acknowledgment of that far-off possibility and the beginnings of an attempt to cope with it.

A second, and probably more reasonable explanation for the plan to shift 70 percent of Japanese armor to Hokkaido might simply have to do with the internal dynamics of Japan's midterm buildup. It is clear that a modern army is an armored army, particularly if at some point it might have to engage in combat on mainland Asia. The slow buildup of armored forces has to have a covering rationale, which cannot be the expectation of new imperial projects. The Soviet threat permits turning Hokkaido's force into an armored force by stripping forces in the rest of the country; this will later justify increased armor procurement.

Certainly, Japan has developed excellent armored vehicles. In fact, it can be said that while the numbers might not be as great as the Japan Self-Defense Forces might want, the quality of the materiel is superior while the quantity is adequate for current needs. For example, Japan currently has 1,190 tanks, 630 armored personnel carriers and armored cars, and 870 artillery pieces.[23] While the numbers are small, the quality of the weapons is excellent. Indeed, the paradox of the GSDF procurement policy is that the weapons they have received are far superior to the mission they are likely to perform, but are produced in numbers too few to cope with absolute confidence with a worst-case scenario such as a Soviet invasion.

One such example is tank procurement, the heart of any modern ground force. It is not clear that Japan has a requirement for heavy tanks; their use in defending Japan against Soviet invasion would be limited. If the Soviets were in a position to force their way across the Sea of Japan, land armored forces, and engage in extensive land combat, the Japanese position would be hopeless anyway, as that would presuppose that the U.S. had been forced out of the waters surrounding Japan and that they had lost air superiority. Under those circumstances Japan would not be in a position to resist.

It is neither economical nor rational for Japan to have designed and produced its own tank, even if we concede to the utility of an armored force, even a heavy main battle tank. American allies like

Belgium, Italy, Greece, or the Netherlands who required similar numbers of tanks invariably found it more economical to purchase foreign equipment, such as Germany's Leopard, France's AMX-30, or an American tank. No one—except the Germans, French, and British, who had armored requirements far in excess of Japanese needs—designed and manufactured their own armored fighting vehicles.

Yet the Japanese decided to produce three heavy tanks, the type 64, type 72, and now an advanced armored fighting vehicle, the type 90, armed with a 120mm gun, appliqué armor, and advanced fire-control systems.[24] Those who have seen the type 90 claim that it has features that make it the finest main battle tank in the world, including a working automatic loading system that Western developers have shunned as too complex for the battlefield, but extremely desirable for low-labor-force countries looking to cut armor crews.[25]

The decision by the Japanese to produce an advanced main battle tank—one at least the equivalent of the American M-1 Abrams tank—is not a rational economic choice. It is, however, an extremely rational political and technological decision. Politically, Japan now controls its own armored production and is in no way dependent on any other country, including the U.S., for its armor. Technically, it has built up a large base of expertise in armored vehicle design and production techniques that would stand them in good stead should they need to expand production, either for their own needs or for their export markets.

The situation is very similar in other ground-weapons systems. The Japanese have developed, or are in the process of developing, a new infantry fighting vehicle (a gunned armored vehicle able to carry a squad of infantry) similar to the M2 Bradley the U.S. produces, as well as a self-propelled antiaircraft gun and several artillery pieces. The infantry fighting vehicle, known as the type 88, is a case in point. Almost the entire vehicle will be Japanese-designed and -manufactured, including laser-guided antitank missiles and the entire chassis and drive system of the tank. The only exceptions to this domestic design and production are the Oerlikon-Buhrle 35mm cannons, which will be purchased from the Swiss but produced in Japan.[26] Here again it would have been much cheaper to purchase off-the-shelf systems directly from allies, but the Japanese consciously decided to produce their own and designed them almost entirely themselves.

The Japanese have therefore developed a substantial expertise in the design and production of key weapons systems for ground forces, particularly in the area of armored vehicles and artillery, which should stand them in good stead in any future eventuality.

The actual equipping of the Ground Self-Defense Force has been spotty at best, the small numbers of weapons procured making production that much more expensive. Indeed, the fact that Japan so far has not exported weapons further increases domestic weapons procurements costs by not allowing larger production runs to average-down the cost per unit. Moreover, many weapons systems that might be desirable have been neglected altogether, such as large-caliber howitzers and lighter armored vehicles. But this much is certain: if Japan decides to create a larger ground force in the future, it has the technological expertise to efficiently design and produce the necessary weapons systems.

This is not to say that the GSDF does not purchase some weapons overseas. For example, they own the Carl Gustav antitank weapon from Sweden, recently made arrangements to purchase the German Panzerfaust III antitank weapon, and so on.[27] They have also purchased American TOW antitank missiles. However, even in the case of antitank missiles, which exist in abundance in the free world, Japan has developed the type 87 antitank missile, with its extremely advanced laser homing system, thoroughly man-portable and reputedly far superior to the U.S. man-portable Dragon system. In other cases, such as helicopter procurement for the GSDF, the Japanese have made licensing and technology transfer arrangements rather than making simple outright purchases.

Thus, Japan has carefully developed the ability to produce a ground force but has not actually produced a particularly useful one. The ability itself is a substantial achievement. Producing a world-class main battle tank—one able to deal with Soviet T-80s, American M-1s, and British Chieftains—is a remarkable feat for a nation that has not been in combat for forty-five years. More important, should Japan find itself forced to develop a substantial ground combat capability, it would be in a position to do so quickly, with relatively little R&D time needed for the key weapons systems.

THE MARITIME SELF-DEFENSE FORCE

The primary mission of the Maritime Self-Defense Force is to possess the "capability required to secure the safety of maritime traffic."[28] Since Japan is both an island nation and a trading state, this is a reasonable and necessary mission for its navy. However, since this mission has generally been carried out in the context of the overwhelming presence of the U.S. Seventh Fleet in the region, and the relative weakness of potential enemy navies, the Soviet Union's in particular, Japanese development of its own forces has not proceeded with great urgency. In general, Japan has left the defense of its sea-lanes to the United States.

However, as has been the case with the Ground Self-Defense Force, the Maritime Self-Defense Force has developed a core technical capability to conduct sea-lane security operations that could, with fair rapidity, be translated into a more fully self-reliant and self-contained force. While the U.S. remains on friendly terms with Japan and bases the aircraft carrier U.S.S. *Midway* and its battle group in Japanese ports, the urgency for greater development is missing. The key, of course, is the notion of remaining on friendly terms with the United States.

The Japanese Navy is organized into escort forces, air forces, and submarine forces, each in turn subdivided into flotillas and air wings. The emphasis on antisubmarine warfare can be seen in the numbers and types of vessels secured:

TABLE 13-3. Number of Major Ships Commissioned Into Service, and Performance and Data.

Number of Ships (As of March 31, 1989)

DIVISION	NUMBER	STANDARD DISPLACEMENT (1,000 TONS)
Destroyer escort	55	149
Submarine	14	30
Mine layer / Minesweeper	41	18
Patrol ship	14	1
Transport	9	12
Special service ship	30	69
Total	163	280

Performance and Data

CLASSFICA-TION	TYPE	STANDARD DIS-PLACEMENT (TONS)	MAXIMUM SPEED (KNOTS)	MAIN EQUIPMENT
Destroyer escort	Shirane	5,200	32	5-inch gun × 2 (High-powered 20mm machine gun × 2) Short-range SAM launcher × 1 Asroc launcher × 1

TABLE 13-3. Number of Major Ships Commissioned (continued)

Performance and Data

CLASSFICA-TION	TYPE	STANDARD DIS-PLACEMENT (TONS)	MAXIMUM SPEED (KNOTS)	MAIN EQUIPMENT
				Triple torpedo tube × 2 Antisubmarine helicopter × 3
	Hatakaze	4,600 (4,650)	30	5-inch gun × 2 High-powered 20mm machine gun × 2 Ship-to-air guided missile launcher × 1 Ship-to-ship guided missile launcher × 1 Asroc launcher × 1 Triple torpedo tube × 2
	Asagiri	3,500	30	76mm rapid-fire gun × 1 High-powered 20mm machine gun × 2 Short-range SAM launcher × 1 Ship-to-ship guided missile launcher × 1 Asroc launcher × 1 Triple torpedo tube × 2 Antisubmarine helicopter × 1
	Yubari	1,470	25	76mm rapid-fire gun × 1 Ship-to-ship guided missile launcher × 1

TABLE 13-3. Number of Major Ships Commissioned (continued)

Performance and Data

CLASSFICA-TION	TYPE	STANDARD DIS-PLACEMENT (TONS)	MAXIMUM SPEED (KNOTS)	MAIN EQUIPMENT
	Yubari	1,470	25	Boforce rocket launcher × 1 Triple torpedo tube × 2
Submarine	Yushio	2,200 (2,250, 2,300)	20	Torpedo tube × 6 (Antiship guided missile launcher)
Minesweeper	Hatsushima	440	14	20mm machine gun × 1 Minesweeping equipment 1 set
Transport	Miura	2,000	14	3-inch rapid-fire gun × 1 40mm twin machine gun × 1

Note: Parentheses show equipment of some ships
(Source: Defense of Japan)

In addition, the Maritime Self-Defense Force has a substantial number of aircraft directly attached to fleet operations, including the P-3C Orion advanced antisubmarine warfare aircraft.

In looking at these weapons systems, with the emphasis on destroyers, counter-mine vessels, and advanced antisubmarine aircraft, the Japanese obsession with sea-lane control and the protection of vessels engaged in sea-lane control becomes obvious.

The Maritime Self-Defense Force (MSDF) is not a small navy; the total strength of its fleet approaches 200 vessels. However, unlike the American Navy, the MSDF is not really a blue-water navy able to project a naval presence at great distance from Japan. This is due to the type of vessel around which the MSDF is organized, the destroyer. The destroyer is the traditional choice for antisubmarine duty owing to its speed, acceleration, and maneuverability; but the weakness of the destroyer is its range and size. Japan's smaller destroyers, such as the Tatsuki and Yamagumo types, displacing under 3,000 tons, are best suited to coastal patrol or duty at a fairly close range to base.

The newer destroyers, however, such as the Shirane type, which displaces 5,200 tons, and the new Aegis-equipped destroyers, which are comparable to the American Arleigh Burke class destroyers, are far more versatile and powerful vessels. The new destroyer will be particularly important for the MSDF when it enters the fleet in 1993.[29] Its effective range at 20 knots will be 5,000 miles, and its weapon systems will include the Harpoon antiship missile, Tartar antiair missile, the towed array sonar system (TASS), and above all, the advanced Aegis antiaircraft system. Most important, Japan is about to construct a class of 7,200-ton destroyers that are fully deep-water capable and are armed with the Aegis air-defense system.[30]

This new class of ship, eight of which will be constructed under current plans, will equal the best of the United States Navy. The decision to license the Aegis system to Japan was extremely controversial in the United States: the transfer of technologies involved in granting the Japanese the right to produce the Aegis system pulled Congress in two directions. On one hand, many who had been pressing for increased burden sharing by the Japanese had to support Japanese willingness to construct these ships. On the other hand, those who were concerned about transferring advanced technologies to the Japanese—usually more out of economic than political fear—tended to be opposed. In addition, there were those, like Louisiana's Senator J. Bennet Johnston, who wanted the sale of Aegis to Japan to depend on the ship itself being built in the United States.[31] In a fight that anticipated the later and much more bitter controversy over the FSX fighter plane, the dispute over the Aegis pointed out the contradictions in the American position on Japan.

The decision to permit Japan to build an advanced destroyer propelled Japan into the forefront of world naval capability. The Aegis system, a complex missile/gun defense system powered by advanced radars and data-processing equipment, had, to this point, been peculiar to the U.S. Navy. No other navy felt it feasible to purchase this extremely expensive defensive system. Even the British, who lost the frigate *Sheffield* in the Falklands War due to air activity, declined the opportunity to purchase the system because of its prohibitive cost.

The Japanese decision to purchase the system has two implications. First, the MSDF expects to see its ships operate in enemy-dominated airspace beyond the radius of land-based aircraft. Second, they regard the technology as important enough to purchase from the Americans immediately, rather than allowing for the development of a native alternative. The willingness to incur costs and the relative urgency of procurement need to be considered carefully.

The Aegis system is not designed to protect only one ship; it is primarily useful as a fleet defense system. For example, when an

American carrier battle group sails, normally the group includes an Aegis cruiser. The task of the cruiser is to coordinate the air defense not only of its own weapons, but of the entire fleet; thus the Aegis system coordinates the antiair weapons of an entire battle group. The key to the Aegis system is neither the antimissile systems nor the close-in weapons systems (CIWS, such as the Phalanx radar-guided 20mm cannon). Rather, the heart of Aegis is the radar and computer system that processes information and targets the missiles and guns. In controlling the fleet's defense posture, Aegis permits the rest of the fleet to concentrate on its mission, be it air superiority or anti-submarine operations.

The purchase of Aegis systems makes no sense for lone destroyers on antisubmarine patrol, nor even for the protection of several lesser destroyers. The system is simply not cost-effective in defending such small vessels. It is only in fleet defense outside the range of ground-based aircraft, against missiles coming in from outside the range of air-superiority fighters, that the Aegis system is useful. In short, it is primarily useful in protecting vast carrier battle groups.

No other ally of the U.S. has purchased Aegis because no other ally (except France) deploys a large and vulnerable carrier battle group. Japan has no aircraft carriers. The acquisition of Aegis clearly indicates that they are contemplating larger fleet operations in distant, hostile waters.

Japan has done as much as possible with land-based surveillance to deal with the problem of operations in contested waters within 1,000 miles of Japan. The purchase of E-2 aircraft and the planned purchase of advanced E-3 AWACS aircraft will provide Japan with vastly enhanced surveillance and control capabilities. That, along with the decision to place advanced radar systems on Iwo Jima, will provide the JSDF with excellent intelligence on activities to the east and south of Japan. What will not be available, however, are sufficient strike aircraft to act on that intelligence, except for the P-3C Orion, which hunts for submarines without using central surveillance systems.

The function of an aircraft carrier is to provide air superiority and sea control in an area outside the radius of one's own land-based aircraft. As Japan extends its patrol zone south toward the Philippines, it will be passing outside the effective radius of its land-based aircraft. Japan's main air-superiority fighter, the F-15, would generally be required for defending Japanese airspace in time of war and would generally not be suited for a maritime strike role under any circumstances. The F-1 ground-attack plane completely lacks the range for sea-lane support.

With the acquisition of P-3C Orion antisubmarine warfare aircraft for long-range patrols, the need for air cover for these highly vulnerable aircraft increases. There has been a debate over acquiring aircraft carriers. In March 1988, Tsutomu Kawara, then Director of the Japan Defense Agency, announced that the government was unified in opposing the acquisition of aircraft carriers. This followed his announcement that Japan, if it chose to do so, could legally acquire aircraft carriers.[32]

This apparent unity was broken just a year later when the chief of the JDA Defense Policy Bureau, its planning section, made it clear that neither the constitution nor Japan's Defense Program Outline of 1976 prohibits the country from acquiring aircraft carriers with vertical takeoff and landing (VTOL) facilities. The context of these remarks is particularly interesting. Policy Bureau Chief Hiyoshi was meeting with Communist members of the Diet, who were expressing concern about continuing rumors that the JDA was planning to construct an aircraft carrier. In speaking directly to the most radical members of the Diet, Hiyoshi was clearly preparing for criticism. When it came from that direction, the Japan Defense Agency appeared arrayed against the Japan Communist Party. Shrewdly, Hiyoshi denied any immediate plans for constructing a carrier but the battle lines were drawn, with the JDA in the stronger position.[33]

The interest in aircraft carriers had to do with the continued vulnerability of Japan's escort system to air attack. The Aegis system goes a long way toward providing security against air attack to any antisubmarine warfare force. But defense against surface vessels, particularly vessels firing antiship missiles from over the horizon, begins with discouraging their approach rather than defending against their missiles.

A sea-control aircraft, capable of engaging the enemy at a distance, is clearly necessary for the Maritime Self-Defense Force. The first and easiest option would be the acquisition of vertical takeoff and landing aircraft, like the British-American Harrier. Indeed, this is the first choice of the MSDF, since, in its early introductory phases, a few might actually be able to operate from the decks of destroyers and not require specialized aircraft carriers. Thus, the MSDF would like to equip their destroyer flotillas with fifty AV-8B Harriers as a first phase in developing a carrier capability.[34]

There is a weakness in all VTOL aircraft: they are generally inferior to more conventional aircraft in weaponry, range, and maneuverability. The parasitic weight of engines powerful enough to lift a dead weight vertically clearly cuts down on payload and aerodynamics. The British and Soviets adopted this approach to aircraft carriers because they were not planning to operate them at extreme distances from land-based aircraft and into extremely hostile environments. Also they were cheap and were the poor man's approach to aircraft carriers.

VTOL aircraft were cheap because the carriers supporting them did not require catapults. Steam catapults, which launch aircraft on American aircraft carriers by providing the energy for horizontal takeoff, also allow conventionally configured aircraft to be launched from carriers. This allows the aircraft to emulate ground-launched aircraft and defeat them in combat.

For Japan to choose the VTOL carrier as a first move into carrier operations is clearly an interim measure. As Japanese forces move farther and farther away from ground-based air support, the need for autonomous naval air power will grow. Indeed, the introduction of VTOL carriers and the decision to begin constructing a catapult-based aircraft carrier will be the clearest indications that Japan feels impelled to begin operating in a wider area than before.

It is important to note that Japan's neighbors would be particularly concerned should it move toward any carrier-based aircraft. Sea-lane control would obviously be only one of the missions an aircraft carrier would be capable of accomplishing. As with U.S. carriers, their primary use is frequently political: putting pressure on smaller nations to capitulate to political demands. On occasion the U.S. has used carriers to bring military pressure, via aerial bombardment or interference with the movement of merchant ships, to bear on other countries. Prior to 1945, Japan used its carrier forces in much the same way—something vividly recalled by China and Korea, among others. Thus, the acquisition of carriers would pose a serious political problem for Japan. It may well be a problem that Japan cannot avoid, but it will be the political threshold beyond which Japan can no longer escape its responsibilities and dangers as a great power.

For now, Japan's Maritime Self-Defense Force has done very much what the Ground Self-Defense Force has done: it has mastered the complexities of development and production of key technologies. With the mastery of the Aegis-class destroyer, Japan has learned the essentials of modern shipboard systems, particularly the integration of advanced radars, fire-control systems, and centralized data processing. Whether done by research and development or acquired by licensing, Japanese engineers now know how to construct a world-class surface ship.

This fact, coupled with proven antisubmarine ability and the integration of advanced destroyers with state-of-the-art antisubmarine-warfare aircraft like the P-3C Orion—produced under license in Japan—makes the Maritime SDF a limited but fully functioning navy. The seriousness with which the Japanese take the problem of submarine warfare is indicated by their expansion in antisubmarine warfare, with the creation of an antisubmarine warfare center and a new generation of sound-measuring ships designed to increase Maritime

SDF detection capabilities.[35] Considering their experience in World War II, this is a sound insight.

Moreover, Japanese expertise in commercial shipbuilding holds tremendous promise for Japan's military construction. Mundane skills, such as the development of oceangoing car carriers, will help Japan enormously in any logistical problems it might encounter during the course of force projection. Indeed, one of the things Japan was willing to do during the Kuwait crisis was to transfer several commercial car carriers to the U.S. for the purpose of transporting military vehicles, including armor.

In more advanced areas the Japanese are in the forefront of high-technology maritime construction. Among the more intriguing examples, the Japanese have established an R&D team to study the design of a high-speed ship capable of moving at sixty knots while carrying a full load of containers. Using superconducting magnets instead of propellers, the technology would also be useful in making superquiet submarines.[36] In short, it could revolutionize surface and submarine warfare.

Whether the superconductor ship is developed or not, three points about the Maritime Self-Defense Force become obvious:

1. The Maritime SDF has already achieved a high degree of competence in the limited and rather prosaic tasks it has assumed.
2. By insisting on designing or producing under license all new naval weapons systems possible, even when not financially reasonable, Japan has developed an advanced industrial base from which it could rapidly improve its naval forces should it choose to do so.
3. Japan's general industrial capability provides the Maritime SDF with a wide array of dual-use technology, designed for civilian use but usable for military purposes.

While Japan currently has a fairly modest navy, the potential for development is enormous and, as is the case with the Ground Self-Defense Force, Japan has planned it that way.

THE AIR SELF-DEFENSE FORCE

The Air Self-Defense Force has two primary missions: first, it must defend Japanese airspace against hostile intrusions; second, it is expected to provide air support to escort operations by the Maritime Self-Defense Force. With the decline of Soviet hostility in the region, the threat of air intrusions over Japan itself declines precipitously. First, no regional land power has an air force large enough and sophisticated enough to threaten Japanese airspace—even North Korea, with a large regional force, cannot, given the political circumstance it finds itself in, be seen as a major threat.

Sea-lane control, however, is a substantial problem for the Japanese. Interference with shipping moving up from Singapore could seriously threaten the Japanese economy and could be carried out with fairly unsophisticated means by countries like the Philippines and China, both of which are internally potentially unstable. Under any circumstances, the Japanese decision to patrol to the south and east to a limit of 1,000 miles requires that air superiority be maintained in these regions.

The Japan Air Self-Defense Force is organized into four functional commands of which air defense—the combat arm—is subdivided into four regional forces. Each air defense force contains three elements: operational combat air units; command, control, and warning wings; and air defense units.

As with armor and destroyers, the Japanese have tried to develop their own weapons systems for their air defense forces. The F-1 was derived from the T-2, the first supersonic aircraft produced entirely in Japan. Manufactured by Mitsubishi Heavy Industries, the F-1 suffered from a relatively light weapons load and a limited range; it was more a learning experience for Mitsubishi and the Japan Defense Agency than a weapon that was expected to bear a major combat role. The F-1 was supplemented by the much more effective American-designed F-4EJ Phantom Jet, produced under license by Mitsubishi and Kawasaki Industries during the 1970s.

The most important development was the Air Self-Defense Force decision to deploy McDonnell-Douglas F-15 aircraft. In many ways the decision was typical of Japanese defense thinking. The purpose of the F-15 was to be an air-superiority fighter, intended to take over from the increasingly obsolete F-4EJ the task of securing Japan's airspace. In that role the bulk of the F-15s were deployed on Hokkaido, where the threat of Soviet intrusions was seen as the greatest. It was also hoped that they would provide air superiority over sea-lanes as a solution to the lack of aircraft carriers. Since this mission was feasible only with the addition of tanker aircraft for refueling on long-distance patrols, the Japan Defense Agency has decided to purchase long-range tankers, probably KC-10s from McDonnell-Douglas. This decision has come under attack from the same factions that oppose the construction of aircraft carriers, because it increases the ability of Japan to project power.

The decision to deploy the F-15 was politically difficult in Japan. On the left, the decision to modernize the Air Self-Defense Force with cutting-edge aircraft was seen as too aggressive for a defense-oriented policy. On the right, the decision to purchase the F-15 rather than develop a native version was seen as a capitulation to American pressure. The fact was that the decision was made with the realization that even with the experience of producing the licensed F-4EJ, Japanese industry did not yet have the technological base to produce its own first-line fighter.

At the same time, the Japanese were not prepared simply to purchase American aircraft off the shelf, even though that would have been the low-cost solution. The decision to assemble most of the aircraft in Japan and manufacture some parts there boosted the price of the project tremendously. The cost of the F-15, $65 million, was over twice what it would have cost to purchase the plane directly from McDonnell-Douglas, but the technological-transfer benefits, as well as the strategic benefits, probably compensated for the additional expense.

Indeed, the Japanese-produced F-15s are expected to have longer effective lives and lower maintenance costs than American-produced versions.[37] The Japanese have also made a number of important improvements in the F-15, the most important being the incorporation of onboard phased-array radars. This is something the U.S. maintains only aboard AWACS aircraft, since the U.S., unlike Japan, has not yet solved the problem of size and weight of the radar system.[38]

Thus, one result of transferring technology to Japan is to give Japan the ability to leapfrog generations of development work in parallel fields as well as in aeronautics. Ironically, many American defense planners approve technology transfers of this sort under the assumption that Japanese assembly plants will be available for American defense purchases in the event of war, and that they will also increase Japanese reliability as an ally. From the Japanese point of view, this both increases Japan's power vis-à-vis the United States and, in the event of a rupture in relations, increases Japan's political and strategic independence from the U.S.

The impression left after the F-15 deal, and confirmed in a 1982 General Accounting Office report, was that coproduction of the F-15 had substantially enhanced Japanese commercial aviation capabilities at the expense of the United States.[39] Indeed, the technology transfers of the F-15 had been much more stringent than the open approach used with the F-4EJ. The atmosphere created by the aftermath of the F-15 decision set the stage for the most important controversy between the U.S. and Japan since 1960: the FSX controversy.

In 1981, after President Reagan and Prime Minister Suzuki issued their joint communique assigning Japan the role of sea-lane control out to 1,000 miles, it became apparent that Japan's forces were not up to the task. One outcome was the purchase of the Aegis system for new-generation destroyers. However, there was also a problem with Japan's aircraft: the F-1 was a low-altitude fighter and the F-15 was not suitable for a maritime attack role. It was clear that Japan needed a new tactical fighter, one that had extended range and re-fueling capability, sophisticated land- and sea-weapons systems, and advanced electronic countermeasure systems to survive in hostile en-vironments into the twenty-first century. Above all, it would have to be a dual-role fighter able to fight its way to a target and deliver a substantial ordnance load.

Japan had two basic strategies it could follow: domestic production, and coproduction with the United States based on some existing aircraft. A third option, but one that was never seriously considered, was coproduction with the Europeans. Japanese industry tended to favor the independent approach. A good deal had happened since the 1970s, when the Japanese felt that they could not produce a first-rate fighter plane and chose the F-15 approach instead. The pro-duction of the XT-4 supersonic trainer, which used advanced carbon-fiber composites as in the most advanced American fighters (for struc-tural endurance and stealth antiradar capability), convinced the Jap-anese that they were capable of competing in the most advanced design criteria.[40]

Mitsubishi Industries had strongly wanted to go it alone and had structured a group of subcontractors to lobby for the project.[41] Ul-timately, however, the Japanese decision to coproduce with the United States was due to American pressure, especially from Con-gress.

American reasoning was not always clear. The most obvious argument—that the U.S. did not want Japan to develop its own ad-vanced fighter because it would decrease Japanese dependence on the U.S.—was never used. Quite the contrary. On one hand, there were complaints that Japan was not pulling its weight in defense matters; on the other hand, the solution to pulling its weight was seen as purchasing American fighters directly. Indeed, this was the first response by many Congressmen: that Japan should purchase its fighter planes directly from the United States.

The Pentagon did not want Japan to develop its own fighter plane either. The surface argument was the fear that there would be in-sufficient interoperability between Japanese and American aircraft on the same bases and in the same airspace.[42] The Pentagon also wanted to reduce its own aircraft development and production costs by sharing them with the Japanese. But the Pentagon had a problem: it knew that it had to replace its fleet of F-15s and F-16s early in the twenty-first century; however, its R&D emphasis had been on the radically new stealth technology aircraft, which it was not prepared to sell to the Japanese or any foreign government. Coproduction meant that they would have to develop a semistealth fighter, a generation behind the ones they were testing, in order to fit the niche that Japan was interested in.

The U.S.–Japanese Memorandum of Understanding signed in November 1988 stated that the General Dynamics Corporation would transfer to Japan airframe technology from its F-16 fighter while the Japanese would transfer, at no cost, any refinements it made on U.S. technologies. Any other technologies held by the Japanese would be available at a fee. The U.S. would do 35 to 45 percent of the project, working with a Japanese consortium that included Mitsubishi, Kawasaki, and Fuji. Japan would absorb all development costs (about $1.3 billion), while General Electric or Pratt and Whitney would provide the engines. One hundred thirty aircraft would be built by 2001, with prototype production beginning in 1991.[43]

The agreement immediately caused an uproar in the United States. Americans felt that the transfer of F-16 technologies to the Japanese gratis would open the door to Japanese civil aviation development that would compete with the United States. The clause which held that U.S. access to prior Japanese technology would be on a fee-for-see basis also angered many. On the whole, the American fear was that the U.S. was once again giving away too much to Japan in return for too little.

This all came out at congressional hearings, where it turned out that the real issue was the balance of payments. Republican Congressman Dan Burton said:

> The first concern that I have is that a technology drain over the past couple of decades has resulted in causing the United States to lose jobs not only to Japan but to other countries. This technology drain should not be allowed to continue if we can help it. The technology drain has lead not only to a loss of American jobs in many industries but it has exacerbated the trade deficit.[44]

Congressman Burton's concerns were reasonable, but he did not clearly spell out the alternatives. If what he wanted was a direct purchase of U.S. technology on a black-box basis—they could operate it but not understand its operating principles—the Japanese would not do that. Indeed, they had no need to do that—they were in a strong enough position technologically to proceed on their own. If what he wanted was for Japan not to purchase any new weapons, Japan might have gone along with that, but the U.S. would have been the chief loser.

The Japanese were flabbergasted at the uproar. First, they had been reluctant to enter into agreements with the Americans on the FSX and had wanted to proceed alone; it was mainly pressure from the Reagan Administration that convinced them to go with coproduction. Second, they felt that the technology flow would go both ways: Japan would pay all development costs and the resulting technologies would go free to the U.S. This would include technologies in composite materials, in which Japan excels, as well as radar and avionics systems. In the end, the U.S. would be able to sell Japan the engines for the aircraft. The Japanese felt they had given away far too much and were being unfairly charged with taking advantage of the Americans. Above all, they deeply resented Americans holding Japan responsible for the U.S. trade deficit and trying to use coproduction as a means for rectifying the problem.

From the Japanese point of view, the unanswered question is whether they could have produced, on their own, an advanced fighter by the year 2000. Opinion inside the Japan Defense Agency is clearly divided on this. A former official of the JDA Technical Research and Development Institute said that Japan can produce defense equipment and ordnance under license, and sometimes better than the original, but it lacks the comprehensive ability to design and develop its own systems due to lack of combat experience.[45]

It is clear that Japan is no more than one generation behind the United States in aircraft production. Indeed, in certain technologies, such as electronics miniaturization—useful in advanced avionics—and fire-control systems, Japan is ahead of the United States. Another area where Japan is at least keeping abreast of the U.S. is hypersonic technologies. An agreement between Japan and other Western nations to conduct research into a hypersonic transport, able to operate at Mach 5, recently broke down. With MITI's help, the Japanese have formed a consortium consisting of Mitsubishi, Kawasaki, and Ishikawajima-Harima to work on the program. The breakdown has again been over the status of technologies to be shared: the Japanese want to share all technology, the others want all technology to remain proprietary.[46] The Japanese are making clear, however, that they will proceed alone if necessary.

THE BEGINNING OF THE FUTURE

The question of technology transfer is continually breaking apart Japanese–American and Japanese–Western projects. There is a generally shared perception that Japanese access to Western technology will be turned to Japanese commercial advantage and an equivalent sense that Japan itself will not make its technology available to others on the same basis, and for the same purpose. The Japanese feeling is that Japan is expected to bear the burden for American defense needs *and* for the inefficiency of the American economy.

At root, the problem is that the reason behind the U.S.–Japanese alliance—the Soviet threat—is gone, and with that demise commercial relations between the two countries have become far more important than military cooperation. Old habits have caused the U.S. Department of Defense and the Japan Defense Agency to smooth over disagreements and force cooperation. However, as the FSX case demonstrated, there was barely enough support to proceed without massive assurances from the Japanese that the project would not be used to make money at America's expense. Had the Soviets really been a threat, there would have been no controversy surrounding the FSX. Getting advanced aircraft into the hands of the Japan Air Self-Defense Force would have been the number-one priority and all other considerations would have been considered frivolous.

The Japanese have avoided the technology-transfer question altogether in the case of the Ground Self-Defense Force by developing their own weapons. The problem has popped up in the Maritime Self-Defense Force, although not as vigorously as in the Air Self-Defense Force, where the question of U.S.–Japanese relations in the post-Cold War era has been put to the test, with the alliance barely surviving.

The real hidden issue was almost never mentioned in the controversy: the future of the U.S.–Japanese alliance after the Cold War. More important, the possibility of trade wars turning into something more direct, more military, was also never discussed. An advanced fighter, along with all other advanced weaponry, could be used by Japan against the United States as well as other countries; Japan's development of a sea-lane control capability, including advanced aircraft, submarines, and Aegis destroyers, can threaten American as well as Soviet submarines.

The issue, never directly addressed during the congressional hearings that raged over the FSX question, is the extent to which the United States wants to build up the technical capabilities of Japan's armed forces. It was once in America's interest to do so, but it is difficult to fathom why it would remain so today.

The general question of Japan's armed forces, therefore, can be summed up in this way: Each of the conventional branches of the JSDF are currently engaged in a substantial qualitative, but not quantitative, buildup. Drawing on domestically developed technologies where possible and on technologies licensed or even copied when domestic development is impossible, Japan has built up an impressive expertise in a wide range of weapons systems.

This expertise has not, to this point, been translated into a large enough force to do very much more than secure the Japanese perimeter. Indeed, Japan is hard-pressed even to carry out its task of patrolling out to 1,000 miles. Moreover, this force is still so heavily weighted toward ground forces that force projection at this point would be virtually impossible. Nevertheless, Japan has established the industrial base, an officer corps, and sufficient trained manpower so that the current JSDF could be rapidly converted into a much larger and more aggressive military force should this become politically feasible. Moreover, the conventional potential of Japan is matched by a very real nuclear potential, as well as by extremely sophisticated delivery systems.

Japan has placed itself in an excellent political position. It has made no overt moves that would threaten either regional powers or superpowers thus far. Therefore, if Japan should find that it can retain its cordial relationship with the U.S. and preserve the Cold War alliance, nothing will have happened to upset that relationship or place Japan in a position where it must assume more of a defense burden than it wishes. In the event of peace or of a renewed Cold War with the Soviets, Japan's position will remain unchanged: under the American umbrella.

On the other hand, should events drive Japan and the United States apart, forcing Japan to become more self-reliant militarily, more able to control its own environment, Japan has taken steps to rapidly create and deploy a military force that would rival those of all other nations. The development of world-class armor, the acquisition of the most advanced warships, the development of advanced fighter planes, and the construction of an advanced intercontinental ballistic missile make it possible for Japan to become at least a regional power in a matter of years, if not months. Japan has laid the groundwork for achieving national power equivalent to its economic power, yet it needs to reach for that power only as necessary.

Obviously, there are several technologies that Japan has not yet mastered. It has diesel-powered submarines but not nuclear-powered submarines; indeed, the entire area of nuclear propulsion for warships will have to be considered if Japan is to develop the ability to project forces as far as Singapore. Catapult-aircraft-carrier technology, the planes to endure that ordeal, and the pilots capable of manning them are all things that Japan must develop; and that will take time.

But in all likelihood Japan has the time to gradually develop the capabilities it may so badly need. Just as it has had time to develop a booster rocket powerful enough to serve as an ICBM, it will have time enough to develop the guidance system necessary to make it a credible deterrent. Japan has time because the coming crisis in international relations will take time to unfold. Just as it took twenty years between the end of World War I and the crisis that led to World War II, so, too, the next cataclysm will take a generation to unfold —that is, unless history has permanently speeded up. But the world was frozen from 1945 until 1990. It will now settle into a new cold war before a hot war threatens.

1. Takashi Kitazume, "Detente Puts Japanese Defenses in New Light," *Japan Times Weekly*, January 13, 1990, p. 5.
2. Ibid.
3. Ibid.
4. Bruce Roscoe, "Japan Puts Priority on Defense," *Jane's Defense Weekly*, December 10, 1988, p. 1479.
5. Japan Economic Institute, "Japan's Defense Planning in an Era of Global Change," September 14, 1990, 35A, p. 4. See also Japan Defense Agency, *Defense of Japan, 1989*.
6. *Washington Post*, March 27, 1990, p. 14.
7. *Defense of Japan, 1989*, pp. 78–79.
8. Japan Economic Institute, "Japan's Defense Planning in an Era of Global Change," September 14, 1990, p. 3.
9. Tetsuya Kataoka and Ramon H. Myers, *Defending an Economic Superpower: Reassessing the U.S.–Japan Security Alliance* (Boulder, 1989), pp. 67–68.
10. "Tokyo Wants Its Arsenal Made in Japan," *Business Week*, September 25, 1989, p. 64.
11. Tai Ming Cheung, "A Yen for Arms," *Far Eastern Economic Review*, February 22, 1990.
12. *Defense of Japan, 1989*, p. 321.
13. Ibid., pp. 142–143.
14. Japan Economic Institute, "Japan's Defense Planning in an Era of Global Change," September 14, 1990.
15. Craig Covault, "Japan Designing Atlas-Class Rocket to Launch Lunar, Planetary Missions," *Aviation Week and Space Technology*, August 20, 1990, p. 68.
16. *Japan Times*, May 28, 1990, p. 5.
17. Craig Covault, "Japan's New H-2 Launch Site Rivals Largest U.S., European Facilities," *Aviation Week and Space Technology*, August 13, 1990, p. 41.
18. John E. Endicott, *Japan's Nuclear Option: Political, Technical and Strategic Factors* (New York, 1975), pp. 132–141.
19. *Defense of Japan, 1989*, p. 305.
20. Michael A. Chinworth, "The Private Sector: Japan's Defense Industry," in *Option 2000: Politics and High Technology in Japan's Defense and Strategic Future*, ed. Ronald A. Morse (Princeton, 1987), pp. 109–111.
21. *Defense of Japan, 1989*, pp. 225–227.
22. *Japan Times Weekly*, September 9, 1989, p. 4.
23. *Defense of Japan, 1989*, p. 300.

24. *Jane's Armour and Artillery, 1984–85* (New York, 1985).
25. Japan Economic Institute, "Japan's Defense Industry," August 3, 1990, p. 6.
26. *Jane's Armour and Artillery*, p. 312.
27. *Jane's Defence Weekly*, "West German Anti-Tank System for Japan," February 18, 1989, p. 255.
28. *Defense of Japan, 1989*, p. 114.
29. *Japan Times Weekly*, July 9–15, 1990, p. 7.
30. Nasanori Tabata, "Government to Launch Defense Plan," *Japan Times*, July 9–15, 1990, p. 1.
31. Japan Economic Institute, "U.S.–Japanese Defense Relations: An Update," October 6, 1989, p. 5.
32. Bruce Roscoe, "Japan Puts Priority on Defence," *Jane's Defence Weekly*, December 10, 1988, p. 1479.
33. See *Japan Times Weekly*, July 8, 1989, p. 3.
34. *Aviation Week and Space Technology*, July 2, 1990, p. 11.
35. *Defense of Japan, 1989*, p. 116.
36. Steven Kreider Yoder, "Japan Plans Speedy Superconductor Ships," *The Wall Street Journal*, August 17, 1988, p. 7.
37. Chinworth, "The Private Sector," p. 108.
38. *Aviation Week and Space Technology*, March 12, 1990, p. 11.
39. *National Journal*, February 20, 1982, p. 333.
40. Richard J. Samuels and Benjamin C. Whipple, *Defense Production and Industrial Development: The Case of Japanese Aircraft* (Cambridge, 1988), pp. 18–21.
41. Masanori Tabata, "Second Thoughts on FSX," *Japan Times*, June 24, 1989, p. 4.
42. Japan Economic Institute, "The FSX Project: Changing the Nature of Defense Technology Transfers," May 26, 1989, p. 5.
43. Japan Economic Institute, *The FSX Project*, pp. 5–6.
44. U.S. House of Representatives, Committee on Foreign Affairs, *United States–Japanese Security Cooperation and the FSX Agreement*, April 1989, p. 7.
45. Tabata "Second Thoughts on FSX," *Japan Times*, June 24, 1989, p. 4.
46. "Agreement on the Japanese SST Engine Program Delayed," *Aviation Week and Space Technology*, March 19, 1990, p. 215.

14

Collision Course

The world has become unglued. For forty-five years history and politics have been frozen, transfixed by the struggle of the continental states, the United States and the Soviet Union. Every struggle, every conflict, every relationship took its bearings from this primordial conflict between the giants. Each of these superpowers was so vast and so powerful that they gave the impression of being eternal and therefore their conflict seemed eternal. Virtually every nation in the world shaped its foreign policy with at least one eye on the superpower conflict. Everyone felt that the arrangements they made or that were forced on them would last for generations.

Japan was one of the nations seeking shelter from the superpowers. The strategy it chose—or more precisely had thrust upon it—was to be an ally of the United States. In many ways, "protectorate" might be a more appropriate term to describe the relationship. Japan was free to administer itself internally but its foreign and defense policies were in American hands. In return for this, the United States provided Japan access to the American free-trade system and to the American market as well. In addition, the U.S. provided guarantees that Japan would have access to the world mineral market, with the right and ability to buy scarce resources at world market prices with delivery guaranteed by the United States Navy.

For Japan this has been a golden age, one that it would like to see continue forever. Japan has lived without the real threat of war and without any responsibility to prepare for war. It has had access to the most lucrative export market in the world and has taken full advantage of it. Indeed, Japan's economy has been constructed out of this access.

With the end of the Cold War, Japan's life as Cinderella must come to an end. Japan must become a normal nation again. It must cease being a protectorate of the United States: Japan must once again have a foreign policy and a military of its own. In a way, it is improper to say Japan "must" have these things; Japan *will* have them because it is historically unavoidable. If Japan is a normal nation again, it will necessarily begin behaving normally.

ECONOMIES IN CONFLICT

Japan's postwar economy has been constructed on two pillars. One pillar is growth. The structure of the Japanese corporation, the structure of Japan's equity markets and banking system, the relationships between corporations and *keiretsu* have placed a premium on growth and made for a relative indifference to profitability. This indifference to short-term profits in favor of long-term growth has been the bane of American competitors and the envy of foreign managers.

Many have hailed this as a grand Japanese achievement. As we have seen, the basis of Japan's economic growth has less to do with vision than with cash flow. Japanese corporations have been caught on a debt-driven treadmill. Having borrowed to the hilt, the Japanese corporation needs to create a strong cash flow to cover debt service (the monthly payment of principle plus interest) and provide operating cash. The indifference of Japanese corporations to short-term profits is not so much the mark of the corporation with a long-term vision as it is the mark of the corporation that is perennially short of cash.

The second pillar of Japan's economy is exports. Historically, dating from the end of World War I, Japan has been incapable of generating sufficient domestic demand to fuel economic growth. The domestic standard of living has historically lagged behind economic growth. One of the reasons for this has been a genuine strength of the Japanese system: high savings rates. But as any good Keynesian can tell you, high savings rates may allow for an investment-driven boom, but sustained consumer demand is the foundation of modern economic success and high savings rates are incompatible with strong consumer demand.

Japan's postwar economic boom began as an investment boom. Only during the mid-1950s was it also driven by consumer spending. Once the Japanese economic infrastructure was in place and it became time to sell end products as well as to manufacture the equipment to make consumer products for sale, the Japanese economy proved inadequate to the task. Japan had two choices. One was to rein in growth—something Japan's financial systems could not permit. The second was to export products, which Japan did with military precision.

This is what has made the Japanese corporation the dreaded monster of American corporate nightmares. When a Japanese corporation enters a new market, American competitors are frequently convinced that the Japanese are "dumping"—selling products at no profit, or even a loss. The American corporation, having to keep its eye on its profit margin, quickly finds itself losing market share to the Japanese, unable to compete on price or able to compete only by cutting quality. In the tradition of Western monopoly formation, dumping was the way in which large, well-capitalized corporations drove competitors out of business before monopolizing the market and driving prices to new, monopolistic heights.

This has been the traditional charge against Japanese price cutting and market-share wars. But, in fact, monopoly has almost never been the Japanese goal. The Japanese corporation has to move units not because of monopolistic conspiracy, but in order to meet debt service. When bank payments are due, many corporations will sell products at deep discounts in order to generate cash. The constant drive to expand market share—at the expense of profit margins—is the Japanese solution to their deep-seated economic needs, not a monopolistic conspiracy against the U.S.

All this, of course, is little comfort to American businesses coping with Japanese competition. Japanese penetration of American markets always seems to take the form of struggles for market share. These are struggles that American corporations must lose because of their dividend-hungry investors and their concern for the bottom line. Market share without profitability means little to American corporations; profitability without sufficient cash flow and growth means little to the Japanese.

Japan's penetration of the American market became noticeable and painful during the early 1970s when Japanese automobiles, textiles, and steel began pushing American manufacturers out of their own markets. The result was agitation to limit Japanese access to the American market or force greater Japanese consumption of American goods. The U.S. was prevented from taking action by political considerations: the Soviet threat. Thus, throughout the 1970s and 1980s enormous defense expenditures by the U.S. limited the capital available for American competitiveness in consumer and industrial goods. Although the American competitive position vis-à-vis the Japanese deteriorated, the importance of Japan's geographical location prevented America from taking political reprisals to compensate for economic weakness.

This willingness to endure economic discomfort for political ends was the hallmark of American foreign policy from 1945 onward. The American obsession with the Soviet political and military threat was the safety net for Japan as well as other countries. The U.S. encouraged Western European development, the creation of the common market, and unification, just as the U.S. encouraged Japanese growth and exports. The reason was political. The U.S. rationally calculated that it would be better to endure the economic pain than the political disaster of a European or Japanese realignment with the Soviet Union.

All of these calculations turned to air once the Soviet Union ceased to be a threat to the United States. The U.S. emerged from the Cold War in spectacular political and military shape and fairly poor—but not by any means disastrous—economic shape. The weakness of the American economic system was caused, in effect, by the Cold War and the American victory in it.

There are two outstanding economic problems posed by the end of the Cold War. The first is the budget deficit. At root, the budget deficit is a political rather than an economic problem. It arose from the inability of the government to resist demands from the American public for more goods and services and lower taxes. In part, this can be traced to the Vietnam War and President Johnson's decision not to raise taxes or cut social spending in order to fight the war. It can also be traced to the 1970s, a time of demographic upheaval, when baby boomers started forming families with a vengeance, entering the credit markets en masse, and requiring increased government services while earning little money and paying very little taxes.

The deficit ought to have been solved as the baby boomers aged and became net creditors instead of borrowers. What made the difference was Ronald Reagan's decision to impose a punishing arms competition on the Soviet Union in an attempt to break its economy. Reagan succeeded. But his decision to nearly double the defense budget while cutting taxes left the United States in a rather nasty economic crisis, although nowhere near the devastating crisis that enveloped the Soviets. Indeed, in the end Reagan won the Cold War by fighting the Soviets economically: a battle of defense budgets.

Derived from the first is the second crisis: the balance-of-payments problem. The arms buildup led to tremendous investment in defense industries and this naturally diverted assets from consumer-oriented industries. During the buildup the U.S. raised its defense spending by nearly 2 percent of GNP. This drained a substantial amount of money out of the consumer-investment sector, thus giving Japan an even greater advantage over the U.S. While there was substantial deterioration in America's economic competitiveness, political solutions to the balance-of-payments problem were also impossible during the Cold War.

Thus, the budget and trade deficits are both symptomatic of the general political condition the United States found itself in during the 1980s. Politically and economically, the struggle against the Soviet Union weakened America's ability to compete with the Japanese. The Japanese, moving according to their own needs and dynamics, necessarily took full advantage of the situation. The conclusion is that the moment of America's political triumph also seems to many to be the preface to America's economic downfall.

FROM TRADE WAR TO POLITICAL RUPTURE

The collapse of Soviet power set in motion a wide range of forces, giving new meaning to already anticipated events. European integration, long scheduled for 1992, had been planned in the context of the Cold War. It was seen as the logical extension of the Common Market sponsored by the U.S. during the 1950s and as an element in the defensive system created to contain the Soviet Union. Nineteen ninety-two was seen as merely a further strengthening of the Western alliance.

With the collapse of the Soviet Union, European integration takes on new dimensions. In the first place, without the Soviet threat it becomes an end in itself rather than a means toward an end. United Europe becomes an autonomous politico-economic entity, rather than merely an anti-Soviet bulwark. In the second place, with the collapse of Soviet hegemony in Eastern Europe and the unification of Germany, the already complex problem of European integration becomes infinitely more difficult.

The former German Democratic Republic, its economy a shambles, is a German responsibility having first claim on Germany's resources. The liberation of East Germany and the general situation east of the World War II armistice line leaves European trade and investment policies in chaos. Since Germany's needs have shifted tremendously, the carefully honed agreements balancing the interests of the members of the EC cannot stand as negotiated. At the same time, European responsibility for stabilizing economic conditions in the east in general requires a careful reconsideration of both investment and trade policies.

Europe will obviously need to strengthen the east in order to guarantee the continued harmlessness of the Soviet Union. In integrating the east—or even only eastern Germany—into its structure, the EC will have to create a system of protection for Eastern Europe's agriculture and infant industries. In due course it will become apparent to the Europeans that only by providing this sort of protection will the east have the breathing room it needs for reconstruction. The only alternative, predatory intrusions by Western European economies into Eastern Europe's crippled economies, will generate tensions within the EC that could wreck not only 1992 but the very solidarity of the EC itself.

In either case, 1992 will kick off a series of trade wars. In one scenario the Europeans will protect Eastern Europe by limiting access to the entire EC market, in particular limiting Japanese consumer goods and American agricultural products. Further, they will construct barriers to American agricultural products far beyond the levels agreed to in GATT talks. In the other scenario, the Europeans themselves turn to squabbling and regional trade wars and, with the Germans in the lead struggling to revive the East German economy, they will throw up a series of national barriers both against other Europeans and against outsiders. The key will be whether the Germans will be able to revive the East German economy in a free-trade environment or whether the eastern zone will require special protection.

Thus, 1992 will find the U.S. being pushed out of markets in Eastern Europe, the Soviet Union, and Western Europe itself. This will occur in the context of a great debate over continued U.S. military presence in Europe and a Presidential election in the United States. Germany's struggle to protect its investments in the east—not just in East Germany—will therefore spark extensive protectionist sentiment in the U.S. It will be bound up with increasing isolationist sentiment as Americans tire of their presence in Europe and Europeans tire of having the Americans there.

As protectionist sentiment rises, Japan will be one of the major victims. It will not have been responsible in any way for U.S. treatment by the Europeans. However, as the largest exporter to the United States and continually pressing to increase its roughly 20 percent share of the American market, Japan is the first exporter that the U.S. will have to deal with as it gets its economic house in order.

To bring both the budget and the trade deficit in line, the American economy will have to grow its way out of the problem. The traditional solution in the U.S. has been to increase domestic consumption. This time, increasing domestic consumption will lead to pressures on the consumer credit markets as well as to further unacceptable declines in savings rates. The U.S. must cut consumption while increasing production.

At least in the short term, the U.S. solution is to emulate the Japanese: hold domestic consumption in check, increase domestic savings rates by higher interest rates, and dramatically decrease imports of finished goods while increasing exports. In this way the U.S. will increase the tax base, thus cutting the budget deficit, decrease the trade imbalance, and increase domestic income and savings. Of course, this is easier said than done.

Increasing exports to Japan is simply not going to happen while the Japanese are struggling with their own growth crisis. Similarly, exports to Europe will not increase while the Europeans are struggling with the problem of integration. Thus, the U.S. must begin thinking of radical solutions to its export problem. One such solution has already begun: construct a regional free-trade zone—resembling the EC—centered on North America and extended to include most of Latin America. It is an opportune moment. For example, Brazil, with an economy closely tied to Europe's, will find itself in a more and more difficult position as its low-cost exports of manufactured goods and raw materials suddenly run against lower-cost production from Poland and Bulgaria, and as its low wage structure is forced to compete with Eastern Europe's wages. Nineteen ninety-two could heavily affect Latin America. Thus, the political moment for striking a long-term deal within the hemisphere might well be at hand. This, along with aggressive attempts to open new markets in nonindustrialized Asia—where American political influence is strong—could create the basis of an export-driven growth surge for the United States.

The second solution is also obvious: the U.S. must, in part or whole, exclude Japan from the American market. The ideological justification for this is of no importance. The point is that American profit-oriented corporations cannot compete with Japanese growth-oriented corporations. At a time when the American domestic market will be kept constant or even shrink, Japanese corporations' aggressive market-share policies will be politically unacceptable. The political sentiment for a greater exclusion of Japanese corporations is already in place and several policies have been proposed in Congress.

First is the proposal of an across-the-board tariff to be imposed on any ally of the United States, equal to the difference between U.S. defense spending and their own. Thus, since U.S. defense spending is 6 percent of GNP and Japanese defense spending is 1 percent of GNP, a 5 percent tariff would be placed on all imports to the U.S. in order to compensate the United States for the cost of "defending" Japan.

Second is the proposal that Japanese corporations selling products to the United States—or corporations producing in the U.S. as Japanese subsidiaries—build into the price of their product a basic profit margin equal to prevailing profit margins in the industry. In this way Japanese indifference to profit and emphasis on growth would not permit Japanese companies "unfair" advantage in the United States.

A third proposal is to require matched sales and purchases. This is where companies from selected countries seeking to do business in the United States would be required to post bonds equal to the customs-clearance value of off-loaded goods. A bond would be cleared when a foreign company purchased an equivalent quantity of goods in the U.S. and cleared them outbound through customs.

In a strictly free-market setting none of these proposals makes very much sense. All appear to be fundamentally counterproductive. But the U.S. has not been a pure free-trade setting since the Cold War began, or since the Japanese corporation and the American corporation began competing for different things: growth or profits.

Things that make little economic sense often make eminently good political sense. During the 1992 Presidential campaign Japan bashing will be good sport, good politics, and fairly bad economics. The United States has been absorbed by politics abroad for the past forty-five years, frequently trading economic benefits for political benefits. After so many years of arguing from a political perspective, arguing now for a purely economic approach to trade policy is not likely to be persuasive. It misses the point that free trade was a political tactic far more than an economic principle for the U.S.

Japan already sees the handwriting on the wall. MITI in its last ten-year plan called for an emphasis on domestic consumption, greater domestic spending on infrastructure, and greater emphasis on the environment. But the Japanese are also caught between a rock and a hard place. The Japanese banking system is the weakest link in the Japanese economy. Its dependency on high savings rates and wide spreads between interest paid to savers and interest collected from borrowers is notorious. For MITI's plans to work, the Japanese must save less and spend more. It is unclear, at least for the next several years, whether the banking industry in Japan can live with such a life-style conversion.

Japan cannot cut its export rate. Its entire growth economy depends on increasing foreign sales at greater and greater rates. For over forty years Japan has had free and easy access to the greatest consumer market in the world; in a way, the Japanese economy was created in order to cater to that market. The most modest American demand that Japanese and American trade be fully balanced would be a cataclysm for Japan, since the surplus generated from U.S. trade is the engine that maintains the growth rate of the Japanese economy. What is an altogether reasonable demand on the American side is a direct assault on Japan.

Thus, there is a fundamental economic divergence between the

U.S. and Japan, a divergence that has been apparent for a decade. The argument that the two economies are linked does not prove that they both benefit from the relationship. With the end of the Cold War, the political constraints limiting American responses have lifted. The weakness of the American trade relationship with Japan is matched by the power of America's political relationship to Japan. Internal political pressures in the U.S. to limit Japan's incursions into the American economy ultimately cannot be resisted by appeals to the principles of free trade nor by claims of mutual interdependence.

By about 1992 the U.S. will be compelled, in the course of the inevitable failure of interminable U.S.–Japanese trade negotiations, to use political power to limit Japanese access to the American market. In addition, the U.S. will turn to exports to fuel its own economic growth. These two decisions will ultimately be as important an event as the fall of Soviet power. The latter ended the old era. The former will begin the new.

JAPAN ON ITS OWN

Japan is now on the precipice of its greatest economic crisis since World War II. The decline of the Tokyo Stock Exchange since 1990 is merely the outward sign of this general problem. The looming inability to meet the capital requirements of the International Bank of Settlements is another sign. The continued growth of the Japanese economy is a fever-like symptom, not a sign of health. Aggressive selling by Japanese corporations is a sign of the urgency of the Japanese cash-flow crisis. The increasing export pressure is a symptom of the underlying instability of the Japanese economy.

Expulsion—or even a capping of the growth of Japan's share of the American market—would be the preface to a huge financial downturn in Tokyo. This is why U.S.–Japanese trade talks are doomed to fail. American negotiators always seem to think that Japan has enough room for maneuver to satisfy American demands, that only misunderstanding, stubbornness, or greed keeps the Japanese from agreeing to proposals that would reduce their trade surplus with America. The fact of the matter is that this trade surplus is Japan's staff of life. Japan cannot negotiate away its share of the American market.

Except for 1973 and the oil embargo, Japan has not had a single recession since the Korean War. It has never had to lay off millions of employees, never had to deal with waves of personal or corporate bankruptcies, has never seen its great financial institutions go bankrupt. The effect of these events on Japan's social and political stability is difficult to imagine. The ruling Liberal Democratic Party coalition, old and tired as it is, has retained its hold by delivering on prosperity and trading on its American connection, just as Prime Minister Yoshida did during the early 1950s. If hard times should come to Japan, particularly as a result of American hostility, the ability of the Liberal Democratic Party to continue governing would be severely undermined.

Japan would have to restructure its foreign and domestic policies. The socialists would call for an abolition of the *keiretsu*, breaking up MITI, emphasizing domestic environmental and infrastructure issues, and ultimately, limiting the growth of Japan's economy. The cost in terms of jobs, growth, and general prosperity would be enormous. While anger at the failures of the ruling elite might extend to breaking up the *keiretsu*, the socialists' anticorporate ideology would also be an antigrowth ideology, something bitterly unpopular with the Japanese electorate, as it would be with most other electorates.

Domestic restructuring would set off economic and political firestorms that the Japanese system would find difficult to contain. A simpler solution, one that would maintain the status quo of a growth-oriented, export-driven economy based on the current corporate structure, would be to find or create new export markets to substitute for the American market.

If limits are placed on the growth of Japanese export sales to the United States, Japan's only real alternative will be to regionalize its economy as the United States and Europe will be doing. As the global economy turns protectionist and regionalizes, Japan will have to find a set of markets large enough to absorb its growing industrial output, capable of providing it with needed raw materials, and outside the reach of the U.S. or Europe.

The natural arena for Japanese economic growth through the 1990s and beyond is the same arena that Japan coveted during the 1930s: East and Southeast Asia. But East Asia has changed tremendously since 1939. South Korea and Taiwan—once Japanese possessions and part of Japan's interior security zones—are now powerful industrial economies in their own right. Indeed, these countries now compete for the same markets as Japan, therefore they clearly would not do as the captive market for which Japan is searching.

As has been shown in Chapters 10 and 11, Indonesia, China, Malaysia, the Philippines, even India are the right markets for Japan in several ways. Collectively they have almost enough raw materials to supply Japan's needs—excepting possibly oil. Together their markets could be developed to create a sufficient demand for Japanese products. Further, Japanese investment in each of these countries could be positioned to increase supplies of raw materials, develop cooperative production ventures, and be used to guarantee trading as well as investment rights.

Constructing a self-sufficient regional trading bloc built on non-industrialized Asia will not be an easy task. Even by excluding all other competitors from these markets and utilizing the bulk of raw materials available from these countries, it will be extremely tight for Japan. The key is the ruthless exclusion of all other competitors; something more political than economic.

The regionalization of economies will intensify the political content of global economic relations. In a way, the depoliticization of trade during the Cold War was an illusion. It was the intense politics of the period that made free trade possible in the first place. However, regionalization will intensify the political content of trade in two ways. First, Japan will need to engage in politics to define and police the limits and integrity of its trading bloc. Second, Japan will have to pay a political price to the members of its bloc in order to have the exclusivity it requires.

Japan will not be able to enter into solely economic relations. It will have to bring arms and political power to the table as well. In a way, this will be a godsend for the Japanese. In shifting markets, Japan will need to retool in order to supply the sorts of things these markets require, and there will have to be a lag between its own investment-fueled boom and the rise of domestic consumption. Weapons sales can bridge that gap. Mitsubishi Heavy Industries and Kawasaki already produce excellent weapons. Merely expanding those production lines would produce substantial cash flow over the first few years of the relationship.

The foundation of any system of enforced economic relationships is political and military power. The foundation of the General Agreement on Tariffs and Trade (GATT) system that governed postwar trade was the overwhelming power of the United States. The foundation of the Soviet bloc's Comecon system was Soviet power. Sometimes these relationships are mutually beneficial so that the iron first is encased in velvet. Sometimes the relationship is exploitative in the extreme and the power is visible and dangerous. But in any large, multinational system of economic relations there must be a political center and some form of ultimate sanction.

The EC may ultimately collapse because no one will be able to accept the only logical claimant for that role: Germany. Then Germany will face the same choice it faced twice before—whether or not to lay claim to hegemonic power by force. In the western hemisphere there is again only one possible claimant: the United States. Here again, the question will be whether the U.S. can make membership in its system attractive economically or whether, as in the past, it will have to resort to political or even military coercion.

In Asia, only one country has the possible power to lay claim to being a regional hegemonist: Japan. Japan would obviously prefer to control by economic means. But it is never that simple. First, the industrial powers of the region, Korea and Taiwan, must take their place in the system or be expelled. Second, outside poachers will seek to exploit the system. Japan can barely survive in Asia if it has complete access to Asia's markets and excludes all others. Poaching will benefit the lesser members of the system and the poachers, but it will not be tolerable to Japan.

In the final analysis, each of these countries, such as Indonesia or the Philippines or even China, is seeking an outside force not only to regulate its economic relations, but even more as guarantor of its regime's stability. Access to weapons, advisors, or the sheer psychological advantage of being backed by a great power are critical in any such relationship. Japan will be expected to play this role, and will be compelled to play the role whether it wants to or not. Political power will be the price Japan will have to pay for a regional trading bloc.

An extremely important relationship will develop between Japan and India. As with the relationships with East and Southeast Asia, there will be a strong economic component. But unlike these other relationships, the one with India will assume a rough political and military equality. In a regionalized world India will emerge as the hegemonic power in South Asia. Its navy, already one of the largest in the world and sporting two aircraft carriers, will clearly be in a position to challenge American control of the Indian Ocean.

For Japan, India's ability to guarantee the security of supply lines from the Straits of Hormuz to Singapore will be an important complement to growing Japanese naval power in the Pacific. Japan's ability to invest in India, purchase Indian exports, and provide weapons and training to Indian forces will be a strong inducement for India to ally with Japan. Similarly, the Indian market and resources and the fact that India's geography is strategically complementary will be a strong inducement to Japan. An Indo-Japanese alliance, merely dreamt of by Japanese planners during World War II, might well make the American presence untenable not only in the Indian Ocean, but in the eastern hemisphere itself.

As the United States forces Japan out of the American market and, indeed, closes off the rest of the hemisphere to Japanese trade, and as Europe raises barriers in order to protect its internal cohesion, Japan will find itself in a position where it will have to create its own regional market. Not accidentally, that market will be the old Greater

East Asia Co-Prosperity Sphere. It will have the same advantage and the same disadvantage for Japan as it had before: its advantage will be that it is near at hand; its disadvantage will be that it is only barely sufficient for Japan's needs.

This relatively modest sphere will, nevertheless, concern the United States. The U.S. will see Japan attempting to force it out of markets that had hitherto been open to the U.S., at the precise moment when the U.S. has made the decision to solve its own economic problems through more aggressive exports. The inevitable conclusion that the U.S. will draw is that Japan intends to close off Asia to American trade and, ultimately, to force the U.S. out of the western Pacific.

The American conclusion will be correct, but not because Japan is consciously plotting against American economic interests and national security. After all, the U.S. will have started regionalization by limiting Japanese access to the American markets. It will be correct because Japan cannot create a viable economic trading zone without some exclusivity built in. Japan will not be able to have this exclusivity without exercising political power to seduce and control Asian regimes. Japan's needs for exclusivity will mean that this political power will be used to force other traders out of the region. Most prominent among these traders will, of course, be the United States.

What will make the clash more frightening for the U.S. is that it will revive the primordial American fear of being physically forced out of the Pacific. The U.S. will respond to the decrease in its economic and political power in the region by increasing its military presence, and converting that presence into the political pressure necessary to try to open up Asian markets to American goods. In short, in the twenty-first century the U.S. will emulate Roosevelt's Open Door policy, replete with figurative gunboats.

The Japanese will respond by increasing their own political activity and constructing an armed force capable of limiting American pressure in the western Pacific. Each country, operating out of a legitimate fear, will increase the ante, trying to protect itself against the other's threat.

REARMING THE PACIFIC

The Japanese are now on the verge of a great political adventure. It is not one of their own choosing. They are also on the verge of a military adventure. This is something they want even less. Indeed, it is something they have thought about even less. History does not always require planning. Japan's only possible response to being limited in their exports to North America will be to seek to trade somewhere else. During the 1990s, such targets will be rare as economies regionalize. Japan will naturally regionalize its economy and its foreign policy as well.

The Japanese will ultimately need an armed force that can carry out the following missions: the ability to land and maintain forces on the Korean Peninsula and on either the Chinese or the Soviet coast simultaneously; the ability to maintain sea-lane control to Singapore; the ability to provide substantial counterinsurgency or covert insurgency support in Indonesia, Malaysia, the Philippines, Micronesia, or Melanesia; the ability to seal off the western Pacific by neutralizing enemy bases and seizing control of critical airfields in Micronesia and Polynesia, as well as Papua New Guinea; and, finally, the ability to detect and deter nuclear attack with minimal exposure to Japan.

Japan will have to be able to suppress instability on the mainland of Asia, particularly in those areas closest to Japan, as well as maintain control of sea-lanes, both against interdiction of Japanese raw materials and American aggression from the central Pacific. In addition, Japan will have to be able to provide forces for stabilizing friendly governments in the region and possess at least a minimal nuclear deterrent.

In order to carry out this mission, Japan would have to substantially increase its armed forces. It would need to increase its total military forces to about 0.8 percent of the population (the current size of Japan's forces is 0.22 percent; the size of German forces is about 0.8 percent). This would give Japan a force of approximately 1 million men: Ground Self-Defense Force of about 350,000; Navy 270,000; Marine Corps 180,000; Air Force 200,000. In addition, a reserve system encompassing 2.2 percent of the population would be created as an emergency force.

Japan would also need to restructure each of the Self-Defense Forces. It would need to create an army consisting of about thirty divisions—twenty armored and mechanized divisions designated for conflict on the mainland; four special forces divisions for counterinsurgency; three tropical divisions, for garrison or equatorial duty; and three arctic divisions. The marines would need fifteen full divisions, which would have the primary mission of being Japan's Rapid Deployment Force, available for service in the Pacific and Indian Ocean basins. The air force would need 50,000 men in the strategic forces, built around the H-2 rocket in hardened silos; they would also be assigned to satellite surveillance and antisatellite missions. The rest would be deployed in tactical fighter and bomber wings built around FSX fighters, designed to protect Japanese airspace, and operate from bases in allied countries.

There would need to be a large naval buildup, including the construction of at least seven aircraft carrier battle groups, four assigned to sea-lane control from Singapore to Japan, and as a political presence in the region; three assigned to screening operations against American incursions from Micronesia. If Japan could create a vertical takeoff and landing (VTOL) aircraft capable of matching conventional aircraft performance, then less expensive carriers or even large destroyers would suffice. Otherwise, Japan will have to create catapult aircraft carriers, which are both more expensive and more time consuming to produce.

Japan would also need to construct a wide variety of marine assault and command ships able to project Marine Corps power in the farthest reaches of its alliance; a sophisticated antisubmarine warfare (ASW) capability, including acoustic monitoring stations running from the Aleutians to New Guinea, as well as along all straits passing from the Indian Ocean; and a small force of submarines with ICBM capability as a second element of Japan's deterrence diad.

A ten-year program, beginning in 1993, would probably cost about $150 to 200 billion a year. This would be about 5 to 7 percent of Japan's 1990 GNP—a substantial amount, but in line with American commitments.

The increase in defense spending would have a beneficial economic side effect. With the growth rate declining because of lack of exports, increased defense spending would be one way to temporarily boost the economy without decreasing savings rates. In addition, it would create a new export market heretofore untapped by the Japanese—international arms trade.

In effect, Japan would become a normal nation, a regional power imposing order on an unruly region and doing what it had to do to protect its own interests. Unfortunately, what Japan will have to do as a normal nation and what the United States will need to do in response will pose a dangerous new equation in the Pacific, an equation not dissimilar to that posed in the 1930s.

AMERICAN RESPONSES TO A NORMAL JAPAN

From the American point of view, the U.S. has never asked for very much from Japan except that it bring its trade into balance with America's. It is, of course, sheer blindness on the part of the U.S. not to recognize that this altogether reasonable demand strikes at the foundation of Japan's economy. On the other hand, not to make this demand would be to make the U.S. a permanent economic extension of Japan's growth policy. The U.S. has to make this demand; Japan must resist.

The American response will be to gradually limit Japanese export growth in the U.S. and force Japan out of the American market. Whether this occurs because of increased American efficiency in production or because of political moves, the results will be the same for Japan. However, given American passions on the subject, the extended nature of the problem with American competitiveness, and the general trend toward regionalization and protectionism that will arise during the early 1990s, it is unlikely that the U.S. will avoid taking substantive political measures against Japan. More important, the U.S. will act to regionalize the trade patterns of its own economy.

Japan will have to respond by regionalizing its own economy and shifting its trade to other Asian partners. This process will be far more difficult for Japan than for the U.S. Imports are much more structurally important to Japan's economy than they currently are to America's. More significant, Japan sends one-third of its exports to the U.S. while the U.S. sends only a little over 10 percent of its exports to Japan. Shifting the American amount to the western hemisphere will be quite a bit easier than shifting Japan's amount to Asia. Given the constraints of the Asian market, Japan could not do this without forcing other nations, particularly the U.S., out of Asia.

For the United States, fear of being forced out of the Pacific is an extremely deep-rooted concern. Access to the Asian markets and rising Japanese naval power caused the U.S. to engage in economic warfare during the 1930s. Rising Japanese economic power in Asia and the western Pacific, occurring in the context of increasing economic tension between the two countries, will inevitably be seen by the American side as a hostile action designed to limit American influence in a region where the U.S. has legitimate rights, particularly in the wake of its victory in 1945. Declining influence in this region will be seen as an economic and political challenge to the United States. It will also be seen as an attempt by Japan to reverse the outcome of World War II.

Rising Japanese economic influence in the region will inevitably translate into political influence and a military presence. American concern over this presence will be ironic because the U.S., ever since the signing of the peace treaty, has encouraged Japan to increase its presence throughout Asia and to increase its military power as well. With the Soviets no longer an important factor, any increase in Japanese power in this region will be seen as a challenge, rather than a benefit, to the United States.

Three factors will combine to disturb Americans. First, there will be a real sense of Japanese ingratitude. With much reason, Americans see themselves as having been particularly gracious victors. Japan's growing assertiveness will be seen as inappropriate behavior, taking advantage of American good nature. Second, the U.S. will be seeking to expand its exports at about the same time that the Japanese will be forcing the U.S. out of the Asian markets. Finally, the fundamental American need to dominate the Pacific will clash with the Japanese need to secure its markets and resources. Thus, psychology, economics, and geopolitics will combine to force an increasingly sharp American response.

This response will have two dimensions. On one side, the U.S. will compete economically with Japan for domination of the Asian markets. However, this competition will not be confined to economics. The key to most Asian markets will be political and military. A long and difficult politico-military competition will ensue. The second dimension will be a Japanese response to American weakness in executing the first. Japan's vulnerability to mineral flows, particularly in oil, will be the ultimate American lever. The American ability to interfere—whether through economic, political, or military means— with the movement of raw materials to Japan will severely constrain Japan's freedom of action and national security. As before World War II, the U.S. will use interference with raw materials as a means for controlling the growth of Japanese power. And, as before World War II, Japan will not accept quiet strangulation.

The American penchant for engaging in economic warfare to solve conflicts has a long history. Iraq, Iran, the Soviet Union, China, Cuba, South Africa are all postwar examples of American attempts to use its economic power to control the actions of others. Imports have become the classic instruments of American foreign policy through freezing of assets in the U.S., limiting access to American markets, organizing boycotts of goods, and blockading through military or political means. They were first pioneered against the Japanese during the 1930s. Indeed, none of these examples are as historically important as America's attempt in the 1930s to control Japanese action in Asia by manipulating Japan's trade.

The first U.S.–Japanese war occurred when Japan sought to resist American economic warfare and found that it had no alternative but military action. The weakness of Japan's mineral position then and now limited Japan's ability to deal with economic coercion through economic countermeasures. Thus, as the U.S. seeks to limit Japanese economic and political hegemony of East and Southeast Asia, Japan will respond using the classic repertoire of "nonmilitary" means. This will be the case particularly when Japan is first forced to use limited military power in imposing its regional hegemony.

Japan will seek to defend its interests by fortifying the political structure of its regional grouping. Behind that will be fortification of Japan's military power. The clash between American economic power and Japan's military power will center on the flow of minerals that are the lifeblood of Japan. The great choke points of Japan's oil and mineral trade—Hormuz, Malacca, Lombok, and the countries that supply Japan's raw materials—will again become an arena for the struggle between Japanese and American interests. Thus, inexorably, the economic conflict will become a political conflict and the political conflict will become military.

PREPARING FOR CONFLICT: AMERICAN OPTIONS

American policy makers continue to evaluate their force structure and deployment based on the Soviet threat. Particularly in the Pacific, American strategic thinking has not yet evolved beyond the Cold War. Decisions such as whether or not to accept Singapore's invitation to base warships there or whether or not to pay the price demanded by the Philippines for continued basing privileges are made on perceptions of the Soviet threat, rather than on any broad considerations of the future.

In part, this myopia is understandable. Nations and their foreign policies are like huge oil tankers. It takes time and space to stop them and turn them around. Generations of diplomats and generals have come of age thinking of certain countries as enemies and other countries as friends. It is not reasonable to expect these views to change quickly. Yet, with 1992 approaching and with decisions being made daily that will have implications for years to come, American readjustment cannot be put off indefinitely.

This is difficult in another sense. Japan is a longtime friend of the United States. It is difficult to imagine it in another role. Moreover, there ought to be a reasonable fear that preparing for conflict with Japan will become a self-fulfilling prophecy. It is reasonable to demand that history—and Japan—show their hand before committing the United States on a fateful policy course.

At the same time, there are relationships and actions that can be taken that do not commit the U.S. to hostility toward Japan. There is, in particular, a set of relationships that the U.S. has had for decades, and others that have been maturing for years, that would be reasonable to pursue in the context of the Cold War and even more useful in any future conflict with Japan. Securing these relationships now would not necessarily be seen by Japan as preparations against its interests. However, not securing them now might prove catastrophic should conflict with Japan occur and Japan preempt the American position in these areas.

A case in point is the Philippines. The U.S. has had important naval and air bases at Subic Bay and Clark Air Force Base since World

War II. These bases were extremely useful for projecting American power on the Asian mainland as well as useful against possible Soviet naval incursions. They may well be unnecessary in a U.S.–Soviet context now that the Cold War has ended. However, Subic and Clark are directly astride Japan's major north-south trade routes. Indeed, today, as during World War II, they are the key to containing the Japanese. Japan's entire military strategy was to get the U.S. out of Manila. The current U.S. government position is to refuse to pay the Philippines' price for retaining the bases. This is clearly conditioned by acceptance of the end of the Soviet threat and failure to appreciate future Pacific threats. Retaining these bases is vital; should a U.S.–Japan confrontation not ensue, nothing would have been lost but a trivial amount of money. However, should such a conflict arise, these bases would be priceless. Retaining them would in no way signal hostility toward Japan. Losing them could be catastrophic.

Singapore is a related case. Singapore is afraid of the future. It is afraid of the Indonesians and the Malaysians. It is also afraid of a world without the Americans. Thus, the U.S. has repeatedly been invited to use Singapore for the Seventh Fleet. The U.S. should accept that offer eagerly. Singapore lies astride the shortest route to Japan from Hormuz. Along with the straits in Indonesia, that is the lifeline of Japan. Hold Singapore and have the ability to deploy a blocking fleet on the northern coast of Indonesia's islands, and Japan is militarily constrained from the beginning. Between Subic Bay, Singapore, and a base in Guam, the U.S. can control the western Pacific against any Japanese naval challenge. In a way, it would give America the combined U.S.–British basing structure prior to World War II. As with the Philippines, accepting Singapore's offer and expanding on it would not at all, at present, signal hostility toward Japan, whereas later it might. Thus, now is the time to enter into historically crucial agreements with Singapore.

Korea is an even simpler matter. The peninsula has traditionally been Japan's first area of security concern. Japan can never feel truly secure if some other power is sitting across the straits from it. The U.S. currently has one division in Korea and is projecting substantial reductions in the coming years, based on a declining Communist threat. The U.S. should maintain its forces in Korea at the very least, and possibly increase them. Should Japan choose an expansionist policy in the region, U.S. forces in Korea would be an effective block against the Japanese. Should Japan remain quiescent, little harm would have been done. Remaining in Korea is an extremely low-cost insurance policy.

In the same spirit, it is an excellent time now for the U.S. to strengthen both political and economic relations with regional Pacific and Asian nations. The U.S. currently has excellent political relations with Indonesia, for example, while Japan has the economic upper hand. It would be extremely useful (a case for a trade-oriented foreign policy) if the U.S. could begin easing Japan out of Indonesia using the American political lever. While it might not work, the political and economic risks are low if this is tried now. A similar policy ought to be followed in China and the rest of Southeast Asia.

The U.S. must refocus its attention on the Pacific islands that it won from Japan in World War II. U.S. neglect of these islands was reasonable during the Cold War, since the strategic significance of the central Pacific was limited. The U.S. permitted the independence of a large number of these island groups, which, along with the Polynesian and Melanesian islands, were given independence by the British and French. Relatively little money goes a very long way in these islands and Japan has emerged as a major economic player in many of them. It is imperative that the U.S. begin programs to increase the stability of the region internally and maximize American political influence and military presence.

All of these policies have three elements in common. First, they are merely extensions or minor variations of existing policies. Second, they would pose no appearance of a threat or hostility toward Japan. Third, each move is vital to a policy of containing Japan. If these steps were taken swiftly and executed effectively, Japan might well find itself blocked on all sides in the event of American economic moves against Japan. While disastrous for Japan, since they would place Japan in a permanently subordinate position to the United States, they could preempt the need for an extended political and military conflict with Japan.

Obviously, the chances of all of these diplomatic moves being attempted by the U.S. in the immediate future is small. All current tendencies are away from this direction. The chances of attempting them and succeeding are even smaller. Therefore, some thought must be given to American military policies that ought to be followed in preparation for a U.S.–Japanese war.

As currently constituted, the United States military was designed to defend Western Europe from a Soviet attack. It has carried out this mission masterfully. So well that, as with the best of victories, it never had to fight at all. Also, as with all victories, after the parades the ingratitude begins. U.S. forces are too heavy, too immobile to carry out their emerging role. The victors of the Cold War must be reshaped, and rather ruthlessly at that.

First, the U.S. should cut its strategic nuclear forces to the bone. If anything was learned during the Cold War, it is the relative uselessness of nuclear weapons. The idea that if the Soviets managed to get enough of an edge to destroy 80 percent of our weapons they would launch a first strike was not only nonsense, but stupidity. A small deterrent force will be enough to frighten any nation, particularly the small nation-states we are now facing. Cutting back to a light mix of land- and sea-based missiles, biased toward the sea, will more than suffice over the next generation. It will also save a substantial amount of money that could be spent on new space-based systems built around advanced speed-of-light technologies.

Second, the U.S. must slash the United States Army. Eighteen standing divisions and another ten available on full mobilization is not nearly enough to fight a war alone in Eurasia. Eurasian allies willing to fight extended wars at the U.S. side are going to be fewer and farther between. Moreover, since the European balance of power ought to keep those nations occupied for the next generation, the need to rush heavily armed troops and fifty-ton tanks to Europe will decline dramatically. The primary function of U.S. Army troops should be as garrison forces. The following force should suffice:

1. Korea: One armored division, plus one in the U.S. as a designated reserve.
2. Panama: One light infantry division for deployment in Central America.
3. Singapore (if mutually acceptable): One division, plus additional Ranger and Special Forces units for regional interventions.
4. Continental reserve: Four divisions, all mechanized.
5. Reserve and National Guard Divisions: Eleven total.

If eighteen total divisions will not solve a problem, then nothing short of full mobilization, conscription, and a 5-million-man army will do the job.

The United States should use the savings from Army cuts to build a Marine Corps at least twice its current size. It should have responsibility for all operations in the Pacific except long-term interventions on the Asian mainland, which should occur infrequently. Pacific operations are amphibious operations at long distances. The U.S. has been contemplating the idea of a Rapid Deployment Force since 1979. The difficulties of Army rapid deployment were made manifestly clear during the Iraqi intervention when the Marines were in place in days while full Army deployment took months. The U.S. has had a first-rate rapid deployment for over 200 years: the United States Marine Corps. As part of the Navy, the Marines do not have to ask another service for a ride; they do not have to train in amphibious warfare—it is their forte—and they carry their own airpower with them. There are several things the Marine Corps needs in addition to more men: a *very* fast landing craft, a good light amphibious tank with a high-velocity gun, a VTOL plane superior to the Harrier, and a good VTOL transport aircraft like the V-22 Osprey. But the Marines are used to carrying out their missions on a shoestring, and since they are already dependent on the Navy, they are a much more cost-effective force.

Most important, the U.S. should resist the temptation to economize by cutting the Navy. The U.S. Navy is the foundation of American strategic policy. The less than $100 billion spent on it annually is nothing compared to the security and prosperity naval power has given America throughout the twentieth century. The list of countries the U.S. has invaded grows; the list of nations that have invaded the U.S. is empty since 1812. To anyone who has lived in a country that has been invaded, this is not a frivolous point.

The Navy should retain fourteen carrier battle groups. Their cost is nothing compared to the cost of losing control of the oceans. The expertise of their crews and the quality of the vessels would be lost if they were kept in mothballs. Certainly, the U.S. is heading into a very temporary lull in carrier operations as it eases out of Eurasian politics after Kuwait. But that could end very quickly.

The number of missile-launching nuclear submarines should be cut. They should be replaced by hunter-killer submarines designed to close sea-lanes. The general emphasis in the U.S. Navy on anti-submarine warfare should be shifted to a sea-lane interdiction program. Against the Soviets the U.S. was the convoyer and the Soviets were the hunters. That relationship reverses itself in the Pacific. Special emphasis should now be placed on coping with Japanese anti-submarine warfare techniques. In particular, the large number of ASW weapons should be cut back in favor of submarines, antiship missiles, and investment in space-based maritime surveillance and even weapons systems.

Finally, the U.S. Air Force's definition of its role must shift. It must accept a far greater responsibility for land-based maritime attack roles. The Air Force obsession with massive land-based operations, such as in Europe, needs to be reconsidered after Kuwait. It must consider redeploying away from Eurasia, toward the Pacific. It must also redefine its primary function away from cooperation with Army plans for deep interdiction and close air support, to cooperation with the Navy on matters of sea-lane control and interdiction, and air support for extended Marine Corps operations. In particular, the scale of its operational conceptions must be reduced to better reflect the smaller force ratios of a Pacific, amphibious environment.

Thus, the Army should be cut to the bone, the marines increased dramatically, the Navy reoriented to sea-lane interdiction, and the

Air Force shifted to a maritime role. These changes along with the policy shifts recommended might give the U.S. such overwhelming power that it could simply impose its will on Japan. But this is doubtful, since no normal country gives up its autonomy willingly.

Japan's will to survive is enormous. No matter how fortuitous the circumstances, its rebound from absolute defeat in World War II is a tribute to Japan and a warning to those who would underestimate it. Thus, there ought to be a suspicion that while preparations might place the U.S. in a better position to deal with Japan, it will not prevent Japan from doing what it must do: survive.

JAPAN AND AMERICA

It is jarring to begin thinking again about the Pacific as a battleground. Japan and the United States have now been tied with bonds of peace and friendship for about two generations. Those who still remember the first U.S.–Japanese war are growing old and memories of exotic names like Iwo Jima, Tarawa, Guadalcanal, and New Guinea are passing into a more distant memory, with names like Gettysburg, Belleau Wood, and Yorktown.

If either nation had its wish, war between them would be inconceivable. However much anger and contempt may condition the thoughts of Americans and Japanese, the deep-seated rage of Frenchmen against Germans or Israelis against Syrians seems to be utterly lacking on either side. Moreover, the issues that divide the U.S. and Japan hardly appear to be worth dying for. The balance of payments is a dry and abstract thing, hardly the stuff of which great wars are made.

But beyond the dry and abstract issue of trade relations and burden sharing there is a fundamental matter at stake. In its first war with Japan, America won a great prize: the Pacific Ocean. For nearly half a century America has ruled this ocean, albeit with a rather indolent hand. Its fleets roamed its waters at will. From California to the Aleutians to the Asian coast and down to Australia, no one could challenge the power of the United States.

When America tried to extend its rule from the Pacific to Asia, it was rebuffed. First China, then Vietnam repulsed the United States. But through all of the Cold War, American domination of the Pacific was never challenged. The security of the Pacific was one of the foundations of America's postwar peace. Whatever happened in Asia, North America could never be menaced from the west.

The United States ordered political relations throughout the Pacific Basin, both internally and externally. Indonesia, the Philippines, Taiwan, and Japan all felt the force of U.S. interventions in their internal political lives. More important perhaps, the U.S. ordered the relations among these nations, determining the hierarchy and prosperity. The U.S. was a good imperialist; most nations benefited from American rule and benevolence. But it must never be forgotten that there has been a great Pacific empire ruled by the United States and that no matter how much others might have benefited as well, the ultimate beneficiary of this empire was the United States.

Japan was one of the greatest beneficiaries. The price it paid was American control over the shape of its internal political life and control over its foreign policy. It was a price Japan happily paid—even assuming it had a choice—for the economic benefits greatly outweighed the loss of autonomy.

Now this era is coming to a close. From the American point of view the economic disadvantages in its relationship with Japan have come to far outweigh the political advantages as the Cold War ends. It is now America's expectation that it will be able to reorder relations in the Pacific to suit America's new needs. In this great reshuffling of its empire, the U.S. expects Japan to accept a much smaller share of the economic pie while continuing to accept American dominion.

Even if Japan were tempted to accept a smaller growth rate or a lower standard of living in order to preserve the peace and the status quo, it is not clear that the matter would end there. The United States is attempting to solve its economic problems at the expense of Japan, using its politico-military power to compel Japan to accept the readjustment. It is easier to force Japan to limit its exports of cars to the U.S. and increase its purchase of American cars than to increase the efficiency of Detroit.

This is the trap of empire. Empire is first won by the most efficient and industrious. It is then maintained by political and military effort, not economic efficiency. Thus, economies atrophy while armies and navies grow. This military power is then used to transfer wealth from colonies and allies, rather than going to the political effort of rebuilding the domestic economy. At each point, the imperialist power has a choice of solving an economic crisis through internal effort or increased exploitation. The latter, being the path of least resistance, is the usual choice. The result is frequently a vast military force with a hollow socio-economic center; an empire in collapse.

The U.S. has not yet traveled very far down this road because the Cold War prevented it from exploiting its dominions. Now, however, the temptation to solve the American economic crisis at Japan's expense is too great to resist. Should Japan capitulate this time, each future American economic crisis will be solved in the same way. Japan will be asked to buy more products it does not want from the U.S. and sell less of what it produces.

Thus, even should Japan be willing to accept subordination, lower economic well-being, and general domination in return for peace, it is not clear that the U.S. would permit this to happen. American demands will grow larger and larger until the price will be the ruination of Japan.

Japan cannot partially resist the United States. The idea that it can resist American economic demands while submitting to American political and military demands is absurd. Ultimately, American political and military power will try to compel Japan to accept American terms. This will become apparent after the U.S. begins expelling Japan from the American market and also takes umbrage at Japanese attempts to find new markets in Asia.

For the U.S., the Pacific Basin is American. Japan's search for markets must be at the expense of American exporters and at the expense of American political interests. Japan does not in any way want this to be the case. But given the structure of the Japanese economy, American demands on Japan will force it to find new markets in a domain, the Pacific, that until now has been American. All trading and all political relationships were American sanctioned and, ultimately, American controlled.

Japan therefore has two choices. One is to submit to the United States and endure an impossible fate. The other is to strike out on its own and accept a collision with American imperialism. The third option, striking out on its own and not colliding with the U.S. is not a possibility unless the U.S. is willing to concede that the Pacific Basin is no longer its indispensable security zone. Since the U.S. is not going to do that without conceding that it is no longer a global power but a very regional one, the collision course is set.

It need not culminate in war. A long, miserable cold war is also possible. But the key to such a cold war is raw materials. Should the U.S. try to cut the flow of raw materials before Japan has strengthened itself, Japan will be forced to submit. Should it cut them after Japan has strengthened itself, then Japan will have to choose between submission and war.

In 1941, under identical circumstances, Japan chose war. It lost. However, fortune smiled on Japan and, rather than ending Japanese history, defeat ushered in a golden age. Now that golden age is at an end. The United States is presenting the bill. The price is high. Japan should pay for the inefficiencies that crept into the American economy during the Cold War with the Soviet Union. Japan might pay the bill, but it will not be the last one.

Thus, Japan must try again. It must once more seek to become an empire on its own, dominating the western Pacific and eastern Asia. Once again the United States stands in its way. Once again the U.S. Navy controls the waters through which the lifeblood of Japan's economy passes. Once again Japan will decide that leaving its fate in the hands of a nation that no longer wishes it well would be catastrophic.

The U.S. means Japan no harm. Like all imperial powers, it means well and frequently does well. But the fact is that American interests and Japanese interests are now opposed. Japan means America no harm. It will create its empire without meaning to harm the U.S. in any way. Japan will ask nothing of America but to be left alone. But America can no more leave Japan alone than Japan can get out of America's way. Intentions, good or bad, will mean nothing.

The coming war with Japan will not arise out of wickedness or mean-spiritedness. It will not arise because of a lack of mutual understanding. It will not arise because Japan and America are similar or different cultures. It will arise because both are reasonable nations living in a dangerous world. Each wants what the other cannot give it. Each would be willing to get out of the other's way, but there is no means of leaving the Pacific and no means of getting out of the way short of national suicide.

Thus, as with most great wars, the coming, second U.S.–Japanese war will occur in spite of the best intentions of all concerned. And one suspects, considering the greatness of these two nations and the vastness of the stakes between them, that no matter who wins the next war it will not be the last. The struggle between Japan and the United States, punctuated by truces, friendships, and brutality, will shape the Pacific for generations. It will be the endless game about which the philosophers have written, the game of nations—the war of all against all.

Bibliography

Primary Sources

Association for Promotion of International Cooperation. *A Guide to Japan's Aid.* Tokyo, 1990.

Bank of Japan. *One Hundred Years of Statistics on Japanese Trade.* Tokyo, 1968.

Bank of Japan. *One Hundred Year Statistics of the Japanese Economy.* Tokyo, July 1966.

Bank of Japan, Economic Research and Statistics Department. *Economic Statistics Annual.* 1949—

Combined Arms and Services Staff School. *E210: Basic Logistical Principles.* Fort Leavenworth, Kansas, 1985.

——— *E709: Organization of the Army in the Field.* Fort Leavenworth, Kansas, November 1985.

Government of Japan. Japan Defense Agency. *Defense of Japan, Annual.* Tokyo, 1989.

——— Office of the Japanese Prime Minister, Foreign Press Center. *Public Opinion Survey on the Self-Defense Force and Defense Problems.* August 1988.

——— Statistics Bureau, Management and Coordination Agency. *Japan Statistical Yearbook.*

Institute of Developing Economies. *Foreign Trade Statistics of Japan Time Series by Partner and Country, 1951–52.* Tokyo, 1974.

International Monetary Fund. *Direction of Trade Statistics Yearbook.* Washington, D.C., 1990.

——— *Primary Commodities: Market Developments and Outlook.* Washington, D.C., July 1989.

JETRO (Japan External Trade Organization). *Nippon: Business Facts and Figures, 1989.* Tokyo, 1989.

——— *White Paper on International Trade.* Tokyo, annual.

Liesner, Thelma. *One Hundred Years of Economic Statistics.* New York: Facts on File, 1989.

Mitsubishi Economic Research Bureau. *Japanese Trade and Industry: Present and Future.* London: Macmillan, 1936.

Navy League of the United States. *Seapower Facts and Figures.* Annual.

Petroleum Association of Japan. *Japanese Oil Statistics Today.* No. 155, Tokyo, May 1990.

SCAP (Supreme Commander, Allied Powers). *Japanese Natural Resources: A Comprehensive Survey.* Tokyo: Hosokawa Printing Co., 1949.

SCAP, Natural Resources Section. *Mineral Resources of Japan Proper, 1925–1945.* Tokyo, 1949.

—— *Natural Resources of Japan.* Tokyo, 1947.

United Nations. *Economic Survey of Asia and the Far East, 1949.* Lake Success, 1950.

—— *Statistical Yearbook.* New York: United Nations, annual.

—— *UNCTAD Commodity Yearbook.* New York: United Nations, annual.

United States Bureau of the Census. *Statistical Abstract of the United States.* Washington, D.C.: GPO, 1989.

United States Department of Defense. *Annual Report, FY 1987.* Washington, D.C., 1987.

—— *A Strategic Framework for the Asian Pacific Rim: Looking Toward the 21st Century.* Washington, D.C.: April 1990.

United States Department of Energy. *World Oil.* Washington, D.C., 1989.

United States Department of the Interior, Bureau of Mines. Preprint for 1987 *Minerals in the World Economy.*

—— *Minerals Yearbook.* (1947–).

United States House of Representatives, Committee on Armed Services. *Hearings Before the Defense Burden Sharing Panel,* September 27, 1988. 100th Cong., 2nd sess. Washington, D.C.: GPO, 1988.

United States House of Representatives, Committee on Foreign Affairs. *United States–Japanese Security Cooperation and the FSX Agreement.* April 1989. Washington, D.C.: GPO, 1989.

United States House of Representatives, Subcommittee on Asian and Pacific Affairs and on International Economic Policy and Trade of the Committee on Foreign Affairs. *Hearings on Developments in United States–Japan Economic Relations.* May 1987. 100th Cong., 1st sess. Washington, D.C.: GPO, 1987.

United States Senate, Committee on Armed Services. *Hearings on International Security Environment (Strategy).* 101st Cong., 1st sess. Washington, D.C.: GPO, 1989.

United States Department of State. Intelligence Research Report IRR No. 156. *Economic Growth of OECD Countries, 1977–87.* March 31, 1987.

United States Tariff Commission. *The Foreign Trade of Japan.* Washington, D.C., 1922.

World Bank. *World Tables.* Baltimore: Johns Hopkins University Press, 1989.

Secondary Sources: Books

Abegglen, James G., and George Stalk, Jr. *Kaisha: The Japanese Corporation.* New York: Basic Books, 1985.

Akao, Nobutoshi. *Japan's Economic Security.* New York: Royal Institute for International Affairs, 1983.

Allen, George C. *Japan's Economic Policy.* London: Macmillan, 1980.

———— *Japan's Economic Recovery.* London: Macmillan, Press, 1958.

Anderson, Irvine. *The Standard Vacuum Oil Company and United States East Asian Policy, 1933–1945.* Princeton, N.J.: Princeton University Press, 1975.

Angell, Norman. *The Great Illusion.* New York: G.P. Putnam's Sons, 1910.

Aoki, Masahiko. *The Economic Analysis of the Japanese Firm.* Amsterdam: Elsevier, 1984.

Aruga, Tadashi. "The Security Treaty Revision of 1960." In *The United States and Japan: In the Postwar World,* ed. Akira Iriye and Warren Cohen. Lexington: University Press of Kentucky, 1989.

Asahi Shimbun staff. *The Pacific Rivals: A Japanese View of Japanese-American Relations.* New York: Weatherhill, 1971.

Axelbank, Albert. *Black Star Over Japan.* New York: Hill and Wang, 1973.

Ball, William MacMahon. *Japan, Enemy or Ally?* New York: John Day, 1949.

Barnett, Robert W. *Beyond War: Japan's Concept of Comprehensive National Security.* Washington, D.C.: Pergamon, 1984.

Barnhart, Michael A. *Japan Prepares for Total War.* Ithaca, N.Y.: Cornell University Press, 1987.

Bisson, T.A. *Zaibatsu Dissolution in Japan.* Berkeley: University of California Press, 1954.

Borg, Dorothy. *The United States and the Far Eastern Crisis, 1933–38.* Cambridge, Mass.: Harvard University Press, 1964.

Boston Study Group. *Winding Down: The Price of Defense.* San Francisco: Freeman, 1982.

Braake, Alex L. *Mining in the Netherlands East Indies.* New York: Institute of Pacific Relations, 1944.

Braisted, William Reynolds. *The United States Navy in the Pacific, 1897–1909.* New York: Greenwood Press, 1958.

———— *The United States Navy in the Pacific, 1909–1922.* Austin: University of Texas Press, 1971.

Brzezinski, Zbigniew. *The Fragile Blossom: Crisis and Change in Japan.* New York: Harper and Row, 1972.

Buck, James H., ed. *The Modern Japanese Military System.* Beverly Hills, Calif.: Sage Publications, 1975.

Buckley, Roger. *Occupation Diplomacy: Britain, the United States and Japan, 1945–1952*. Cambridge University Press, 1982.

Burstein, Daniel. *Yen: Japan's New Financial Empire and Its Threat to America*. New York: Simon and Schuster, 1988.

Butler, James R.M. *Grand Strategy*. London: H.M. Stationary Office, 1956.

Butow, Robert J.C. *Japan's Decision to Surrender*. Stanford; Calif.: Stanford University Press, 1954.

Bywater, Hector C. *Sea Power in the Pacific: A Study of the American–Japanese Naval Problem*. Boston: Houghton Mifflin, 1921.

Castle, Emery N., and Kenzo Hemmi, eds. *U.S.–Japanese Agricultural Trade Relations*. Washington, D.C.: Resources for the Future, 1982.

Chapman, J.W.M., R. Drifte, and I.T.M. Gow. *Japan's Quest for Comprehensive Security*. New York: St. Martin's Press, 1982.

Chinworth, Michael A. "The Private Sector: Japan's Defense Industry." In *Option 2000: Politics and High Technology in Japan's Defense and Strategic Future*, ed. Ronald Morse. Princeton, N.J.: Woodrow Wilson International Center for Scholars, 1987.

Chu, Chin-ning. *The Asian Mind Game*. New York: Rawson Associates, 1991.

Clinard, Outten Jones. *Japan's Influence on American Naval Power, 1897–1917*. Berkeley: University of California Press, 1947.

Cohen, Jerome B. *Japan's Economy in War and Reconstruction*. Minneapolis: University of Minnesota Press, 1949.

Cohen, Theodore. *Remaking Japan*. New York: The Free Press, 1987.

Conant, Charles A. *The United States in the Orient: The Nature of The Economic Problem*. Port Washington, N.Y: Kennikat Press, 1900.

Conroy, Hilary. *The Japanese Frontier in Hawaii, 1868–1898*. Berkeley: University of California Press, 1953.

Costello, John. *The Pacific War: 1941–1945*. New York: Rawson, Wade, 1982.

Courdy, Jean-Claude. *The Japanese: Everyday Life in the Empire of the Rising Sun*. New York: Harper and Row, 1984.

Crawford, John, and Saburo Okita. *Raw Materials and Pacific Economic Integration*. Vancouver, B.C.: University of British Columbia Press, 1978.

Dingman, Roger. *Power in the Pacific: The Origins of Naval Arms Limitation, 1914–1922*. Chicago: University of Chicago Press, 1976.

Dorn, Frank. *The Sino-Japanese War, 1937–41: From Marco Polo Bridge to Pearl Harbor*. New York: Macmillan, 1974.

Douhet, Giulio. *Command of the Air*. New York: Coward-McCann, 1942

Dower, J.W. *Empire and Aftermath: Yoshida Shigeru and the Japanese Experience, 1878–1954*. Cambridge, Mass.: Harvard University Press, 1979.

Dunn, Frederick S. *Peace Making and the Settlement With Japan.* Princeton, N.J.: Princeton University Press, 1963.

Dunnigan, James F. *How To Make War.* New York: William Morrow, 1982.

Duus, Peter. *The Rise of Modern Japan.* Boston: Houghton Mifflin, 1976.

Duus, Peter, Ramon H. Myers, and Mark R. Peattie, eds. *The Japanese Informal Empire in China: 1895–1937.* Princeton, N.J.: Princeton University Press, 1989.

Egner, Philip. *Grand Strategy.* New York: C. Fisher, 1915.

Emmerson, John K. *Arms, Yen and Power: The Japanese Dilemma.* New York: Dunellen, 1971.

Emmerson, John K., and Leonard A. Humphreys. *Will Japan Rearm?* Washington, D.C.: American Enterprise Institute, 1973.

Endicott, John E. *Japan's Nuclear Option: Political, Technical and Strategic Factors.* New York: Praeger, 1975.

Eyre, James K. *Japan and the American Annexation of the Philippines.* New York, 1942.

Fearey, Robert A., and Edwin M. Martin. *The Allied Occupation of Japan, Second Phase: 1948–50.* New York: Macmillan, 1950.

Friedman, Edward, and Mark Selden, eds. *America's Asia: Dissenting Essays on Asian-American Relations.* New York: Random House, 1971.

Fukodome, Shigeru. "The Hawaii Operation." In *The Japanese Navy in World War II.* Annapolis: Naval Institute Press, 1986.

Fukutake, Tadashi. *The Japanese Social Structure.* Tokyo: University of Tokyo Press, 1982.

Goldsmith, Raymond W. *Comparative National Balance Sheets: A Study of Twenty Countries, 1688–1978.* Chicago: University of Chicago Press, 1985.

Goodman, Grant K. *The American Occupation of Japan: A Retrospective View.* Lawrence: University of Kansas, 1968.

——— *Imperial Japan and Asia: A Reassessment.* New York: Columbia University, 1967.

Greene, Fred. *Stresses in US–Japanese Relations.* Washington, D.C.: Brookings Institution, 1975.

Guillain, Robert. *The Japanese Challenge.* Philadelphia: J.B. Lippincott, 1970.

Gunston, Bill. *Allied Fighters of World War II.* New York: Arco Publishing, Inc., 1981.

Haffa, Robert P., Jr. *Planning U.S. Forces.* Washington, D.C.: National Defense University Press, 1988.

Hamill, Ian. *The Strategic Illusion: The Singapore Stategy and the Defence of Australia and New Zealand, 1919–1942.* Singapore: Singapore University Press, 1981.

Harries, Meiron, and Susie Harries. *Sheathing the Sword: The Demilitarization of Japan.* London: Hamish Hamilton, 1987.

Hitler, Adolf. *Mein Kampf.* trans. J. Murphy. London: Hurst and Blackett, 1939.

Holland, Harrison M. *Managing Defense: Japan's Dilemma.* London: University of America Press, 1988.

Holtom, Daniel C. *The National Faith of Japan: A Study in Modern Shinto.* London: Kegan Paul, Trench, Trubner, 1938.

Hosoya, Chihiro. "Japan's Search for an Independent Foreign Policy." In James W. Morley, ed., *Deterrent Diplomacy.* New York: Columbia University Press, 1976.

———. "Yoshida Letter to the Nixon Shock." In *The United States and Japan in the Postwar World,* ed. Akira Iriye and Warren Cohen. Lexington: University Press of Kentucky, 1989.

Hunsberger, Warren S. *Japan: New Industrial Giant.* New York: American–Asian Educational Exchange, 1972.

Ienaga, Saburo. *The Pacific War, 1931–1945.* New York: Pantheon, 1978.

Ike, Nobutake. *Japan's Decision for War: Records of the 1941 Policy Conferences.* Stanford, Calif.: Stanford University Press, 1967.

Ikuhiko, Hata. "The Army's Move Into Northern Indochina." In *The Fateful Choice,* ed. James W. Morley. New York: Columbia University Press, 1980.

Iriye, Akira. *The Cold War in Asia.* Englewood Cliffs, N.J., Prentice-Hall, 1974.

——— *Pacific Estrangement: Japanese and American Expansion, 1897–1911.* Cambridge, Mass.: Harvard University Press, 1972.

——— "The Ideology of Japanese Imperialism: Imperial Japan and China." In *Imperial Japan and Asia: A Reassessment,* ed. Grant K. Goodman. New York: Columbia University Press, 1967.

Iriye, Akira, and Warren Cohen, eds. *The United States and Japan in the Postwar World.* Lexington: University Press of Kentucky, 1989.

Ishikawa, Tsuneo, and Kazuo Ueda. "The Bonus Payment System and Japanese Personal Savings." In *The Economic Analysis of the Japanese Firm,* ed. Masahiko Aoki. New York: North-Holland, 1984.

Jane's Armour and Artillery, 1984–85. New York: Jane's, 1985.

Jansen, Marius. *Political Development in Modern Japan,* ed. Robert Ward. Princeton, N.J.: Princeton University Press, 1968.

Johnson, Chalmers. *MITI and the Japanese Miracle.* Stanford, Calif.: Stanford University Press, 1982.

Johnson, Sheila K. *The Japanese Through American Eyes.* Stanford, Calif.: Stanford University Press, 1988.

Jones, F.C. *Japan's New Order in East Asia: Its Rise and Fall, 1937–45.* London: Oxford University Press, 1954.

Kahn, Herman. *The Emerging Japanese Superstate.* New York: Prentice-Hall, 1969.

Kaplan, Morton, and Kinhide Mushakoji, eds. *Japan, America and the Future World Order.* New York: The Free Press, 1976.

Kataoka, Tetsuya, and Ramon H. Myers. *Defending an Economic Superpower: Reassessing the U.S.–Japan Security Alliance.* Boulder, Colo.: Westview Press, 1989.

Katsuii, Nakagane. "Manchukuo and Economic Development." In *The Japanese Informal Empire in China, 1895–1937,* ed. Peter Duus, Ramon H. Myers, and Mark R. Peattie. Princeton, N.J.: Princeton University Press, 1989.

Kauffman, William W. *A Thoroughly Efficient Navy.* Washington, D.C.: Brookings Institution, 1987.

Kawai, Kazuo. *Japan's American Interlude.* Chicago: University of Chicago Press, 1960.

Kawakami, Kiyoshi Karl. *Japan and World Peace.* New York: Macmillan, 1919.

———*Japan in World Politics.* New York: Macmillan, 1917.

——— *American–Japanese Relations: An Inside View of Japan's Politics and Purposes.* New York: Fleming H. Revell, 1912.

Kennan, George. *Memoirs.* 2 vols. Boston: Little, Brown, 1967.

Kennedy, Paul. *The Rise and Fall of the Great Powers.* New York: Random House, 1987.

Kosai, Yutaka. *The Era of High Speed Growth.* Trans. J. Kaminski. Tokyo: University of Tokyo Press, 1986.

Kosai, Yutaka, and Yoshitaro Ogino. *The Contemporary Japanese Economy.* Armonk, N.Y.: M.E. Sharpe, 1984.

Krause, Lawrence B., and Hugh Patrick, eds. *Mineral Resources in the Pacific Area.* San Francisco: Federal Reserve Bank of San Francisco, 1977.

Lewe Van Aduard, E.J. *Japan, From Surrender to Peace.* The Hague: M. Nijhoff, 1953.

Lincoln, E.J. *Japan: Facing Economic Maturity.* Washington, D.C.: Brookings Institution, 1988.

———*Japan's Unequal Trade.* Washington, D.C.: Brookings Institution, 1990.

Louis, William Roger. *British Strategy in the Far East.* Oxford: Clarendon Press, 1971.

Low, A. Maurice. *Japan and the World's Future.* Providence: delivered before The University Club, 1905.

Lowe, Peter. *Great Britain and the Origins of the Pacific War.* Oxford: Clarendon Press, 1977.

Lu, David J. *From the Marco Polo Bridge to Pearl Harbor.* Washington, D.C.: Public Affairs Press, 1961.

Mackinder, Halford J. *Democratic Ideals and Reality: A Study in the Politics of Reconstruction.* New York: Holt, 1942.

Martin, Edwin M. *The Allied Occupation of Japan.* Westport, Conn.: Greenwood Press, 1972.

Matsukawa, Michiya. *The Japanese Trade Surplus and Capital Outflow.* Occasional Paper No. 22, Group of Thirty. New York, 1987.

Matsuoka, Toshio. *Japan 1983: An International Comparison.* Keizai Koho Center, 1983.

McIntosh, Malcolm. *Arms Across the Pacific.* New York: St. Martin's Press, 1988.

——— *Japan Rearmed.* New York: St. Martin's Press, 1986.

McMichael, R. Daniel. "Strategic Minerals: The Public Policy Process." In *Strategic Minerals and International Security,* ed. Uri Ra'anan and Charles M. Perry. Washington: Pergamon, Brassey's, 1985.

McNelly, Theodore. "The Constitutionality of Japan's Defense Establishment." In *The Modern Japanese Military System,* ed. James H. Buck. Beverly Hills, Calif.: Sage, 1975.

McCormick, Frederick. *The Menace of Japan.* Boston: Little, Brown, 1917.

Medlicott, W.N. *The Economic Blockade,* Volume II. London: Her Majesty's Stationer's Office, 1959.

Millard, Thomas. *Japan and the "Irrepressible Expansion Doctrine."* Shanghai: The Weekly Review of the Far East, 1921.

Miyazaki, Masayoshi. "Theory of East Asian Federation (1936)." In Joyce C. Lebra, *Japan's Greater East Asia Co-Prosperity Sphere in World War II: Selected Readings and Documents.* Kuala Lumpur, Malaysia: Oxford University Press, 1975.

Morgenthau, Hans. *Politics Among Nations: The Struggle for Peace and Power.* 4th ed. New York: Knopf, 1967.

Morishima, Michiko. *Why Has Japan Succeeded.* Cambridge: Cambridge University Press, 1982.

Morley, James W. *Japan's Foreign Policy: 1868–1941.* New York: Columbia University Press, 1974.

Morley, James W., ed. *The Fateful Choice: Japan's Advance into Southeast Asia, 1939–1941.* New York: Columbia University Press, 1980.

——— *Japan Erupts: The London Naval Conference and the Manchurian Incident: 1928–1932.* New York: Columbia University Press, 1984.

——— *Dilemmas of Growth in Prewar Japan.* Princeton, N.J.: Princeton University Press, 1971.

——— *Deterrent Diplomacy: Japan, Germany and the USSR, 1935–1940.* New York: Columbia University Press, 1976.

Murota, Yashuhiro. "Options for a Resource Poor Country—Japan." In *Mineral Resources in the Pacific Area,* ed. Lawrence B. Krause and Hugh Patrick. San Francisco: Federal Reserve Bank of San Francisco, 1977.

Myers, Ramon H., and Mark R. Peattie, eds. *The Japanese Colonial Empire, 1895–1945.* Princeton, N.J.: Princeton University Press, 1984.

Nakamura, Takafusa. *Economic Growth in Pre-War Japan.* Trans. Robert Feldman. New Haven, Conn.: Yale University Press, 1983.

Nish, Ian. *Alliance in Decline: A Study in Anglo-Japanese Relations, 1908–1923.* London: Athlone Press, 1972.

Nitobe, Inazo. *Bushido: The Soul of Japan.* Tokyo; Rutland, Vt.: Charles E. Tuttle, 1969.

Nye, Joseph S., and Robert O. Keohane. *Power and Interdependence: World Politics in Transition.* Boston: Little, Brown, 1977.

Oi, Atsushi. "Why Japan's Antisubmarine Warfare Failed." In *The Japanese Navy in World War II*, ed. David C. Evans. Annapolis: Naval Institute Press, 1986.

Okazaki, Hisahiko. *A Grand Strategy for Japanese Defense.* Washington, D.C.: University Press of America, 1986.

Ono, Gichi. *War and Armament Expenditures of Japan.* New York: Oxford University Press, 1922.

Osgood, Robert E. *The Weary and the Wary.* Baltimore: John Hopkins University Press, 1972.

Ouchi, William G. *Theory Z: How American Business Can Meet the Japanese Challenge.* Reading, Mass.: Addison-Wesley, 1981.

Packard, George. *Protest in Tokyo.* Princeton, N.J.: Princeton University Press, 1966.

Panda, Rajaram. *Pacific Partnership: Japan–Australia Resource Diplomacy.* Rohtak, India: Manthan, 1982.

Parrott, Lindsey. "The Touchy Issue of Peace With Japan." In *The Korean War*, ed. Lloyd Gardner. New York: Quadrangle Books, 1972.

Passin, Herbert, ed. *The United States and Japan.* 2d ed. Washington, D.C.: Columbia Books, 1975.

Patrick, Hugh, T. "The Economic Muddle of the 1920's." In *Dilemmas of Growth in Prewar Japan*, ed. James W. Morley. Princeton, N.J.: Princeton University Press, 1971.

Patrick, Hugh, and Henry Rosovsky. *Asia's New Giant: How the Japanese Economy Works.* Washington, D.C.: Brookings Institution, 1976.

Peattie, Mark R. *Nanyo: The Rise and Fall of the Japanese in Micronesia: 1885–1945.* Honolulu: University of Hawaii Press, 1988.

Pepper, Thomas, Merit E. Janow, and Jimmy W. Wheeler. *The Competition: Dealing With Japan.* New York: Praeger, 1985.

Perry, John Curtis. *Beneath Eagle's Wings: Americans in Occupied Japan.* New York: Dodd, Mead, 1980.

Perry, Charles. *The West, Japan and Cape Route Imports: The Oil and Non-Fuel Mineral Trades.* Cambridge: Institute for Foreign Policy Analysis, 1982.

Prestowitz, Clyde W. *Trading Places: How We Are Giving Our Future to Japan and How to Reclaim It.* New York: Basic Books, 1988.

Reed, Robert F. *The U.S.–Japan Alliance: Sharing the Burden of Defense.* Washington, D.C.: National Defense University Press, 1983.

Richmond, Frederick W., and Michael Kahan. *How to Beat The Japanese at Their Own Game.* Englewood Cliffs, N.J.: Prentice-Hall, 1983.

Roberts, John G. *Mitsui: Three Centuries of Japanese Business.* New York: Weatherhill, 1973.

Roscoe, Theodore. *United States Submarine Operations in World War II.* Annapolis: U.S. Naval Institute, 1949.

Royama, Masamichi. *Foreign Policy of Japan: 1914–1939.* Tokyo: University of Tokyo Press, 1941.

——— *Japan's Position in Manchuria.* Paper presented at the Third Biennial Conference of the Institute of Pacific Relations, Kyoto, 1929.

Sakurabayashi, Makoto, and Robert J. Ballon. "Labor-Management Relations in Modern Japan." In *Studies in Japanese Culture: Tradition and Experiment.* Monumenta Nipponica Monograph No. 23. Tokyo: Sophia University, 1963.

Samuels, Richard J., and Benjamin C. Whipple. *Defense Production and Industrial Development: The Case of Japanese Aircraft.* Cambridge, Mass.: MIT, 1988.

Scalapino, Robert. *Asia and the Major Powers.* Washington, D.C.: American Enterprise Institute, 1972.

Schaller, Michael. *The American Occupation of Japan.* New York: Oxford University Press, 1985.

Shiels, Frederick. *Tokyo and Washington.* Lexington, Mass.: Lexington Books, 1980.

Shinjiro, Nagaoka. "Economic Demands on the Dutch East Indies." In *The Fateful Choice*, ed. James W. Morley. New York: Columbia University Press, 1980.

Shinohara, Miyohei. *Industrial Growth, Trade and Dynamic Patterns in the Japanese Economy.* Tokyo: University of Tokyo Press, 1982.

Stone, P.B. *Japan Surges Ahead.* New York: Praeger, 1969.

Stuart, Douglas T., ed. *Security in the Pacific Rim.* Brookfield, Vt.: Gower, 1987.

Swearingen, Rodger. *The Soviet Union and Postwar Japan.* Stanford: Hoover Institution Press, 1978.

Takahashi, Seizaburo. *Japan and World Resources.* Tokyo, 1938.

Tatsuo, Kobayashi. "The London Naval Treaty, 1930." In *Japan Erupts: The London Naval Conference and the Manchurian Incident: 1928–1932*, ed. James W. Morley. New York: Columbia University Press, 1984.

Taylor, Jared. *Shadows of the Rising Sun.* New York: William Morrow, 1983.

Utley, Jonathan G. *Going to War with Japan.* Knoxville: University of Tennessee Press, 1985.

Vernon, Raymond. *Two Hungry Giants: The United States and Japan and the Quest for Oil and Ores.* Cambridge, Mass.: Harvard University Press, 1983.

Vogel, Ezra F. *Japan as Number One.* Cambridge, Mass.: Harvard University Press, 1979.

——— *Comeback.* New York: Simon and Schuster, 1985.

Ward, Robert E., and Sakamoto Yoshikazu, eds. *Democratizing Japan.* Honolulu: University of Hawaii Press, 1987.

Warden, John A., III. *The Air Campaign: Planning for Combat.* Washington, D.C.: National Defense University Press, 1988.

Watkins, James D. *The Maritime Strategy.* Annapolis: Naval Institute Press, 1986.

Weinstein, Martin. *Japan's Postwar Defense Policy, 1947–1968.* New York: Columbia University Press, 1971.

Wescott, Allan, ed. *Mahan on Naval Warfare.* Boston, 1948.

White, John Albert. *The Diplomacy of the Russo-Japanese War.* Princeton, N.J.: Princeton University Press, 1964.

Wildes, Harry. *Typhoon in Tokyo: The Occupation and its Aftermath.* New York: Octagon Books, 1978.

Williams, Justin. *Japan's Political Revolution Under MacArthur.* Athens: University of Georgia, 1979.

Willmott, H.P. *Empires in the Balance.* Annapolis. Naval Institute Press, 1982.

Wolf, Marvin J. *The Japanese Conspiracy: The Plot to Dominate Industry Worldwide—And How to Deal With It.* New York: Empire Books, 1983.

Wolferen, Karel van. *The Enigma of Japanese Power.* New York: Knopf, 1989.

Zumoto, Motosada. *Japan and the World.* Tokyo: The Herald Press, 1928.

Journal Articles

"Agreement on the Japanese SST Engine Program Delayed." *Aviation Week and Space Technology,* March 19, 1990.

Agnelli, Giovani. "The Europe of 1992." *Foreign Affairs,* Fall 1989.

Akaha, Tsuneo. "Japan's Response to Threats of Shipping Disruptions in Southeast Asia and the Middle East." *Pacific Affairs,* 59:2 (Summer 1986).

Anderson, Irvine H., Jr. "The 1941 Defacto Embargo on Oil to Japan: A Bureaucratic Reflex." *Pacific Historical Review*, 44:2 (May 1975).

"Anglo-American Combine to Check Japan Urged." *The Oriental Economist*, 3:1 (January 1936).

Association of the U.S. Army. *The 1989–90 Green Book*, 39:10 (Arlington, Va.: 1989).

"Australia's Defence Capabilities: The Dibb Review." *Australian Foreign Affairs Review*, June 1986.

Blakeslee, George H. "The Establishment of the Far Eastern Commission." *International Organization*, 5 (August 1951).

Buck, James H. "The Japanese Self-Defense Forces." *Asian Survey*, 7:9 (September 1967).

Business Week/Harris Poll. *Business Week*, August 7, 1989.

Cheung, Tai Ming. "A Yen for Arms." *Far Eastern Economic Review*, February 22, 1990.

Clark, Dan E. "Manifest Destiny and the Pacific." *The Pacific Historical Review*, 1 (1932).

Covault, Craig. "Japan Designing Atlas-Class Rocket to Launch Lunar, Planetary Missions." *Aviation Week and Space Technology*, August 20, 1990.

———— "Japan's New H-2 Launch Site Rivals Largest U.S., European Facilities." *Aviation Week and Space Technology*, August 13, 1990.

Denson, John. "Must We Rearm Japan?" *Colliers*, 126, September 9, 1950.

Ebata, Kensuke. "Japan Warns on Soviet Build-up." *Jane's Defence Weekly*, September 23, 1989.

Eyre, James K., Jr., "Japan and the American Annexation of the Philippines." *Pacific Historical Review*, April 1942.

Fallows, James. "Containing Japan." *The Atlantic Monthly*, May 1989.

George, Aurelia D. "The Japanese Farm Lobby and Agricultural Policy Making." *Pacific Affairs*, 54:3 (Fall 1981).

Hadley, E.M. "Trust Busting in Japan." *Harvard Business Review*, July 1948.

Holt, Thaddeus. "Joint Plan Red." *Military History Quarterly*, 1:1 (Autumn 1988).

Hormats, Robert D. "Redefining Europe and the Atlantic Link." *Foreign Affairs*, 68:4 (Fall 1989).

Howarth, H.M.F. "Singapore's Armed Forces and Defense Industry." *International Defense Review*, 16:11 (1983).

Ikle, Fred Charles, and Terumasa Nakanishi. "Japan's Grand Strategy." *Foreign Affairs*, Summer 1990.

Ikuhiko, Hata. "Japan Under the Occupation." *The Japan Interpreter*, p. 362.

"Japan's Banking Uncertainties." *The Economist*, June 30, 1990.

Kitazume, Takashi. "Detente Puts Japanese Defenses in New Light." *Japan Times Weekly*, January 13, 1990.

Livermore, Seward W. "American Naval-Base Policy in the Far East, 1850–1914." *Pacific Historical Review*, 13 (June 1944).

Lloyd, Bruce. "Indonesia's Mineral Resources." *Resources Policy* 1:6 (December 1975).

Marx, Daniel. "Shipping Crisis in the Pacific." *Far Eastern Survey*, X, May 5, 1941.

McNelly, Theodore. "The Renunciation of War in the Japanese Constitution." *Armed Forces and Society*, 13:1 (Fall 1986).

Mearsheimer, John. "The End of the Cold War." *Atlantic Monthly*, August 1990.

Morris, Ivan I. *The Nobility of Failure: Tragic Heroes in the History of Japan*. New York: Holt, Rinehart, Winston, 1975.

Morton, Louis. "War Plan ORANGE: Evolution of a Strategy." *World Politics*, 11:2 (January 1959).

Murphy, Taggart. "Power Without Purpose: The Crisis of Japan's Global Financial Dominance." *Harvard Business Review*, March–April 1989.

Nakasone, Yahurio. "Toward Comprehensive Security." *Japan Echo* 5:4 (1978).

Pollard, Robert T. "Dynamics of Japanese Imperialism." *Pacific Historical Review*, 8 (March 1939).

Purcell, David C. "The Economics of Exploitation: The Japanese in the Mariana, Caroline and Marshall Islands, 1915–1940." *Pacific Studies*, 6:1 (Fall 1982).

Quigley, Harold S. "The Great Purge in Japan." *Pacific Affairs*, 20:3 (September 1947).

Roscoe, Bruce. "Japan Puts Priority on Defence." *Jane's Defence Weekly*, December 10, 1988.

Russett, Bruce. "Dimensions of Resource Dependence: Some Elements of Rigor in Concept and Policy Analysis." *International Organization*, 38:3 (Summer 1984).

Sakurabayashi, Makoto, and Robert J. Ballon "Labor-Management Relations in Modern Japan." *Studies in Japanese Culture: Tradition and Experiment*, Monumenta Nipponica Monograph No. 23 (Tokyo, 1963).

Spencer, Edson W. "Japan as Competitor." *Foreign Policy*, March 1990.

Tabata, Masanori. "Government to Launch Defense Plan." *Japan Times Weekly*, July 9–15, 1990.

Tabata, Masanori. "Second Thoughts on FSX." *The Japan Times*, June 24, 1989.

Tarnoff, Peter. "America's New Special Relationships." *Foreign Affairs*, 69:3 (Summer 1990).

Tokyo Broadcasting System polls, 1985–89. Cited in Japan Economic Institute, "American and Japanese Polls on the Bilateral Relationship: Trends and Implications." March 2, 1990.

"Tokyo Wants Its Arsenal Made in Japan." *Business Week*, September 25, 1989.

Weinstein, Martin. "Defense Policy and the Self-Defense Forces." *The Japan Interpreter*, 6:2 (Summer 1970).

"West German Anti-Tank System for Japan." *Jane's Defense Weekly*, February 18, 1989.

Williams, Justin. "From Charlottesville to Tokyo: Military Government Training and the Democratic Reforms in Occupied Japan." *Pacific Historical Review*, 51:4 (November 1982).

Yamashita, Isamu. "Tackling Foreign and Domestic Problems Under the Leadership of the LDP." *Keidanren Review*, No. 121 (February 1990).

Yoder, Steven Kreider. "Japan Plans Speedy Superconductor Ships." *Wall Street Journal*, August 17, 1988.

Yoshida, Shigeru. "Japan and the Crisis in Asia." *Foreign Affairs*, 29:2 (January 1951).

Periodicals Cited

Aviation Week and Space Technology
Business Week
Jane's Defence Weekly
New York Times
Newsweek
Oriental Economist
The Japan Times

Index

About the Authors

George Friedman is currently Professor of Political Science at Dickinson College in Carlisle, Pennsylvania. He is the author of *The Political Philosophy of the Frankfurt School* (Cornell University Press, 1980) and has published numerous articles on defense issues, political philosophy and U.S.–Japan relations. He lives in Columbia, Maryland, with his wife and two children.

Meredith LeBard has her B.A. and M.A. from the University of Sydney and lived in Sydney, Australia, until 1976 when she moved to the United States. She is a free-lance writer who teaches writing and has published articles on relations between the U.S. and Japan, as well as several works of fiction and poetry. She currently lives in Columbia, Maryland, with her husband and two children.